Derivatives

The risks that remain

edited by

Elizabeth Sheedy and
Sheelagh McCracken

ALLEN & UNWIN
Macquarie Series in Applied Finance

The Macquarie Series in Applied Finance is an occasional series on the issues and practice of applied finance in the Asia-Pacific, published in association with the Centre for Studies in Money, Banking and Finance, Macquarie University.

First published in 1997 by
Allen & Unwin
9 Atchison Street
St Leonards NSW 1590
Australia
Phone: (61 2) 8425 0100
Fax: (61 2) 9906 2218
E-mail: frontdesk@allen-unwin.com.au
Web: http://www.allen-unwin.com.au

National Library of Australia
Cataloguing-in-Publication entry:

Derivatives: the risks that remain.

Bibliography.
Includes index.
ISBN 1 86448 324 5.

1. Derivatives securities. I. Sheedy, Elizabeth A. II. McCracken, Sheelagh. (Series: Macquarie series in applied finance).

332.645

Set in 10/11 pt Sabon by DOCUPRO, Sydney
Printed and bound by Southwood Press, Marrickville, New South Wales

10 9 8 7 6 5 4 3 2

Foreword

Derivatives have grown rapidly in recent years, in Australia and world-wide. Unfortunately major losses have arisen at times from their misuse. There is a need to place these losses in perspective. Contributors to this book identify lessons from these experiences, drawing on skills in a number of disciplines. Their work is both instructive and opportune.

Regulators, both nationally and internationally, have done much to establish minimum procedures and systems for banks dealing in derivatives. It is important that all parties, not just banks, involved in the derivatives markets understand and implement equally appropriate systems and procedures for these valuable instruments.

This book is the first in the Macquarie Series in Applied Finance from Macquarie University's Centre for Studies in Money, Banking and Finance. Under its Director, Professor Bill Norton, the Centre is a leader in applied finance teaching and research. Its Master of Applied Finance program is offered in financial centres in Australia, Hong Kong, Japan and Singapore. This series illustrates the Centre's commitment to research in applied finance.

M.A. (Tim) Besley, AO, FTS, Chancellor
Macquarie University

Contents

Contributors

Richard Allan, *BCom MA Melb., PhD ANU, MAppFin Macq.*
Associate Professor, Centre for Studies in Money, Banking and Finance
Richard Allan is Associate Professor in Applied Finance and Deputy Director of the Centre for Studies in Money, Banking and Finance at Macquarie University. Dr Allan's previous experience includes six years in CSR Ltd's Treasury, where he was in charge of foreign exchange and money market exposure management. Banking experience was gained at ANZ and UBS Australia Ltd.

Nuncio D'Angelo, *LLB BJuris UNSW*
Solicitor of the Supreme Court of New South Wales
Partner, Mallesons Stephen Jaques
Visiting Fellow, Centre for Studies in Money, Banking and Finance
Nuncio D'Angelo is a banking and finance partner with Mallesons Stephen Jaques in Sydney. He is also a part-time lecturer in finance law in the Master of Applied Finance program at Macquarie University.

Sarah Dow, *BEc Syd, LLB (Hons) UTS*
Solicitor of the Supreme Court of New South Wales
Sarah Dow is a solicitor with Mallesons Stephen Jaques in Sydney.

Peter Humphrey, *MAppFin Macq.*
Vice President, Union Bank of Switzerland, Singapore
Peter Humphrey is Vice President at UBS Singapore with responsibility

for trading and sales systems for East Asia. Prior to this he has held various middle office, trading and systems roles within UBS and other banks. He received a Master of Applied Finance degree from Macquarie University in Singapore in 1996.

Kevin Jameson, *BSc Adel.*
Senior Fellow, Centre for Studies in Money, Banking and Finance
Kevin Jameson joined Macquarie University in 1994, after 15 years experience in the Treasury and Capital Markets fields. He was formerly Managing Director of NatWest Markets in London, responsible for global capital markets trading, structuring, sales and product development activities. He has also held various posts with the National Westminster banking group in the Asian region, and has been a Director of the Sydney Futures Exchange.

John Jarratt, *BA Otago, McSc, PhD Warwick*
As Deputy Treasurer of Westpac, John Jarratt has further developed an interest in the quantification of risk. His extensive academic and banking career has featured an interest in financial mathematics as applied to derivative products. He has previously taught 'Derivative Products and Markets' in the Master of Applied Finance program.

David Lynch, *MA Dublin, MAppFin, PhD Macq.*
Director of Policy, International Banks and Securities Association of Australia
Prior to joining the International Banks and Securities Association of Australia, David Lynch was a Research Associate with the Centre for Studies in Money, Banking and Finance at Macquarie University. Research undertaken to complete his doctoral studies analysed the development of financial markets in the Asian region. Prior experience was gained in stockbroking and central banking.

Sheelagh McCracken, *MA Cantab, PhD Syd.*
Solicitor of the Supreme Courts of New South Wales, Hong Kong, England
Associate Professor, Centre for Studies in Money, Banking and Finance
Having initially qualified and practised as a solicitor with a major commercial firm in the City of London, Sheelagh McCracken has held various academic appointments and legal consultancies in Paris, Singapore and Sydney. She is currently responsible for the legal component of the Master of Applied Finance program at Macquarie University. Her research interests include rights of set-off and netting in common law jurisdictions, insolvency law

and banking and financial institutions law generally. She has published widely.

Max Morley, *BEc Qld*
Visiting Fellow, Centre for Studies in Money, Banking and Finance
Head of Financial Markets, Westpac Banking Corporation—New Zealand
Max Morley has gained extensive experience in the financial markets of London, Australia and New Zealand. He has been employed by Westpac Banking Corporation since 1981, specialising at various times in capital markets, swaps, risk management and fixed interest. He teaches 'Swap Book Management' as part of the Master of Applied Finance program at Macquarie University.

Elizabeth Sheedy, *BComm UNSW*
Fellow, Centre for Studies in Money, Banking and Finance
Prior to joining Macquarie University, Elizabeth Sheedy was an Associate Director at Macquarie Bank Ltd where she marketed funds management and derivatives products to institutional clients. Her teaching responsibilities include 'Strategic Marketing in Finance' within the Master of Applied Finance program. Ms Sheedy is currently undertaking doctoral studies on risk measurement for fund managers.

Abbreviations

ABAFRA	Australian Bankers' Association forward rate agreements
AFIC	Australian Financial Institutions Commission
AFMA	Australian Financial Markets Association
AIRS	Australian interest rate swap
APEC	Asia Pacific Economic Cooperation
ASC	Australian Securities Commission
ASX	Australian Stock Exchange
BFS	Barings Futures (Singapore) Pte Limited
BIS	Bank for International Settlements
BoBS	Board of Banking Supervision
bp	basis point
BSJ	Barings Securities Japan
BT Co.	Bankers Trust Co. Singapore
BTI	Bankers Trust International plc
BUGS	basket of unhedged gold stocks
CAD	capital adequacy directive
CASAC	Companies and Securities Advisory Committee
CFTC	US Commodity Futures Trading Commission
CMO	collateralised mortgage obligations
CP	commercial paper
CPI	Consumer Price Index
DEM	Deutschemark
DSS	PT Dharmala Sakti Sejahtera
FRA	forward rate agreement
FRN	Floating Rate Note
FX	foreign exchange

GARCH	Generalised Auto-Regressive Conditional Heteroscedasticity
GATS	General Agreement on Trade in Services
GBP	Great Britain pound
GDP	gross domestic product
GIC	guaranteed investment certificate
InTech	InTech Asset Consulting Pty Ltd
IO	interest only
IOSC	International Organisation of Securities Commissions
ISC	Insurance and Superannuation Commission
ISDA	International Swaps and Derivatives Association Inc.
JGB	Japanese Government Bond
JPY	Japanese yen
LEPOs	low exercise price options
LIBOR	London inter-bank offered rate
MG	Metallgesellschaft AG
MG Corp.	Metallgesellschaft Corporation
MGRM	Metallgesellschaft Refining and Marketing
MIML	Macquarie Investment Management Ltd
MTN	medium term note
NIKKEI	Nikkei Stock Average
NPV	net present value
NYMEX	New York Metals Exchange
OSE	Osaka Securities Exchange
OTC	over-the-counter
P/E	price/earnings ratio
PO	principal only
QSL	Qantas Superannuation Ltd
RAPM	risk adjusted performance measurement
RBA	Reserve Bank of Australia
RICO	anti-racketeering legislation
RMS	risk management statement
S&P	Standard & Poor's stock market index
SEC	US Securities and Exchange Commission
SFE	Sydney Futures Exchange
SIB	UK Securities and Investments Board
SIMEX	Singapore International Monetary Exchange
SIS	Superannuation Industry (Supervision) Act
SYCOM	Sydney Computerized Overnight Market
TIFFE	Tokyo International Financial Futures Exchange
USD	US dollar
VAR	value-at-risk

List of tables and figures

Tables

Figures

Introduction

SHEELAGH McCRACKEN

The forgotten derivatives crisis

The collapse of Barings on 27 February 1995 capped over a year of significant losses in the world of finance, most of which were blamed on derivatives. For a time, names such as Metallgesellschaft, Procter & Gamble, Orange County and Barings made headlines in the financial press. In 1995 a joke running through New York's financial circles defined a derivative as 'any investment that loses a lot of money'. Yet two years later the evidence of an industry in crisis is ambiguous.

Although the 1995 *Corporate Finance* (Brady 1995) poll of global foreign exchange activity suggested a move away from corporate derivatives usage, other surveys such as that of *Institutional Investor* (March 1995) painted a more positive picture. Despite a decline in the use of exotic derivative instruments, barely three per cent of institutional investors and corporate treasurers surveyed expected to reduce their derivatives activity in 1995. In the event, the International Swaps and Derivatives Association (ISDA) reported fast growth in derivatives during 1995 (Conway 1996). Over-the-counter (OTC) transactions outstanding reportedly increased by 57% during the calendar year. Subsequent surveys have shown that use of derivatives has increased in the period since 1994/95 (see for example Ernst & Young, ASCT, ANZ 1996).

These figures suggest that, in some respects, reaction to events such as the collapse of Barings was short-lived. The figures do not, however, provide information about management practice, which is the focus of this book. It is still far from clear that the lessons of 1994 and 1995 have been learned. There is, in our view, a risk that industry participants will forget what happened. With that loss of collective memory there may also disappear the opportunity for management to learn. In the rapidly developing derivatives markets of the Asia-Pacific region, it is easy to grow complacent about risks. Nonetheless the authors of this book suggest that much still remains to be done if future disasters are to be avoided.

Assessing the risks

We agree with the Group of Thirty (1993) that 'derivatives by their nature do not introduce risks of a fundamentally different kind or of a greater scale than those already present in the financial markets'. Financial disasters such as those in 1994 and 1995 have taken place throughout history, without the aid of derivatives.

An early example, often cited and neatly illustrative of the point, is that of the 'tulip crisis'. In the mid-1500s, some enterprising commercial genius introduced the tulip to western Europe. It was a novelty and popular attention focused on it, as it often does on anything new in the commercial arena in any era (to whit, futures and swaps in the current context). By the 1630s appreciation of the tulip had blossomed and the introduction of new and particularly beautiful hybrids led to accelerating price increases. The concept of value was overwhelmed by the greed of market participants who borrowed to buy yet more tulip bulbs, thus pushing the price ever higher. People mortgaged their houses and other assets to leverage their participation in the market. Single bulbs changed hands for upwards of $60,000 in today's currency before the inevitable collapse.

The seventeenth century tulip crisis may seem far removed from the twentieth century collapse of Barings. Yet in almost any case of significant financial loss, common factors can be found at the core of the problem: excessive leverage, lack of understanding and inadequate management controls. Mistakes of history are often repeated in the world of finance, just as they are in other spheres of life. In a growing market in particular it is easy to delay or ignore the implementation of management and legislative reforms that at the time of the particular crisis seemed so vital.

While much has changed since the large losses of 1994 and 1995, we are far from convinced that such events will not be repeated.

Objectives and theme

This is not a book primarily aimed at describing the events of 1994 and 1995. Rather, it is the consequence of these events that interest us. The nature of the derivatives industry has changed. Providers can no longer regard their activities as exempt from scrutiny or discussion; users must consider carefully their method of operation as well as their relationship with providers. Those concerned with the integrity of firms and markets, be they managers, boards, or supervisors, must appreciate the risks involved. These are the issues central to this book.

Our objectives are threefold:

- to identify the problems confronting the derivatives industry;
- to determine to what extent the industry in the Asia-Pacific region is vulnerable to risk; and
- to consider how that risk might best be managed.

While there is undoubtedly evidence of reform and increasing professionalism, the principal theme of this book is that further reforms are necessary to reduce risks and to enable the industry to grow further within a sound structure.

We have divided the book into three sections, as follows:

Part 1 provides an up-to-date context for discussion of the derivatives industry. It describes the events and issues which have arisen in recent times and considers the longer-term trends in the Asia-Pacific region currently shaping the industry as a whole.

Part 2 reviews the process of transition presently occurring in each segment of the derivatives industry. Issues are examined from the perspective of both providers and users of derivatives, and attention is drawn to common pitfalls in the marketing and legal relationships between these two groups. *Part 2* highlights a greater awareness of risk in its many guises: in particular, market risk, credit risk, agency risk, reputational risk, legal risk and operational risk. Many of these risks have not yet been fully analysed, let alone addressed.

Part 3 explores the path to improved risk management, both at a company level and for the economy as a whole. Topics include the measurement and management of market and credit risk, regulation and new product development. Resolving these issues will assist in moving the industry to secure, well-managed ground.

We conclude with a discussion of the future of the derivatives industry, drawing on recommendations from earlier chapters. The need for ongoing vigilance and a risk management culture throughout the industry is emphasised. Such a culture is, in our view, the best long term insurance against further losses.

References

Brady, S. 1995, 'Relationships Matter—At Last', *Corporate Finance*, October

Conway, O. 1996, 'OTC Market On The Up and Up', *Risk*, vol. 9, no. 8, August

Ernst & Young, Australian Society of Corporate Treasurers, ANZ 1996, *1996 Corporate Treasury Survey*

Group of Thirty 1993, *Derivatives: Practices and Principles*, Global Derivatives Study Group, Group of Thirty, Washington DC, July

Derivatives defined

SHEELAGH McCRACKEN

Discussion of the derivatives industry is often clouded by issues of terminology. Even the term 'derivative' has been a source of some confusion.

A derivative is an instrument whose value depends on the values of other underlying variables. It can be 'derived from' almost any variable, from the price of corn to the amount of rainfall at a certain location. Most often, however, the variables are prices of traded financial assets such as shares, bonds, foreign currency and commodities. Derivatives thus include a wide range of instruments, such as futures, forwards, swaps and options (see *Chapter 1*). At one end of the spectrum are the derivatives such as currency forwards that are well understood and commonly used by many companies. In contrast, more complex derivatives such as leveraged swaps and structured notes are used by a smaller group of institutions that are, generally speaking, sophisticated users.

Given the broad scope of derivatives, there is a danger in generalisations. There is, however, a common thread in derivatives products—the concept of a 'replicating portfolio'. When the underlying variable is a traded asset (like equity in a public company), the derivative can be replicated by a portfolio containing that (and other) assets. That is, a portfolio can be found that will have approximately the same value and approximately the same risk profile as the derivative security in all circumstances. Such a portfolio is called a replicating portfolio.

For example, a forward contract on a particular equity issue can be replicated by borrowing to finance a purchase of equities. Similarly, a call option on a particular equity issue can be replicated by borrowing and investing in stock, although in this example the amount of stock purchased changes continuously as the stock price changes (described as a dynamic replication strategy).

Many participants who trade derivatives may be unaware of the replication concept. Yet the concept is central to understanding derivatives for four reasons:

- it is at the heart of the way derivatives are valued and their risks managed;
- it provides ways to construct new derivatives products or to manufacture an existing derivative. Alternatively, it allows underlying securities to be recreated;
- it underlies the main economic purpose of a derivatives contract: namely, to attempt to create (or modify) a particular risk-return profile in the most efficient way; and
- importantly, it enables the 'derivatives crisis' of 1994 and 1995 to be placed in context, for it shows that most derivatives strategies can equally be implemented using only physical securities. Consequently, it underscores the point that there is nothing intrinsically new about the risks of derivatives.

Although the same effect as that produced by derivatives can be achieved using simpler instruments, derivatives can confer positive advantages, particularly efficiency. Market participants wishing to achieve an investment aim may use either derivatives or the underlying securities. They will choose the instrument with lowest transaction costs. These transaction costs include the costs of physical trading (such as costs of gathering information, bid-ask spreads, commissions and fees), potential costs of counterparty default, and the costs of taxation, accounting and other regulatory compliance. Derivatives may reduce such costs and offer a more efficient alternative than their underlying counterparts. Providers of derivatives products attempt to engineer customised solutions to match their customers' needs.

Part 1

The context for change

Part 1 provides a framework for understanding the current state of the derivatives industry, juxtaposing favourable long-term industry trends with crises such as the Barings collapse. We find that growth continues notwithstanding the problems of 1994 and 1995.

Participants in, and observers of, the derivatives industry often adopt either an unduly optimistic or pessimistic view. Prior to 1994, and again very recently, there has been confidence in the growth prospects of the industry and its ability to withstand or avoid losses. Yet, in the immediate aftermath of the Barings and Procter & Gamble cases, the use of derivatives was questioned and debated vociferously. In our view, a more balanced approach can be gained by considering the 'disasters' in a long-term context. This is the objective of *Part I*.

Chapter 1 considers the industry from a broad perspective. What are the long-term trends driving development in derivatives in the Asian region? Generally speaking, the diverse derivatives markets of Asia are enjoying a long-run growth phase, despite occasional hiccups. This growth is initially driven by deregulation which leads inevitably to volatility in market prices and hence the need for risk management. The events of 1994 and 1995 show, however, that despite positive growth trends, there are significant management challenges for the industry. To ensure that long-term growth continues, these challenges must be met. Three of these 'derivatives disasters' are described in *Chapter 2*, providing background for later discussions. The cases exemplify management issues which we believe should remain of concern to participants in the industry.

Chapter 1 highlights the risks for participants in less-developed derivatives markets, although it is ironic that the events described in *Chapter 2* occurred in developed countries with more sophisticated market infrastructure. Both *Chapters 1* and *2* emphasise that problems in one country are unlikely to be peculiar to that country. Within a book of this size, it is not possible to detail the experience of all the countries surveyed in *Chapter 1*. The remaining chapters focus on the experience of selected centres in the Asia-Pacific region, in particular Australia, Japan, Hong Kong and Singapore. Nonetheless the lessons to be drawn from these centres apply more widely.

1

Growth in Asia-Pacific markets

DAVID LYNCH

Editors' Note

This chapter sets the scene for discussion of the industry, examining the nature of derivatives and exploring not only what types of institutions use such instruments but also the reasons for their use. It becomes evident that derivatives are complementary to other types of financial instruments and, if used properly, are simply part of the necessary armoury for effective financial management, providing a means for managing market risk.

Interestingly, the demand for derivatives has not been uniform across countries, particularly in the Asia-Pacific region. Despite the potential availability of the relevant technology, active trading has been inhibited by factors such as the absence of underlying financial markets of sufficient breadth and depth to support derivatives, lack of trained personnel, high counterparty risk and inadequate competition between financial institutions. Nonetheless, it is argued that derivatives markets in the region's developed countries will follow global trends. These trends include reviews of the relevant regulation, greater education of users and the development of more sophisticated risk management systems. The development of an adequate risk management culture is seen as critical to the stable growth of derivatives markets, irrespective of their location.

1.1 Introduction

Derivatives markets in Asia-Pacific countries cover the complete spectrum of development, selectively ranging from the deepest and most sophisticated markets in world terms to nascent markets that trade basic risk management products on an *ad hoc* basis. At the advanced end, derivatives markets in Australia, for example, are well organised, deep and trade a broad range of quite sophisticated or 'exotic' derivatives. At the other end of the spectrum, derivatives in Indonesia are basic and trade much less frequently. Such diversity makes these markets of immense interest to financial economists and offers a great challenge to derivatives practitioners to expand their regional business. This chapter provides a description of derivatives markets in Asia-Pacific countries, with a focus on the factors that determine their current structure and are likely to drive their future development.

To begin, it is necessary to establish what derivatives are, who uses them and why they use them. This approach is useful because often too much emphasis is placed on the technical application of derivatives and the ultimate objective of using derivatives is given insufficient attention. This matters from a commercial perspective, as derivatives market strategists must understand the key drivers of the market's development in order to identify potential opportunities for new business. This done, the operations area can implement a strategy to capitalise on these opportunities.

This framework can be used to trace the origin of derivatives and understand their development in the Asia-Pacific region. The pattern of derivatives market development across countries that emerges from the analysis is a little unusual, in that neither the largest nor most developed economies necessarily have the most developed derivatives markets. Financial sector deregulation, economic restructuring, innovation, technology and globalisation of markets are identified as significant factors shaping derivatives markets. Against this background, opportunities for derivatives market development in various countries can be identified and strategies put in place to grasp them. An immature risk management culture prevails in many countries and so it is vital that proper account is taken of individual entity and sectoral risks from growth in derivatives use. Education and caution are required by derivatives providers, users and regulators, who will jointly shape a market's development. Recognition of this interdependence will provide a solid platform for emerging markets.

1.2 Nature and scope of derivatives

1.2.1 *What are derivatives?*

As stated in the introduction, a derivative is an instrument primarily for trading risk. Its current value is ultimately derived from, or varies in accordance with, the value of underlying good, instrument, rate or index, or some combination of these.

There are two basic types of derivatives: forwards and options. Forward contracts are symmetrical obligations; one party to the contract must buy and its counterparty must sell an underlying instrument for a given price, at a set future time. Options are asymmetrical because option purchasers have a right, but not an obligation, to transact at a contracted price: the exercise price. A call option is the right to buy the underlying instrument and a put option is the right to sell it, at the exercise price. Option sellers (or writers) are obliged to give effect to the purchaser's decision. Some options can be exercised before maturity of the contract is reached. As pointed out in the introduction, derivatives can be replicated using underlying assets and cash. However, forwards and options are, themselves, key building blocks of other more complex derivatives. For example:

- a currency swap is equivalent to a simultaneous spot purchase and forward sale of a currency;
- a swaption is an option on a swap; and
- a warrant bond is a straight bond with a stock option attached.

The building blocks themselves are interdependent. For example, a portfolio comprising a bond and a long put option at a given price is equivalent to a single long call option at that price. Decomposition of derivatives into their simpler parts assists practitioners in several ways. For example, it helps identify derivatives' risk characteristics that in turn promotes more accurate product pricing and facilitates better design of risk management strategies, including stress testing.

Therefore, the value of a derivative is ultimately derived from, or varies in accordance with, the future value of the underlying commodity, instrument, rate or index, or some combination of these. The liability created by a derivative is settled between the parties before, or at, its maturity. Derivatives are mainly based on financial products, such as interest rate securities, foreign exchange and company shares, and their value responds to price changes in these products. There is also a large range of commodity derivatives based on a great variety of products like oil, gold and wool. Derivatives contracts may be deliverable (for example, a bank-accepted bill may be delivered to satisfy an obligation under a bank bill futures contract) or, alternatively, they may be closed out by a cash settlement. The latter is much more likely.

Derivatives are traded on both organised exchanges and over-the-counter (OTC) markets. Futures are forward contracts traded on organised exchanges, like the Singapore International Monetary Exchange (SIMEX) and the Sydney Futures Exchange (SFE). Exchange traded derivatives usually have standardised terms, guaranteed settlement arrangements exist and novation (similar to netting of contracts) occurs. These characteristics help generate market liquidity. OTC derivatives are more flexible and can be customised to meet specific transactor needs, though at the cost of higher counterparty and operational risks and lower liquidity. Legal risk on OTC markets is usually reduced by the use of standardised documentation, like that of the International Swaps and Derivatives Association (ISDA). Similar derivatives frequently trade alongside each other in the OTC and exchange traded markets. Indeed, the markets are often interdependent; for example, forward rate agreement (FRA) traders in Australia use bank bill futures as a means to hedge positions and manage their market risk.

Derivatives have long been a part of standard economic and financial transactions, though not always transparent as such. For example, a capped interest rate loan is equivalent to the sum of a variable rate loan and an interest rate option. Non-financial derivatives are also common place; for instance, a mining licence that affords the holder flexibility to determine the production level is effectively an option to produce a considerable amount, a modest amount or nothing—the outcome depends on the underlying commodity price. Thus, although derivatives can be complex and have an air of mystery about them, they occur frequently in normal transactions.

1.2.2 *Who uses derivatives?*

Surveys of derivatives trading across countries and across markets uniformly identify financial institutions, primarily banks, as the major users of derivatives. Corporate and other users account for a much smaller portion of turnover but this understates their importance in a number of other respects, especially as a source of profit for banks. Table 1.1 presents the breakdown by counterparty of trading with banks in the OTC markets in Australia in

Table 1.1 Trading of OTC derivatives in Australia by counterparty

		Year to mid-1996			
Interest rate products	**Turnover $ billion**	**In-house %**	**Banks %**	**Government %**	**Corporate & other %**
FRAs	664	29	49	10	12
Interest rate swaps	265	46	36	6	12
Cross currency swaps	83	54	29	5	12
Interest rate options	28	------11------		------89------	
Caps/floors	25	48	9	4	39
Swaptions	5	19	14	0	67
Foreign exchange products					
Options	175	13	58	2	27
		Domestic dealers %	Overseas banks %	Corporate & other %	
Outright forwards	551	17	33	50	
Swaps	8,597	35	46	19	

Source: Figures are derived from material prepared by the Financial Products Research Group and published in the *1996 Australian Financial Markets Report*, AFMA, Sydney (1996). Foreign exchange figures therein are derived from Reserve Bank of Australia data.

the year ended mid-1996. This is a typical profile of participants in derivatives markets in developed countries, as presented in reports by the Group of Thirty and others.

FRAs and swaps are easily the highest volume interest rate derivatives products and banks (including 'arm's length' internal deals) account for around 80 per cent of total trading. Government and corporate customers account for the remainder. Non-bank entities have a much greater share of the options market. It is notable that governments are just as important as corporations in derivatives markets. By far the greater part of interest rate derivatives are denominated in Australian dollars. Non-residents are modest players in the market.

Close to half of foreign exchange derivatives transactions in Australia are accounted for by foreign banks and about the same proportion involves currencies other than the Australian dollar. Around half of all trading in Australian dollars took place in offshore centres (especially London and New York) in the mid-1990s. These characteristics reflect the inherent global dimension to foreign exchange trading, the international integration of the

Australian economy and capital markets, the role of the Australian dollar as a 'commodity' currency and Australia's place in the international time zone. The market for outright forwards, which is less than one tenth of the size of the swaps market, is notable for the high proportion of business there accounted for by non-bank customers.

The SFE accounts for a large chunk of derivatives trading in Australia, principally through its interest rate futures and options contracts. A counterparty breakdown of business on the futures exchange is not available, but anecdotal evidence suggests that it is similar to that for the OTC markets, bearing in mind that it does not trade foreign exchange contracts.

Larger companies are more active users of derivatives. Surveys of Australian corporations, by the Australian Society of Corporate Treasurers and others, find a positive correlation between company size and both the level of corporate hedging and its degree of sophistication. International studies similarly report a positive link between firm size and the sophistication of cash and foreign exchange management practices.[1]

The economic role of Australian fund managers increased markedly over the last decade and by the mid-1990s they held the greater part of household savings. Nonetheless, they are relatively much less important players in the derivatives market and rely primarily on exchange traded derivatives. Research by the Financial Products Research Group suggests that fund managers account for around 8 per cent of the interest rate OTC derivatives market and 31 per cent of foreign exchange swaps and outright forwards. Their use of derivatives is growing, however, and becoming more sophisticated. In this context, it is interesting to note that an international survey of developed country investment managers in 1995 found that fund managers are conservative users of derivatives. Many do not use them at all, and those that do tend to have greatest reliance on forward foreign exchange contracts and futures (Ernst and Young 1995).

In summary, though there is some variation across products, it is evident that derivatives markets primarily service the needs of financial institutions, governments, corporations and overseas entities. Derivatives markets are large in developed countries and their widespread use across sectors illustrates their central place in modern economies.

1.2.3 *Why do they use derivatives?*

Derivatives facilitate the trading of risk, so that risk is transferred

Table 1.2 Risk management potency of selected financial instruments

	Liquidity risk	Credit risk	Market risk: Share price	Market risk: Interest rate	Market risk: Exchange rate
Bank facilities—customer view					
Deposit	✓✓✓	✓✓✓	×	✓	×
Foreign currency deposit	✓✓✓	✓✓✓	×	✓	✓✓
Overdraft	✓✓✓	×	×	✓	×
Term loan	✓✓	×	×	✓	×
Futures/forwards					
Equity index	✓	×	✓✓✓	×	×
Interest rate	✓	×	×	✓✓✓	×
Currency	✓	×	×	×	✓✓✓
Options					
Equity index	×	✓	✓✓✓	×	×
Interest rate	×	×	×	✓✓✓	×
Currency	×	×	×	×	✓✓✓
Warrant bond	✓	✓	✓✓	×	✓
Emerging instruments					
Credit derivatives	×	✓✓✓	×	×	×

Risk management potency: ✓✓✓ : Strong; ✓✓ : Modest; ✓ : Weak; × : None

to those entities most willing to hold it at the market price. A simple example is an importer with future foreign exchange expenses, who buys foreign exchange on the forward market from an exporter who has future foreign exchange receipts. In doing so, both eliminate their exposure to unfavourable exchange rate movements and benefit from greater certainty, at the cost of forgoing potential benefits from favourable movements.

Derivatives facilitate risk trading by splitting synthesised risks. For example, fixed interest corporate bonds embody market risk from movements in bond yields and credit risk from issuer default. A bond investor can purchase an interest rate forward, or option, to eliminate the market risk and retain only the idiosyncratic (or company specific) credit risk. Derivatives are also used to re-configure the risk-return profile of investments. For example, debt-equity hybrids, like convertible bonds, include an options feature for purchasers to exchange their bonds for shares in the issuing company, so they can participate in company returns under certain conditions. *Table 1.2* provides an overview of the risk management qualities of traditional bank products and derivatives. The table is qualitative and captures the essence of each instrument's characteristics, not every eventuality.

Bank deposits and loans have valuable liquidity management attributes; for example, deposits can be drawn down, or loan stand-by facilities arranged, to satisfy demand for short term funds. Depositors benefit directly from banks' high credit standing and indirectly from credit diversification and banks' comparative advantage in managing credit risk. Turning to market risk (from movements in financial prices), foreign currency deposits (loans) can hedge foreign currency liabilities (assets), but are inflexible and not suitable for variable foreign currency cash flows. As a rule, traditional bank products are ill-suited for active risk management.

In contrast, derivatives have excellent market risk management features, described in detail in the following chapters, but quite limited credit and liquidity risk management attributes. Credit derivatives are a recent innovation that may change this. For example, credit swaps can be used to separate credit risk from the underlying loan instrument, in a similar manner to the splitting of interest rate risk from a bond through swaps. Credit derivatives are nascent but, given growth in loan securitisation, they may establish a foothold in the financial sector.

It can be concluded that if market risk, or price volatility, is low then there will be little demand for derivatives. On the other hand, if market risk is high, active markets for derivatives should emerge. Finally, it is clear that derivatives are largely complementary to other financial instruments and complete the tool-set for effective financial management.

a) Financial institutions

As discussed, banks are easily the largest users of derivatives. This is because their core business activity involves taking and managing financial risks, which they accept from their customers for a charge. Derivatives are an essential tool to manage the resultant risk that accrues to their account. Banks internally offset the individual customer's financial risks that they purchase; for example, by selling foreign exchange forward to an importer while at the same time buying foreign exchange forward from an importer. There are still, however, sizeable residual net interest rate and exchange rate exposures to be managed by banks. This is done by selling part, or all, of the residual risk back into the market. With new customer business constantly being written, there is an ongoing need for banks to re-balance and hedge their foreign exchange and interest rate positions. Derivatives facilitate the transfer of risk between banks, in much the same way as the interbank money market re-distributes liquidity between banks.

Banks also undertake arbitrage trading and run open interest rate and exchange rate positions (in other words speculate) to generate profit. This reflects their supposed comparative advantage in trading which, some claim, is obtained through superior information, size and scale factors. Derivatives are an important instrument through which banks implement their risk management strategy. Consequently, banks are both large producers and large consumers of derivatives.

Fund managers operate investment trusts, superannuation funds and the like on behalf of their clients, usually in accordance with pre-determined criteria. For example, limits may be placed on the allocation of investment funds between different asset classes and the fund manager must maximise returns within these constraints. Their character is different to that of banks because they manage clients' funds on a best endeavours basis and, on average, have a much longer investment horizon than deposits. Consequently, the emphasis of their derivatives usage is different to that of banks. Derivatives are used by fund managers to help diversify investment portfolios, hedge investment positions, enhance returns through a variety of mechanisms (including arbitrage) and reduce transaction costs, amongst other things. For example, restricted access to a foreign share market, like that of Korea in the mid-1990s, may be overcome by building an equity exposure by acquiring convertible or warrant bonds. These issues are considered in detail in *Chapter 5*. Commercial pressures dictate that derivatives are increasingly used by fund managers to improve their performance.

Lower transaction costs in portfolio management and trading of risk is one of the most important benefits that derivatives afford to users, especially banks and fund managers. This is neatly illustrated in *Figure 1.1*, which summarises the results of research by Gary Gastineau of Salomon Brothers. *Figure 1.1* compares estimated transactions costs in the UK, the US and Japan for a USD50 million index-replicating portfolio transaction in equities and that portfolio's risk equivalent in equity index options and futures. Transaction costs include brokerage charges, the bid-offer spread and taxes. Clearly, in each case, futures and options entail much lower transaction costs than trading in physical equities.

The reduction in transaction costs afforded by derivatives is less accentuated for interest rate instruments than for equity products but, nevertheless, is tangible. Derivatives provide substantial additional liquidity to the interest rate markets, which acts

Figure 1.1 Transaction costs for equities, options and futures—Japan, UK and USA

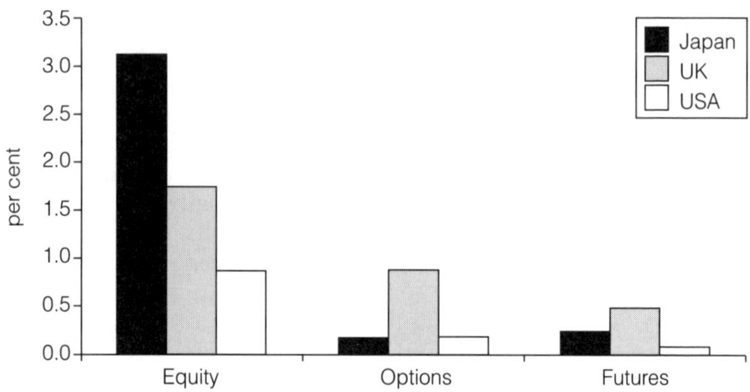

Source: Gary Gastineau, *Portfolio Trading, Futures and Options*, Salomon Brothers (1991).

to reduce bid-offer spreads and to lower the impact of individual trades on market prices. The mechanisms for trading are also easier and the cost of holding physical stock is reduced, as banks' bond portfolio interest rate exposures can be continually adjusted without buying or selling bonds. The increased flexibility this affords is useful in several ways; for example, banks can hold bonds to satisfy monetary authority liquidity regulations without carrying the associated interest rate exposure.

Derivatives assist entities by promoting better identification of risk and more accurate pricing of risk, as well as improving their ability to hedge and manage risk. These attributes are critical to almost all financial institutions, given the range of financial risks that they face. Derivatives also enable financial institutions to offer customers a wider range of products; for example, banks can offer a wider range of retail mortgage facilities to home purchasers, while fund managers can provide tailored investments for superannuants.

It is important to bear in mind that, while offering benefits to financial institutions and their corporate and government clients, derivatives' leveraged character and complexity pose serious operational risks for their users. Management of these risks is an important theme in this book. Management controls (like setting risk limits), procedures (like reporting), operations (like exposure identification), external factors (like legal uncertainty), systemic risk (like loss of market liquidity) are areas where serious problems can occur.[2] The leveraged nature of derivatives creates a particularly difficult incentive structure to manage and there is potential for small problems quickly to get out of control. All entities using derivatives must bear the cost of implementing safety controls.

b) Companies

Companies mainly use derivatives to hedge financial exposures arising from their business operations (see *Chapter 4*). Hedging can be defined as the use of financial and other instruments to reduce the variability of an entity's value. That is, hedging reduces covariance of the entity's value with the price of the variable being hedged. One explanation of hedging is that lower volatility of net income through hedging reduces volatility of the company's (discounted) value and increases the welfare of its owners, if they are risk averse. Hedging also helps preserve smooth dividend payments, that companies and investors seem to prefer.

In theory, this should be unnecessary as investors can replicate company hedging strategies and independently adopt their desired risk profile. In practice, there are significant operational costs and transactions costs to managing risk. Frequently, the most efficient way to manage some risks, especially those of a short-term nature, is for the company to manage them directly on behalf of the shareholders. Practical advantages of this include quicker company access to more complete information. Another benefit from hedging is that it allows companies to concentrate on their core business activity, where their comparative advantage lies, and provide their shareholders with the business exposure that they presumably desire.

While hedging can reduce the covariance of a company's income stream with variables like the exchange rate, it cannot eliminate long-run exposures to them. For instance, if a currency is devalued substantially, an importer is protected from the exchange rate change only as far out in time as the hedge cover exists. Beyond that point, the importer must adjust its operations to the new exchange rate level. Hedging eliminates transitory fluctuations and gives time to adjust to new circumstances in the event of a sustained change. This can have significant benefit, if adjustment costs are high; for example, if capital stock is made obsolete. The optimal time profile of hedging minimises adjustment costs to transitory shocks and, at the same time, facilitates adjustment to long term changes.

Of course, derivatives are usually only one element in a company's hedging strategy. Re-pricing agreements and fixed contract prices are more traditional methods of reducing short term price volatility. In the long term, plant relocation overseas, mergers and new financing sources are alternative ways that are frequently used by corporations to hedge.

In addition to providing risk management facilities, derivatives can reduce company cost of funds. This is more complicated than sometimes portrayed. Derivatives are of no benefit if the apparent reduction in the cost of finance achieved by application of derivatives is offset by a less transparent economic cost. For example, warrant bonds have a lower interest rate cost than straight bonds, but the difference is simply the value of the stock option sold to the bond holder—assuming that the option is priced at fair value. On the other hand, a company that issues short term debt and swaps it for long term fixed rate finance reduces its exposure to interest rate changes, without having to pay the standard long term debt premium. This is because it is kept on a financial discipline 'leash' by its short term debt holder. Thus, derivatives have an inherent value for companies and their creditors.

In practice, transaction costs and other distortionary factors also create opportunities to lower funding costs by using derivatives. For example, swaps can lower access barriers to markets. Hedging is a means to reduce the amount of tax payable, if the tax-earnings schedule is convex.

A minority of companies use derivatives to speculate; that is, their corporate treasury department operates as an independent profit unit within the company. This is only sustainable if the company has some comparative advantage in the trading of financial instruments. The margin between hedging and speculation is fine, which experience shows sometimes causes inadvertent position taking. While proficient company hedging reduces the likelihood of insolvency, deficient hedging can lead to unintended speculation and heighten insolvency risk.

c) Government

Government enterprises have similar risk management motivations as private companies, though their relations with government (in areas like tax, guarantees and subsidies) can greatly qualify their need for derivatives. Central government departments and agencies

Figure 1.2 An overview of global derivatives markets—amount outstanding USD000 billion

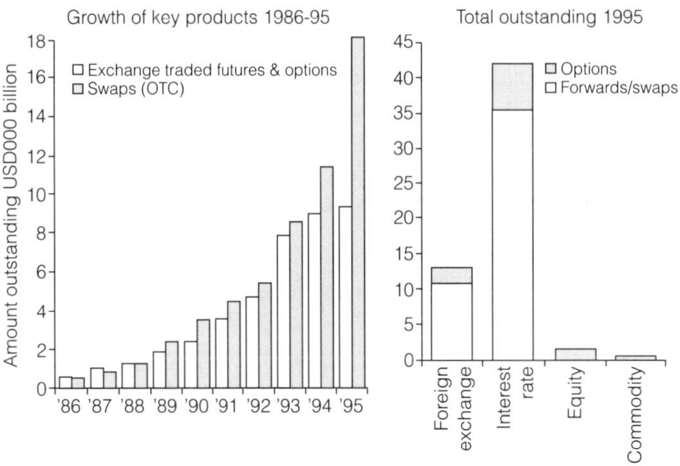

Source: Data for 1986–95 are from Bank for International Settlements (BIS) *Annual Reports*. Total outstanding data are for end–March and were collected in a BIS co-ordinated survey of global derivatives markets. Monetary authorities in the world's developed countries participated in the survey. The survey data cover a wider range of instruments than *Annual Report* data and include OTC options, foreign exchange forwards/swaps and FRAs.

usually have substantial debt and asset portfolios (notably the official external reserves) to manage, for which derivatives provide significant cost and flexibility advantages. The scale of their operations can create specific problems and requires sensitive management of their portfolios. Derivatives can assist in this regard. Futures, for example, allow government debt managers to alter aspects of their debt portfolio, like duration or convexity, without unduly disrupting the primary market for their debt. The use of derivatives by the government sector involves a range of complex control issues that differ from those facing private companies. These are beyond the scope of this chapter.

1.3 Market size and range of derivatives in Asia-Pacific countries

In principle, the above factors apply to banks and companies in all countries in the Asia-Pacific region. In practice, the extent of risk to be managed varies greatly across countries, so demand for derivatives is not uniform. Derivatives require a sophisticated infrastructure, which is a constraining influence on the supply side. This section outlines the depth and breadth of Asia-Pacific derivatives markets in the mid-1990s. An overview of the markets in a global context is followed by information on the size of the markets. Finally, the range of products traded on exchanges and on OTC markets is separately considered. This sets the scene for *Section 1.4*, which explains the cause of the cross-country pattern of development and presents a view on the outlook for derivatives markets in Asia-Pacific countries.

1.3.1 *An overview of derivatives markets*

Developed derivatives markets are liquid, highly competitive, have low transaction costs, offer a broad range of products and have a wide user base. They are founded on a secure legal and regulatory framework and a financially sophisticated commercial community. In contrast, emerging derivatives markets are illiquid, with trading on an *ad hoc* basis, have high transaction costs and an uncertain legal and regulatory basis. They exist in economies where the risk management culture is in the early stages of development.

Market turnover, the amount outstanding and the range of products traded are a reasonable guide to the level of development of a country's derivatives markets.

The global derivatives market expanded rapidly over the decade to the mid-1990s. As shown in *Figure 1.2*, both the OTC and exchange traded components grew strongly. Markets in the Asia-Pacific region mirrored this growth, as reflected in the rapid expansion of the OTC foreign exchange and exchange traded interest rate futures markets. Derivatives trading in developed Asia-Pacific countries (Australia, Hong Kong, Japan, New Zealand and Singapore) accounted for about one-third of the global derivatives market in 1995.[3] Institutions in Japan accounted for over two-thirds of the regional total, largely on the back of exchange traded interest rate futures. Derivatives markets outside of the developed countries are small and largely restricted to foreign exchange forwards and swaps.

Successful financial futures and options exchanges that actively trade a range of contracts are well established in the region's developed countries. Exchange traded financial futures were introduced in Malaysia and Korea in 1996. Large OTC derivatives

Table 1.3 Overview of derivatives markets in Asia-Pacific centres (notional amount outstanding, end–March 1995, US$ billion)

	Interest rate		Equity		Foreign exchange		Commodity	
	ET	OTC	ET	OTC	ET	OTC	ET	OTC
Developed countries (by location of trading entity)								
Australia	246	346	7	2	0	581	0	26
Hong Kong	189	477	1	5	4	966	1	1
Japan	4,211	5,099	53	0	0	3,211	0	0
New Zealand	15	20	n/a	n/a	n/a	38	n/a	n/a
Singapore	542	680	n/a	n/a	n/a	988	n/a	n/a
Other countries (by location of trade)								
Indonesia	×	–	×	–	×	1	×	×
Korea	×	–	×	–	×	<1	×	×
Malaysia	×	–	×	–	×	<1	–	×
Philippines	–	–	×	–	–	<1	–	×
Taiwan	×	0.2	×	–	×	1	×	×
Thailand	×	–	×	–	×	<1	×	×
Global	15,674	26,645	645	599	120	13,153	142	317

Developing country foreign exchange data are estimated average daily turnover.

Notes: ET stands for 'exchange traded' and OTC stands for 'over-the-counter', '×' means that no market exists and '–' means that a very small market exists. Exchange traded excludes convertible and warrant bonds.

Sources: Data are derived from material released by monetary authorities that participated in the BIS global survey of derivatives. Information on other countries is drawn from a range of sources, including industry associations and monetary authorities.

markets exist alongside of the futures exchanges in the developed countries, with Australia easily having the most advanced set of markets, though not the largest, within this group. Modest trading in foreign exchange forwards and swaps comprise the OTC markets in Taiwan, Korea, Malaysia, Thailand and Indonesia. Interest rate and other derivatives are traded on a patchy or *ad hoc* basis outside of the developed countries.

The great variation in the size of derivatives markets is illustrated in *Table 1.3*, which provides an overview of derivatives transactions by entities located in each country in the region. Markets of material importance exist only in the developed countries, of which Japan has by far the largest markets in US dollar terms. There are three important points of qualification.

Firstly, derivatives markets in Hong Kong and Singapore are international markets handling derivatives contracts that are largely denominated in US dollars and Japanese yen. For example, only 3 per cent of interest rate derivatives turnover in Hong Kong is denominated in Hong Kong dollars. In contrast, derivatives markets in Japan, Australia and New Zealand mainly service the domestic economy and most contracts are denominated in the local currency.

Secondly, nominal measures of the size of derivatives markets have limited application in cross-country comparisons. If account is taken of the underlying economic base (for example, by measuring market turnover of domestic derivatives in terms of Gross Domestic Product (GDP)) and the range and sophistication of products actively traded, then Australia has the most developed derivatives market in the region. The variation in annual turnover can be great too, mainly reflecting changes in price volatility of the underlying instruments.

Thirdly, care must be taken in interpreting derivatives data from a risk assessment perspective, as the market value of derivatives contracts outstanding is a small and variable percentage of the notional amount outstanding. For global markets in April 1995, the percentages were 4 per cent on average: 2 per cent for interest rate derivatives, 9 per cent for equity and commodity derivatives and 8 per cent for foreign exchange derivatives. These percentages vary across countries and across time, as well as across markets; for example, the above normal market value of foreign exchange derivatives is caused by unusually high exchange rate volatility in early 1995. Thus, notional outstanding amounts are not necessarily a guide to market value and outstanding risk. The global figures are representative of those for the region's developed countries.

Interest rate and foreign exchange forwards and options are easily the largest derivatives markets. *Table 1.4* summarises transactions in OTC and exchange traded interest rate derivatives by entities located in the developed countries.[4] Taiwan is included as an example of a country with nascent derivatives markets (it is atypical, however, of many developing countries in that it collects data on derivatives transactions). Both turnover and amounts outstanding are presented, from which it is clear that sizeable markets exist in each country. Turnover is highest on futures markets but novation and the short term to maturity of contracts act to greatly reduce the amount outstanding, relative to the OTC market.

Swaps dominate trading in foreign exchange derivatives, which are almost entirely OTC based; see *Table 1.5*. Most foreign exchange swaps have a maturity of less than a week. This is in contrast to interest rate swaps, which usually have a maturity of one to five years. Forwards and options are much less common.

Table 1.4 Interest rate derivatives in Asia-Pacific centres (USD100 million, April 1995)

	OTC			Exchange traded	
	FRAs	**Swaps**	**Options**	**Futures**	**Options**
Turnover daily average					
Australia	20	5	3	313	32
Hong Kong	16	18	1	134	10
Japan	23	128	112	4,333	174
New Zealand	1	*	*	7	*
Singapore	50	111	1	236	3
Taiwan	*	*	*	0	0
* Less than US$50 million					
Amount outstanding					
Australia	887	2,319	253	2,060	62
Hong Kong	1,195	3,315	252	1,829	314
Japan	1,739	45,163	3,779	37,737	4,378
New Zealand	47	95	61	n/a	n/a
Singapore	1,333	5,398	71	n/a	n/a
Global	45,970	182,830	35,480	124,360	32,380

Notes: Local monetary authorities in the above countries participated in a global survey of foreign exchange and derivatives activity organised by the Bank for International Settlements. Data in this table are derived from material released by the local monetary authorities. Data for Singapore are taken from the MAS Annual Report 1994/95 and are daily average data for the year 1994.

Foreign banks are the counterparty for the majority of trades and the corporate sector usually accounts for 10 to 20 per cent of transactions. Around half of foreign exchange transactions are denominated in local currency in Australia, New Zealand and Japan but local currency accounts for just under a fifth of the market in Hong Kong and one twentieth of the market in Singapore, reflecting their more important roles as international financial centres.

Foreign exchange trading in developing markets is dominated by spot transactions. Foreign exchange derivatives emerge through modest trading in near-term forwards and subsequently evolve towards longer-dated forwards and swaps as the market develops. Options trading comes at a much later stage in the process of financial sector development. Thailand has the most liquid of the developing markets. For some countries, like Malaysia, the offshore market for their currency is more liquid than the local market, because it is less regulated.

Equity and commodity derivatives are much less important than interest rate and exchange rate derivatives in terms of turnover and amount outstanding; see *Table 1.6*. Nonetheless, the

Table 1.5 Foreign exchange derivatives in Asia-Pacific centres (turnover, daily average, USD100 million, April 1995)

		OTC			ET	
	Total	**Forwards**	**Swaps**	**Options**	**Futures**	**Options**
Australia	229	13	209	8	–	–
Hong Kong	564	29	527	6 (includes futures)		–
Japan	1,122	-----1,064-----		58	0	0
New Zealand	41	4	36	1	0	0
Singapore	630	48	582	(included in forwards)	0	0
Taiwan	12	3	8	1	0	0
Global	7,026	969	5,497	407	126	27
Developing countries—Local currency turnover in each centre						
Indonesia	13	7	6	0	0	0
Korea	<1	<1	0	0	0	0
Malaysia	<2	-----<2-----		0	0	0
Philippines	<1	0	0	0	0	0
Thailand	<15	----<15-----		0	0	0

Notes: See *Table 1.4* for sources for developed countries and Taiwan. Developing country turnovers are based on April 1995 data. Indonesia's data cover interbank business only and are derived from Bank Indonesia's *Annual Report 1994/95*. Other data are based on market review and analysis in the financial press.

markets are still sizeable and provide an important risk management service to customers, who are the counterparty in the majority of transactions. The bulk of equity derivatives is exchange traded and based on share price indices, like Japan's Nikkei index. Commodity derivatives markets are particularly well developed in Australia, where more than two-thirds of the amount outstanding is based on gold.

Convertible bonds are quasi-derivative instruments traded in both developed and developing countries, though the markets are quite small in all cases, except Japan and Korea. Several countries are developing this area of the market; a good example is Thailand, where reforms stimulated the emergence of a small market in convertible and warrant bonds in the mid-1990s.

1.3.2 *Exchange traded derivatives products*

A list of futures exchanges in the region and the main financial futures and options contracts that they trade is given in *Table 1.7*. Australia led market development with the establishment of the Australian Options Market in 1976 and the SFE in 1979. SIMEX commenced trading in 1984 and was followed later by the other

Table 1.6 Equity and commodity derivatives in the main centres and Taiwan (amount outstanding, USD100 million, April 1995)

	Equity			Commodity			
	OTC Options	ET Options	ET Futures	OTC Forwards & swaps	OTC Options	ET Futures	ET Options
Australia	20	56	10	216	44	1	0
Hong Kong	50	1	4	--------11-------		-------6-------	
Japan	–	434	90	0	0	0	0
Taiwan	0	0	0	0	0	0	0
Global	5,470	4,500	1,950	2,080	1,090	920	500

Notes: See *Table 1.4* for sources. Data are not available for New Zealand.

exchanges. Although the growth of new exchanges had tapered off by the mid-1980s, the established exchanges continued to develop new products to meet evolving demands. The Manila International Futures Exchange began trading financial futures in 1990 but the market has been slow to develop. A second phase of exchange development emerged with the establishment of the Kuala Lumpur Financial Futures and Options Exchange and the Malaysian Monetary Exchange and the introduction of equity futures on to the Korean Stock Exchange in 1996. A futures exchange (linked with the Chicago Board of Trade) is planned to operate in Taiwan from mid-1997 and a market is also mooted for Thailand before the end of the decade.

Some futures exchanges also trade commodity futures and options contracts. Contracts traded are based on energy products, like Brent crude oil and high sulphur fuel oil contracts on SIMEX, and on primary commodities, like wool and wheat on the SFE. Commodity futures have a longer history than financial futures in the region. In addition to the exchanges listed in *Table 1.7*, there are exchanges, like the Tokyo Commodity Exchange, that trade commodities futures only. Their contracts are quite diverse, so for the sake of brevity this chapter focuses on financial derivatives.

Notable characteristics of the futures and options markets include:

- interest rate futures contracts dominate the other markets;
- futures based on equity indices are common and generally have good liquidity;
- options markets across all categories are much less active than futures contracts; and

Table 1.7 Main financial futures and options contracts traded on Asia-Pacific exchanges

Exchange		Turnover—1995 ('000) Futures	Options
Sydney Futures Exchange (trading commenced in 1979)	Bank accepted bills	6,173	713
	3 year Treasury bonds	8,821	434
	10 year Treasury bonds	5,741	604
	Share Price Index	2,476	653
	Individual shares	131	×
Australian Stock Exchange	Individual shares	×	9,146
Hong Kong Futures Exchange (trading commenced in 1985)	Hang Seng Index	4,547	646
	Rolling USD Forex DM	13	×
	Rolling USD Forex Yen	9	×
	Individual shares	n/a	n/a
Tokyo Stock Exchange (trading commenced in 1988)	Government bond 10 year	14,010	2,017
	Government bond 20 year	3	×
	TOPIX (equity index)	2,745	17
	US T-Bond	102	×
Osaka Securities Exchange (trading commenced in 1988)	Nikkei 300	2,319	122
	Nikkei 225	7,221	5,175
Tokyo International Financial Futures Exchange (trading commenced in 1989)	Euroyen 3 months	36,330	362
	Euroyen 1 year	25	×
	USD/JPY	14	×
Korea Stock Exchange (trading commenced in 1996)	KOSPI 200 (equity index)	new market	×
			×
Kuala Lumpur Futures & Options Exchange (trading commenced in Dec. 1995)	KLCI (equity index)	new market	×
Malaysian Monetary Exchange (trading commenced in 1996)	KLIBOR	new market	×
			×
Manila International Futures Exchange (trading commenced in 1990)	USD/DM	96	×
	USD/YEN	180	×
	GBP/USD	55	×
	USD/CHF	99	×
New Zealand Futures and Options Exchange (trading commenced in 1986)	Bank bills	478	18
	Government bond 3 year	27	0
	Government bond 10 year	8	0
	NZSE-40 (FIF)	4	0
	NZSE-10 (TOP)	3	0
	Share options	×	137
Singapore International Monetary Exchange (trading commenced 1984)	Euroyen 3 months	6,549	129
	Eurodollar	8,395	5
	Japanese govt bond 10 year	297	35
	Nikkei 300	174	3
	Nikkei 225	6,547	1,943
	Deferred spot USD/YEN	59	×
	Deferred spot USD/YEN	109	×

Note: 'X' indicates that no contract is traded. The notional monetary value of contracts differs markedly by contract type.

Source: Material provided by relevant exchanges.

- the market for foreign exchange contracts is very small, relative to the other markets.

These characteristics are common to those of the global markets. SIMEX is unusual in that it trades no contracts based on its local currency, Singapore dollars, and international customers account for 80 per cent of its business.

Table 1.7 does not fully capture the ongoing innovation of the region's futures exchanges. New products are continually being introduced; for example, share futures were introduced by the SFE in 1994 and the Hong Kong Futures Exchange in 1995. New trading and margining systems are being developed; for example, the 1989 introduction of an after-hours automated dealing system (SYCOM) extended the SFE's trading coverage up to 21 hours.[5] In another example, Tokyo International Financial Futures Exchange (TIFFE) introduced a new margining system in 1996 based on a system developed by the Chicago Mercantile Exchange, to reflect the actual risk on participants' portfolios. Links are being established across exchanges in the region and across the world to extend the range of products traded and lengthen the trading day for contracts; for example, SIMEX, TIFFE and the London International Financial Futures Exchange trade Euroyen futures.

1.3.3 *OTC derivative products*

It is evident from *Table 1.4* that OTC derivatives products are actively traded by entities located in each of the region's developed countries and that markets (other than foreign exchange) are nascent elsewhere. This is not, however, necessarily a good guide to the range of instruments available in each centre and the extent of activity in those instruments. For example, Singapore dollar derivatives trading is tightly controlled and small, though institutions based in Singapore are large traders of third currency derivatives. *Table 1.8* allays this problem by providing an outline of OTC derivatives products available in Asia-Pacific currencies at mid-1996. The table is subjective and provides a broad benchmark of OTC derivatives development. Market descriptions have regard to the size of the local financial sector and the economy.

Rather than separately considering derivatives in each currency, it is more efficient to concentrate on the broad pattern of development across the region and focus on common characteristics and particular points of interest. Not surprisingly markets in developed country currencies are most advanced, with the exception of Singapore dollar derivatives. The markets in Korea,

Taiwan, the Philippines and Malaysia have been similarly affected by official regulation. The Indonesian market is more open but other factors, like inadequate financial sector infrastructure, have combined to restrict market development. Thailand has the most advanced derivatives market of the developing countries but it is still emerging.

If a country's domestic foreign exchange market is tightly regulated, it is common for an active market in its currency to develop offshore, especially in Singapore and Hong Kong. A liquid Malaysian ringgit offshore market, for example, evolved for this reason. Foreign exchange risk management instruments are more readily available across currencies than are facilities to manage interest rate risk, though markets of some form exist in all countries. Active trading in options generally emerges after forward contracts are established, so the markets in foreign exchange and interest rates are relatively less developed. Exotic derivatives entail complex financial engineering, usually through a combination of forwards, options and underlying instruments, and are at the advanced end of the development spectrum. As they require mature markets in basic derivatives, they are actively traded in only a few developed countries.

In summary, the pattern of derivatives market development across countries is similar to that of futures exchanges: risk management facilities are most advanced in the developed countries. OTC derivatives do have, however, a wider currency coverage than exchange traded instruments, though the illiquid character of the market for some products makes the cost of hedging high in some cases. Typically, bid-offer spreads (if they are available) and option premiums are high in less liquid markets. These costs can fall quickly as markets develop.

1.4 Perspectives on derivatives development in Asia-Pacific countries

Derivatives markets emerge through *ad hoc* OTC transactions, develop into active exchange traded futures markets and near maturity offer a broad range of basic and complex instruments to manage risk. What explains this pattern of derivatives market development across countries in the region? This section examines the origin of modern derivatives markets in the industrial countries and identifies a set of macro factors that shape their development. The observed pattern in the region is then explained by reference

Table 1.8 Foreign exchange and interest rate OTC derivatives Asia-Pacific markets in mid-1996

	Foreign exchange		Interest rate			
	Forward/ swaps	Options	FRAs	Swap	Option	Exotics
Developed countries						
Australian Dollar	✓✓✓	✓✓✓	✓✓✓	✓✓✓	✓✓✓	✓✓✓
Hong Kong Dollar	✓✓✓	✓✓	✓✓	✓✓✓	✓✓	✓✓✓
Japanese Yen	✓✓✓	✓✓✓	✓✓✓	✓✓✓	✓✓✓	✓✓✓
New Zealand Dollar	✓✓✓	✓✓	✓✓	✓✓	✓✓	✓✓
Singapore Dollar	✓	✓	✓	✓	✓	✓
Other countries						
Indonesian Rupiah	✓✓	✓	✓	✓	×	×
Korean Won	✓	✓	✓	✓	×	×
Malaysian Ringgit	✓✓	✓	✓✓	✓✓	✓	
Philippine Peso	×	✓	✓	×	×	×
Taiwanese (New) Dollar	✓✓	×	✓	✓	×	×
Thai Baht	✓✓	✓✓	✓✓	✓✓	✓	×

Key:
✓✓✓ Strong market
✓✓ Reasonably active market
✓ Small/emerging market
× No market

to these factors and the likely future development of derivatives in the region is assessed within this framework.

1.4.1 *The origin of derivatives*

Several factors combined to stimulate development of derivatives and risk management techniques in the industrial economies during the late-1970s and 1980s. On the demand side, structural changes in the economy and in the financial sector were important. On the supply side, technology developments and financial innovation facilitated growth.

Financial sector liberalisation accompanied economic deregulation in industrial economies during the 1970s and 1980s. Features of domestic financial sector reforms typically included greater competition, elimination of credit controls and more freely determined interest rates. The break up of the Bretton Woods exchange rate agreement in the early-1970s preceded domestic financial sector deregulation (and contributed to it). Greater international mobility of capital and more rapid assimilation of information by markets, together with fewer restrictions on financial prices, led to a well-documented sharp increase in exchange rate volatility. Interest rate volatility also jumped, as shown in

Table 1.9 International interest rate volatility—an historical view

		UK	USA
Short term			
Bretton Woods	1950–70	0.31	0.21
Floating	1973–90	0.76	0.74
Long term			
Bretton Woods	1950–70	0.12	0.12
Floating	1973–90	0.47	0.40

Note: Volatility is estimated by the standard deviation, using monthly data. Data are taken from McKinnon (1990).

Table 1.9, and levels became more dispersed across countries. The rise in volatility of financial prices was probably the most important factor in the development of derivatives and expansion of risk management.

Financial sector deregulation reduced market segmentation and relaxation of exchange controls freed up international portfolio capital flows, which expanded rapidly. Increased trading on deregulated money, bond and foreign exchange markets provided an essential piece of infrastructure for derivatives. Price reliability and liquidity were most important in this regard as derivatives providers hedge their residual exposure in the physical market. There is positive feedback between derivatives and physical markets, because active derivatives markets improve pricing accuracy and increase notional market turnover, partly due to lower transaction costs.

Product innovation and technology each made a major contribution to development of derivatives and the financial sector in general. Technological advances in communications and computing were applied by financial institutions to improve information flows, lift trading efficiency, reduce transaction costs, measure risk, develop new products and design new trading techniques. For example, computer software has been developed to price complex financial instruments and their speed of execution facilitates more active trading. Other problems, like ongoing accurate measurement of exposures, have been transformed as discussed in *Chapter 8*. There have also been significant theoretical advances in areas like the pricing of derivatives.

In summary, a variety of economic and financial developments combined to alter dramatically the financial and operational exposures facing companies. Competition at home and abroad intensified, real economy relationships became more uncertain and financial prices became more volatile. In response, companies and financial institutions undertook more active risk management, which generated demand for hedging products. The technical development of financial markets, from regulatory, organisational and technological perspectives, was rapid and facilitated construction of suitable instruments to manage risk. Trading in derivatives exploded in the 1980s, though the bulk of this trading was confined to a small set of countries.

1.4.2 *Explaining derivatives markets in Asia-Pacific countries*

The observed pattern of development of derivatives markets in the Asia-Pacific region can be explained by the relative potency of similar demand and supply factors. On the demand side, the base of economic activity exposed to financial prices and the volatility of financial prices varies greatly across countries, while the infrastructure necessary to support active derivatives markets is equally diverse.

The region experienced rapid economic growth and development for a sustained period well into the 1990s. This involved structural change in the production base, which impacted on financial markets. Greater sophistication in production technology and organisation embedded in economic development was matched by larger and more complex financing requirements, at both an individual and an aggregate level. This is akin to evolution from sole traders to shareholder companies, and a shift from internal (self) finance towards external finance. Economic development also involved a substantial expansion of international trade in merchandise goods and non-financial services derivatives. In addition, the region became the focus of significant inward foreign direct investment from both within the region and from the USA and Europe. These events have combined to create new financial exposures, while scale factors opened up the opportunity for active management of the resulting risks. In this environment, demand for derivatives is largely dependent on the volatility of financial prices.

Exchange rate volatility in Asia-Pacific developing economies is considerably lower than that in developed economies, as shown in *Figure 1.3*. One reason for this is the heavy weight given to the US dollar in exchange rate mechanisms in the region. A second reason is the controlled nature of many regimes. Even where exchange controls are limited, monetary authorities have a heavy hand in the foreign exchange market; for example, Indonesia and Singapore. The cross-country difference in exchange rate volatility declines as the horizon over which volatility is measured

Figure 1.3 Exchange rate and interest rate volatility

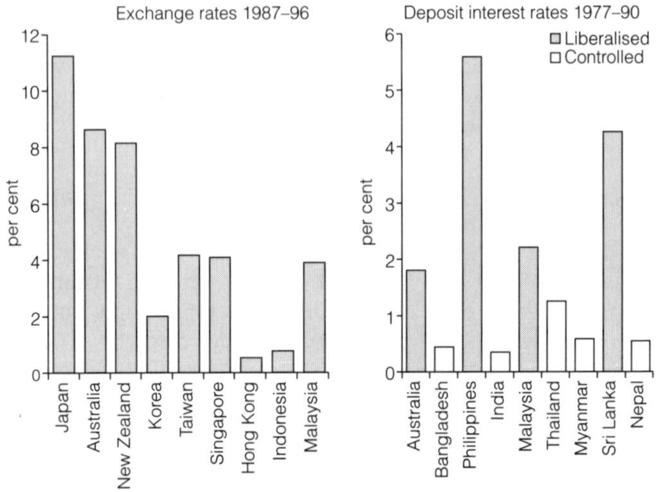

Note: Volatility is estimated by the average standard deviation of monthly percentage changes for rolling twelve month periods (annualised). Bilateral US dollar exchange rates to mid-1996 are used in the foreign exchange calculations. Data are taken primarily from the International Monetary Fund's *International Financial Statistics* and the Reserve Bank's *Bulletin* database.

is lengthened. One possible interpretation of this is that managed exchange rate regimes limit short-term exchange rate movements, but do not contain longer term volatility. In contrast, exchange rate derivatives generally protect against the former, but not against the latter.

What are the implications of all this for derivatives and risk management? Short-term risk from exchange volatility is lower in the developing economies than it is in developed economies. Thus, demand for derivatives to manage foreign exchange risk in developing Asia-Pacific countries is lower. In effect, intervention by the monetary authorities absorbs part of the risk posed by exchange rate movements, but the trade-off is occasional, large one-off adjustments if macroeconomic performance deviates from the required balance.

Financial sector liberalisation generates new financial risks for economic entities, some of which derivatives are equipped to deal with (in principle, at least). In particular, interest rate risk rises if tightly controlled interest rates are replaced by more flexible market determined rates that change in response to economic developments. Most Asia-Pacific countries have undertaken deregulation of this sort and experience shows that interest rate volatility jumps by a factor of two to three, and sometimes more, once controls are removed (see *Figure 1.3*).

The competitive dynamics of financial sector development increase corporate access to debt securities, whose interest rates are more volatile than rates on standard bank loans. Thus, the mix of corporate borrowing switches towards instruments with higher price volatility. More importantly, after financial markets are liberalised, private sector debt and financial savings in the economy rise significantly. This means that not only do average interest rates on financial instruments become more volatile, but they also apply to a significantly larger base.

International capital markets are more widely used to raise finance by companies in developing Asia-Pacific economies than are local markets. This can be an offset to business operational exposures, or may widen the exposure to be managed.[6] The rising exposure of foreign investors to financial markets (mainly equity markets) in the region, through portfolio investment, is a further stimulus to demand for derivatives. Many of these investors are familiar with complex risk management instruments, from their operations in their domestic markets.

Economic and financial developments in the region point to a complex web of domestic and external financial exposures that will require more active risk management in the future. Therefore, demand for derivatives is likely to rise. There are, however, important supply side constraints that limit their development. The principal inhibiting factors are:

- inadequate infrastructure in most developing Asia-Pacific economies;
- the absence of financial markets of sufficient breadth and depth to support derivatives through continuous and robust pricing, low transaction costs, residual hedging and liquidity. Interest rate derivatives are most affected; see *Table 1.10* for market turnover. Taiwan made most progress on this front during the first half of the 1990s;
- a lack of trained personnel and the absence of a 'risk management culture'. This affects all developing countries and is reflected in inadequate legal systems, poor internal management controls and doubtful corporate discipline that inhibit derivatives trading and make it more risky. For example, the legal status of derivatives in Indonesia is unclear and Taiwan has yet to promulgate derivatives laws. Disclosure

Table 1.10 Turnover on financial markets in Asia-Pacific centres (times GDP) 1993/94

	Money market		Government bond market	
	Physical	ET derivatives	Physical	ET derivatives
Australia	9.9	11.0	4.50	3.79
Hong Kong	13.8	0	0.72	0
Japan	9.7	9.2	2.12	3.11
New Zealand	4.9	2.9	0.76	0.31
Singapore	8.8	0	0.51	0
Indonesia	0.3	0	0	0
Korea	3.5	0	–	0
Malaysia	4.6	0	0.06	0
Philippines	1.8	0	0.41	0
Taiwan	6.5	0	2.29	0
Thailand	0.9	0	–	0

Notes: Money market data are for 1994, except for Hong Kong, New Zealand, Singapore and Taiwan (1993) and Korea (1991). Government bond market data are for 1994, except for New Zealand, Singapore, Taiwan and Korea (1993). Some data on the physical money market are estimated. Data are principally derived from the bulletins and annual reports of the monetary authorities and futures changes.

requirements are inadequate and regulators have insufficient technical expertise. Developed countries suffer from these problems to a much lesser extent, especially since a concerted effort in the first half of the 1990s to reduce risks associated with derivatives trading;

- high counterparty risk is a feature of volatile or depressed economies and controlled regimes that fail to enforce financial discipline. Poor accounting systems and scarcity of credit ratings make credit assessment difficult. The risks are that a counterparty may not be able, or may not be willing, to meet its contract obligations. There are many reported cases of institutions in Asia-Pacific countries refusing to meet losses arising from derivatives trading. In one instance, Bankers Trust was forced to sue an Indonesian company when it refused to make payments in relation to a swap agreement (see *Chapter* 7). The company alleged that Bankers Trust had breached its duty of care to it by failing properly to explain the nature of the transaction. The company's argument was rejected by the English High Court. Another example is Lehman Brothers who have been involved in several actions against Chinese companies that base defences on errant traders and unaccountable subsidiaries. These problems exist in developed countries too (for example, the Procter & Gamble case described in *Chapter*

2), but are much less accentuated there because both corporate discipline and legal controls are tighter; and
- inadequate competition between financial institutions in some economies reduces the incentive to innovate. For example, Korea has suffered in this regard and is lessening government controls in an effort to introduce more competition. To counter the absence of domestic risk management instruments, companies frequently trade on overseas derivatives markets. For example, offshore trading of Malaysian ringgit currency derivatives is several times larger than the domestic market. In another example, the authorities in Taiwan approved the main overseas exchanges (and their listed contracts) as suitable for domestic companies to trade on, through locally regulated brokers. This is seen as a pre-cursor to the introduction of domestic futures markets. The inexperienced nature of these companies creates significant risks for their derivatives transaction counterparties.

Other factors on the supply side, such as technology and product design innovations, are readily transferable across national boundaries and available to developing countries but are insufficient to support active derivatives trading in the face of the other problems.

It follows that dealing in derivatives in the developing economies is difficult and entails significant legal, operational and market risks. Transaction costs are high, market liquidity is uncertain, hedging is difficult and government regulation can be capricious. These factors must be balanced against the returns from dealing in the markets and being a part of the market's development. Further, particular care must be taken when dealing with companies from these countries as a counterparty in overseas derivatives markets. Aside of the commercial risks, these companies cannot be assumed to have the same level of sophistication as the average industrial country company. Hence the courts may be more willing to hold that banks owe a duty of care to these clients.

1.5 The future of derivatives in Asia-Pacific countries

Derivatives markets in the region's developed countries will follow global trends. The focus of change may be a little different than in the past. In particular, mechanisms are being put in place to improve the operation of the markets, rather than increase their size, *per se*. At the macro level, these include a review of regulation of derivatives markets and their users, improvements to company reporting standards for derivatives and international co-operation by regulators and industry bodies. At the micro level, they include education of users (at all management levels) and development of more sophisticated risk management systems, as well as design of new products. The developed countries are likely to provide a base from which emerging derivatives markets in the region can draw experience and resources. The framework provided by the General Agreement on Trade in Services (GATS) and APEC is useful in this regard, even though it is quite incomplete.

A range of economic and financial developments have significantly increased the potential user base for risk management tools in the region's developing countries in recent years. The amounts exposed to foreign exchange, interest rate and other market risks have increased significantly in most economies. In addition, liberalisation of financial markets led to a marked increase in interest rate volatility, though exchange rate volatility is lower than in developed economies. On the supply side, most developing country financial sectors have inadequate infrastructure to provide financial derivatives, except on an *ad hoc* basis. Progress in developing underlying physical markets is being made in many countries. Competition in financial markets within the region is likely to intensify, as countries cannot counter pressure from the globalisation of markets.

The pieces are coming together that will support active derivatives markets across a wider range of Asia-Pacific markets. It is, however, dangerous to move too quickly in the introduction of derivatives markets. Premature introduction of derivatives markets can be counter-productive. An example is the introduction of bond futures on the Shanghai Stock Exchange in December 1992. The market was suspended in March 1995 after speculation destabilised it. Such an event was inevitable as essential market infrastructure, like a deep physical market and natural commercial interest rate exposures, did not exist as interest rates are predominantly controlled. In addition, experience in the industrial countries, especially Japan, is that adjustment to a liberalised financial environment with more active risk management is tricky, with substantial losses made by many entities along the way. This is not a reason to halt the development of derivatives, as this will impair the efficient operation and competitiveness of the financial and corporate sectors in the long run. Rather, it means that the path of advancement must be trodden cautiously, as it has many pitfalls.

There are many new opportunities emerging for both providers and users of derivatives in the Asia-Pacific region. A secure risk management culture will take time to evolve in the developing countries; indeed, it is not yet entirely in place in the developed countries. A key element of this is a solid institutional and regulatory foundation, that enhances participants' trust in the integrity of the markets. It is upon this trust that the future of the region's markets lie.

References

Ernst and Young 1995, *Derivatives Usage by Investment Funds*

McKinnon, R. 1990, 'Exchange Risk and Interest Rate Volatility in Historical Perspective', paper presented to The American Economics Association, Washington DC, December

Soenen, L. and Aggarwal, R. 1989, 'Cash and Foreign Exchange Management: Theory and Corporate Practice in Three Countries', *Journal of Business and Finance*, vol. 16, no. 5, Winter, pp. 599–619

Notes

1. For example, a study of corporate treasuries in Belgium, the Netherlands and the UK by Soenen and Aggarwal (1989) finds a positive link between firms' size and the sophistication of their cash and foreign exchange management practices.
2. See *Part 3* of this book for further information.
3. Derivatives trading by institutions located in the region's developed countries accounted for 36 per cent of global interest rate and foreign exchange derivatives turnover recorded in the Bank for International Settlements' co-ordinated survey in April 1995.
4. This differs from *Tables 1.7* and *1.8*, which present data compiled according to the location of the transaction. For example, in *Tables 1.4, 1.5* and *1.6* a Euroyen futures transactions on SIMEX in Singapore by a Hong Kong-based bank is recorded in the data for Hong Kong, not Singapore.
5. SYCOM stands for the Sydney Computerised Overnight Market.
6. Euromoney Bondware data show a rise in bond issuance (including FRNs) on international markets by Asian entities from USD 4 billion in 1990 to USD14 billion in the first ten months of 1994. Corporations, banks and governments are all important issuers. Significant corporate bond issues are from companies domiciled in a range of countries, including Korea, Taiwan, China, the Philippines, Indonesia, Hong Kong, Singapore and Malaysia.

2

Case studies: catalysts of change

RICHARD ALLAN AND KEVIN JAMESON

Editors' Note

This chapter recounts three case studies which are potentially, if not already, catalysts of change for the industry world-wide. Although the factual circumstances of each are very different, they provide powerful illustrations of the disastrous consequences which abuse of derivatives in various guises may provoke.

The case studies disclose all too clearly that the problem is not simply a question of the opportunity derivatives may provide for fraud by an individual, although that remains always possible. Rather, and more worryingly, they suggest that misuse has occurred through a lack of knowledge and understanding of the operation of derivatives within the industry generally, and the presence of a misplaced complacency within management in particular. They also show that no one participant, be it a provider or end-user, can claim to be immune from the threat of loss.

The repercussions of these three case studies are already being felt to some extent. As discussion in subsequent chapters indicates, practitioners are currently engaged in re-evaluating their practices and policies, while regulators consider to what extent legislation may assist in preventing repetition of such events. Nevertheless, we believe that further lessons can be drawn from these cases.

2.1 Introduction

At times it is hard to comprehend the extent of the financial failures of the 1990s. In 1996 alone, two Japanese corporations reported losses which stretch credibility. Daiwa Securities lost USD1.1 billion as a result of dealings in US Treasury Bonds from Daiwa's New York office and Sumitomo lost USD2.6 billion on copper trading. In both cases, losses appear to have been built up over at least a decade. In the case of Daiwa, a single employee lost, on average, over USD400 000 per day every working day for eleven years. In Sumitomo's case, the average daily loss over ten and a half years exceeded USD1 000 000. There is not yet sufficient published material to provide detailed analysis of either of these cases, but unfortunately there is no lack of others for which there is considerable evidence. From this plethora of red ink, three companies have been selected because of their particular importance as catalysts of change: Barings, Metallgesellschaft and Procter & Gamble.

2.1.1 *Barings*

Barings, a 240-year-old British bank, collapsed in February 1995 following revelations of losses of around USD1.4 billion. As is well known, these losses were attributable to one person, Nick Leeson, a Singapore-based dealer operating in the futures and options markets in Asia.

The impact on participants in the financial markets was profound. For example, the editorial of the UK-based Association of Corporate Treasurers' monthly journal for May 1996 commenced as follows:

> In the same way that most of us remember where we were when President Kennedy was assassinated, most treasurers who practised through 1995 will remember the effect that the Barings debacle had on their business. (Jones 1996)

The markets were stunned by the speed of Baring's demise as well as the apparent unawareness of senior management that such an event was possible. The complacency of many firms was badly shaken.

2.1.2 *Metallgesellschaft*

Over a period of approximately two years, MG Refining and Marketing, a US subsidiary of the German company Metallgesellschaft, built up a position in oil and oil products futures and swaps (against long term sales contracts), which eventually were liquidated at a cost of around USD1.3 billion.

The case attracted world-wide attention. Even Merton Miller, a Nobel prize-winning economist, became involved in a very public debate as to whether the liquidation of what were designed to be hedges, not speculative positions, was justified, bringing into the spotlight the whole issue of the efficacy of the use of derivatives by corporations.

2.1.3 *Procter & Gamble/Bankers Trust*

In this case, an American conglomerate lost USD150 million in a set of interest rate swaps with Bankers Trust (BT), all of the losses being incurred over a three month period. While swaps are extremely common financial instruments, the amount of leverage involved was remarkable, resulting in a very rapid deterioration of Procter & Gamble's position.

Litigation quickly commenced, with BT and Procter & Gamble becoming embroiled in a long and very public court case, revelations from which seriously embarrassed both companies. Public debate proliferated on the ethics, efficacy and efficiency of the derivatives markets. If two such respectable organisations could find themselves in such an invidious position, who else could suffer a similar fate?

Each of these cases will now be examined in more detail.

2.2 Case study—Barings

The demise of Barings on 27 February 1995 represents the ultimate nightmare of financial institutional executives—to wake up one morning and find that your conservative, respected and apparently highly profitable organisation has virtually collapsed overnight, with losses beyond comprehension. A single dealer, Nick Leeson, apparently lost the firm over USD1 611 000 000 through unauthorised trades in Asian equity derivatives and the only certainty was bankruptcy.

The fact that a single organisation with a capital base of USD615 million could hold positions with a nominal face value of USD6 680 million is in itself difficult to comprehend, but the size of the position alone does help explain how the end could come so quickly, with realised losses of around USD1 420 million. On the surface, the collapse of Barings Futures (Singapore) Pte Limited (BFS) and the subsequent rapid demise of the Barings group should not have been possible, as the futures markets on which virtually all of Nick Leeson's positions were transacted are designed to ensure that losses are effectively realised each day. That is, cash is required for margin calls should any positions show a loss on their mark-to-market value.

In the two months prior to its receivership in February 1995, Barings companies in London and Tokyo had transferred USD835 million in cash to meet margin calls made by SIMEX. Yet it took Nick Leeson's flight from Singapore eventually to trigger the collapse.

2.2.1 *The facts of the case*[1]

BFS was incorporated in Singapore in 1986 with operations initially limited to non-clearing functions, executing orders from Barings Securities Japan (BSJ) through floor members of SIMEX. The Japanese operations of Barings were particularly active in trading the Nikkei 225 futures contract, an equities-indexed contract dealt on the Osaka Securities Exchange (OSE), and the Japanese Government Bond (JGB) futures contract through the Tokyo Stock Exchange. The three-month Euroyen futures contract was also traded on TIFFE, as were various options in each of the three types of futures contracts in Tokyo and Osaka.

Since the Nikkei 225, the JGB futures and the three-month Euroyen futures are also traded on SIMEX, there was the potential for arbitraging differences in prices between markets. These arbitrage operations are designed to be high in volume but low in risk, as they are meant to involve the purchase in one market and simultaneous sale in the other market of equal positions, allowing Barings to benefit from the small price differentials existing between the two exchanges.

At the outset, the Japanese operations of Barings initiated all deals, with Singapore being effectively an administrative centre, principally involved in the processing of BSJ's transactions on SIMEX. To the extent that Barings Singapore operations were filling orders from Japan, there was only the need for back office operations (which were managed by Nick Leeson). As volumes increased, however, it made sense to apply for floor membership, rather than to continue using agents. In July 1992 SIMEX granted BFS full corporate clearing membership, with Nick Leeson being one of two BFS employees registered as floor traders. This was Leeson's first experience as a futures trader.

Surprisingly (incredibly, in hindsight), Leeson continued in his position as head of settlements, thus giving him authority over both front and back offices. Yet, if his role as a trader was merely to execute orders originated in Japan, and if these orders were confined to arbitraging the markets, then there is some justification for breaching what is a fundamental principle of operational control. It was to prove to be a fatal mistake.

In 1993, to reduce costs, the arbitrage activity was moved to SIMEX because it had lower margin requirements than OSE. It was following this move that Leeson apparently began proprietary trading, that is, initiating deals rather than simply filling orders. This meant that he began to take open positions rather than automatically offsetting any initial position with the opposite position in another market.

Leeson's activities appeared at first to prosper; BFS's modest 1993 profits of GBP800 000 increased to around GBP8 million in 1994. To quote the Report of the Board of Banking Supervision (BoBS) Inquiry into the Circumstances of the Collapse of Barings (BoBS, 1995, para 7.12): '[Barings Staff stated] "Because he [Leeson] was so trusted, he was regarded as almost a miracle worker. He had a lot of free rein to do what he had to do".'

In fact, Barings was only being told part of the story. Central to the deception which Nick Leeson was able to continue for over two and a half years was the existence of Account 88888. This was ostensibly an error account set up in July 1992 whose main function was to allow for the temporary transfer of amounts which could not be immediately reconciled with client orders, or errors made in filling orders by Barings' dealers. Shortly after its establishment, on the pretext that it was not, therefore, part of the client reporting requirements, Leeson arranged for the programmers to remove Account 88888 from all internal reports. Yet reports provided to SIMEX did include Account 88888 in order to reconcile the exchange's margin requirements on futures and options contracts.

Leeson reportedly used Account 88888 artificially to generate reported profits in other accounts in three main ways:

- by transferring trades originally booked in other Barings group accounts in order to inflate the profits in these accounts;
- by adjusting the prices of trades in other Barings accounts against Account 88888, generating profits in the former matched by losses in the latter; and
- by booking fictitious trades between Account 88888 and other Barings group accounts.

The fact that London-based management did not know of the existence of Account 88888 meant that they were receiving a

Table 2.1 Leeson's positions as at end February 1995

	Number of contracts* Nominal value in USD million		Actual position in terms of open interest of relevant contract
	Reported	Actual	
Futures			
Nikkei 225**	Matched 30,112 $2,809 m	Long 61,039 $7,000 m	49% of March 1995 24% of June 1995
JGB	Matched 15,940 $8,980 m	Short 28,034 $19,650 m	85% of March 1995 88% of June 1995
Euroyen	Matched 610 $26.5 m	Short 6,845 $350 m	5% of June 1995 1% of September 1995 1% of December 1995
Options			
Nikkei 225	Nil	Short 37,925 calls $3,580 m	
Nikkei 225	Nil	Short 32,967 puts $3,100 m	

Source: Chew (1996)
Notes:
* Number of contracts are expressed in terms of SIMEX contract sizes.
** Reported matched positions means that the number of contracts were said to be held long on one exchange with an equivalent number held short on another exchange.

fictitious view of the position in Singapore. They only saw an increasingly profitable operation rather than a highly risky and capital-consuming speculative position.

Given the status and staying power of Barings, it might be believed that it would take an earthquake to topple the company. As it turned out, there was, and it did.

On 17 January 1995 the Kobe earthquake struck, triggering among other things a plummeting of the Nikkei stock index, which on 21 January fell over 1000 points to under 17 800. This also heralded the end of Barings, for the bulk of the losses occurred in the period following the earthquake. Nick Leeson's position before the earthquake had been based on the Nikkei's stability. He had long positions of around 3000 contracts on the Osaka exchange—a position which suffered if the Nikkei fell. Leeson appears to have attempted to try single-handedly to reverse the decline of the Nikkei by aggressively purchasing further long futures positions. He built his open position to over 19 000 contracts by mid-February, having a notional value of over USD3000 million.

This position on the Osaka exchange was not offset by the reverse position in Singapore. In fact, Leeson had almost the same sized position in Singapore as in Osaka but on exactly the same side, thereby doubling his exposure. This was pure speculation; it had none of the characteristics of the low-risk, arbitrage trades for which Barings' operations had originally been designed. By the end of February 1995, his actual position was as set out in *Table 2.1*.

The huge position created by Leeson had to be funded, with payment requests reaching up to USD150 million in a single day. The size of margin calls had been flagged as early as June 1994, as evidenced in a note by Ron Baker, head of Financial Products Group at Barings and the person operationally responsible for Leeson:

> One specific concern in the futures area is the level of margin calls paid by BSL London without knowing precisely on who's [sic] behalf the cash is being paid. Citibank are our SIMEX clearing bank. A margin variation payment is made from our account each day. If our account in Singapore does not carry sufficient funds for a margin call, BSL London pays the difference (could be as much as $10 million).
>
> The BSL treasurer simply receives a request for USD to make up the shortfall and has to satisfy the demand at very short notice, sometimes even during SIMEX trading hours. The request is in a lump sum form and the payment is debited to a 'Loans to Customers' account. Tony would at least like to know how much of the payment is for house positions and how much is for customers. (BoBS 1995, para 9.8)

The end finally came when an experienced settlements officer arrived from London on 13 February 1995 with a brief to investigate the reason for the size of the margin calls. He finally succeeded in his attempts to talk to Leeson on 23 February. That afternoon Leeson walked out of Barings and was out of Singapore the same day. He faxed his resignation from Malaysia and only re-emerged when arrested at Frankfurt Airport one week later. Nine months later, back in Singapore, he was jailed for eight years

Table 2.2 Barings' cumulative losses on liquidation

	GBP millions
Cumulative trading loss at 27 February 1995	827
Additional losses to close out	42
Foreign exchange loss	55
SIMEX costs	3
Cumulative loss after liquidation	927

Source: BoBS (1995) Paragraph 4.14 and Figure 4.5

after pleading guilty to a range of charges. Behind him lay a total loss of GBP927 million (USD1420 million).

2.2.2 *Conclusion*

Barings' losses were due to a failure of management and internal controls of the most basic kind. Leeson had responsibility for both the front and the back offices so that reconciliations and other control procedures in BFS were ineffective. This allowed him to:

- conceal the true nature of the transactions;
- manipulate the profitability reporting;
- obscure the level of open positions;
- hide the level of funding;
- ignore contact with SIMEX;
- operate Account '88888'; and
- direct the reporting of trading activities to management.

There was seemingly no independent check on any of these functions by anybody within BFS or Barings' senior management. There appeared to be no independent revaluation of the open positions nor reconciliation with the exchanges to agree positions. Even at a more senior level apparently no responsibility was taken for analysing the composition of the balance sheet or the business rationale for individual businesses or their revenue contribution.

The BoBS report states 'it is absolutely essential that top management understand the broad nature of all the material activities of the institution . . . and that product management have a detailed understanding of all activities that they manage'. Ron Baker, head of Financial Products Group, one of the product managers, admitted that his 'lack of experience in the area [equity derivatives] was a contributing factor to what happened' and that if he had had ten years experience in exchange traded options then the situation at BFS would not have occurred. The fact that such large profits were generated from supposedly risk-free operations appears to have been accepted, regardless of the warning signs (BoBS, paras 1.68–1.70).

The Chairman of Barings International Investment Bank asserted that he believed that Leeson's trading was low risk. The Singapore Ministry of Finance's investigation (San and Kuang 1995) rejected this claim, stating that this was in its opinion 'implausible and demonstrates a degree of ignorance of market reality that totally lacks credibility'.

2.3 Case study—Metallgesellschaft

One of the best summaries of what happened to Metallgesellschaft AG, then the 14th largest corporation in Germany, was provided in the company's Annual Report for the 1992/93 fiscal year (to September 1993):

> **Losses Threaten Group's Existence:**
> In the past fiscal year and the current 1993/94 fiscal year, the North American subsidiary *Metallgesellschaft Corp*, New York, generated losses which are threatening the Metallgesellschaft Group's existence. Metallgesellschaft Corp has tried to hedge long-term delivery commitments towards customers who had concluded fixed price contracts with short-term revolving oil futures dealings. As a result of the declining oil price, serious losses originated from the realisation of the individual futures contracts and their rollover. Metallgesellschaft Corp burdened the consolidated result before taxes with DEM–770 million in the past fiscal year (previous year DEM78 million). (Metallgesellschaft 1993, p. 9)
> **To our staff**
> Against the background of the planned massive reduction of workforce and the cutback of voluntary pays above the collective agreements pay scale, special hardship will have to be borne by our employees. To restore our Company's earnings strength, a large number of staff will lose their jobs. Those retaining their working place in the Company will have to accept losses. We trust our employees will understand the severity of this situation. (Metallgesellschaft 1993, p. 14)

2.3.1 *The facts of the case*[2]

Metallgesellschaft AG (MG) traditionally operated in the mining and smelting of non-ferrous metals. In the 1980s they diversified into such areas as explosives, chemicals and machine tools. One of their new ventures was into the US energy market, which it entered through its US subsidiary Metallgesellschaft Corporation (MG Corp.) and MG Refining and Marketing (MGRM). Reflecting the strategy expressed in the parent's annual reports, MG Corp. aimed to become a large and integrated operator in the market. It also wanted to achieve this goal with a limited amount of risk.

The idea was to lock in all levels of raw material and production costs against long term sales contracts, thereby achieving a low cost, high volume business. The first step in this operation was to acquire a 49 per cent interest in Castle Energy, a US oil exploration company which they helped to develop into an oil refiner. MGRM effectively agreed to guarantee the 'crack spread', or the margin between crude and refined products (eg heating oil and gasoline) for periods of up to ten years (Power 1994). MGRM also organised long term arrangements for transportation, as set out in the affidavit of Arthur C. Benson (the then chief executive officer of MGRM), who subsequently sued MG for wrongful dismissal (Benson 1994).

The main selling strategy of MGRM was to concentrate on longer-term fixed price refined sales of oil products, with some forward delivery as far out as ten years. MGRM's strategy was based on two main products. The first was its 'firm-fixed' contract, where MGRM offered long term supply contracts for energy products such as gasoline, heating oil, diesel and jet fuel at fixed prices and quantities on a monthly basis as far out as ten years. A second, smaller 'firm-flexible' program was similar, except the timing of delivery was at the customer's discretion—although products not ordered by the end of the contract had to be accepted at that time.

The final link in the core business strategy was to lock in the price of oil, in order to cover the exposure to energy prices themselves. If this price risk could be eliminated or at least reduced to a more acceptable form of risk (such as basis risk where the hedging instrument is similar to, rather than the same as, the underlying exposure), then MGRM could confidently continue to grow the business in a niche where there was little, if any, competition.

Ideally, if MGRM had arranged long term sales of products such as heating oil, diesel, gasoline and jet fuel for fixed periods on a monthly basis out to five and ten years, it should hedge with long term futures/forwards contracts to the same date. Such long term contracts were, however, virtually non-existent and accordingly MGRM adopted a 'stack hedge' strategy.

If MGRM had been able to neutralise its exposure to oil price involvement, it would have locked in a margin of around USD4 a barrel, or around USD640 million over the ten years against contracted sales of around 160 million barrels (Edwards and Canter 1994, p. 213).

Because of the thinness of longer term forward markets, MGRM engaged in a 'stack and roll' technique. This involved buying short term futures to cover all exposures, regardless of date of maturity and rolling the contracts forward as they neared expiry except where there was a revenue offset. Some contracts were to be rolled for up to 120 months.

One of the problems in this strategy, or indeed in any use of futures markets to hedge long-term sales, was the possibility that the futures would require funding for margin calls. In the present case margin calls would arise if crude oil/gasoline, heating oil prices fell, whereas the gains would not be realised until the long term contracts matured.

For the funding of margin calls to be an issue, one of two scenarios must apply. Either the energy futures markets must be in contango (forward prices exceed spot prices) and this contango must exceed any increase in spot oil or, alternatively, the fall in oil prices must exceed any gain via backwardation (the reverse if it is contango, with forward prices less than spot).

Since the energy markets were normally in backwardation, that is, MGRM could purchase crude oil, gasoline and heating oil at forward prices lower than the current or 'spot' prices, MGRM usually made a cash profit from such rollovers. Thus the market's pricing structure was initially working for them. They assumed that it would continue to do so.

In early 1993 a study of the past ten years of the relevant energy futures markets showed that: 'the average monthly rollover gain far exceeds the average monthly rollover loss' (Edwards and Canter 1995, p. 221).

Energy markets had a history of backwardation, so this result was not surprising. MGRM assumed that it would, on average, continue to be the pattern over the ten years of its current exposures. For any one year, the probability of *cumulative* losses also appeared to be small. An occurrence of twelve consecutive months of contango, making funding of rollovers an absolute issue, was unlikely. According to research done:

> the probability of a string of contango months occurring in the particular months in which they occurred in 1993 is extremely small—in the order of zero. (Edwards and Canter 1995, p. 225)

Finally, even if there were large margin calls, difficulties would arise only if MGRM was unable to gain access to these funds. Theoretically, this should not have happened, for three main reasons:

- MG was largely owned by institutions. Deutsche Bank and Dresdner Bank, the two largest German banks, directly owned 33.8 per cent between them. In addition, they had control over Daimler Benz, which owned a further 10 per cent of stock (Roe 1993). Presumably if the banks had been convinced

of the efficacy of the hedges, short term funding would have been available;
- MGRM had a DEM1.5 billion (approximately USD850 million) unrestricted credit line with 48 banks, first established in May 1992 (Euromoney 1994); and
- MGRM had the potential to use the forward sales as collateral for funding. In fact, in December 1993 Chemical Bank had discussions about securitising the forward supply contracts (Eckhardt and Knipp 1994).

Overall, the probability of funding risk appeared small to MGRM in early 1993, when their major exposure commenced. They had even organised stand-by financing to cover this and other contingencies.

In order to hedge its risk, MGRM had to have access to the futures and swaps markets. There is, however, normally a limit of 24 000 contracts applying to any single party. This limit is designed to protect the integrity of the market. MGRM arranged with the New York Metals Exchange (NYMEX) to have this limit waived due to the existence of the long term sales and, therefore, the non-speculative hedging nature of their transactions. Thus, by December 1993 MGRM had approximately 55 000 contracts—equal to 55 million barrels of crude—outstanding on NYMEX (around 16 per cent of total open interest according to Energy Risk 1994). NYMEX did have the ability to revoke this exemption at any time, as well as impose additional liquidity requirements if it deemed these necessary. This was a risk that MGRM believed that it was willing to take.

Strategically, therefore, MGRM was aiming to secure a margin between all-up-costs and sales; it was not holding open positions in energy products. The major issue was whether or not it could tactically achieve these strategies.

2.3.2 *What went wrong*

The program commenced in March 1992 with the fixed price set by MGRM at a level slightly higher than current market prices. There were modest sales as some customers took advantage of the historically relatively low prices to lock in long term certainty of both supply and price. During 1993, however, sales rocketed in an environment of low and falling energy prices. By the middle of 1993 MGRM had locked in around 185 million barrels (equivalent) (*The Economist* 1995, p. 83). Unfortunately, there was also a serious negative feature emerging in the market; the oil futures markets moved from backwardation to contango.

Futures contracts converge to the prevailing spot price as they approach expiry. When the market was in backwardation, MGRM would sell the contracts on expiry and re-establish the hedge in the next contract month at a lower price, thereby locking in a rollover profit. When the market moved into contango the situation was reversed and MGRM sold the near contract at a lower price than it could buy the next month's contract, resulting in rollover losses.

A second serious event was the sharp fall in energy prices in the second half of 1993, increasing the possibility of default in MGRM's existing contracts with end-users and heightening concerns about the viability of the program. In addition, because MGRM's positions were widely known to the market, market-makers were able to position themselves in order to benefit from the very large and predictable requirements of MGRM. MGRM appeared to miscalculate the impact on profits of their very public position and suffered accordingly.

Growing concerns regarding the size of MGRM's position also led NYMEX, firstly, to impose additional margin calls on the company and, secondly, to reduce its contracts. When this happened, MGRM had to try to take positions on the over-the-counter (as compared to the exchange-traded) markets. This proved to be difficult and expensive.

By November 1993 the situation was becoming unstable. This was not helped by the differences in the way the transactions were reported. Using American accounting procedures, Arthur Andersen reported a USD61 million profit before tax for MGRM in the fiscal year to September 1993, while KPMG reported, under German accounting conventions, a loss of USD291 million for the same period (Eckhardt and Knipp 1994). The main reason for the difference was that the US standards permit the unrealised profits on the forward sales to offset the realised and unrealised losses on the hedges, while the German standards do not. Thus MGRM was reporting profits, while the supervisory board was seeing losses.

On 19 November 1993, MG's supervisory board extended the contract of the Chairman of MG for an additional five years. Four weeks later the same board fired him (Eckhardt and Knipp 1994). During December 1993 they also authorised the termination of all of MGRM's outstanding contracts, thereby realising all underlying losses on the contracts. Thus the board, in one month, decided both the future of the program and the timing of its demise. Overall, the losses of this action and the subsequent settlement with Castle Energy to cancel long term contracts amounted to

USD1.5 billion dollars (USD1.27 billion and USD0.25 billion respectively).

2.3.3 *Conclusion*

While there were other issues and other risks involved in the rise and fall of MGRM, two facts are clear:

- without the existence of derivatives markets, MGRM would not have been able to embark on its long term sales strategy, without taking on extremely speculative positions; and
- there was a major change in the supervisory board's attitude to MGRM in November/December 1993, resulting in the eventual termination of MGRM's positions and underlying operations.

The case highlights the importance of communications within an organisation as to the nature and purpose of financial risk management. It also emphasises the need for risk managers to ensure that their strategies are resilient and able to adapt to changing market conditions.

2.4 Case study—Procter & Gamble/Bankers Trust

This case study differs from the previous two cases in that it deals with a small number of transactions rather than with an ongoing series. As a result, a somewhat different approach is taken in describing the background to the transaction and its ramifications. More emphasis is placed on the mechanics of the key deal than in the first two cases because it is the details rather than the strategic nature of the deal that were at issue and on which the subsequent court case was based.

2.4.1 *The background*

Procter & Gamble is a large Cincinnati-based manufacturer, ranking in the top 50 of the Standard & Poors 500 stock exchange listings. At the time of the transaction (late 1993) the company was a large scale user of derivatives, running a profit-centre Treasury. It had a track record of using complex derivative transactions in order to generate a low cost of funds. Company policy implicitly encouraged the use of such aggressive tactics to achieve a targeted cost of funds significantly below that readily available to corporate borrowers.

According to the claim lodged by the company with the US

District Court[3] they had a maturing swap which had helped generate funds at the Commercial Paper rate (CP) less 0.40 per cent per annum (CP–0.40%). Procter & Gamble wanted to replace this swap to ensure continuity of the low cost of funds. Discussions took place between the company and Bankers Trust, a financial institution active in the development and marketing of complex derivatives.

2.4.2 *The transaction*

Bankers Trust proposed a number of transactions, but discussion eventually focused on a swap with the following characteristics:[4]

- Face value US$200 million
- Term of 5 years, commencing 2/11/93
- Procter & Gamble to receive a fixed rate (which proved to be 5.3%) for 5 years on a semi-annual basis
- Procter & Gamble to pay a floating rate for the first 6 month period based on CP–0.75%
- Procter & Gamble to pay a floating rate for the following 4½ years based on the formula CP–0.75%+margin, where the margin is the greater of zero and the result of the expression:

  $$((98.5 * (i_5/5.78\%)) - P_{30})/100 \qquad (1)$$

  where i_5 and P_{30} are the yield of a 5 year constant maturity Treasury and the price of a 30 year Treasury bond (6.25% of 8/2023) respectively.

There are a number of observations that can be made about this swap.

- The margin was to be set as at the end of the 6 month period, and was to be constant for the rest of the life of the swap. In addition, the margin set was to depend on 5 and 30 year rates in six months.
- Procter & Gamble's cost of funds would be either CP–0.75% for the last 4½ years of the swap or it would be greater. No further improvement then was possible. If both rates fell, stayed constant, or even rose to a limited extent, expression (1) would be negative and hence the margin over CP–0.75% (being the greater of zero and this negative number) zero.

In effect, Procter & Gamble was selling an option which would either expire worthless (and, therefore, they would achieve CP–0.75%) or would pay out at a highly leveraged rate. Bankers Trust, on the other hand, could either partially or fully offset its exposure by taking the opposite positions through options and securities in the financial markets. For Procter & Gamble, the concept behind the swap was attractive. If the interest differentials behaved as predicted, they would achieve a much better rate (CP–0.75%) than their targeted borrowing cost of CP–0.40% for 4½ years. In summary, the transaction implied a six month view that medium and long term rates would not rise significantly.

Discussions took place between Procter & Gamble and Bankers Trust about the possibility of close out before the end of the 6 month period, with Procter & Gamble looking to lock in a less aggressive margin but to accept exposure to interest rate risk for a shorter period. Unfortunately, this discussion was never documented, and became a major point of dispute as Procter & Gamble insisted that such an early close out at CP–0.40% was guaranteed by Bankers Trust. Bankers Trust in turn responded that any early close out was to have occurred at market rates. Because close out would involve Procter & Gamble buying back options on the 5 and 30 year rates, the company was not only exposed to 5 and 30 year rates, but also to the volatilities of 5 and 30 year rates and the correlation between 5 and 30 year rates.

It should also be noted that, due to the complexity of the pricing, Procter & Gamble was unable to mark the transaction to market. This meant that management were not receiving timely information about the state of what amounted to a large trading position, and were therefore not receiving any warning signals alerting them to the rapid deterioration of their position.

2.4.3 *What went wrong*

For a while, nothing happened. However, following a rise in official US rates prompted by the Federal Reserve, US (and global) bond rates increased sharply and consistently. The general view at the time was that this was not a long term trend. In fact, rates continued to rise, and conversations began between Procter & Gamble and Bankers Trust as to the margin against CP to be paid for the last 4.5 years were it to be set before the end of 6 months.

Very quickly it became clear that the cost of funds had gone from CP–0.75% if rates did not change, to CP+4.5% by 22/2/94 (for example) when rates had risen by roughly 0.5%. Nonetheless, Bankers Trust assured Procter & Gamble that if the increases in rates stopped there, they would still lock in CP–0.75% in May 1994. This statement looks wrong but in fact was quite correct. It reflected the fact that rates has risen almost exactly to the breakeven point. If rates rose no further, they would escape (barely) with no additional margin. The gearing of the transaction meant, however, that even small further increases in rates led to large increases in the margin.

Unfortunately, rates continued to rise, and after various conversations between Procter & Gamble and Bankers Trust, the swap was closed out in 3 tranches. The final result was that Procter & Gamble had an obligation to pay CP+14.12% for the last 4½ years of the swap. In present value terms, the loss attached to this swap was approximately $130 million pre-tax.

In May 1994, Bankers Trust had an obligation to make a (net) payment to Procter & Gamble, and did so. In November 1994, Procter & Gamble had an obligation to make a (net) payment to Bankers Trust, but did not do so. Bankers Trust eventually exercised its right to terminate the swap.

In the meantime, Procter & Gamble lodged a suit seeking to have the swap declared invalid on the basis of 'fraud, misrepresentation, breach of fiduciary duty and negligence'. The basis of the claim was that Bankers Trust had led staff to believe that the 40 basis point margin below CP was in some sense 'risk free' at some point during the first 6 months, while in fact they had entered into risks that had not been adequately explained. In particular, Procter & Gamble claimed that Bankers Trust used a proprietary model to calculate the value of the margin at an early close-out date to which they had not agreed.

Bankers Trust responded by stating that it was always clear to Procter & Gamble that this was a risky transaction. In particular, it had been made clear to them that this transaction had option-like characteristics, and that at all times Procter & Gamble showed they were aware of the impact of market movements on the position.

As part of the discovery process, highly damaging tapes and other material became public which involved conversations between dealers at Bankers Trust talking about this and similar transactions. Procter & Gamble claim that this material was evidence of a 'pervasive pattern of fraud', and increased the stakes by seeking to invoke anti-racketeering (RICO) legislation which could have resulted in triple damages being awarded against Bankers Trust. Bankers Trust responded that the RICO suit was being used for its 'in terrorem' effect.

In addition, Procter & Gamble sought to have disclosed to them the results of official investigations following transactions with some similar features with Gibson Greeting Card Co., which resulted in adverse findings including those of 'serious fraud and misrepresentation'.

2.4.4 *Conclusion*

The case was finally settled out of court in May 1996, with Procter & Gamble paying Bankers Trust a total of USD49 million, consisting of USD35 million in cash and the assignment of the terminated swap valued at USD14 million (against the initial claim of USD150 million).

Some specific issues can be highlighted:

- Insufficient understanding that although this was called a swap and was documented like a swap, its financial implications were quite unlike a standard swap. The transaction was much more akin to the sale of a very large volume of 6 month options on 5 and 30 year bonds;
- A speculative approach to treasury management by Procter & Gamble, combined (it would seem) with insufficient reports, controls and inappropriate benchmarks. There appeared to be insufficient identification and appreciation of the consequences of gearing, particularly by management;
- Inadequate documentation of the early close-out feature of the transaction;
- Alleged aggressiveness of Bankers Trust's sales practices in respect of this and similar transactions. Transcripts of conversation in the Bankers Trust dealing room have encouraged this point of view. This has helped drive a re-examination by banks of the nature of their relationship with, and responsibilities to, customers when complex derivative transactions are proposed; and
- Insufficient appreciation of the potential non-financial consequences of the transaction. Procter & Gamble and Bankers Trust are both sufficiently large companies that this transaction would never have seriously damaged their financial viability. Nevertheless, both have suffered to an extent well beyond the monetary values in dispute, in areas such as management distraction and, in particular, damaged reputation in the eyes of many including employees, shareholders, rating agencies and regulators.

2.5 Review of the case studies

In each of the three case studies the companies failed to understand the potential downside of their strategies. In each case, prior to the crisis, there is justification for arguing that risks were 'reasonable':

- **Barings:** Futures markets require daily cash settlement of losses, so it could be argued that there should have been an automatic warning system built in, triggered by the request for cash funding of positions;
- **Metallgesellschaft:** Futures markets were again used, but to hedge positions rather than to take outright exposures to oil price movements. In the long run, short positions were designed to offset long positions, with no outright exposures; and
- **Procter & Gamble:** This transaction was designed as a replacement funding for a transaction which had been highly successful over the past few years. As such, it was repeat business rather than a major change in risk-taking. Additionally, Procter & Gamble had the ability to set the rate at any time within the first six months; there was thus an additional safeguard built into the exposure.

In many other regards, the transactions were very different. Barings' transactions were understood by management to be in the nature of arbitrage. MGRM's futures contracts were designed to be hedges, offsetting exposures created by their clients' contracted purchases of oil products. In the case of Procter & Gamble, the transaction represented a speculative view on the direction and volatility of interest rates and interest rate differentials.

Taken together, the three cases illustrate the potential power of derivatives radically to alter the financial health of both providers and end-users. Each used derivatives to solve their unique requirements within an apparently seamless world financial market infrastructure covering Singapore, Germany, Britain and the USA. Yet in each case the end result was disastrous in terms of financial and reputational losses, with world-wide interest in the reasons behind the failures. Like high-performance motor cycles, derivatives can produce remarkable results in the right hands and in the right climate, but they can also have extremely serious consequences in the wrong hands or should conditions change substantially.

References

Benson, W. A. 1994, affidavit of W. Arthur Benson vs. Metallgesellschaft Corp. (and others) (1994): USDC Maryland, Civil Action No. JFM–94–484, filed 13 October

BoBS 1995, 'Report of the Board of Banking Supervision Inquiry into the

Circumstances of the Collapse of Barings', *Bank of England* (London, HMSO 18 July)

Chew, L. 1996, *Managing Derivatives Risk*, John Wiley & Sons, Chichester

Culp, Christopher. L. and Miller, Merton. H. 1995, 'Metallgesellschaft and the Economics of Synthetic Storage', *Journal of Applied Corporate Finance*, USA, Winter., vol. 7, no. 4, pp. 52–76

Eckhardt, L. and Knipp, T. 1994, 'Metallgesellschaft: Neue Probleme in den USA', *Handelsblatt*, 4 November

The Economist 1995, 'Germany's Corporate Whodunnit', 4 February, p. 84

Edwards, Franklin R. and Canter, Michael. S. 1994, 'The Collapse of Metallgesellschaft: Unhedgeable Risks, Poor Hedging Strategy or just Bad Luck?', *Journal of Applied Corporate Finance*, USA, Spring, vol. 8, no. 1, pp. 87–105

Energy Risk 1994, 'Postmortem of MG Corpse', vol. 1, no. 3, pp. 3–4

Euromoney 1994, 'In the Line of Fire', March, pp. 40–9

Fay, S. 1996, *The Collapse of Barings*, Richard Cohen Books, London

Jones, G. 1996, 'Editorial: Treasurer: risk or risk manager', *The Treasurer*, May, p. 1

Metallgesellschaft 1993, *Annual Report 1992/93*, Metallgesellschaft A.G.

Power, W. 1994, 'Metallgesellschaft Ripples Are Rocking Castle Energy', *The Wall Street Journal*, 8 January

Roe, M.J. 1993, 'Some Differences in Corporate Structure in Germany, Japan, and the United States', *The Yale Law Journal*, vol. 102, pp. 1927–98

San, M.L.C. and Kuang, N.T. 1995, *The Report of the Inspectors Appointed by the Minister for Finance*, Barings Futures (Singapore) Pte Ltd, Investigation pursuant to Section 231 of the Companies Act, Chapter 50, Ministry of Finance, Singapore

Notes

1. This material is based on Chew (1996) and Fay (1996).
2. This material is based on Power (1994), Edwards and Canter (1994) and Euromoney (1994).
3. US District Court, Southern District of Ohio, Western Division, Case C–1–94–735.
4. Note that further transactions also took place, and in fact this swap was slightly restructured after it was entered into. However, in this discussion we will focus only on the 5/30 year swap.

Part 2

Analysing the risks

Part 1—The context for change examined the issues that shape today's derivatives industry. As described, the trend in the industry is one of rapid growth, driven by financial sector deregulation, product innovation, technology and the volatility of financial prices. The rapid growth in the volumes and sophistication of derivatives traded can create a sense of invincibility. This optimism and confidence has been tempered by the cases described in *Chapter 2*.

Part 2 reflects on the state of the derivatives industry two years after the events of 1994 and 1995 and highlights the unresolved issues. To some extent, industry participants have re-examined their motives, objectives, policies and procedures. Nonetheless, risks remain.

To better understand the evolution of the derivatives industry we examine the key participants in turn. The protagonists in the industry are the providers of derivatives (usually banks) and end-users. Providers and end-users differ in their approach, facing disparate issues and problems. For the former, participation as a principal in the derivatives industry is an end in itself, as described in *Chapter 3*. For the latter, the use of derivatives is normally a means to achieving broader business goals.

End-users may be further segmented into corporations and fund managers (including superannuation funds, life offices, unit trusts and hedge funds). While corporate treasurers were once the main users of derivatives, they are now rivalled by fund managers in terms of volumes traded and the sophistication of instruments used, especially in major financial centres. The dissimilarity in approach to derivatives (and also derivatives losses) by these two groups is a function of their diverse purposes, as shown in *Chapters 4* and *5*. Each of the three groups (banks, corporations and fund managers) is examined, to explore the current issues shaping the use, misuse, and non-use of derivatives.

After examining the participants in the derivatives industry *Part 2* considers the relationship between the protagonists and the legal framework in which they operate. Since derivatives are generally transacted in the context of a relationship, an understanding of both areas is fundamental. To the extent that problems remain unresolved in the industry, they are often most evident at the point of contact between bank and client. An effective legal framework is essential for productive derivatives relationships. Such a framework can help avoid the unwelcome and costly possibility of court action. *Chapter 6* explores the pressures on relationships and unresolved issues facing marketers. *Chapter 7* examines the legal environment within which participants operate, focusing on the legal risks they run and examining the responsibilities and obligations they assume.

Key themes in this section are as follows:

- *The impact of derivatives disasters.* Overall the disasters have been a catalyst for change, but the process of change is incomplete.
- *Growing professionalism is evident within each group of participants.* Examples include the requirement for greater technical expertise for individuals and greater emphasis on enunciating policies and objectives for the use of derivatives.
- *Senior management involvement in derivatives.* Directors and senior managers can no longer afford unquestioning trust in the abilities of derivatives specialists. Increased managerial oversight is a feature of today's industry.
- *Increased awareness of legal risks.* Providers and end-users are realising the legal risks in these transactions and appreciating that failure to address these risks may result not only in the invalidation of a transaction but also in the imposition of liability.
- *Push for regulation.* Immediately following the events of 1994 and 1995 there were demands for further regulation. New regulations are now being debated or implemented in many areas.
- *Erosion of trust in relationships.* Just as senior management

and regulators no longer have blind confidence in derivatives specialists, trust has eroded between the key protagonists. For example, derivatives clients seem less inclined to rely on advice offered by banks who are often perceived as biased.

- *Agency problems.* Conflicts of interest mitigate consistent and sound risk management practice. For example, performance measurement criteria applied to both providers and end-users may encourage excessive risk-taking. Such agency issues remain to be resolved in each segment of the industry.

3

At the dealing desk

MAX MORLEY

Editors' Note

Of all the participants in the derivatives industry, derivatives providers have the most at stake. Derivatives are not just a means to an end, but an end in themselves as a source of profitability to the financial institution. Driven by fierce competition, new technology and the need for effective risk management, derivatives providers have experienced a metamorphosis. While certainly not the only impetus for change, the events of 1994/95 have hastened the pace of the transition.

Chapter 3 *describes how attitudes and practice have changed over time. The author argues that derivatives providers have become increasingly professional in their approach, as a natural consequence of product maturity. Yet many issues remain to be fully resolved and best practice is far from universal. Remaining issues of concern are noted in the context of recent positive developments.*

3.1 Introduction

Recent years have witnessed significant developments in derivatives, not only in the increasing sophistication of the products but also in the transformation of the industry. Whereas most of the knowledge of derivatives once resided on the derivatives dealing desk, knowledge is now widely dispersed among a range of professionals. The largely transparent way in which derivatives transactions are now priced and dealt, together with increased end-user awareness of the nature of the products and pricing techniques, is vastly different from the early days of derivatives. An alternative title for this chapter could have been 'The Disappearing Black Box'. This phrase succinctly describes the key change. The 'black box' on the derivatives dealing desk is being steadily dismantled and reassembled in the full light of day in the offices of those professionals who have brought their specialisations to bear on the industry: lawyers, accountants, tax advisers, credit assessors, regulators, risk managers, compliance officers and senior managers, to mention but a few.

It is the process by which this change has occurred which is the subject of this chapter, along with some consideration of impediments to its completion. As we will see later, there is always the risk that as fast as the wider industry catches up with the expertise on dealing desks, radically new products are developed which open the gap again. The Procter & Gamble/Bankers Trust transaction, described in *Chapter 2*, is a case in point.

A central theme of this chapter is that much of the change in both the role and the function of a professional derivatives dealing desk is inevitable. Evolutionary change is the natural consequence of the maturing of most products. Therefore, it is argued that a transformation of the derivatives industry would have occurred regardless of the highly publicised and comparatively recent 'derivatives disasters' outlined in *Chapter 2*, although these have clearly assisted in accelerating the timing and pace of the evolution. An example of the transformation relates to the role of market personnel who fifteen years ago dealt with early forms of derivatives transactions. They now find themselves involved in complex issues of product suitability, attempting to determine the appropriateness of derivatives for end-user applications. The shift in knowledge from the few specialists to the many professionals is a further example of change. It is this writer's view that we have seen a classic, albeit extreme, manifestation of the life-cycle of a mature financial product. The role of the disasters has been to accelerate this evolutionary life-cycle. Yet generalisations about the life-cycle of derivatives should be made with caution. The term 'derivative' actually encompasses a family of specific product groups. Each of them is, in fact, at a different point in its own evolution.

In order to understand how significant the change has been

it is important to consider both the industry and the dealing functions from an historical perspective. This discussion will take place in *Section 3.3*, following an overview of the role of the dealing desk in *Section 3.2*. The derivatives professional does not, however, work in isolation. *Section 3.4* will examine parallel developments in a number of related disciplines such as law, accountancy and tax that have affected the daily work practices of the derivatives dealer. The evolution of the role of the risk manager is discussed briefly here and in *Section 3.7*, along with other significant management issues.

A useful barometer of the major influences on the derivatives dealing business has been the way in which sources of revenue have changed and developed. Accordingly the interaction between dealing desk and end-users is examined in *Section 3.5*. Specific relationships between the dealing desk and financial engineers, risk advisors/sales desks and the professional hedging markets are reviewed. Dealing desk activity is also affected by product innovation; the impact of this process is scrutinised in *Section 3.6*.

It should be noted that most of this discussion focuses on over-the-counter (OTC) interest rate and exchange rate derivatives. Much of the argument, however, is also relevant to equity and commodity derivatives. Exchange traded derivatives are not treated separately, although reference is made to them where appropriate.

3.2 The role and functions of the professional derivatives desk

For the purposes of this discussion, the traditional function of the derivatives dealing desk can be described as:

- provision of interest rate and foreign exchange risk management products to end-users;
- price-making to achieve both portfolio liquidity (through market access) and profitability (by retaining the bid-offer spread);
- taking 'on desk' proprietary risk proactively.

The primary role of the dealing desk is thus to earn income through performance of the above functions. Rewards earned must constantly be balanced against risks incurred. These functions broadly define the sources of revenue for a contemporary derivatives desk, which will be considered in more detail in *Section 3.5*. It is important to recognise, however, that it is the nature of these functions that has changed (as described in *Section 3.3*) and will doubtless continue to evolve further over time.

No mention has been made here of the marketing function, as this is specifically addressed in *Chapter 6*. It should not be forgotten that marketing strategy is relevant to both the development of the product and the creation of sources of revenue.

3.3 An historical perspective

Derivative products can be broadly classified into four groups:

- forward-based products;
- option-based products;
- correlation-based products;
- leveraged derivative products.

The two basic groups, forwards and options, were introduced in *Chapter 1*. More recently, products utilising correlation and leverage have emerged, although it should be noted that these new groups retain the essential features of the earlier groups. It should further be noted that the development of these groups and the products within them did not take place strictly sequentially.

- *Forward-based* derivatives were the first generation of derivatives commonly traded. As discussed in *Chapter 1*, products in this category have a comparatively simple pay-off profile. They include well known and widely used FRAs and interest rate and currency swaps.
- The *option-based* group introduced the need for a more mathematically competent dealer (and one cognisant with the Greek alphabet!). This resulted in a change in the composition of the derivatives desk since a proportion of derivatives 'traders' were replaced by mathematicians often sourced from the engineering corps (hence the term 'rocket scientist'). It is not many years ago that comparatively few bank or corporate treasury dealers had any in-depth knowledge of option theory, despite the widespread use of the product group. Now 'option literacy' is virtually a prerequisite to working in a corporate treasury or bank dealing room, let alone to becoming a derivatives practitioner.
- *Correlation-based* products are a more recent variant on the basic forward/option concept. The payoff of the product depends not only on the level of interest rates (say), but also on relationships between different types of rates, prices or

indexes. Even within this group there are further sub-categories of products. For example, the degree of correlation risk undertaken in most basket options is considerably lower than that in the more exotic 'quantos'. It is this latter genre which now carries the 'black box' tag from the point of view of many potential end-users.

- The so-called *leveraged* or geared derivative is essentially an offshoot of the previous groups. This type of instrument may incorporate features borrowed from any or all of the previous three groups of derivatives. It is probably the least understood by end-users, not only in terms of 'fair value' but also in its potential impact on market liquidity. It is often to be found embedded in securities transactions. The evolution of the leveraged derivative and its impact in new product innovation is considered in Section 3.6. This product group has generated considerable concern among regulators on account of the threat of systemic risk which it potentially poses.

The transaction between Procter & Gamble and Bankers Trust described in *Chapter 2* has elements of all of these categories. Its value rose and fell with interest rates, in the same way as a forward transaction. Furthermore, its value rose and fell with interest rate volatility like an option transaction. Even more dramatically, the value of the transaction was linked not only to the level and volatility of 5 and 30 year rates, but also to the correlation between them, making it a correlation product. Finally, all of these effects were exaggerated by the leverage of the transaction. As rates rose (beyond a certain point) for example, the transaction lost value roughly 20 times faster than an ungeared or unleveraged transaction.

As noted in *Table 3.1*, each new generation of derivatives has ushered in a significant change in the expertise required of the derivatives dealer. Yet even within a generation the functions performed by the desk have themselves developed considerably. Interest rate and currency swaps provide an example of a first generation derivatives product. As part of the 'forward product' group of derivatives, they are now furthest advanced in their life-cycle and in fact have entered the 'commodity' phase in sophisticated financial centres. Hence an examination of swaps provides insight into the degree of change which has taken place in 'on desk' dealing functions.

Early swaps were entered into directly between end-user counterparties in order to take advantage of anomalies created by market regulation. Restrictions on the international or even

Table 3.1 Derivatives product life-cycle

Event	Sources of revenue	Effect on dealing desk functions
First generation derivatives		
broking/intermediating swaps	arrangement fees	strong management of deal pipeline to match
	spread for credit risk	credit—intermediating (still 'matching')
		legals/documents negotiated 'on desk'
		accruals accounting-based reporting
positional risk/hedged positions	bid-offer spread for trading risk	add interest and currency trading skills from bond and FX markets
		most derivative desks part of capital markets department
		mark-to-market accounting treatment
zero curves/technology advances		front office valuation; back office still accruing (systems lagging); transparency of 'fair value' issue for many end-users
genuine risk management services offered to clients	trading movement in swap spreads	interpreting the impact of end-user flows on the level of swap spreads
trading liquidity in some derivatives outstrips liquidity in the underlying instrument	outright positional risk	proprietary risk function added
documentation issues		focus on legal issues shifts from dealer to legal specialist
master agreements developed		market practice becomes codified; dealing desk no longer sole custodian of market practice
Hammersmith & Fulham		process hastened; counterparty credit issues more starkly identified; transfer of derivatives product knowledge from 'on desk' to credit and legal functionaries

Second generation derivatives		
option pricing theories put into practice	volatility trading income	hedging becomes mathematically based/model driven
writing options—capacity to deal issues revisited in various industry segments		'on desk' knowledge of counterparty's legal position increases
Third generation derivatives		
new products: basket options	correlation risk income	product design for end user acceptance; statistical analysis of risk
new products: quantos	supernormal income from 'fair value' translucency	strong innovation emphasis added to desk
Fourth generation derivatives		
leveraged derivatives	liquidity risk income	product design for end-user v. product design to shift unsavoury risk positions
derivative product vehicles set up	importance of access to market 'flows' of business recognised	issues surrounding capital required to support derivatives dealing business debated and clarified; ratings agencies enter the derivatives industry
industry disasters; Barings		impetus to creation of segregated risk manager role; more 'dealer' knowledge of risks distributed 'off desk'
		senior management awareness of derivatives enhanced; strategic planning for derivatives business moves away from dealing desk towards senior management

sub-national flow of capital created pricing imperfections. Early swap transactions were arranged on a 'matched basis' to satisfy the offsetting needs of end-users to their mutual benefit. It soon became apparent that the requirement to 'match' the needs of two end-users was restricting swap transactions which would have been consummated but for timing, volume, tenor or other structural discrepancies. Unwillingness of end-users to deal directly with each other, due to credit or other considerations, saw the early dealers assume the function of credit intermediary (charging a credit type spread for standing between two end-users). It was, however, the subsequent recognition that an informed intermediary could take on 'unmatched' swap positions with a view to laying them off (matching them out) at a later date which created the first OTC derivatives dealing desk. The primary function of this desk was to act as principal in a swap transaction while being aware of, and even managing, a 'pipeline of potential deals' against which the original deal could be matched.

Expertise grew quickly, with abnormal (in economic terms) profits being available to these early derivatives desks. Short-term hedging techniques were developed (or rather imported) from bond markets to lengthen the effective periods for which swaps could be held unmatched. Early forms of mark-to-market-based accounting were introduced as it became apparent that accrual methodologies were inappropriate. The search for suitable valuation methodologies, combined with technological progress, provided the dealing desk with the capacity to value swaps on a discrete cash flow basis. The previously academic notion of the zero coupon curve was thereby put into practice; 'on desk' knowledge of this concept moved from zero to expert in a very short period. This probably represented the largest single factor in the emergence of the modern dealing desk.

Steady growth in acceptance of zero curve techniques provided the derivatives desk with considerably more scope in terms of the types of transaction it could undertake. It also stimulated trading liquidity in the derivatives products themselves. Early 'transaction matching' dealers were already being forced to modify their practices to accommodate the move to the 'mark-to-market' environment.

This liquidity opened up other activities for the derivatives dealing desk. It could now seek to retain a bid-offer spread in a trading (as opposed to credit) sense. In other words, derivatives desks were no longer forced to match transactions exactly for hedging purposes. A 4-year swap might, on occasion, be hedged by a 3-year or a 5-year swap, or some combination of the two, with some additional (yet quantified) risk and a great deal more flexibility in book management.

The primary source of revenue continued to change. Interaction between derivatives markets and capital markets increased and opened the door for derivatives desks to take proprietary risk. This represented a significant shift in the role and functions of a desk which originally had arranged transactions on a matched basis from a pipeline of interested end-users.

While counterparty credit issues initially predominated, market risk and liquidity risk progressively assumed importance. The interaction between derivatives and the underlying physical markets also became significant as volumes grew. Derivatives dealers built skills in the area of managing access to market liquidity as volumes started to outstrip the liquidity available in the underlying instruments. Continuing technological advances brought the capability to carry out sophisticated simulations and stress tests which supported the development of complex derivatives including leveraged transactions.

Futures and options exchanges initially perceived this growth of OTC derivatives as a threat to the viability of exchanges, fearing volumes and liquidity would be drawn away from the regulated exchange environment. In fact, the reverse generally occurred, with the OTC derivatives practitioner contributing to the liquidity available in the relevant exchange-traded instrument.

Over time the abnormal profits which had been available in the early part of the product life-cycle diminished, with the result that the vanilla forward and option-based derivatives became commodities. As with any commoditisation process, the emphasis thereupon shifted to non-price differentiation. This inevitably prompted a marked increase in marketing activity as derivatives were incorporated into the relationship banking framework (see *Chapter 6*). Derivatives were no longer the province solely of specialist sales staff; rather, they became part of the set of products promoted by generalist financial markets staff and relationship managers. The end-user market was consciously expanded. With the base product now distributed by a generalist salesperson, the specialist derivatives team became free (or forced) to concentrate on 'cutting edge' product variations. This in turn led to the development of leveraged derivatives for sophisticated end-users. The derivatives dealing desk, in search of a new source of revenue to compensate for the commoditisation of the base product, developed new products accordingly.

It is important to understand that this process at best becomes an engine for innovations and ideas, but at worst can result in complication for its own sake. Despite organisation-wide objectives, the individual parts of most larger organisations are loath to give up their revenue stream, or very existence. As products become 'commoditised' and move away from the specialist dealing desk, there is an imperative to replace them with new products. This gives rise to some significant management challenges, and leads us to a discussion of the relationship between innovation and suitability in *Section 3.6* and in *Chapter 11*. The whole issue of the relationship between the trading desk, specialist and generalist sales staff and relationship managers is outside the subject area of this chapter, but must be dealt with if an organisation is to maximise bank-wide rather than dealing desk profitability.

3.4 Shifting product knowledge to the support profession

As with any rapidly developing and growing product, knowledge among the support professions tended to lag behind the 'state of the art' practised or trialled by the product specialist. That this was true of the derivatives industry is an understatement. The existence of this timelag and the consequential discrepancy in levels of understanding within the legal, accounting and taxation professions arguably contributed to the high profile derivatives disasters discussed in *Chapter 2*. It is important to consider the reasons for this timelag. The skills and understanding were initially revolutionary and simply did not exist in the support areas. This is understandable, but in many organisations the process by which the specialist knowledge was transferred was poorly managed. People who gained those skills tended to move from the support areas to the dealing desk, as such individuals were in short supply in a growing market. This migration was exacerbated by a culture that provided dealing desk personnel with much higher salaries, bonuses and status than support staff. It is only recently that dealing desk management has realised that it is in its own interest to ensure, firstly, that skills are transferred to support areas in a managed way and, secondly, that the remuneration of support staff reflects their skills and their scarcity in a market-wide sense.

The position is now changing, especially as the product has moved into the vanilla or 'commodity' phase. On the one hand, the dealer has had to become more specialised in the trading of the product itself and has lost the more general knowledge of industry issues held by predecessors. On the other hand, there has been an increase in product knowledge within the supporting professions which has stemmed from their need to address issues raised by derivatives in their own specialist areas.

In the legal field the advent and broad acceptance of master agreements was pioneered by the International Swaps and Derivatives Association, Inc. (ISDA), previously known as the International Swap Dealers' Association, Inc. ISDA published its first master agreement—the 'Interest Rate and Currency Exchange Agreement' and 'Definitions'—in 1987. Prior to the promulgation of the first ISDA Master Interest Rate and Currency Swaps Agreement, derivatives dealers had to have a working knowledge of the accepted terms and conditions of a swap agreement and would have been expected to clarify any unusual documentary requirements at the time of dealing. In practice, many discrepancies were debated after the event, but nonetheless it was the derivatives dealer who was central to the debate. As the legal profession and industry associations caught up with the issues surrounding the explosive growth of derivatives usage, responsibility for addressing the legal niceties switched from being an 'on desk' function to a back office/legal function. This switch spawned the growth of a generation of legal 'derivatives specialists'. Today that knowledge is spread even more widely, to the point where most commercial lawyers have at least some working knowledge of the derivatives industry, assisted no doubt by the high profile cases which have come before the courts.

The transfer of this responsibility from the dealing desk into the specialist profession began through the efforts of the industry itself (via ISDA). The decision of the English court in the *Hammersmith & Fulham* case, however, exposed deficiencies in industry practice regarding the assumed enforceability of transactions (see *Chapter 7*). This decision was therefore instrumental in hastening the emergence of derivatives expertise in the legal profession.

Taxation of derivatives products lacked an internationally accepted framework and approach, with taxation professionals initially attempting to apply existing structures and policies. These were not necessarily appropriate and did not always take account of the true economic impact of derivatives (in part, because this impact was not widely understood by tax specialists themselves). The existence of anomalies, both between and within jurisdictions, led to 'arbitrage' behaviour. The tax knowledge of the average derivatives dealer increased substantially during this time in the relevant area of 'arbitrage'. Legislators are now addressing the anomalous treatment of derivatives, especially those that impact on the tax revenue base. In the interim, however, a whole generation of tax specialists has had to become 'derivatives literate' in order to understand the economic impact of derivatives and hence to determine the appropriate taxation treatment. Conversely 'on desk' knowledge of taxation issues has come and gone in response to available opportunities and the growth of 'off desk' product knowledge.

A similar shift has occurred in the area of accounting and is still occurring with respect to financial reporting. The initial shift from accrual to mark-to-market accounting treatment was relatively painless conceptually, but tended to be delayed or complicated by the lack of availability of suitable systems. Derivatives dealers became skilled at 'shoe-horning' transactions into inadequate existing systems. The process required dealers to have sufficient knowledge of the accounting system to ensure derivatives transactions were 'booked' so as to generate the correct accounting result. As 'off-the-shelf' systems have become available, so the level of accounting expertise available (or necessary) 'on desk' has diminished. Accounting issues within the derivatives field have now largely, and appropriately, been mastered by accounting professionals.

With the accounting treatment of derivatives becoming fully integrated into an organisation's accounting systems, the quality of high-level financial reporting of derivatives risks and exposures will continue to improve. In part, this is because the lack of reporting of such risks and exposures has been a major embarrassment to management associated with high profile losses. Once again, the shift in knowledge from the derivatives desk into the complementary profession, accountancy in this case, is evident.

Another group of professionals now working feverishly to address its lack of product familiarity is the senior management of professional derivatives houses and of users alike. Awareness of derivatives at senior levels emerged slowly, causing discomfort to some organisations. This, combined with the regulatory need for improved financial risk disclosure and reporting, has hastened the introduction of the specialist risk manager, or 'middle office' as discussed in *Chapter 9*. The middle office is specifically charged with identifying and monitoring risks in a business, reporting on those risks, and making senior management aware of those risks. The creation of the risk management 'profession' is not solely an outcome of the progress of the life-cycle of derivatives, but the vigour with which this new profession is growing and the importance placed on it are, in large part, due to developments within the derivatives industry. Once again, the impact on the derivatives desk has been to transplant a portion of the existing 'on desk' derivatives product and industry knowledge into a specialist 'complementary' profession: in this case that of the new and increasingly important risk manager.

3.5 Changing sources of revenue

No single measure of the changing role of the derivatives desk reveals as much as the tracking over time of shifts in the main sources of desk revenue. The manner in which these sources of revenue change is driven by derivatives practitioners' perceptions of opportunities. Changing areas of profitability are therefore indicative of the wider changes taking place in the industry itself.

It is more clearly evident here than elsewhere that derivatives were originally the result of arbitrage of regulatory inconsistencies. Initially derivatives desks sourced revenue by acting as brokers or matchers of end-user interests. This revenue was essentially brokerage, earned through the ability to identify and match offsetting counterparty positions. The primary role of the (yet-to-be-so-named) derivatives desk was 'transaction matching' and 'pipeline management'. This revenue which was derived from a 'broking' activity should be distinguished from a later development where revenue was generated from a credit intermediating activity. In the latter case a 'matched' transaction cannot proceed but for the willingness of an intermediary to interpose itself between the end counterparties, thereby accepting 'performance' exposure on each party. The former role of broking end-users has now disappeared as a source of revenue. The latter role of credit intermediary, while originally performed 'on desk', is now more likely to be a source of revenue for corporate financiers.

The next change in revenue source saw the broking income replaced by revenue attributable to a willingness to incur market related risk. This can be broken down into a number of elements. As houses began to mismatch positions, the derivatives desk became more focused on hedging positions to retain the 'bid-offer' spread, a concept which connotes the development of a trading market with elements of liquidity. With the establishment of trading/hedging activity there came an element of proprietary risk-taking which was a further new revenue source. The role of the desk changed considerably at this juncture from hedging to active management of market risk.

With increasing sophistication and technological advances the transition from simple mismatching to fully blown warehousing, or portfolio management, was made. At this point revenue sources changed composition yet again, with the result that the focus of a swap warehouse was as much on the likely future direction of swap spreads (to government yields) as it was on bid-offer retention and proprietorial risk. The growing popularity of option-based and later correlation-based products added revenue sources by introducing volatility and correlation exposures, but did not displace these existing revenue activities.

Increasing competition pushed desks to seek new sources of revenue. This pressure contributed directly to the advent of the 'financial engineer' as a spin-off from the now well-developed capacity to warehouse many varieties of market risk. While this was initially an activity associated directly with the derivatives desk, it has since tended to develop into a specialisation of its own. Similarly, the area of product innovation and variation gained importance as a revenue source for the derivatives desk. The advent of the risk manager has generally seen this activity removed from the desk and established either as a separate specialist activity or as a process managed 'off desk'. It carries with it a brief which extends beyond simply the derivatives product group to much broader spheres of innovation.

As the industry has developed, so the role of the derivatives desk has altered. The changing sources of revenue, as identified above, reflect both the drive of the derivatives practitioner to search out new revenue sources and the consequential developments in the industry itself.

3.6 New products and innovation

The leveraged derivative (described in *Section 3.2*) is a prime example of a new product which has been designed around a market impediment. Although liability managers (predominantly corporate treasurers) had the legal ability to use derivatives comparatively freely, asset managers were in a different position. Many asset managers operated under trust deeds drawn up well before OTC derivatives became commonplace. As a result, they did not expressly provide for such transactions and thus restricted the authority of fund managers and certain institutional investors to enter into OTC derivatives contracts. This was to the detriment of both the asset managers and derivatives providers. Asset managers were viewed by derivatives professionals as a large untapped source of potential business and the asset managers themselves were reportedly keen to take advantage of the 'new' hedging and income generation possibilities offered by derivatives.

These same trust deeds usually, however, permitted broad 'investment' activities. It was perhaps inevitable that a way would be found to bring derivatives within the overall definition of 'investments', to the mutual satisfaction of both sets of interested parties. This has been accomplished primarily through embedding features of derivatives in debt or equity instruments to meet the investment criteria of the asset manager. The move to incorporate leveraged derivatives in securities was simply a logical progression to enable the asset manager to access the OTC derivatives market in this de facto fashion.

An unfortunate consequence was the over-exuberant promotion of this type of product to many end-users whose underlying risk position or risk appetite made the 'leveraged' product inappropriate. This enthusiasm may be attributed, at least in part, to the 'sales commission' style of remuneration common to the industry and to the overriding need to differentiate products. The suitability of derivatives products to an end-user's circumstances quickly became an issue for the organisation (derivatives desk) promoting the product and became rapidly and inextricably linked to the issue of price/risk transparency.

The accusations which have been levelled at the derivatives industry have brought a marked and swift response. Measures to ensure that products are suitable to individual end-users' circumstances and levels of sophistication were quickly implemented and, simultaneously, steps were taken to make pricing and risk more transparent. New product development became the function of a specialist group, removed from the 'vested' interest of the derivatives desk. In addition, most derivatives desks now operate under an express code of conduct which is designed to ensure (among other things) that the derivatives activity is focused on delivering products consistent with an end-user's own risk framework/philosophy, as opposed to just 'pushing the latest innovation'. This is best expressed as a shift from 'buyer beware' of a new product to 'seller take care'; particularly in light of the reputational risks highlighted recently. These issues are discussed more fully in *Chapters* 6 and 7.

3.7 Management issues

The public profile of the derivatives industry in recent years is disproportionate to the underlying level of public understanding of the general product area. This awareness of derivatives has manifested itself in a number of ways:

- increased management scrutiny of derivatives activity;
- a shift towards re-regulation of the industry;
- emphasis on ethical behaviour both internally and externally and the implementation of professional codes of conduct; and
- acknowledgement of reputational risk as a key issue for the industry.

These factors have combined to create a demand for the dissemination of knowledge previously centred on the derivatives desk. While legal, accounting, taxation and management professionals have been called upon to play their part in this process, it is the creation of the new 'risk management' profession which represents the most significant recent development. Just as the catalogued developments in the derivatives industry were a catalyst in changing products, so they have also triggered the appointment of specialist 'risk managers' in most major professional derivatives houses. This new specialisation is described in detail in *Chapter 9*. Furthermore, skills developed by these professionals are now being applied to areas outside derivatives.

The initial focus of the newly appointed risk manager was driven by the need to understand, monitor and report to senior management (in an easily understood form) the market risk which derivatives businesses incurred. The interrelationships between derivatives and other financial products have, however, led to the role of the risk manager encompassing many other risks: viz credit, legal, transactional, operational and reputational risk, to name but a few. In addition, the risk management profession is (quite rightly) being drawn into new product design and launch processes as well as broader compliance issues. Thus the derivatives industry has been a major contributor and catalyst to the birth and subsequent growth of the modern risk management profession.

For senior managers, the challenges of overseeing a derivatives business are immense and varied. For example, it usually falls to senior management to arbitrate in the inevitable conflicts occurring between business units. The management of dealing desks within banks and similar organisations is a broad topic, worthy of a significant chapter of its own. However, this chapter would not be complete without some mention of the major issues involved, which include:

- how to manage the competing desires to introduce new products quickly, while having sufficient controls and support in place before such an introduction;
- how to ensure co-operation between derivatives dealing desks (including specialist sales staff) and the rest of the bank

(including non-specialist salespeople and broader banking staff responsible for the management of customer relationships);

- how to structure derivatives dealing desks. Should a bank have one desk for all derivatives (interest rate, foreign exchange, commodity and equity, say) or multiple desks? The former has benefits of integration and it confers the ability to exploit anomalies and opportunities across markets, but is unwieldy and in practice cuts across the traditional management structure within banks which would tend to make some or all of the product areas quite separate units;
- how to ensure that the operations, accounting, credit, market risk and other similar procedures and processes within the bank, primarily developed for vanilla products, are also appropriate for 'cutting edge' products or dealing desks; and
- how to manage the remuneration of dealers (and in particular a culture of significant bonuses) in such a way as to reward performance and to reflect market forces, while at the same time being equitable within the organisation, defensible to other stakeholders, and structured so that behaviour which benefits the organisation as a whole (and its customers) is encouraged and the opposite behaviour discouraged.

3.8 Conclusion

The role of the derivatives dealer has changed markedly as the product has developed. Originally the sole repository of product knowledge, the dealer has now focused on the narrower market as other professionals have taken responsibility for the more specialised issues. This process has an air of inevitability as the derivatives product matures through its life-cycle.

There will continue to be innovation and new variants of derivatives will appear, many of which will offer genuine advantage to the customer. More fundamental changes to the role of the derivatives desk can already be foreseen as new product delivery channels evolve. The derivatives desk will have to adapt to accommodate 'electronic' delivery and execution of transactions. Traditional market boundaries will continue to become more blurred.

These developments, however, will impact all financial market products—not just derivatives. Derivatives dealing desks no longer hold a special position among other financial market activities. Derivatives dealers have become fully integrated into the modern treasury dealing room and the 'black box' has been almost completely dismantled. Significant management issues remain to be fully addressed as enumerated in earlier sections. These issues are, however, no longer specific to derivatives but apply to all financial instruments traded by financial institutions. Risks can therefore be addressed within the broader contexts of business strategy, trading room management and customer relationships, rather than being seen as unique to the derivatives market.

4

Inside the corporate treasury

RICHARD ALLAN

Editors' Note

A transformation has occurred in corporate treasuries in the past decade caused, in part, by the losses that have rocked the industry. Changes in this field in some ways mirror the evolution in professionalism of financial institutions described in Chapter 3. *Yet, in other respects, change has been even more extensive in the corporate arena.*

Corporations have questioned the use of derivatives at a fundamental level. Directors and treasurers are asking themselves basic questions about the role of risk management that have enormous implications for the way in which derivatives are used, if at all. Many have also questioned the ability of directors to oversee their treasury functions adequately. A symptom of the transformation is the dramatic reduction in the number of corporate treasuries operating as profit centres.

The author argues in favour of the use of derivatives in corporate financial risk management provided a number of conditions are met. These conditions include managerial capacity to understand derivatives, comprehensive risk assessment across the firm in order to understand its true risk profile and appropriate performance measures for the treasurer.

4.1 Introduction

Financial disasters such as those which befell Metallgesellschaft and Procter & Gamble were powerful catalysts for change in corporate treasuries world-wide. It should be noted, however, that the process of change predates those cases. A number of watershed cases came even earlier which, in hindsight, proved to be defining moments in the evolution of corporate attitudes to derivatives in the Asia-Pacific region. Thus evolution was hastened by, but began prior to, the events described in *Chapter 2*.

In Australia, for example, the pivotal case came relatively early. As a small open economy with a freely floating exchange rate, there was great incentive to learn about controlling financial risk. The particular company involved was a medium-sized electronics company, AWA Limited, which in 1987 suffered realised foreign exchange losses of AUD49 million through the activities of its sole foreign exchange dealer. The losses completely wiped out the company's profits for the year and resulted in a reassessment Australia-wide of the role of corporate treasuries.

In Japan there have been a number of significant cases, including that of Showa Shell, a Japanese refiner and distributor 46 per cent owned by Royal Dutch Shell. In early 1993 it disclosed a JPY125 billion (USD1.1 billion) loss in currency forward contracts, a loss equal to 82 per cent of the capital base of the company.

While it is clear that the primary reasons for the complete reversal of profitability related to the downturn in world markets, the collapse in interest rates and the extreme strength of the yen (and therefore the weakness of foreign-denominated investments), there is an important point of more widespread application for companies to note. By turning a secondary function, treasury, into a main corporate strategy, Japanese companies drifted away from their core business, which they both understood and could manage successfully, into areas in which they had no real comparative advantage.

Experiences such as those mentioned above have led many corporate boards to examine not just the use of derivatives within their organisation but also the more basic question as to their whole attitude to risk and the role of financial risk management within their organisations. The fact that risk management can be a high risk activity in itself has led to its very nature being brought into question. Accordingly, after surveying the extent of the use of derivatives by companies in the mid-1990s, this chapter will focus on examining four crucial underlying questions:

- should a company manage financial risk?
- if so, what risk should be managed?
- what should be the role of the treasurer? and
- what methods and instruments should be employed?

It is contended that it is not derivatives themselves which are the cause for concern, but rather the manner in which financial risk generally is managed within the corporation.

4.2 The extent of derivatives usage

The most recent international survey of the corporate use of financial derivatives was released by Price Waterhouse in October 1995. It covered 386 major corporations over 16 countries, mainly from Europe but including Australasia (90 respondents) and Hong Kong (12 respondents) (see Price Waterhouse 1995). Although the survey did not extend to commodity options, which were a key issue in such disasters as Metallgesellschaft (discussed in *Chapter* 2), it disclosed that 73 per cent of all respondents used derivatives to manage their interest rate exposures (especially swaps, FRAs, caps and collars) and that 96 per cent used currency derivatives, with forward contracts the most commonly utilised of all (in 90 per cent of cases). Options were used by approximately 58 per cent of companies. Overall, the picture which emerges is of a very high use of derivatives in the surveyed countries.

A very different picture is revealed in a second survey carried out by the Wharton School (Smithson 1996). This survey was much larger, covering 2158 firms but it related only to non-financial firms in the USA and it received only a 16 per cent response rate (350 firms). According to the survey, the percentage of American firms using derivatives increased from 35 per cent in 1994 to 41 per cent in 1995 (a usage rate of less than half that of the non-US companies covered in the Price Waterhouse survey). It appears that firm size has been a major factor in derivatives use by American firms, with only 13 per cent of firms with market value of less than USD50 million using them, rising to 59 per cent of those worth more than USD250 million. Of those firms using derivatives, 76 per cent used them for managing foreign exchange exposures and 73 per cent used them for interest rate management. Only 37 per cent used derivatives for commodity exposure management and 12 per cent for equity exposures. Of the US-based firms not using derivatives, the three most cited reasons for this were:

- lack of significant exposure (65 per cent of respondents);
- an excess of expected costs over the perceived benefits; and
- concerns about the perceptions of derivatives among investors, regulators and the public.

The users had concerns as well. The major three were:

- credit risk (33 per cent);
- difficulty in evaluating the risks of derivatives (32 per cent); and
- uncertainty over accounting treatment (30 per cent).

These surveys suggest that there appears to be a very large divergence in the use of derivatives not only between countries but also within countries. There is also a large range in the reasons cited for each firm's behaviour. Both surveys suffer, however, from a major defect if they are to be used as a guide to the extent of corporate use of financial risk management. Financial derivatives as marketed by financial institutions or traded on exchanges are only a fraction of the total use of risk management techniques employed by most companies. As such, all surveys which ignore embedded options seriously underestimate the extent of financial risk management actually carried out by firms. Options are embedded in everything from sales contracts to loan contracts. In terms of the impact on the value of a firm, it makes no difference whether a sales contract contains a currency revaluation clause or whether a firm replicates this clause through the purchase of a foreign exchange option, unless there are taxation or legal issues to be taken into consideration.

But should any financial risk management take place, embedded or otherwise? This question has assumed new prominence in the wake of losses incurred by Metallgesellschaft and Procter & Gamble.

4.3 Should a company hedge financial risk?

There is a crisis of confidence within many companies concerning the efficacy of active risk management. This is in part due to a re-examination of the fundamental goals of risk management. At the core of this issue is the question as to why firms hedge their exposures in the first place.

Most portfolio models assume that the total variation in value of a share can be divided between two types of risk:

- systematic, or non-diversifiable risk: This type of risk is economy-wide and cannot be removed by diversifying risk across a portfolio of assets. It results from factors such as the state of the economy, droughts and floods; and

- unsystematic, or diversifiable risk: This is a type of risk which is company or industry specific, and which can be largely eliminated by diversifying investments across a basket of assets. Factors such as strikes, technology changes and currency fluctuations may contribute to unsystematic risk.

Systematic risk cannot, by definition, be diversified away. Unsystematic risk can, although this may be done by the investor him/herself to the degree required. Removing all risk may not, however, leave the individual with the desired risk-return profile. In fact, it might be argued that portfolio management should make hedging by any individual firm unnecessary. Why, for example, should an Australian gold company hedge its USD-based gold sales, given that the investor may be presumed to wish to invest in gold and to select a portfolio mix accordingly? Consider in this context the New York Stock Exchange's BUGS, or Basket of Unhedged Gold Stocks, which enables investors to purchase a pure gold risk, since the portfolio is restricted to shares in companies which do not use financial derivatives.

It is argued that there are three major reasons why the firm itself, rather than the investor, might hedge, namely:

- Tax: Tax is not assessable/deductible until the cash actually flows. This can result in some significant mismatches between the firm's tax position and company accounts or exposure reports. In addition, hedging can change the tax profile and further, by reducing volatility, hedging can also reduce the expected tax payable. National and international tax management is often a significant part of financial management within a firm;
- Bankruptcy: The corporate risk/return trade-off is not symmetric. The chance of bankruptcy decreases if cash flow is less variable, so companies often prefer more certain flows which may result from hedging. Further, a more certain cash flow will be attractive to potential lenders such as banks or financial institutions. If companies are managing their cash flows, they may be perceived to be less vulnerable to a liquidity crisis and therefore be more acceptable credit risks. This can increase the company's debt capacity and therefore its potential for growth; and
- Agency Effects: There are stakeholders other than shareholders who have a vested interest in ensuring that the firm is not

subject to significant downside risk. Management is generally risk-averse and unable to diversify personal risk associated with poor company performance. It is often less costly to allow managers to engage in low-cost hedging than to raise their compensation. In fact, the greater the separation of ownership and control, the greater the potential strength of such agency influences on corporate strategies.[1]

Additionally, there are factors such as the imperfection of markets, competitor behaviour and accounting considerations which encourage firms to hedge risks.

Ultimately, the decision as to the extent of financial risk management is a decision for the board of directors. However, unless the characteristics of derivatives are clearly understood at board level, they are genuinely dangerous and their misuse can result in serious loss to the company as well as possible unwanted shareholder and regulatory responses. This was certainly the experience of all the companies cited above and in *Chapter 2*.

While derivatives are remarkably flexible and varied, they are not risky in themselves. On the contrary, they allow risk to be transferred from the risk-averse to the risk-tolerant at a fair price. Yet, just as not everyone is proficient in driving a car, not all companies can be relied upon to handle derivatives.

There are three special risks associated with corporations which directors are especially prone to misconstrue. The first two are disclosure (or accounting) risk and non-disclosure (or audit) risk. These two risks are not the inverse of each other, but are closely related. They can only be fully understood when put into the context of a third type of risk—exposure risk. Each will be examined in turn.

4.3.1 *Disclosure (or accounting) risk*

One of the great weaknesses of many corporate reporting systems is the bias that can be introduced by focusing on the accounting reports rather than the underlying exposures. An example may help to illustrate this point.

An importer has an underlying exposure to movements in the exchange rate. Diagrammatically, this can be shown in the pay-off profile in *Figure 4.1*.

In order to cover part or all of this exposure, the company can use forwards, futures options, capital markets or commodity-based exposure management techniques. Just one of many solutions would be to purchase the right to sell the local currency (or buy the foreign currency) at a pre-set price, say $M in *Figure*

Figure 4.1 Importer's currency exposure

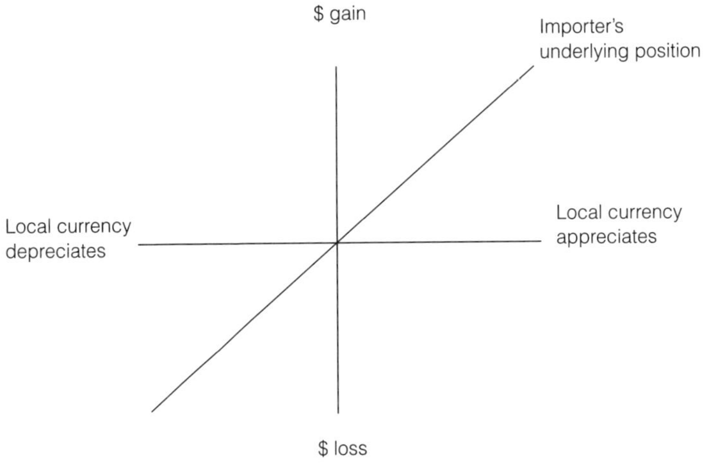

4.2. The effect of the option (technically, a put on the local currency) is illustrated diagrammatically in *Figure 4.2*.

This option will be exercised if the local currency depreciates below $M. Thus the final exposure of the corporation is shown in *Figure 4.3*.

Note that if *only* the option is considered, the company appears to benefit from a devaluation. When combined with the underlying exposure, the company in fact benefits from the reverse situation: namely, an appreciation of the local currency. In the above case, this gives the appearance of exactly the reverse risk/return trade-off for the company from what is actually the case (from *Figure 4.3*, line Y is reported, not line Z). This is potentially a major issue for corporations, as some of the accounting standards, both current and proposed, require derivatives to be reported separately. Furthermore, some accounting regimes allow forward sales/purchases to be offset against derivatives, while others do not. In the case of Metallgesellschaft, for example (see *Chapter* 2), under US accounting rules the American subsidiary reported a USD61 million profit at the end of the fiscal year 1993, while the German reports, under German regulations, did not allow forward sales to offset derivatives and reported a $271 million loss.

Accounting reports compartmentalise returns and present 'snapshot' valuations. This contrasts with the continuous nature

Figure 4.2 AUD put options

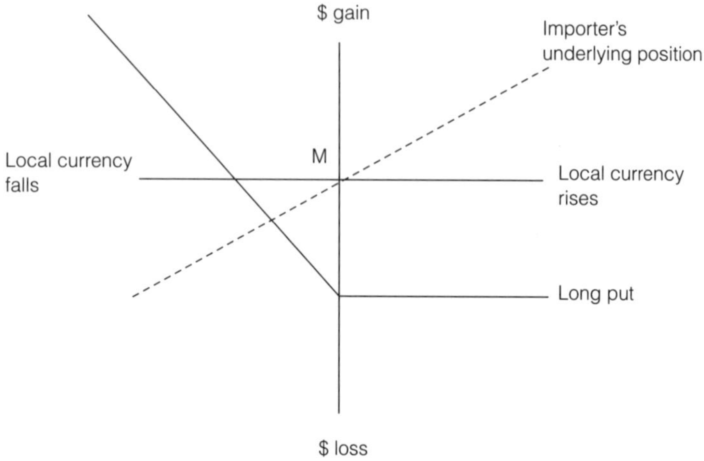

of cash flow management. For example, under accounting regulations both unrealised and realised gains/losses on Foreign Exchange (FX) borrowings are recorded in the profit and loss account, while only the realised gains/losses affect cash flow and tax. *Table 4.1* illustrates the different roles and perspectives of accounting reports and risk management.

The Profit and Loss Account is an historical report; there is no risk left in it since the reported profit is a known amount. The Balance Sheet provides a snapshot of a company at the end of the financial year, giving some indication of the financial health of a company and its general structure. Risk managers need, however, to focus on future cash flows, for these are the only cash flows which they can influence. The emphasis on profit and loss effects, rather than on the cash flow effects, can have major implications for both the treasurer and the company. As a leading US academic puts it:

> Difficulties in distinguishing between the accounting description of foreign exchange risk and the business reality of the effects of these risks can cause corporate executives to make serious errors of judgment. In few other areas (outside the treatment of depreciation) is such a large divergence possible between a company's actual and reported results. (Shapiro 1989 pp. 240–1)

Figure 4.3 Importer's position after hedging

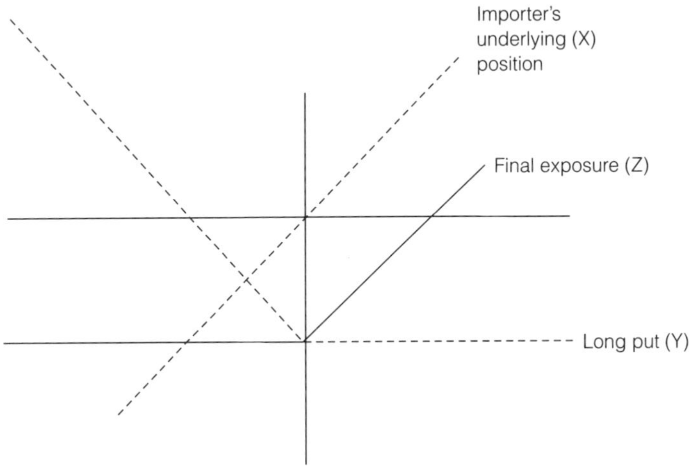

4.3.2 *Non-disclosure (audit) risk*

This second type of risk relates to the bias introduced by failing to account for underlying exposures. The bias is towards the non-management of exposures since they are not recognised in the first place. Further, this can again lead to management perceiving the wrong picture. Assume a company has a $100 million currency exposure related to export sales. On account of a belief that these export sales will benefit from currency movements, 90 per cent is left uncovered but 10 per cent is hedged using forwards. Should the view (of an appreciation of the foreign currency) prove to be correct, all the hedges could lose money. An audit which concentrates only on the derivatives would conclude that the policy had been unsuccessful. Conversely, if the currency view had been wrong, all the hedges could be in profit (while the value of the 90 per cent of the underlying exposures left unhedged would be eroded).

Table 4.1 Accounting reports and risk management

	Past	**Present**	**Future**
Result	Reported profit	Financial health	Actual profit
Aim	Share price	Borrowing power	Robustness
Target	Profit & loss	Balance sheet	Risk management
Influence	Accounting	Accounting	Economic

4.3.3 *Exposure risk*

Exposure risk, the company's sensitivity to its underlying business position, underlies all corporate exposure management. Only if it is properly understood and forms the basis of board decisions can the use of derivatives be properly assessed at board levels. Companies are not banks and to treat them as such in terms of the reporting of derivative positions and their pricing is folly. If the hedge or derivative is divorced from the business-based exposure it is protecting or varying, the overall or final exposure of the firm to financial price movements cannot be determined.

Overall, an inadequate reporting structure can result in the wrong signals being given to the board. The current emphasis is on marking derivatives to market and reporting the positions without reference to the underlying exposures. Such erroneous signals may result in serious losses, for the boards are tending to shoot the messenger (that is, ban derivatives) rather than to comprehend the message.

4.4 What risk should be managed?

Increasingly, corporations are interested in the use of derivatives at a company-wide level, rather than at a specific commodity or loan level. As a result, the way that derivatives are utilised changed significantly in the mid-1990s. The new focus is on modelling all of the risks a firm faces to construct a comprehensive risk profile. Derivatives may or may not then be selected as a suitable tool to manage this profile.

David Cromwell, Treasurer of the British Post Office, highlights the key issue:

> Treasurers have increasingly widened their portfolios of risk management to include the management of retained and transferred risk as embodied by insurance and physical risk management. Then, when you add tax, project finance, corporate finance, banking relationships, cash management and pensions, the definition of risk activities can be seen to be very extensive, both as a result of the complexity of activities corporates engage in and the matching development of products, techniques and markets which have evolved to manage them.
>
> What concerns me, however, is that . . . however extensive the list above is, it probably does not match the risk profile of the company. (Cromwell 1996)

Cromwell lists eight major risks faced by corporations of which only the first two—or possibly three—are normally managed by treasuries:

- interest rate risk;
- foreign exchange risk;
- commodity risk;
- strategic risk;
- operational risk;
- technological risk;
- product risk; and
- political risk.

It is not the function of this chapter to describe these risks in detail. The aim of listing them is to highlight the fact that a concentration on financial risk may be insufficient or even counterproductive. This view is reinforced by surveys such as that of Copeland and Joshi (1996a), entitled 'Why derivatives don't reduce FX risk'. Their study of 190 large firms found that only one firm would have reduced its ten year income volatility risk (as measured by volatility of cash flows) by hedging by more than 20 per cent and only 20 firms would have reduced their income volatility by more than 10 per cent.

> How can it be that hedging programs that appear so elegant in theory don't work in practice? The reason, we believe, is that the theory assumes a static world in which all factors apart from FX rates stay exactly the same. In real life, however, a host of other variables—demand for parts and products, supply of new materials, regulatory frameworks, cost and productivity of labour and capital—all change just as FX rates change. (Copeland and Joshi 1996a)

The new emphasis on comprehensive risk modelling has been aided by the quality, availability and cost effectiveness of computer software and hardware. There is an increasing tendency for companies to require (and financial intermediaries to provide) company-wide risk management analysis as well as the tools to manage these risks. Under these systems, which use basic models of the firm, the effects of various scenarios are simulated. The objective is to determine the likelihood of the occurrence of firm-wide targets being missed, met or exceeded. Strategies which can be modelled include:

- the use of forwards or options in effecting company targets, such as return on equity or return on funds employed;

Figure 4.4 Financial risk management

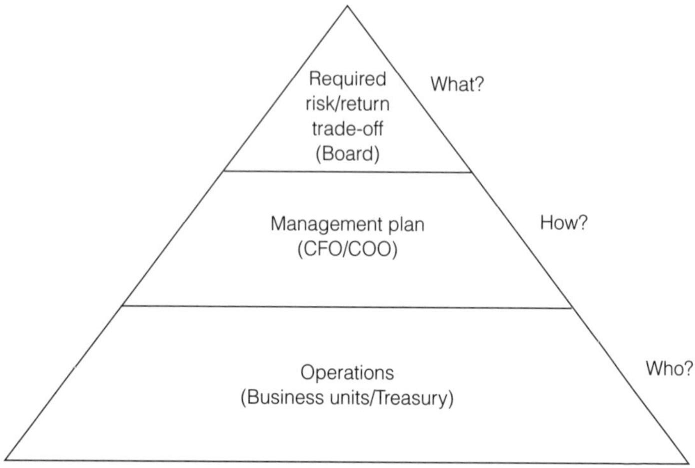

- the costs and benefits of risk management of the firm's overall exposure as well as that of individual business units or specific exposures; and
- the identification of significant levels of risk or critical currency, commodity and interest rate levels and the costs of managing them.

Thus, financial risk management is carried out in the context of company-wide risk, as illustrated in *Figure 4.4*.

Once corporations have determined their actual risk profiles and have also identified how this varies from their required risk profiles, they can then determine the appropriate methodology of risk management. It is at this stage that derivatives can be utilised, due to their ability to specifically price each category of risk.

4.5 The changing role of the treasurer?

It is not only the use of derivatives by companies which has reached a watershed but also the position of corporate treasuries within the risk management framework. The role of the corporate treasury is an evolving one, varying dramatically between countries and between firms. Within firms, the function of the treasury is largely a function of the risk return profile within which the company is comfortable, together with the company's own degree of maturity. Like the dinosaur, the treasury has to evolve or face extinction.

Prior to the AWA case a significant number of Australian corporations operated their treasuries as profit centres, including Coca-Cola Amatil, Consolidated Press and Elders IXL. In the aftermath, the number of treasuries acting as profit centres suffered a sharp decline, until by 1996 there remained only one major corporation with a full profit centre treasury (Asea Brown Boveri). The fact that an apparently conservative company such as AWA could lose so much so quickly had a profound effect on the attitude of many directors in Australia, especially as the loss occurred through the use of one of the most basic derivatives of all—currency forwards. Similarly, the Showa Shell case in Japan exemplifies the risks of profit centre style treasuries.

According to the company's President, the problems for Showa Shell began in 1989 when staff began purchasing US dollars at a rate of around USD/JPY130. When the loss was announced, the rate had fallen to USD/JPY117, with contracts totalling USD6.4 billion. This was despite an annual import bill of under USD1 billion. There were, however, two more general factors which affected Showa Shell. First, until mid-1992, the Ministry of Finance allowed companies to roll over their forward contracts indefinitely, thus keeping them off-balance sheet. Secondly, and more significantly, it was involved in Zaiteku, which may be roughly translated as financial engineering or financial arbitrage. During the mid-to-late 1980s, approximately two-thirds of Japanese companies were so involved. Their treasuries engaged in everything from simple interest rate plays such as borrowing money at a lower rate than they were able to invest it (for example, via Euromarket capital raisings swapped back into the Japanese market), to outright speculative equity market plays (Lynch 1993). Zaiteku was originally meant to refer to the management of surplus corporate funds. Opportunities for cross-market arbitrage developed, however, through the freeing up of some financial markets, and significant Zaiteku actively commenced. By 1986, the top ten Zaiteku (including Toyota, Nissan, Sharp, Sony and Mitsubishi) were earning Zaiteku earnings which accounted for between 47 per cent and 151 per cent of profits. Some companies would thus have made losses without their Zaiteku operations.

Yet by 1992 Zaiteku had become a tainted word. In fact, Mitsubishi, Nissan and Sony all lost money on Zaiteku, and losses among the major Zaiteku now rival the profit levels of the 1980s.

In 1993 Mitsubishi, for example, had to rescue its financial subsidiary, MC Finance, which had incurred JPY28 billion (USD235 million) in unrealised losses or securities investments. Examples such as these have encouraged many treasurers to focus on primary corporate strategies, rather than making treasury a separate business unit.

According to surveys carried out by executive search firms such as Russell Reynolds, the requirements for corporate treasurers are changing across Asia as well as in western countries. Ten years ago a treasurer was normally an accountant and/or a cash manager, but by the mid-1990s the role increasingly had become that of a financial strategist. In little under a decade the previously control-dominated treasury became result orientated and the treasurer's role became pivotal within both corporate and public authority structures. The treasurer emerged as a professional.

The 1980s generation of treasurers were largely recruited from administrative and accounting backgrounds, with duties largely reflecting the monitoring and control aspects of treasury operations as well as the crucial fund raising responsibilities. In this latter area, treasury was often treated as the 'can do' component of the company: fund raising without regard to risk or even return. It was entrepreneurship *sans frontiers*.

Table 4.2 compares this 1980s-based profile with that of the early and mid-1990s.

The 1980s list of qualities most demanded by companies recruiting a corporate treasurer were largely accounting-based and somewhat pedestrian. However, the financial disasters of the late 1980s and early 1990s forced a broadening of the requirements, with much more emphasis on financial skills and communications. This was partly caused, and indeed partly driven, by the considerable expansion of derivatives markets. Companies now had the means by which to manage risk on an ongoing basis, along with an increasing supply of individuals proficient in the pricing and use of these instruments.

A further phase in the evolution of financial risk management now appears to be under way, driven by the emergence of company-wide risk management technology and databases. This new direction is reinforced by evidence that managing financial risk independently of other company risks is ineffective.

4.6 What methods and tactics should be employed?

There are many differences between the risk management activities

Table 4.2 The changing role of the corporate treasurer

Mid-1980s
CONTROL-ORIENTED CFO SKILLS
Financial Accounting
Cost Control
Financial Analysis
Budgeting
Treasury
CPA Qualifications
Compliance Experience
Early 1990s
TREASURY-ORIENTED CFO SKILLS
Cash Management
Risk Management
Investment Analysis
Banking Relations
Investor Relations
Acquisitions/Divestitures
Currency Management
Accounting Control
Degree Qualifications
Late 1990s
RISK MANAGEMENT-ORIENTED CFO SKILLS
Risk Analysis
Liquidity Management
Investment Analysis
Acquisition/Divestitures
Risk Management (FX/Interest Rates/Commodities)
Financial Audit and Control
Postgraduate Qualifications

Source: Based on information from Russell Reynolds Associates

of corporations (as end-users of derivatives) and of financial institutions (as providers of derivatives). The chief distinction relates to their underlying exposures. Misunderstanding of this crucial factor has led to serious errors of judgment by both corporations themselves and by financial institutions in their efforts to assist the management of corporate exposures.

When a financial institution's treasury starts dealing it normally has no underlying exposures. It then proceeds to trade in financial instruments, valuing these either individually or as a portfolio, using market prices to determine changes in the value of their operations and the level of risk being assumed. Methodologies such as Value-At-Risk (VAR) can be used to value the instruments and assess potential risks. (See *Chapter 8* for a detailed account of the application of VAR.)

By contrast, when a corporate treasury commences operations, there is already in existence a set of commodity and probably currency exposures. In respect to achieving the overall goals of the company, treasury is an intermediary, functioning as a means to an end, rather than being an end in itself. Even the 7 per cent of firms which have established treasuries as profit centres (Price Waterhouse 1995) have this core underlying role. It is the underlying business that is at the centre of the exposure management issue, whether this be electronics, primary production, motor vehicle manufacturing or the provision of technical services. Many of these have no easily calculated market value and are difficult to manage. Each of these basic exposures comes replete with financial exposures. Simply to reach the core position, a treasurer should go through the steps outlined in *Figure 4.5*.

As is illustrated, it is the board that sits on top of the structuring of risk and return within a firm. Well before financial markets are introduced into management strategies, the firm needs to evaluate the extent to which there are internal offsets before establishing company goals. Whether or not the company requires an adjustment of the risk by way of a different business configuration or via risk restructuring is again a decision for the board. Once these have been decided, it is a matter of determining how these goals are achieved.

The firm then needs to examine its overall exposures—or 'apparent exposures', as shown in the diagram. These should be, firstly, identified by the business units in terms of their face value (eg export receipts, debt servicing costs) and then, secondly, aggregated in order to allow for offsets.

It is also crucially important that a risk audit be carried out to determine whether there are any 'embedded options' and to what extent these affect overall exposures. Directors often baulk at the introduction of derivatives to their operations, yet have no qualms about using what amounts to the same thing in many of their contracts or funding agreements.

Three examples are as follows:

- Repricing Clauses
  Sales contracts often contain restrictions on the extent to which prices (interest rates, commodities or foreign exchange rates) can vary before one or other party has the right to change the conditions of supply. In the case of AWA, for example, while its underlying exposure was around AUD200 million pa, this fell to 'about AUD100–125 million net after taking into account the cover from contracts with the

Figure 4.5 The exposure management process

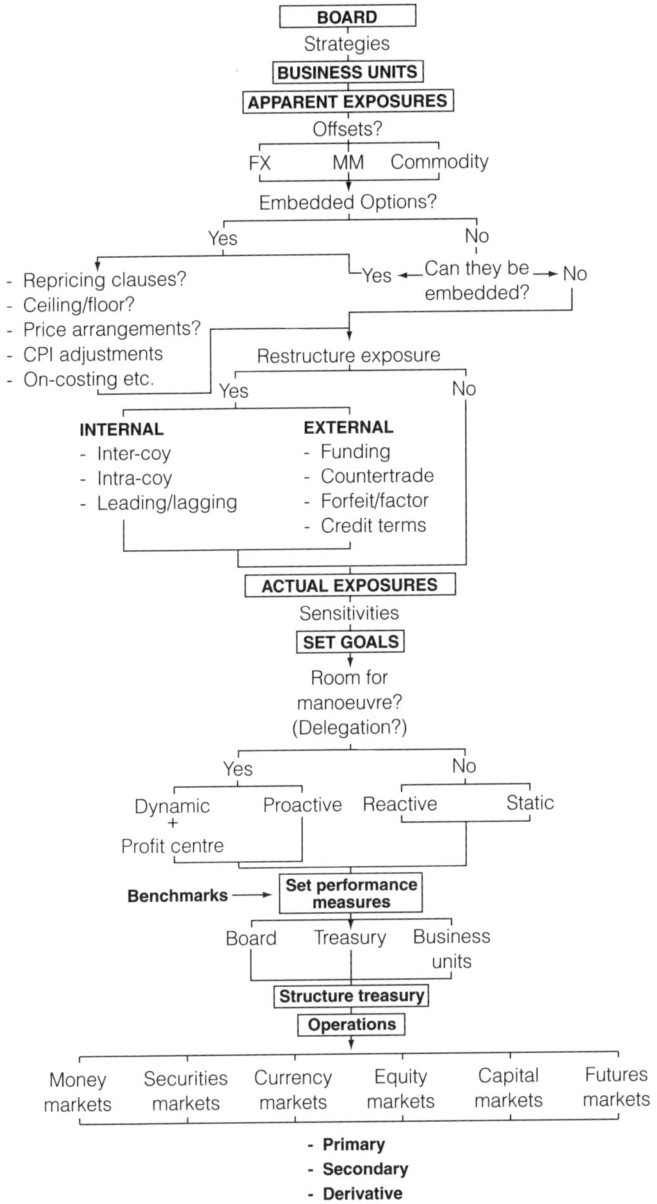

Department of Supply'. (Mr Justice Rogers in *AWA Ltd v Daniels*, pp 34–5)

In other words, AWA directors actually had the ability to re-invoice the Department of Supply where the exchange rate deviated from that rate agreed in the contracts. Yet on no occasion did they exercise this option. Nor did they, or their bankers, ever value these options. Even had they not wanted them, they could have sold the rights embedded in them to a third party.

- Ceiling/floor price arrangements
  These are another group of embedded options, where maximum and/or minimum prices are set in sales or funding contracts. For example, a board might reject the purchase of an interest rate cap against a two year FRN at 6 per cent per annum, but accept a loan at 6.4 per cent per annum floating which includes a clause guaranteeing rates will not exceed 8 per cent over the life of the loan.
- Inflation adjustments
  Some government and semi-government operations have pricing arrangements linking maximum price increases to movements in the Consumer Price Index (CPI). Thus they are directly, and their customers indirectly, subject to ceilings and/or floors. Alternative arrangements revolve around repricing of contracts should CPI exceed a pre-set level.

Where firms have been unwilling to purchase or sell options, financial institutions and other companies have been able to achieve the same results indirectly by embedding them. In many cases there is no attempt to price them properly. In others, there is clearly an advantage to the party because of over-or-under pricing of the option. Each step is important in ensuring that the corporation has a clear understanding of the nature and extent of its exposure. Further, the corporation also needs to determine the extent to which it then wants to modify this exposure in order to achieve its corporate goals.

The methods and tactics employed by treasury depend crucially on the performance measures which have been set. Inappropriate benchmarks can have dire consequences for the firm, as exemplified by the Procter & Gamble case (see *Chapter 2*). In that case it was reported that borrowing targets for 1994 were set at treasury bills minus 60 basis points and lending (investing targets) at treasury plus 140 basis points. Achievement of these goals necessitated considerable risk-taking, as was documented in *Chapter 2*. It is unlikely that the board was aware of the extent of the risk assumed, but by setting goals for treasury functions along the lines of financial institutions, high risk-taking was an inevitable consequence.

The final stage in the exposure management process (see *Figure 4.5*) is the implementation of appropriate trades in the market place. Even if all of the planning processes in *Figure 4.5* are adequately addressed, hedging may fail in its objectives due to operational problems. The Metallgesellschaft case (see *Chapter 2*) illustrates how hedging programs may fail at the implementation stage. In this case, the company did not appreciate the extent to which poor market liquidity and high funding costs could defeat an otherwise sensible exposure management strategy.

4.7 Conclusion

The current use of derivatives by corporations needs to be seen in the context of financial risk management generally in the 1990s. The discussion above suggests that financial risk management has evolved from an adjunct of the accounting function to an organisation-wide strategic issue. Accordingly, board-level decisions are now required, both as to the extent of the need for financial risk management as well as the extent to which derivatives are appropriate for that particular firm in undertaking financial risk management. This highlights the importance of corporate governance. With a plethora of well-publicised losses by highly regarded firms, boards have had good cause to question their ability to oversee derivatives-based risk management operations. Their vulnerability has appeared to increase as derivatives markets continue to develop, producing products which are so sophisticated that there appears to be no valid corporate use for them. In the context of the heightened importance of corporate governance, however, these products have in some ways outsmarted themselves; extremely few board members have the expertise to comprehend the real risks of these derivatives. From a board perspective such products become too risky to accept.

While there are many ways in which the educated use of derivatives could be encouraged, four straightforward but important suggestions are offered to help improve the efficiency of a company's use of derivatives and hopefully to encourage their acceptance by corporations as a powerful risk management tool:

- encourage directors' liability insurance premium discounts for boards which have undertaken due diligence courses in derivatives. Directors subject to potential claims under directors' liability claims should be able to show that they have taken reasonable steps to grasp the core characteristics of derivatives;

- require reporting of cash flow at risk, not mark to market of derivatives. In other words, allow exposure offsets to be permitted when assessing a firm's vulnerability to movements in interest rates, commodity prices and exchange rates—preferably on a portfolio basis;
- require external auditors to report unhedged as well as hedged positions and to provide a written statement as to the adequate separation of dealing and control/settlement functions; and
- impose ethical caps on the remuneration payable to derivative and other securities traders, including disclosure of compensation packages similar to that currently required of company directors.

References

Copeland, T.E. and Joshi, Y. 1996a, 'Why derivatives don't reduce risk', *McKinsey Quarterly*, February, no. 1

—— 1996b, 'Why derivatives don't reduce risk', *Corporate Finance*, May, pp. 35–41

Cromwell, David 1996, 'Treasurers: are we really managing all the risks that matter?', *The Treasurer*, December 1995/January 1996

Lynch, D. 1993, *The Impact of Financial Sector Reform on Corporate Treasuries: Some Lessons from Japan*, Working Paper no. 93–3, March, Centre for Japanese Economic Studies, Macquarie University, Sydney

Price Waterhouse 1995, *Corporate Treasury Control and Performance: An International Study*, London, October

Shapiro, A.C. 1989, *Multinational Financial Management*, 3rd edn, Allyn and Bacon Inc., Boston

Smithson, S. 1996, 'Who uses what', *Risk*, vol. 9, no. 5, May, pp. 49–51

Notes

1. Parenthetically, one of the reasons for the lack of trust between companies and their financial institutional counterparts is the sheer size of the compensation packages of some of the bankers. Companies are wont to muse over who, in the end, is actually paying for those salaries.

5

Within the institutions

ELIZABETH SHEEDY

Editors' Note

Chapter 5 *explores the current status of derivatives use in the funds management industry. Fund managers have been forced to grapple with the impact of derivatives losses in 1994 and 1995 due to concerns from both investors and regulators. These events have forced institutions to reflect on many policy and procedural issues. Fund managers have necessarily re-examined the usefulness of derivative strategies, and found that derivatives are an essential tool for effective funds management. If anything, derivatives are still under-utilised in this industry.*

The funds management industry has unique fiduciary responsibilities, creating very different pressures to those discussed in Chapter 4. *Regulation has been a dominant issue for this industry which has the responsibility of managing the retirement savings of its many financially naive members. The critical question is whether the funds management industry is unduly exposed to risk from derivatives. If so, can regulation help to reduce risk? The chapter describes an industry struggling to ensure that derivative strategies can be appropriately and prudently implemented, thus maximising the efficiency of funds management.*

5.1 Introduction

This chapter focuses on whether the funds management industry is unduly exposed to risk from derivatives. Derivatives, it is argued, are an essential tool for effective funds management. Yet derivatives, like many powerful tools, can be misused. A series of incidents in the funds management industry in recent years illustrates the potential for loss, and therefore the need for careful management of derivatives. As a result, risk management standards, both externally and self-imposed, are improving. Nonetheless vigilance is required at all levels of management and by all participants (including clients) to provide genuine protection for investors.

The reason for concern becomes obvious when the size and growth of the funds management industry is examined. In June 1996 the consolidated assets of Australian life offices, public unit trusts, superannuation funds and rollover funds reached $310 billion (Assirt 1996), compared to a figure of $190 billion in December 1990. As superannuation becomes a significant source of funding for retirement the stakes grow higher. Fund performance is critical to the future of millions of investors who are ill-equipped to manage and assess risk. Yet managed funds remain relatively unregulated when compared to banks, the traditional home of savings for the unsophisticated.

The use of derivatives by fund managers has raised questions about appropriate risk management standards and the suitability of particular investment strategies. In order to assess the industry's exposure to risk from derivatives the chapter has been divided into four parts. *Section 5.2* explores the extent and nature of derivatives use in the industry. While the use of derivatives is common, there is potential to apply these instruments further and thus enhance fund performance, especially in Asia. *Section 5.3* provides evidence of derivatives misuse in the industry. Recent examples are cited and lessons drawn. *Section 5.4* considers reaction to the derivatives losses in 1994 and 1995, both in the short and medium term. Initial panic created demand for new regulations in the industry, which are only now being implemented. This chapter concludes with a discussion of the industry's vulnerability to derivatives misuse. Notwithstanding recent progress, the conclusion is reached that a prudential control focus is still not as widespread as it could be.

5.2 Use of derivatives by professional fund managers

The use of derivatives by superannuation funds, unit trusts, hedge funds and insurance companies is widespread. A recent international survey of portfolio managers by Coopers & Lybrand (1995) finds that almost 80 per cent of respondents use derivatives for hedging purposes, 65 per cent use derivatives for asset allocation and almost 50 per cent use derivatives for yield enhancement. Most research into the extent and nature of derivatives use is for the US market. Derivative strategies arguably penetrate funds management to a greater degree there than in Australia and Asia. Even in the US, however, there is potential for more widespread use of derivatives. This is considered likely as fund managers' skills increase and as investors reduce their constraints on derivatives use.

This section highlights the benefits of derivatives use to funds management, benefits which are often overlooked by those wishing to restrict the use of derivatives. Legitimate uses of derivatives are also an important point of reference for the misuses later discussed in *Section 5.3*. While not attempting to be exhaustive, *Section 5.2.1* describes some popular applications of derivatives in this industry. The appropriateness of any derivative strategy can only be determined with reference to the investment aims of the institution. Thus *Section 5.2.2* discusses the institutions in the funds management industry, and their various requirements for derivative instruments. Features of the Asian funds management scene are discussed in *Section 5.2.3*.

5.2.1 *Applications*

It is this author's view that derivatives can add significantly to fund performance. Eight examples below show how derivatives, used appropriately, can enhance investor welfare. Hence, failure to use derivatives arguably disadvantages investors.

Derivative strategies may be used to achieve the following:

a) Improve returns on liquid assets

Most managers hold a portion of funds in liquid assets. Expected returns from cash are, however, lower than those in growth assets such as equities. A fund can achieve effective exposure to equities by holding a futures contract and posting a margin (Millman 1995). The remaining funds that would have been needed to invest in equities are made available to be invested in liquid assets. Thus the fund can simultaneously achieve the objectives of liquidity and higher expected return.

b) Minimise transaction costs

Changes in asset allocations increase transaction costs. Fund managers who frequently change asset allocations may find resultant gains offset by these costs. Fund managers can use swaps and futures to adjust their asset allocations, leaving physical asset holdings unchanged. Since transaction costs for derivatives are often lower than for equivalent physical stock, net fund returns may be enhanced (Millman 1995).[1]

c) Take advantage of preferential taxation/legal regimes

Swaps and structured notes can be used to gain exposure to markets while minimising taxes and avoiding other local laws (Schwimmer 1995). Rather than directly purchasing securities with adverse taxation and legal consequences, a manager can use derivatives to achieve an effective exposure. The manager can thus obtain the positive characteristics associated with certain investments without adverse consequences.

In Australia, for example, franking credits are available to domestic shareholders but not to overseas-based shareholders. Overseas investors in Australian shares may however partially benefit from these franking credits by entering into an equity swap with a domestic counterparty.

d) Diversify investment portfolios

Portfolio diversification is aided by using a range of investment styles. Accordingly, innovative investment approaches may be employed on the basis of their low correlation with other traditional investments (Peters 1994; Schneeweis et al. 1996).

For example, the returns of managed futures (that is, professionally managed investments in futures, options and forward contracts) are generally unrelated to those of traditional investment strategies. In a similar vein, hedge funds (see *Section 5.2.2d*) are frequently characterised by unconventional investment styles. Returns from hedge funds and managed futures funds may be highly volatile when considered in isolation, but can potentially reduce risk in a balanced investment portfolio.

e) Create investment vehicles with upside potential but low risk of capital loss

Investment strategies with low risk (of achieving negative returns) generally attract low expected returns. Such capital stable investments tend to underperform growth assets during periods of high returns. A synthetic capital stable investment can be structured by combining growth assets with protective put options (Cerulli and Casey 1995). In favourable market conditions the investor will realise the high returns associated with growth assets, less an insurance premium. Thus the investment may outperform traditional capital stable portfolios, yet the return of capital at a fixed time is assured by the use of the put options.

f) Hedge against adverse market movements

Derivatives may be used to protect investors against adverse market movements (Gastineau 1995). Hedging may apply to existing assets, or may be implemented prospectively. That is, a manager may choose to hedge in relation to an expected inflow of funds. A common use of currency forwards is to hedge overseas asset portfolios against a depreciation in foreign currency (appreciation in domestic currency). This can be implemented directly by the fund, or by an overlay manager with specialist expertise in the field of currency.

g) Enhance returns

A wide range of derivative strategies can be used to enhance returns, usually at the expense of higher levels of risk (Bensman 1994; Simon 1994; Schwimmer 1994). At the conservative end of the spectrum, derivatives can be used to exploit inconsistencies in prices of various securities. For example, 'Index Plus' managers aim to achieve a minimum return equal to that of a predetermined stock index. Extra returns can be generated by exploiting arbitrage opportunities with derivatives securities.

Managers with greater risk appetite may sell options to generate premium. They may also invest in structured notes with potential for high returns, depending on movements in a range of assets including equities, commodities and bonds. Inverse floaters are securities whose value increases as interest rates decline. Potential for loss is exaggerated if such instruments are leveraged. In some cases significant gains/losses may result from quite minor market movements. Low levels of liquidity for structured instruments can further contribute to risks.

Mortgage backed securities (or pass-throughs) are also purchased by money-market and fixed-income funds to achieve higher returns. A mortgage-backed security is either an ownership claim on a pool of mortgages or an obligation that is secured by such a pool. Such securities allow mortgage lenders to sell packages of loans in the secondary market. Lenders continue to collect principal and interest payments from borrowers, but *pass-through* these payments to the holders of mortgage backed securities. Often the payments are packaged separately with some investors buying Principal Only (PO) strips and others buying Interest Only (IO) strips.

The risk of such pass-through securities is that borrowers have some control over the duration of the borrowing. For example, when interest rates fall, borrowers are more likely to prepay their mortgages, thus reducing the duration of pass-through securities. Conversely, as interest rates increase, borrowers will extend the term of fixed rate borrowings for as long as possible. Hence the risks are often greater than those associated with traditional bonds.

h) Exploit investment specialities

Overlay services have become popular in the last five years as part of the trend to investment specialisation (Layard-Liesching 1994; Sy 1996). Specialist fund managers can manage currency risk (currency overlay) or manage asset allocation decisions (tactical asset allocation overlay). These strategies are implemented by using derivatives. Physical investments are established by specialists in each asset class ie equities, fixed income and international assets. Currency hedging or asset allocation decisions are 'overlayed' on the physical assets using derivatives such as forwards, swaps, options and futures. The use of overlays does not affect the physical assets but provides an effective overall investment process.

5.2.2 *Institutional requirements*

The funds management industry can be broken into segments based on institutional type. Unique characteristics of the various institutional groups lead to different approaches to derivatives.

a) Insurance companies

Insurers can be divided into two groups: first, life insurance and second, property and casualty insurance. Cummins et al. (1996)

investigate the extent to which US insurance companies use financial derivatives contracts to manage risk. They also examine the determinants of derivatives usage and motives for hedging. Such analysis is possible because US insurers are required to provide an annual statement of derivatives usage. The sample has 1207 life insurers and 2063 property and casualty insurers. The study finds derivatives use by insurers is quite low, but increasing.

According to the study, 12 per cent of life insurers and 7 per cent of property and casualty insurers use derivatives.[2] Greater use of derivatives by life insurers is due to a higher degree of interest rate exposure. Interest rate exposure for life insurers results from an investment component in many life insurance contracts combined with the interest rate sensitivity of policy holders. Participation in Guaranteed Investment Certificates (GICs)[3] is another source of interest rate exposure. According to Sullivan (1995), derivatives are used by life insurers to hedge annuity portfolios supported by bond investments. When interest rates rise and bond prices fall, an annuity underwriter is exposed to potential loss.

Property and casualty insurers' liabilities are also interest rate sensitive, but are of a shorter-term nature than those of life insurers. All insurers face interest rate risk on the asset side of the balance sheet arising from investments in bonds. Typically insurers face a positive duration gap.[4]

Cummins et al. (1996) found that the size of the insurer is an indicator of derivatives use due to economies of scale in human capital investment and derivatives trading. An insurer is also more likely to use derivatives if other companies in the same group use derivatives. The use of swaps and futures is correlated with holdings of Collateralised Mortgage Obligations (CMOs). This could be explained by the fact that institutions are hedging the duration gap between CMOs and GICs since the former typically have poor liquidity. The organisational form (ie a publicly listed structure or a vehicle with a mutual form of ownership) was also a significant factor in derivatives use. Publicly listed insurers are more likely to use derivatives, as they are more likely to be involved in complex and/or risky lines of business that give rise to the need for hedging.

For property and casualty insurers, size is also positively correlated with derivatives use. Derivatives use is, however, negatively correlated with general liability and workers' compensation insurance. These lines of business have long payout tails, providing a natural hedge for interest rate risk in the asset portfolio.

Insurance companies are regulated closely in most jurisdictions.

For example, since 1992 life companies in Australia have been required to provide quarterly statutory reports which encompass the effect of derivatives in portfolio management (Insurance and Superannuation Commission 1993). This supervisory regime helps reduce potential losses from the misuse of derivatives.

b) Unit trusts (mutual funds)

Unit trusts (or mutual funds as they are termed in the United States) pool the limited funds of small investors into large amounts, thereby gaining the advantages of large-scale trading. They invest in a range of separate asset classes including bonds, money market instruments, equities and overseas assets, as well as combinations of the above. Professional managers are employed to make investment decisions according to their prospectuses and trust guidelines. They issue shares to investors entitling them to a pro rata portion of the income generated by the funds. The unit trust concept has become so popular with investors that there are now more mutual funds available in the United States than listed shares.

In October 1993 the Investment Company Institute surveyed 1728 long-term mutual funds in the United States (Simon 1994). More than a quarter reported that they held derivatives. The survey concluded that the funds most likely to employ derivatives are fixed-income and balanced funds.

Koski and Pontiff (1996) studied the use of derivatives by 675 equity mutual funds. Twenty-one per cent of the funds analysed use derivatives, with the majority claiming to use futures and options for hedging purposes. The study found no systematic differences in the distribution of returns for funds that use derivatives as opposed to those that do not. The use of derivatives did, however, affect the correlation between volatility (ie standard deviation of returns) and fund performance. Funds which do not use derivatives tend to experience low volatility after good performance and increased volatility after poor performance. The use of derivatives dampens the negative correlation between fund volatility and past performance.

Investors rely on the fact that unit trusts are fairly priced and on the ability to trade units at all times. The use of derivatives is influenced by these concerns. Unit trust managers tend to prefer investments that are liquid and easily valued (Association of Unit Trusts and Investment Funds 1995). In this respect exchange-traded derivatives have advantages over over-the-counter instruments due to their price transparency, liquidity and lower counterparty risk.

Of all the segments analysed in this chapter, unit trusts are the least regulated. It is therefore not surprising that the majority of derivatives mishaps have occurred in this segment.

c) Superannuation funds (pension funds)

Superannuation funds (or pension funds as they are known in the United States) are used by investors saving for retirement. In Australia superannuation funds are sponsored by employers, unions (often referred to as industry funds) and life companies (Clark et al. 1996). Employer and union sponsored superannuation funds generally employ professional fund managers to make investment decisions subject to specified guidelines. Thus it is unusual for superannuation funds to trade directly in derivatives. Rather, any derivatives transactions are undertaken by a professional manager on behalf of the fund. The investment strategy for the fund (including the use of derivatives) is often guided by asset consultants.

The two basic fund types are defined contribution plans and defined benefit plans (Bodie et al. 1996). The former are tax-deferred retirement savings accounts established by the sponsor in trust for its members. The member bears all the investment risk and receives all investment returns net of fees. In a defined benefit plan, the sponsor holds all the investment risk since the sponsor is responsible for paying a predetermined retirement benefit. The assets of the fund serve as collateral for the liabilities of the sponsor.

Superannuation funds generally have a long-term investment horizon. Traditionally, higher volatility investment strategies have been justified on this basis, with a large proportion of funds invested in growth assets.[5] Greater perception of risk tolerance has also typically reduced the incentive to use derivatives for hedging purposes. Further, the use of derivatives is frequently discouraged by the existence of strict investment guidelines. Many Australian superannuation funds, especially those established prior to the derivatives era, do not empower managers to invest in derivatives.

It is difficult to estimate the number of superannuation funds that currently use derivatives. According to surveys in the UK and Canada (Guthrie 1994; Williams and Grossi 1995) 57 per cent and 37 per cent (respectively) of pension funds use derivatives. However, these surveys may underestimate the importance of derivatives in superannuation as the larger funds are more active users. Over time, acceptance of derivatives is trickling down from large, well-resourced schemes to the smaller ones.

In Australia, superannuation funds are governed by the Superannuation Industry (Supervision) Act 1993 (SIS). The SIS legislation prevents superannuation funds from borrowing (Superannuation Industry (Supervision) Act 1993, Sections 67, 95 and 97). Funds may not use derivatives to circumvent these limitations. In other words, superannuation funds may not leverage their portfolios using derivatives. In addition, further guidelines have been introduced for the use of derivatives by superannuation funds: see *Section 5.4.2*.

In 1994 Australian fund managers were surveyed on their use of derivatives (Australian Investment Managers' Association and Sydney Futures Exchange 1994). The thirty-seven respondents account for approximately 80 per cent of all managed funds in Australia. Most of these respondents manage superannuation funds and a significant minority also offer unit trusts. The survey uncovered widespread usage of derivatives, especially exchange traded derivatives on the SFE.

The most popular equity derivatives are the SFE's Share Price Index contracts (used by 91 per cent of respondents) and the Australian Stock Exchange's (ASX) equity option contracts (used by 81 per cent of respondents). Similarly, 88 per cent of respondents use the 10 and 3 year bond futures and options contracts on the SFE. Over-the-counter products such as FRAs, Interest Rate Swaps and Swaptions were less popular; less than one-third of managers use these instruments.

d) Hedge funds

The original hedge funds were so named because they took a combination of both long and short stock positions, thus creating a 'hedged' or market-neutral portfolio. As a result, they could potentially perform well in a variety of market conditions, depending on stock selection skill. According to Caldwell (1995), the first hedge fund was established in this manner by Alfred Winslow Jones in 1949. Loomis' 1966 article in *Fortune* magazine described Jones' successful investment approach in glowing terms, leading to the proliferation of hedge funds. George Soros was among hundreds who established hedge funds at this time.

Jones observed that short selling does not sit comfortably with the mindset of most equity managers. In the bull market of the late 1960s, hedging portfolios through short selling became less appealing. Jones' insight proved correct, with most managers abandoning the 'hedge' approach early on.

A range of investment strategies are now used by so-called hedge funds (see below). Hedge funds today tend to be characterised by a particular investment style rather than by any one strategy. They employ unconventional and aggressive investment styles with few constraints. To the extent that the law permits, hedge funds have typically refused to reveal the precise nature of their investment strategies.

According to Van (1995) there are more than 3000 hedge funds in the US and fewer offshore. The funds avoid US regulation by limiting each fund to 99 investors who typically invest more than USD1 million each. These investors may be wealthy individuals or superannuation funds seeking diversification. The manager of the fund receives incentive fees of around 20 per cent of profits, plus a management fee based on a percentage of assets. The fee structure is an important element of the hedge fund ethos because it creates incentives for high return and (therefore) high risk strategies.

Investment strategies have evolved over time so that the term 'hedge fund' is a misnomer in most cases. Jaffer (1994) describes a range of investment strategies used by hedge funds, including:

- aggressive growth—manager buys stocks with high P/Es, low/no dividends;
- value—emphasis on company assets and cash flow;
- market neutral—a true 50 per cent long, 50 per cent short hedge that theoretically reduces market risk substantially but relies heavily on stockpicking; and
- macro—manager exploits shifts in global interest rates, exchange rates (George Soros's Quantum fund is typical of this style).

Hedge funds tend to make liberal use of leverage which adds to the volatility of investment returns. Derivatives are used in a variety of ways: for example, to create gearing, to implement arbitrage strategies and to exploit market views.

The popularity of hedge funds peaked in early 1994 after their spectacular success in the early 1990s (Galarza 1996). From 1991 to 1993 Soros's Quantum fund produced a compounded annual return of 62 per cent while the S&P 500 grew at a compounded annual rate of 16 per cent. During the heyday of hedge funds in September 1992, Soros is reputed to have boasted that his fund caused the withdrawal of the British pound from the European Monetary System and its subsequent devaluation.

5.2.3 *Use of derivatives by Asian fund managers*

The largest funds management centre in Asia is Japan. The Australian Embassy in Tokyo estimated that at the end of March 1995, Japanese pension fund assets stood at JPY213.5 trillion (AUD3285 billion). Hong Kong is another significant Asian funds management centre, being the regional base for many international managers. According to the Hong Kong Investment Funds Association there are over 60 fund managers in Hong Kong. In many respects the Asian funds management industry is less sophisticated than in North America or Australia. For example, the use of investment benchmarks, specialist managers and derivatives is not yet widespread in either Japan or Hong Kong.

In a conversation with the author, Justin Pascoe of Jardine Fleming Investment Management (Hong Kong) explained that derivatives are under-utilised for several reasons. Firstly, there is a lack of suitable exchange traded instruments with the depth of liquidity required by fund managers. High volatility in many Asian markets leads to high option premiums and deters potential purchasers. Superannuation trustees often lack understanding of derivatives and tend to award investment mandates restricting or prohibiting the use of derivatives. Finally, the fund managers themselves often lack appropriate expertise and systems. Many do not have the ability to report effective investment exposure including derivatives. Pascoe believes that lack of derivatives use by fund managers produces inefficiencies. Hedge funds and arbitrage desks operated by banks in Asia are taking advantage of opportunities passed over by fund managers.

The exception to this rule is the popularity of warrants which are traded actively. Even though warrants are essentially long-dated options, they are not generally regarded as derivatives in Asia. Portfolios would normally include warrants under the same heading as traditional equities. Foreign currency forwards may also be used at times to hedge foreign exchange risk.

Greg Cooper of Towers Perrin, an asset consultant who advises superannuation fund trustees in Hong Kong, notes that there is little regulation in Hong Kong for derivatives. Under the Occupational Retirement Scheme Ordinance governing superannuation funds, there is no mention of derivatives. Legislation is being drafted to govern the new Mandatory Provident Fund. It is expected that the new legislation will restrict the use of derivatives.

Unit trusts in Hong Kong are regulated by the Securities and Futures Commission. According to the Code on Unit Trusts and Mutual Funds (Securities and Futures Commission 1995), a unit trust may invest in options, warrants and futures for hedging purposes. The value of a scheme's investments in derivatives not held for hedging purposes may not exceed a fixed percentage of total net asset value. In addition, the writing of uncovered options is prohibited. The writing of call options on portfolio investments may not exceed 25 per cent of a scheme's total net asset value in terms of exercise price. The Code also sets out detailed regulations governing specialist warrant funds and futures and options funds whose principal objective is to invest in derivatives.

Turning to Japan, the use of derivatives is shaped by the regulatory and accounting regime. Yoshinobu Kono of William M. Mercer explained in a conversation with the author that these factors have caused the use of derivatives to lag that in other funds management centres. The use of book value accounting to date has created little incentive for fund managers either to hedge portfolios against risk or to maximise returns.[6] The funds management culture has not emphasised performance as investment restrictions ensure that the majority of assets are invested in domestic cash and fixed interest.[7] The only performance benchmark generally applied is a 5.5 per cent actuarial discount rate which is used regardless of market conditions.

Given the limited use of derivatives, it is not surprising that there have not been any large-scale derivatives disasters in the two large Asian funds management centres. Cooper, Pascoe and Kono were not aware of any publicly known misuse of derivatives by fund managers. The collapse of Barings and other high-profile disasters such as those discussed in *Section 5.3* had little impact since fund managers and trustees were already conservative in their use of derivatives. If anything, the events of 1994 and 1995 confirmed their existing suspicions, delaying the rate of growth in such investment strategies.

5.3 Misuse of derivatives

Misuse of derivatives should be of concern whether it results in gains or losses to the investor. Evidence of derivatives misuse generally arises only after losses have been incurred; investors rarely complain if derivatives misuse results in unusual profits, although this is often a warning of future losses. In several examples cited below, portfolio managers were praised and won awards for strategies which subsequently came unstuck. It should also be remembered that derivatives losses may not necessarily indicate misuse. Some short-term losses may be acceptable to risk-tolerant investors.

The cases discussed in *Chapter 2* have had a significant impact on the funds management industry, despite the fact that none relate directly to participants (see *Section 5.4*). There have in fact been derivatives cases specific to this industry which raise important concerns. *Section 5.3* explores derivatives management issues peculiar to the funds management industry by examining these cases. The majority of funds management derivatives debacles uncovered by this writer have occurred in American unit trusts. This sample may, however, be biased, for two reasons: firstly, the ready availability of information on the American market and secondly, the widespread proliferation of so many unit trusts.

According to Simon (1994), about a dozen money market funds were heavily hit by derivatives related losses, despite their image as low volatility investments. Bond funds using derivatives suffered losses up to 15 per cent greater than those funds that did not when the bond market collapsed in early 1994. The misuse of derivatives in unit trusts has been blamed on competitive pressures (*The Economist* 1994). Competition has encouraged fund managers to use more exotic derivatives in an attempt to outperform rivals.

The misuse of derivatives is exemplified by six case studies described below. This section concludes with a summary of the lessons to be learnt from these events.

5.3.1 *PaineWebber*

PaineWebber's flagship short-term bond fund lost USD268 million after investing in derivatives strategies to enhance returns. The parent company later offset losses by topping up the fund. In this case the misuse of derivatives related to the fact that investments were inconsistent with the investment strategy sold to investors.

The PaineWebber Short-Term US Government Income Fund attracted USD1.6 billion from retail investors in its first year of operation (Bary 1994b). Investors were encouraged to invest in this fund as a high-yielding, slightly higher-risk alternative to money market funds. During the bear market in the early part of 1994 almost all money market and bond funds performed poorly as bond prices fell. As a general rule, the longer the term of assets held by the fund, the greater is the sensitivity to market prices. The PaineWebber fund performed relatively well with a loss of 1.3 per cent for the first four months of the year. Then on Friday 6 May 1994, the value of the fund fell by 4 per cent in one day, an unprecedented loss for a quasi money market fund. In fact, the fund performed worse than unit trusts investing in long-term securities.

The bond market fell on that day on publication of higher unemployment figures. This market decline cannot explain losses of such magnitude since the average maturity was two to three years. The firm attributed these losses to the result of a sale of securities. This explanation failed to impress market commentators who pointed out that if the assets were valued fairly, their sale could not affect the portfolio value. Instead, many suspect the fund held volatile mortgage derivative issues that were not correctly valued.

Bary (1994b) claims that the PaineWebber fund held companion bonds, a form of pass-through securities. Promoters of these securities estimated the life of these issues at two to three years. As interest rates rose in 1994, borrowers adjusted their refinancing behaviour, resulting in an increase in the effective duration of the securities to more than 10 years. As interest rates rose on 6 May 1994, significant losses were incurred.

While these rumours have not been substantiated, the fund's half yearly report dated 30 November 1993 provides some clues. At that time the fund held USD200 million in illiquid derivative securities such as inverse IOs and POs. Depending on the term and exact nature of these securities, considerable losses may have eventuated.

Liquidity is a major concern in the use of derivatives by unit trusts. Normally fund managers provide daily valuations of all securities held in their portfolios. Illiquidity of some structured derivatives products has reduced the validity of these daily valuations. As some derivatives rarely trade, fund managers may need to use internal price estimates which are open to bias or error. In the PaineWebber case the sharp decline in fund value on 6 May 1994 raised questions about the validity of valuations prior to that date. According to Bary (1994b), buyers of the fund from early February may have the right to a rebate on part of their purchase price because the fund's assets appear to have been overvalued.

5.3.2 *Piper Jaffray*

Piper Jaffray's bond funds suffered massive losses after buying mortgage-backed securities similar to those that contributed to the PaineWebber losses (Bary 1994a). The critical issue here, as in the PaineWebber case, was the use of derivatives in a manner inconsistent with the investment policy understood by investors.

In March 1994 Worth Bruntjen of Piper Jaffray was named a runner-up in a portfolio management competition. He was described as a visionary, one of very few portfolio managers who could successfully negotiate the complex mortgage-backed securities market. In 1993, Bruntjen's five funds achieved returns double those of their peers in the mortgage market.

The value of the funds collapsed when American interest rates rose in early 1994. By mid-May of 1994 the Piper Jaffray Institutional Government Income Portfolio, marketed as a short-term government fund, had lost 26 per cent for the year. The loss compared adversely not only with other short term funds, but also with the most risky long-term bonds. For the same period 30-year zero-coupon Treasury bonds lost 18 per cent. The significant losses are blamed on liberal use of leverage and volatile mortgage derivatives.

In 1993 Bruntjen correctly predicted that rates would decline, resulting in significant refinancing by home-owners. He purchased POs and inverse floaters to exploit this view. When the trend reversed in early 1994, gains turned to significant losses. The firm eventually agreed to pay USD70 million to compensate investors for about 40 per cent of their losses (Willoughby 1995). The Piper Jaffray experience exemplifies the common problem that high risk derivatives strategies are only scrutinised after losses occur.

5.3.3 *Investors Equity*

Although insurance companies are highly regulated, safeguards have not entirely eliminated the misuse of derivatives. Losses in the bond market caused problems for Investors Equity, a small insurer domiciled in Hawaii (Sullivan 1995). Disaster was precipitated by the use of 30-year bond futures to create a leveraged position. Initially bond futures were used to hedge annuity liabilities. Brokers allowed the company to trade derivatives with margins as low as 2 per cent of the effective exposure. However the hedging strategy later evolved into speculation. The company was able to create an effective position of USD20 billion through futures transactions. As market prices moved adversely, the company lost USD90 million in the first 5½ months of 1994. A company spokesman estimated that between 40 and 50 per cent of the asset base was lost during the same period.

The Investors Equity case is an isolated instance of derivatives misuse by insurers. The level of regulation in the industry generally results in conservative investment strategies. In fact, the Investors Equity losses occurred just a few months before a scheduled examination by regulators. The role of rating services also diminishes the likelihood of derivatives misuse. Analysts from ratings agencies look for volatility in earnings as a sign of inappropriate use of derivatives (Sullivan 1995). Major losses in the insurance industry linked to derivatives have been minimal when one considers losses incurred in junk bonds and real estate.

5.3.4 *State of Wisconsin Investment Board/Wisconsin Retirement System*

Turning to superannuation, one finds further evidence of derivatives misuse. According to Barr (1995), the State of Wisconsin Investment Board lost USD95 million using swaps. The USD30 billion Wisconsin Retirement System had USD1.1 billion invested in the fund and suffered losses of around USD16 million. After analysing the losses, the State's Legislative Audit Bureau advised that losses resulted from lack of care by investment staff in analysing the original investments and poor handling of initial losses.

The losses resulted from speculative positions on currency swaps unrelated to the fund's exposures (*The Economist* 1995). The Board had used interest rate swaps since 1991 to enhance yield. While the Board's guidelines prohibited speculative investments, speculation was not defined. Earlier transactions had resulted in profits with the result that concerns were not aroused until the loss occurred.

According to the September 1995 report in *Global Investor*, the Board did not mark-to-market and failed to appreciate that some swap transactions were leveraged. The value of one contract was based on the difference between yields on US and Mexican government bonds, known as the MexSpread.

The counterparty to the swap, Bankers Trust, expressed the payout on the swap as follows:

$10 million x (2.95%–MexSpread)/2.95%.

Investment staff were criticised for failing to notice the leverage inherent in this formula. The leverage becomes more obvious once it is appreciated that division by 2.95 per cent is equivalent to multiplication by 33.898. The formula could therefore have been rewritten as follows:

$10 million x (2.95%–MexSpread) x 33.898.

Despite the fact that Bankers Trust provided the Board with sensitivity analysis showing projected gains and losses, staff failed to notice the leverage. After the leverage factor was eventually discovered, the swap was restructured. As a result, the potential for loss was effectively tripled. The Legislative Audit Bureau criticised the highly decentralised management structure and recommended establishment of an independent internal audit unit.

5.3.5 *Qantas Superannuation*

The Australian superannuation industry has also experienced losses from derivatives misuse. In 1995 a dispute arose between Qantas Superannuation Ltd (QSL) and an external fund manager, Legal & General Investment Management Ltd (Legal & General).[8] Legal & General had been appointed as an investment manager in 1988 and made investment decisions in accordance with the Investment Agreement between the two parties.

QSL brought an action against Legal & General for losses from derivatives investments in excess of AUD5 million. QSL made several claims: that the manager traded derivative transactions in breach of the Investment Agreement; that the investments were not of a type specified in the Investment Agreement and did not conform with directions regarding risk and size; that Legal & General staff were not qualified to manage derivatives transactions; and that the latter failed to monitor adequately open positions and to respond expeditiously when losses were first incurred. QSL further charged that the transactions were speculative; outside the agreed parameters of risk; and contrary to or in disregard of Legal & General's own view of anticipated interest rate volatility. Legal & General denied these claims.

5.3.6 *Granite Fund*

In the early 1990s some hedge funds had spectacular returns, benefiting both the investors and the managers who earned substantial fees. However in early 1994, failed bets in the currency and bond markets saw some equally spectacular losses. Between December 1993 and December 1994, assets invested in hedge funds fell from USD100 billion to USD75 billion due to a combination of poor performance and asset withdrawals (Celarier 1995).

The infamous Granite Fund lost most of its assets after taking highly leveraged positions in mortgage-backed securities. The manager, David Askin, is reported to have assured investors that he invested in high-quality mortgage securities using a low-risk, low-leveraged 'market neutral' strategy. Investors later sued Askin and several brokerage firms for USD700 million (Willoughby 1996).

Contrary to his assurances, Askin had effectively leveraged his equity more than two times and had invested in illiquid, hard to price securities. While Askin's funds management abilities were later proved suspect, his marketing abilities are undoubted. In 16 months, he took assets under management from USD110 million to USD600 million. According to Lappen (1994), Askin promised investors that the fund would return 15 per cent regardless of interest rate movements.

Controversy regarding hedge funds in general has arisen in several areas. Firstly, investors are increasingly demanding disclosure regarding the nature of investment strategies. Complaints have arisen regarding undisclosed changes in investment style, breaches in compliance, shaky administration and inadequate custodial arrangements. Secondly, many are concerned about the practice of paying significant incentive fees which may encourage excessive risk-taking. The problem is compounded when incentive fees are paid on recent good performance but when past losses have not yet been recouped. Investors are demanding that incentive fees should only be paid once a hurdle rate has been achieved, and on the basis of long-term rather than short-term performance.

5.3.7 *Lessons from derivatives misuse*

The examples given in this chapter raise the following issues:

- are derivatives used in a manner consistent with investment guidelines and marketing materials? (see PaineWebber, Piper Jaffray, Legal & General, Granite Fund);
- are derivatives liquid and valued accurately on a mark-to-market basis? (see PaineWebber, Wisconsin Retirement System, Granite Fund);
- is helpful and intelligible information available to investors on the risk of investment strategies? (see Piper Jaffray, PaineWebber, Granite Fund);
- do investment guidelines clearly delineate the purposes for which derivatives may be used? (see Investors Equity, Wisconsin Retirement System);
- are investment staff equipped to analyse and manage derivatives? (see Wisconsin Retirement System, Legal & General);
- are limits and other procedures in place to prevent small losses growing large? (see Wisconsin Retirement System);
- what internal checks and balances are needed to review the

actions of individual traders? (see Wisconsin Retirement System);

- do fee structures provide appropriate incentives for fund managers? (see Granite Fund); and
- are strategies scrutinised even when returns are unusually favourable? (see Piper Jaffray, Wisconsin Retirement System).

5.4 Impact on attitudes

The events of 1994 and 1995 alarmed many investors and fund trustees. Initially some avoided derivatives entirely. Demands for more disclosure and tougher regulation were strident. This initial phase is discussed in *Section 5.4.1*. *Section 5.4.2* describes the new regulations which have resulted from these demands. The medium term impact of the crisis is discussed in *Section 5.4.3*, first from a fund manager's perspective and thereafter from that of an asset consultant.

5.4.1 *Initial alarm*

After the incidents described in *Chapter 2*, some plan sponsors over-reacted. For many, the fear of featuring in the media as a disaster story was a driving factor. According to one fund manager: 'I have been asked by clients to sign affidavits attesting that we will not use any derivative product' (Millman 1995).

In July 1995 it was reported that around a dozen states in the US were considering bills to ban or severely limit the use of derivatives by local government entities such as pension funds (*The Economist* 1995). In May the Oklahoma legislature repealed a law that had previously allowed state pension funds to invest in derivatives. In a radical Californian proposal, fiduciary responsibility was to be imposed on any institution doing financial business with a state entity.

Fortunately the majority of observers did not take an extreme view. A more common response was to continue use of derivatives, but under much stricter controls and avoiding high-risk strategies. According to Millman (1995), a survey of fund managers shows that the only derivatives product to lose popularity was the structured note. In 1993, 49 per cent of fund managers invested in these products, while in 1994 the proportion fell to 38 per cent. Another area to lose business was the issuance of pass-through securities. Yet there was no change in the number of managers using futures, swaps and options. If anything the market for simpler derivatives grew.

In early 1996 *Pensions & Investment Age* reported a new conservativeness regarding derivatives (Barr 1996). Conservative uses of derivatives (eg enhanced indexing and currency hedging) were still expected to grow. Nonetheless, pension executives were reported as more vigilant about the use of derivatives, implementing tighter investment guidelines and increasing their oversight.

Pension World reported the withdrawal of both Eastman Kodak and Virginia Retirement System from the use of managed futures (Bergsman 1996). In both cases, the pension fund trustees felt uncomfortable with the degree of volatility compared to potential returns. Concerns were expressed about the cost of controls and transaction costs associated with high turnover levels. The Eastman Kodak pension fund reduced the use of derivatives in the pension plan, consistent with company policy. This occurred despite reports of favourable past returns.

5.4.2 *More regulation*

One of the most far-reaching reactions has been the trend to greater regulation of fund managers in their use of derivatives. While investor protection is the rationale, some forms of supervision may actually reduce investor welfare. This writer would argue on the basis of *Section 5.2.1* that restricting use of derivatives by fund managers would reduce the efficiency of investment portfolios. Regulations may limit investor choice by disallowing the high risk strategies preferred by some investors. Limits on the use of derivatives would be useless since, by definition, any derivative strategy can be replicated with a portfolio comprised of physical assets (see *Derivatives defined*). Further, regulation can create a moral hazard by giving investors and managers a false sense of security that risks have been adequately controlled. To the extent that further regulation is introduced, it should encourage, rather than restrict, the appropriate use and management of derivatives.

This section examines regulatory trends in several segments of the industry.

a) Unit trusts

A report on the use of derivatives in investment funds was tabled at the Investment Funds Conference in Paris in October 1995 (Association of Unit Trusts and Investment Funds 1995). The document recommends internal management and external regulatory control systems on the use of derivatives. The report draws on experience in Austria, Canada, Denmark, France, Germany, Japan, Italy, Luxembourg, Spain, the United Kingdom and the United States.

The 1995 report highlights the variation internationally in the permitted use of derivatives. Some countries (eg USA, Canada, Japan, UK and Luxembourg) have liberal legislation allowing the use of all or most derivatives. Other countries impose prescriptive product rules which allow the use of some derivatives but prohibit others. Many jurisdictions impose stringent limits on the gearing of portfolios. Disclosure of derivatives usage is regulated in only some jurisdictions.

Recent derivatives losses have encouraged regulators to consider further regulation of the industry. Predictably, this is a trend opposed by most fund managers. The 1995 report did however highlight the need for intelligible and relevant disclosure to aid investors in assessing risk. It acknowledged the serious lack of participation of senior management in exercising controls over derivatives. For example, the issue of segregation of duties between front office and back office was highlighted by the Barings crisis, discussed in *Chapter 2*. The 1995 report recommended that segregation of duties be made mandatory.

b) Superannuation funds

In April 1996 the Australian Insurance and Superannuation Commission (ISC) released guidelines for superannuation funds that use derivatives (Insurance and Superannuation Commission 1996). While an assessment of their impact on the industry cannot yet be made, their introduction has been welcomed in principle. The new guidelines have generally been well received because they do not attempt to prevent or limit the use of derivatives. Rather, they put the onus on senior management to determine the suitability of any investment strategy and to implement appropriate controls. A similar approach has been adopted in Japan. From 1996 Japanese plan sponsors are required to formalise investment guidelines, including the use of derivatives.

The new Australian guidelines are intended to assist trustees with investment decisions and to ensure derivatives are used for *bona fide* purposes. According to the ISC Guidelines there have been no significant problems with derivatives in Australia to date. Rather, the objective is to avoid potential problems similar to those experienced elsewhere.

Under Section 52 of the Superannuation Investment (Supervision) Act (1993) trustees are required to formulate and give effect to an investment strategy in the best interests of beneficiaries. ISC guidelines encourage funds with derivatives to review regularly investment and risk management policies in order to ensure the covenants in Section 52 are satisfied at all times.

Central to these guidelines is the concept of a Risk Management Statement (RMS) to be issued by all superannuation funds. The RMS identifies all cases where derivatives are used by the fund, either directly or by external managers. Where external fund managers are authorised to use derivatives, they too must complete an Investment Manager RMS.

The guidelines assume that ultimate responsibility for all investments lies with the trustees. Trustees must determine that derivatives are permitted under the governing rules of the fund. Trustees must also ensure that the investment strategies of each external manager regarding derivatives are consistent with fund guidelines, both individually and in combination.

The RMS must explain the objectives for which derivatives are used as part of the overall investment process. Emphasis is placed on the policies and processes to restrict and manage the use of derivatives. The RMS should describe risk controls, systems, processes for dealing, administration and settlement of derivatives. Most importantly, the issues of market risk, liquidity risk, counterparty risk and operations risk must be addressed.

One strength of the ISC approach is that it has forced all fund managers to adopt reporting of effective exposures. Derivatives must not be considered in isolation but as part of the overall investment strategy. Net exposure, including both physical and derivatives holdings, must be monitored so that market risk[9] can easily be assessed. The ISC has specifically recommended the use of stress testing to highlight potential losses that could be incurred given a range of adverse risk scenarios.

c) Life insurance regulation

Regulation of derivatives in the Australian life insurance industry was outlined in a circular issued in 1995 (Insurance and Superannuation Commission 1995). New requirements on life insurers relating to derivatives take effect for financial years after 31 December 1995. The ISC does not restrict the use of derivatives in the investment process. The onus is on directors to determine appropriate investment strategies and risk controls.

Prior to this circular the ISC required regular reporting on the effect of derivatives use via Quarterly Statutory Fund Returns (see *Section 5.2.2a*). The new arrangements state that life insurers must implement risk controls in relation to derivatives. These controls should be evidenced by an RMS. Risk management practices must be codified in a single document approved by the board of directors. The nature of the RMS is described in an appendix to the circular. Life companies must ensure compliance with the RMS via internal and external audits.

5.4.3 *Opinions on medium term impact*

a) Interview with Macquarie Investment Management Ltd (MIML)

An interview was conducted by the author with an Australian fund manager to gain insight into the medium term impact of the derivatives crisis. MIML exemplifies fund managers in the industry who have taken seriously the issue of risk management for derivatives.

MIML is an Australian fund manager with more than AUD13 billion in funds under management. MIML has used derivatives effectively for some years, subject to parameters agreed with each client (Macquarie Investment Management Limited 1996). Prudential risk controls at MIML are considered to be of a high standard by asset consultants who scrutinise MIML and other fund managers.

Derivatives are used by MIML as part of the asset allocation process to implement short-term tactical asset allocation changes. Futures and options are used to meet target weightings of portfolios, and to enter or exit markets at a defined price level. Derivatives are also used within asset sectors as appropriate. For example, in equity portfolios derivatives are used to switch between overvalued stocks and the market. Share options and futures may be used to effect stock selection in lieu of physical shares. Fixed interest managers use bill and bond futures and options to manage duration risk. Volatility is traded in equities, interest rate and currency overlay portfolios through the use of options. Futures and options are used to hedge market risk in all asset classes. Arbitrage opportunities between the futures and physical market are exploited in cash, bond and equities portfolios. Finally, as a specialist currency overlay manager, MIML uses currency forwards and options to hedge against currency risk.

The Prudential Management team, headed by Virginia Malley, monitors derivatives transactions and is independent of the trading group. Malley comments favourably on renewed interest in controls since the events of 1994 and 1995. The industry is now more aware of the risks of derivatives and has moved to reduce these risks. Since derivatives controls had already been the subject of scrutiny at MIML for some time, the ISC guidelines did not necessitate any change in MIML's risk management practices.

Immediately after the Barings collapse, a number of trustees approached MIML with concerns about the use of derivatives. Questions related to the controls used to monitor derivatives, enforcement of those controls and compliance with investment mandates. In every case these concerns were satisfied. There were no cases of clients wishing to withdraw from, or limit the use of, derivatives.

Since that time, prudential controls have increased throughout the industry worldwide. Principles and processes for the use of derivatives have been reviewed at MIML and further measures taken to avoid potential loss. One such measure has been the introduction of the Prudential Management team, within Financial Control Division, to monitor derivatives and other issues.

Each fund has limits on the use of derivatives approved by the client and the internal Risk Committee. In every case gearing of funds using derivatives is prohibited. Derivatives may only be used if they explicitly comply with fund deeds, fund mandates, investment strategies, fund management agreements, terms of life policies, ratings criteria, relevant regulatory policies, relevant legislation, derivatives exchanges dealing agreements, and master agreements for trading OTC instruments. Portfolio managers have to ensure compliance with derivatives guidelines. However, Prudential Management independently monitors adherence to these controls with the aid of computer systems. The system monitors compliance with over 1000 rules per day and reports breaches daily to Management Committee.

Further checks and balances exist to attempt to ensure that derivatives cannot be misused. For example, internal audits are conducted on an annual basis by Macquarie Bank's Internal Audit Division. External audits are conducted annually, and regulatory audits are conducted by the Australian Securities Commission (ASC), SFE and ISC. Since some investment funds are rated, ratings agencies also conduct independent reviews.

Since 1995 prudential controls have featured in marketing strategies. Malley encourages clients, prospective clients and asset consultants to tour MIML's Prudential Management area. Prior to the Barings collapse financial control was not considered exciting, but now clients and asset consultants are genuinely interested.

b) An asset consultant's perspective

InTech Asset Consulting Pty Ltd (InTech) advises Australian superannuation funds and other investors regarding investment strategy and related issues. Brett Elvish, Senior Consultant, is a specialist in the area of fund custody and prudential management. In this role he assesses many fund managers with regard to investment process and business risk. His opinions were sought by the author on the medium-term impact of the derivatives crisis in the industry.

In the last two years he has observed a general improvement in risk management by fund managers. Back office and middle office teams are better resourced and independent of trading areas. Management attention is more focused on prudential controls. Nevertheless there are examples of poor management practice even amongst the largest managers. For example, fund managers should have integrated computer systems incorporating both physical and derivatives positions. Some managers still monitor derivatives positions using PC-based spreadsheet packages.

Reactions to the events of 1994 and 1995 have been piecemeal according to Elvish. While some clients of fund managers are concerned about prudential controls, many are not sure what questions to ask or how to assess expertise. Some assume that the more derivatives are used the riskier will be the fund. Indeed the opposite may be true, as funds using derivatives to a limited extent may be riskier since they lack expertise in this area. Elvish has not observed any diminution in the use of derivatives, but introduction of new derivatives-based products has been delayed due to trustee nervousness. One example is the use of Tactical Asset Allocation Overlays favoured by Elvish. Some trustees have shied away from such services in the current environment.

Elvish is concerned that the ISC's recent guidelines may be an inadequate response to risk management concerns. For example, the guidelines focus solely on the use of derivatives. Since derivatives are only one aspect of risk, a broader-based treatment would have been more appropriate. He also points out that fund managers can easily comply with the 'letter of the law' by issuing a glossy RMS. The 'spirit of the law' can easily be avoided by providing superficial, irrelevant or incomplete information. In some cases the RMSs have lacked substance, giving little insight into the fund manager's operations. It appears that some have been copied verbatim from the ISC guidelines, suggesting that little thought or effort has been taken to consider the issues at stake.

According to Elvish, the ISC response to derivatives was driven by political imperatives. The industry needed to be seen to be doing something to address perceptions of safety after the high-profile derivatives losses. The risk is that the new guidelines become a 'box-ticking' exercise rather than a catalyst for genuine change. The passage of time will reveal whether or not fund managers can successfully implement the lofty principles expressed in their policy statements.

5.5 An industry at risk?

It is evident from this study that derivatives are an increasingly important feature of professional funds management. The application of derivatives is in fact far from exhausted, with many still not using derivatives at all or only to a limited extent. One could argue that managers without access to derivatives are working with their hands tied behind their backs. Derivatives, used effectively, greatly enhance the potential for effective funds management. Any attempt to restrict their use is likely to reduce investor welfare and would in any case probably be ineffective.

Notwithstanding these positive aspects, derivatives have been misused by fund managers on a number of occasions. Losses have jolted the industry into an awareness of risk. With this new awareness, systems and controls have been scrutinised more thoroughly than ever before. For the true professionals in the field, the bar of prudential management has been raised to higher levels. The use of complex high-risk strategies by the unskilled has diminished. New regulations in the superannuation and insurance industries have addressed some of these management issues in an attempt to give investors greater protection, but there is no room for complacency.

Increased regulation will not of itself eliminate derivatives misuse. Rather, it should ensure that participants are aware of the risks involved before they enter into an investment strategy. The task of comprehensively addressing risk is complex and requires vigilance at all levels and in all areas of funds management. Many of the highly publicised losses did not result from the failure of sophisticated controls, but from deficiencies in basic risk management procedures.

Some excellent risk management guidelines have been developed to guide end-users in establishing suitable controls, such as those developed by the UK Futures and Options Association (Futures and Options Association 1995). A cursory glance at an extensive document such as this indicates the enormity of the task that lies ahead of those who are serious about managing risk. The report of the Futures and Options Association emphasises the limitations of government regulation.

> What is needed, therefore, is voluntary action on the part of those involved in the use of derivatives to establish high standards of risk management practice which do not treat derivatives in isolation but integrate them with an organisation's other risk exposures.

Industry participants interviewed for this paper reveal that risk management practices range from exemplary to superficial to elementary. For example, many managers still do not have computer systems that can integrate derivative and physical positions. Many do not have the ability to run stress tests[10] on a portfolio-wide basis. Senior managers and directors are often poorly equipped to understand and scrutinise complex strategies. These issues are magnified many times over in the less sophisticated financial centres where expertise in derivatives is rare.

Clients, as well as managers, have a role to play in helping to avoid risk. Very often disaster has struck when clients have sought unrealistically high returns, with little regard for the high risk which inevitably follows. In cases where unusually high returns are promised, some responsibility must rest with the client to determine whether the downside risk is acceptable. Through this process of questioning, unwanted or inappropriate risk-taking may be avoided.

The best regulatory regime can never rule out the possibility of loss. What is required is a change in the mindset of both clients and fund managers, from the chief executive to the humblest clerk. Prudential risk management must be a top priority, higher even than fund rankings and inflows. Risks of derivatives should not be isolated, but integrated into an overall risk management policy which is taken seriously at all levels of the organisation. While this paradigm shift has already occurred within some institutions, there is need for further change throughout the funds management industry.

References

Assirt Pty Ltd 1996, *Market Share Report*, Sydney

Association of Unit Trusts and Investment Funds, 1995, *Report on the use of derivatives in investment funds*, Investment Funds Conference, Paris

Australian Investment Managers' Association and Sydney Futures Exchange 1994, *AIMA/SFE Survey of derivatives usage by Australian Fund Managers—Summary of Results and Analysis*, Sydney

Barr, P. 1995, 'Poor oversight cited in Wisconsin swaps loss', *Pensions & Investment Age*, vol. 23, no. 7, p. 35

——1996, 'Execs wary of derivatives', *Pensions & Investment Age*, vol. 24, no. 1, pp. 2, 26

Bary, A. 1994a, 'Paying the piper', *Barrons*, vol. 74, no. 15, pp. 15–16

——1994b, 'Trading points: Derivatives undo a popular PaineWebber fund, triggering 4% one-day drop in its value', *Barrons*, vol. 74, no. 20

Bensman, M. 1994, 'New strategies for selling volatility', *Global Finance*, vol. 8, no. 10, pp. 30–2

Bergsman, S. 1996, 'Why Virginia and Kodak got out of managed futures', *Pension World*, vol. 32, no. 3, p. 31

Bodie, Z., Kane, A. and Marcus, A. 1996, *Investments*, Irwin, Boston

Caldwell, E. 1995, 'Introduction: The model for superior performance', *Hedge Funds—Investment and Portfolio Strategies for the Institutional Investor*, Eds Jess Lederman and Robert A. Klein, Irwin Professional Publishing, New York

Celarier, M. 1995, 'Clipped', *Euromoney*, vol. 320, December, pp. 42–6

Cerulli, K. and Casey, G. 1995, 'Looking for stable value? Several choices available', *Pension World*, vol. 31, no. 5, pp. 50–1

Clark, G., Burkitt J., Caldow, W. and Jobling, M. 1996, *The Superannuation Industry in Australia*, Australian Housing and Urban Research Institute, Working Paper 7, Melbourne

Coopers & Lybrand Banking & Finance Industry Group 1995, 'Derivatives and funds managers: in control?' *On Banking*, pp. 1–6.

Cummins, D., Phillips, R. and Smith, S. 1996, *Corporate hedging in the insurance industry: The use of financial derivatives by US insurers*, Wharton School, University of Pennsylvania, Philadelphia

The Economist 1994, 'Mutual funds' derivatives dilemma', vol. 332, no. 7879, pp. 69–70

——1995, 'Derivatives: To ban or not to ban', vol. 336, no. 7924, pp. 67–70

Futures and Options Association 1995, *Managing derivatives risk: Guidelines for end-users of derivatives*, London

Galarza, P. 1996, 'Time to hedge again', *Financial World*, vol. 165, no. 9, pp. 59–61

Gastineau, G.L. 1995, 'The currency hedging decision: A search for synthesis in asset allocation', *Financial Analysts Journal*, vol. 51, no. 3, pp. 8–17

Global Investor 1995, 'Lessons from Wisconsin: The importance of elementary mathematics', vol. 85, pp. 26–7

Guthrie, J. 1994, 'Derivatives: Rocket scientists set course for planet pensions', *Pensions Management*, September 1994, pp. 55–61

Insurance and Superannuation Commission 1993, *Circular No. 302*, 13 July, Canberra

—— 1995, *Derivatives—Use, Management and Control*, Canberra

—— 1996, *Risk Management Statements for Superannuation Entities Investing in Derivatives—Guidelines*, April, Canberra

Jaffer, S. 1994, 'How to choose a managed derivatives fund', *Global Investor*, vol. 77, November, pp. 18–20

Koski, J. L. and Pontiff, J. 1996, *How are derivatives used? Evidence from the mutual fund industry*, University of Washington, Seattle

Lappen, A. 1994, 'Did dealers gang up on David Askin?', *Institutional Investor*, vol. 2, no. 7, pp. 84–5

Layard-Liesching, R. 1994, 'Currency overlays', *Euromoney* (Currencies Supplement), March, pp. 69–72

Loomis, C.J. 1966, 'The Jones nobody keeps up with', *Fortune*, April, pp. 237–47

Macquarie Investment Management Limited 1996, *Risk Management Statement, Part B*, Sydney

Millman, G. 1995, 'Why investors need to understand derivatives', *Global Investor*, vol. 81, pp. 10–13

Peters, C. 1994, 'Managed Futures win pension foothold', *Pension World*, vol. 30, no. 5, pp. 28–30

Samuelson, P. 1994, 'The Long-term Case for Equities', *Journal of Portfolio Management*, vol. 21, no. 1, Fall

Schneeweis, T., Spurgin, R. and Potter, M. 1996, 'Managed futures and hedge fund investment for downside equity risk management', *Derivatives Quarterly*, vol. 3, no. 1, pp. 62–72

Schonfeld, E. 1995, 'Any derivatives in your portfolio?' *Fortune*, vol. 131, no. 6, pp. 60–4

Schwimmer, A. 1994, 'Structured note buyers turn to new exotic play', *Investment Dealers Digest*, vol. 60, no. 34, p. 9

—— 1995, 'Derivatives may come back in fashion with pension funds', *Investment Dealers Digest*, vol. 61, no. 12, pp. 12–13

Securities & Futures Commission 1995, *Code on Unit Trusts and Mutual Funds*, February 1995

Simon, R. 1994, 'Don't get socked by those #?@!* derivatives', *Money*, vol. 23, no. 8, pp. 26–9

Sullivan, S. 1995, 'Insurers go mano a mano with derivatives', *Life Association News*, vol. 90, no. 7, pp. 76–84

Sy, W. 1996, 'Tactical Manoeuvres', *Journal of the Securities Institute of Australia*, July, pp. 2–9

Updegrave, W. and Misra, P. 1994, 'Funds with hidden risks', *Money*, vol. 23, no. 12, pp. 132–8

Van, G. 1995, 'Taming hedge funds', *Pension World*, vol. 31, no. 8, August, pp. 20–4

Williams, P. and Grossi, F. 1995, 'The top 100 pension funds', *Benefits Canada*, vol. 19, no. 4, pp. 41–53

Willoughby, J. 1995, 'Piper Jaffray shakes up execs, expands oversight role on top', *Investment Dealers Digest*, vol. 61, no. 39, pp. 3–4
—— 1996, 'Investors in Askin funds sue Street for $700 million', *Investment Dealers Digest*, vol. 62, no. 14, p. 3

Notes

1. It should be noted that there are risks associated with trading futures as a substitute for physical assets. For example, futures prices may differ from their theoretical values. In addition, basis risk can mean that futures are an ineffective substitute for physical assets. For example, Share Price Index futures based on the All Ordinaries Index may be an imperfect match for a share portfolio invested in a subset of stocks in the All Ordinaries Index.
2. Derivatives in this study include options, caps, floors, collars, swaps, forwards and futures. However, structured securities such as mortgage backed securities are not considered to be derivatives.
3. A GIC (guaranteed investment certificate) is a bond-like obligation issued by insurance companies which pay fixed interest rates for periods ranging from 3 to 5 years.
4. Total long-term assets exceed total long-term liabilities.
5. Recently the belief that a long investment horizon justifies higher risk has been challenged by Samuelson (1994).
6. From April 1997, mark-to-market accounting will be introduced to pension funds for the first time.
7. The 50/30/20 rule states that more than 50 per cent of assets must be invested in domestic cash and fixed interest, less than 30 per cent in domestic equities, less than 30 per cent in overseas assets, and less than 20 per cent in real estate.
8. Information was obtained from a Statement of Claim lodged with the Federal Court of Australia, Federal Court Number G271 of 1995.
9. Market risk is the risk of adverse market movements including asset prices, volatility and changes in yield curve, as discussed in *Chapter 8*.
10. Scenario analysis to test the performance of the fund under extreme market conditions.

6

Changing market relationships

ELIZABETH SHEEDY*

Editors' Note

One barometer of change in the derivatives industry has been the transformation in relationships between providers (banks) and clients (end-users). Since derivatives are usually marketed in the context of a relationship, this transformation is of vital importance. The comfortable and stable bank/client relationships which characterised the banking industry of former years have been replaced by pragmatic and volatile associations.

The events of 1994 and 1995 were an influence in this evolution. In particular, the dispute between Procter & Gamble and Bankers Trust both typified and hastened the erosion of trust between banks and their clients. However it could be argued that a more pragmatic and self-seeking approach to relationships was inevitable as the industry matured and competition increased.

This chapter explores the changing nature of the bank/client relationship and the factors causing change. In so doing, the difficulty of profitably running a derivatives business in today's competitive environment becomes evident. Outstanding issues confronting the derivatives marketer are highlighted.

* Thanks to students in Sydney and Hong Kong 'Strategic Marketing in Finance' classes in 1996. Their assistance with market surveys was invaluable.

6.1 Introduction

Relationship marketing emphasises long-term relationships between providers and customers, rather than individual transactions. For at least fifteen years commercial banks have pursued relationship banking programs to target key corporate and institutional clients.[1] More recently, the relationship concept has been adopted in a range of industries beyond financial services, and extended to other customer groups including retail customers. Benefits of relationship marketing are sung by many marketing academics and practitioners. For example, Christopher et al. (1991) claim that:

> relationship-based marketing and the resulting long-term retention of customers' attention leads to significantly improved financial and market performance. Relationship marketing represents a new opportunity for organisations to gain a competitive edge in the turbulent business environment of the 1990s.

According to the marketing literature, the derivatives industry is ideally suited to relationship marketing. Relationship banking promises various benefits to providers of derivatives, such as higher profits, greater differentiation between providers, and reduced price sensitivity. Yet recent developments in the derivatives[2] industry in 1994 and 1995 highlight potential problems in relationship marketing. Litigation between Procter & Gamble and Bankers Trust (see *Chapter 2*) is *prima facie* evidence of relationship breakdown and possibly suggests a general deterioration in bank/client relationships.

Accordingly, this chapter evaluates the success of relationship banking in the derivatives industry. To the extent that problems exist, what are their causes? What are their broader implications for relationship marketing in financial services and other industries? To answer these questions the study explores derivatives marketing by banks to corporate and institutional clients in Sydney and Hong Kong. This was achieved by interviewing participants in the derivatives industry in both centres.[3]

The paper is divided into four sections. *Section 6.2* defines relationship banking and explains why it has been advocated in the derivatives industry. *Section 6.3* details the results of market surveys in Sydney and Hong Kong. The surveys provide evidence that the relationship approach has not delivered many of the benefits promised in the marketing literature. *Section 6.4* explores why these failings are inevitable given the current industry structure. *Section 6.5* summarises the lessons from the study and suggests avenues for further research.

6.2 Relationship banking—What is it? Why is it advocated?

Relationship banking literature dates back to the early 1980s. Moriarty et al. (1983) describe relationship banking as 'a recognition that the bank can increase its earnings by maximising the profitability of the total customer relationship over time, rather than by seeking to extract the most profit from any individual product or transaction'.

Relationship banking is described as the antithesis of 'transaction banking'. The objective is to build long-term profitability by maintaining and enhancing client relationships. Bankers hope to achieve the position of lead banker or a preferred supplier of banking services.

One of the key elements of relationship banking is the role of the 'account manager' or 'relationship manager' as described by Watson (1986) and Moriarty et al. (1983). Not only is this individual a co-ordinator or facilitator of sales efforts, but also a quasi-ombudsman for the customer's interests. The account manager encourages the customer to use a broader range of bank services, thus extending the equity of both parties in the relationship.

Since relationship banking emphasises cross-selling, relationship pricing is an important facet of the relationship process. Ennew et al. (1995) describe relationship pricing as the practice of offering advantageous prices to users of multiple services. Not to be confused with loss leading, relationship pricing relies on the economies of scope associated with relationship banking. Relationship pricing may also incorporate the notion of cross-subsidisation. That is, banks are prepared to provide some services for free or below cost in order to gain the opportunity to bid for more profitable transactions.

The relationship approach evolved from several strands of the marketing literature including industrial marketing, services marketing and the customer retention literature. All of these elements are relevant to the derivatives industry. However, unique aspects of derivatives further support the application of a relationship approach. This section explains why the relationship approach is advocated for derivatives with reference to each strand of the literature. Arguments in favour of relationship marketing for derivatives are summarised at the end of the section.

6.2.1 *Industrial marketing*

Relationship banking draws on the interaction and network approach to industrial marketing developed in the 1960s. Hakansson (1982) describes industrial marketing as a flow of both goods and information between buyer and seller. Both financial and social exchanges occur in the context of a relationship. More recently, McKenna (1991) has proposed that customers be integrated into the value-generating process. He emphasises the reciprocity and interdependence of customer and provider so that the relationship can be seen as a strategic alliance. In a similar vein, Zineldin (1995) examines relationship banking as a complex pattern of interactions between the parties.

Marketing to industry (as opposed to retail consumers) is characterised by:

- a relatively small number of large and geographically concentrated buyers;
- complex technical and economic considerations;
- a longer and more structured purchase process;
- larger numbers of people involved in the purchase process;
- customised transactions to meet specific problems; and
- interdependence between buyer and seller.

These characteristics are clearly seen in the banking industry. Many derivatives providers promote their ability to develop solutions tailored to specific client concerns and market conditions. The derivatives transaction disputed between Procter & Gamble and Bankers Trust is an example of such a customised solution.

The process of searching out a suitable provider, negotiating a contract and customising a transaction can be protracted in industrial marketing. Therefore it is usually in the interests of both parties to repeat the transaction on more than one occasion, or to enter into a long-term contract. Levitt (1983) draws an analogy between such a business relationship and marriage. According to Levitt:

> A purchase decision is not a decision to buy an item (to have a casual affair) but a decision to enter a bonded relationship (to get married) . . . The era of the one-night stand is gone. Marriage is both necessary and more convenient. Products are too complicated, repeat negotiations too much of a hassle and too costly. Under these conditions, success in marketing is transformed to the inescapability of a relationship.

Industrial marketing researchers highlight the issue of risk and anxiety in the purchase process. The larger and more complex the transaction, and the longer the time-frame over which the contract will be completed, the greater are the customer's anxieties and expectations. Buyers are purchasing a promise which may take years to fulfil. Levitt likens the purchase process to a courtship. The seller is attempting to build trust and demonstrate the qualities which will hopefully become apparent after the wedding.

6.2.2 *Services marketing*

The relationship concept is further supported in the services marketing literature. The intangibility of services means that clients buy a promise as services are high in 'experience' or 'credence qualities'. According to Levitt (1981), clients are not able to judge the quality of the purchase until after experiencing it.

Intangibility immediately suggests the importance of trust between buyer and seller. Maister (1991) highlights the fact that service purchasers often experience feelings of personal risk and anxiety during the purchase process. This element of risk is linked with the concept of intangibility discussed above.

Maister claims that technical skill is a necessary but not sufficient condition for selection by clients. Many firms possess technical skills which are indistinguishable from each other in the eyes of the client. Therefore trust, confidence and professionalism in the context of a relationship are touted as the imperatives for marketing success.

6.2.3 *Customer retention literature*

Relationship banking is given further impetus by the interest from the late 1980s in customer retention. Reichheld and Sasser's influential 1990 paper boasts that companies in the finance sector can boost profits by as much as 100 per cent by retaining just 5 per cent more of their customers. Their argument assumes that most costs associated with a relationship occur in its early stages. Customers generate increasing revenues over time, and can generate new business through referrals. Reichheld and Sasser argue that a lower defection rate results in longer average customer relationships and therefore a dramatic increase in profits. Some of their arguments have been challenged (Carroll 1991), but customer satisfaction and retention are now an important element of relationship banking programs.

Storbacka et al. (1994) highlight the benefits to the bottom line of a relationship orientation. A link between interactive marketing and customer satisfaction is established by File et al.

(1995). Juttner and Hans (1994) see a link between relationship banking and competitive advantage:

> The common superior objectives of all strategies are enduring unique relationships with customers which cannot be imitated by competitors and therefore provide sustainable competitive advantage.

6.2.4 *Relationship marketing*

Since the 1980s, the relationship marketing literature has flourished. Gummesson (1987) claims that traditional marketing concepts should be replaced by a 'new marketing concept' based on relationships. An emphasis on interaction and relationship management has developed in services and industrial marketing. Gummesson claims that this emphasis has wider application. In a similar vein, Gronroos (1994) refers to a paradigm shift that is occurring in marketing centred around the relationship concept.

The concept of trust is linked to relationship marketing. Moorman et al. (1992) define trust as 'a willingness to rely on an exchange partner in whom one has confidence'. The same authors claim that the need for reliance on the provider is critical in information-based relationships such as banking. Trust influences the quality of interactions and the commitment of the buyer to the relationship.

The literature does not recommend a relationship style of marketing for every industry or segment. Gronroos (1994) refers to a marketing continuum where some businesses are more suited to a relational (as opposed to transactional) style. He concludes that services marketing and industrial marketing are more likely to be relationship oriented. The research described below on the banking industry further supports the application of relationship marketing to derivatives.

6.2.5 *Special characteristics of derivatives marketing*

Derivatives marketing can partly be explained in terms of the services marketing literature, the industrial marketing literature and the customer retention literature. In addition, there are special characteristics of the derivatives industry that warrant discussion. These characteristics are outlined in the following paragraphs.

The key to success in banking is *information*. Information about the needs of transactors is collected and then used to price, structure and distribute securities (Eccles and Crane 1988). Studies have highlighted the need for information (obtained through an effective customer base) to make trading rooms profitable (Braas and Bralver 1990). Speculative position taking is not the most important source of profit in most trading rooms as is commonly supposed. Rather, trading with customers is the primary source of revenue and profit.

A great benefit of customer business is the fact that it uncovers information which can then be used to further generate profits. The provider's capacity not only to recommend and design a product but also to *manufacture* it profitably will depend crucially on the availability of information. 'Being in the deal stream' improves a provider's pricing and distribution capabilities. Access to good information can establish a virtuous cycle in the finance industry, as the information from one transaction can be used to help with the next and so on.

The insatiable requirement for information explains why most banks offer a broad range of services, even when some are not profitable in their own right. Some vanilla products may offer little opportunity for profit in isolation, but may be valuable in the relationship development process. This has been one of the criticisms of Bankers Trust in the past (Shirreff 1995). Bankers Trust had consciously followed a strategy of specialising in exotic high margin derivative products and avoiding vanilla (and less lucrative) business opportunities.

Credit assessment is another driver for good relationships in derivatives. Haubrich (1989) advocates long term relationships as a means of monitoring borrowers, gathering information needed for credit assessment and enforcing contract compliance.

Customers are involved in the creation of commercial banking services (File et al. 1995). Since customers participate in the manufacturing process, relationships and communication are essential. Task-oriented communications are associated with higher satisfaction, probability of repurchase and intent to give referrals.

Relationships also help to overcome the 'loose linkage' problem identified by Eccles and Crane (1988). The 'loose linkage' exists between value provided to customers and revenues generated. Most derivatives providers give information, advice and ideas to clients or potential clients. There is no direct payment for these services. Rather, the bank is compensated over time through transactions. An ongoing relationship is necessary to ensure that adequate compensation is received over time.

6.2.6 *Summary—Benefits of relationship banking*

To sum up, customer benefits from relationship banking are:

- greater assurance of credit when needed (Holland 1992);

- an advocate in the bank ie the account manager (Watson 1986);
- tailored proposals through greater knowledge of client needs (Eccles and Crane 1988);
- efficient use of time. The relationship concept should help minimise time taken by corporate treasurers to explain their needs to bankers (Eccles and Crane 1988);
- reduced risk of purchasing unsuitable services (Moriarty et al. 1983);
- special treatment and free services. These include free information and education (Moriarty et al. 1983);
- quick response to funding needs and other services (Holland 1992);
- privileged access to rationed opportunities and new ideas, priority treatment in any conflict of interest situation (Holland 1992); and
- lower costs of banking services. Relationship pricing should result in lower costs and therefore greater profitability (Holland 1992).

The literature suggests that a bank may achieve the following advantages from relationship banking:

- customer loyalty. Increased customer satisfaction should result in customer loyalty and hence improved profitability (Storbacka et al. 1994 and File et al. 1995);
- lower costs. Cross-selling of multiple services should result in economies of scope, thus further enhancing profits (Turnbull and Gibbs 1987);
- a competitive advantage in the market place (Juttner and Hans 1994 and Zineldin 1995);
- greater trust by the customer. Trust enhances the commitment of the buyer to the relationship (Moorman et al. 1993);
- higher margins. The customer is less price sensitive, resulting in greater and more stable profits (Moriarty et al. 1983);
- preferred supplier status. Strong relationships can confer the right to bid on new business and to rebid to meet competitors in some cases (Moriarty et al. 1983);
- privileged information. Information from relationship clients can be used for product development (Eccles and Crane 1988 and Moriarty et al. 1983). Information can also be used to help price and distribute securities (Eccles and Crane 1988);
- avoidance of 'loose linkage' problem (see *Section 6.2.5*). The link between customer revenues and the costs of providing service is often loose. A relationship approach tightens this

linkage, thus ensuring overall profitability (Eccles and Crane 1988); and

- improved credit risk management. The bank gains an 'early warning system' to monitor credit risk (Haubrich 1989).

Greater profitability is claimed as a benefit both for bank and client. These claims may not be mutually exclusive provided that there are genuine economies of scope in offering multiple services. The literature implies that both parties share these benefits to some extent.

In summary, the ultimate reason for a bank to practise relationship banking is the promise of greater long-term profits through interdependence. As will be shown in *Section 6.3*, relationship banking is generally accepted in the industry as the most appropriate way to market derivatives to corporate clients.

6.3 The relationship concept gone wrong

The following study on relationship banking in derivatives is prompted by the events of 1994 and 1995 which provide *prima facie* evidence of relationship breakdown.

The objective is to examine developments in relationship banking in light of these events. To what extent has the relationship concept succeeded in the derivatives industry?

6.3.1 *Background events in the derivatives industry*

From a marketing perspective, the incidents of greatest interest are those relating to Bankers Trust. In several high-profile court cases Bankers Trust was accused of inducing customers to purchase unsuitable complex derivatives deals, and misrepresenting to clients the pricing, value and risks of the products it sold (*Business Week* 1995; Brady 1994). These cases have the potential to damage the relationship concept by suggesting to end-users that derivatives providers cannot be trusted.

The dispute between Gibson Greetings and Bankers Trust (Loomis 1995) illustrates these issues. Gibson Greetings claimed in their suit against Bankers Trust that derivatives sales people lied to treasury staff on the extent of losses sustained in a derivatives transaction. These claims were supported by incriminating taped telephone conversations. The Procter & Gamble case further exemplifies the relationship breakdown.

One of the key issues at stake in the Procter & Gamble case (see *Chapter* 2) was the suitability of the transaction for the company, given its risky characteristics. This strikes at the heart of relationship banking: the ability of the provider to create customised solutions which match the client's requirements. According to *The Economist* (1995):

> Bankers Trust was shamed by further revelations about its derivatives sales practices in 1993–94 following a court ruling on October 3rd which made public previously sealed documents and tapes relating to the Procter & Gamble case . . . Staff refer to a 'rip-off' factor when describing deals involving leveraged derivatives. One BT salesman described how he would 'lure people into that total calm and then totally fuck them.' Perhaps worst of all a training video shown to new employees includes a description of how a swap works: Bankers Trust can 'get in the middle and rip them [the customers] off'.

Other 'derivatives disasters' occurred at about the same time including Metallgesellschaft and Barings (see *Chapter* 2). Bank/client relationships were not the primary concern in these latter cases. Nevertheless this series of events may have shaken the confidence of end-users of derivatives generally.

6.3.2 *Methodology for study*

In-depth interviews were conducted with both providers and end-users of derivatives in Sydney and Hong Kong in April–June 1996. These two markets are representative of western and eastern banking centres in the Asia-Pacific region. This study is an analysis of notes taken from the interviews. The purpose of the study was to determine whether watershed cases in 1994 and 1995 caused, or were indicative of, a more widespread deterioration in relationships.

In Sydney, 18 end-users and 16 providers of derivatives were interviewed. While this sample is small, the derivatives market in Australia is dominated by less than 200 market participants. It is estimated[4] that 80 to 90 per cent of market volume is accounted for by professional and semi-professional users including price-making banks, fund managers, government business enterprises and very large corporations. Ninety per cent of those surveyed represented this dominant group. The 15 providers interviewed represented institutions based in Australia, Europe, USA and Japan.

In Hong Kong, 11 interviews were conducted with end-users of derivatives and 10 with providers. The providers were comprised of 5 of European origin, 3 banks of North American origin, 1 Japanese and 1 Chinese bank.

All of the derivatives providers interviewed claimed to implement a relationship approach to marketing derivatives. Similarly, all but 2 end-users stated that they gave preference to relationship banks in their derivatives purchasing decisions. The interviewees were asked a series of open-ended questions. Due to the small sample, a case study method was adopted. Formal statistical tests were not used.

6.3.3 *The impact of 'derivatives disasters' on relationship marketing*

As noted earlier, the study was partially prompted by allegations of aggressive and unethical marketing practices in derivatives. These issues were central to the dispute between Bankers Trust and Procter & Gamble. According to the survey there is no evidence that such marketing practices are common in Australia and Hong Kong. Interviewees were unanimous in their belief that the Asia-Pacific derivatives market is very different to that in the US. The 'aggressive' marketing tactics which contributed to the misuse of derivatives in the US were not evident in this market. End-users in the survey generally praised banks for taking care in explaining the implications of complex structures.

The overwhelming impression from the survey was the extent to which market participants claim to support the relationship concept. Many interviewees described a trend 'back to relationships'. Three of the providers surveyed describe significant internal structural changes to support a renewed commitment to relationships.

This renewed emphasis on relationships throughout the industry was further evidenced by promotional strategies employed by bankers. An advertisement appearing in *The Far Eastern Economic Review* of 16 November 1995 for Swiss Bank Corporation had the following copy beside a picture of a Roman bronze finger key:

> The key to relationship . . . Just as the ring symbolises trust, at Swiss Bank Corporation a personal relationship with our customers is the key requirement for confidence . . .

The 7 December 1995 issue of the same magazine carried an advertisement for Hong Kong Bank in a similar vein.

> Everything has changed. Except the relationship, and the barbecued duck. In Asia, there are always new markets and new opportunities. And there are always new ideas, new products

and new technologies. But there are also old ties and long relationships.

The interviewees posited a range of explanations for this trend, namely:

- the events of 1994 and 1995 have created renewed interest in relationships as trust has become more highly valued;
- the major local trading banks now have derivatives capability comparable to foreign/investment banks. There is no need to go beyond the relationship circle to satisfy most requirements;
- derivatives have reached a mature phase of the product lifecycle in the corporate market. The derivatives market is currently over-serviced. Banks are attempting to differentiate their services through relationships; and
- Australian and Hong Kong-based corporations tend to be more reliant on banks for funding than their North American or European counterparts. As a result, they tend to have stronger bank relationships.

Notwithstanding this renewed commitment to relationship banking, there was evidence that the events of 1994 and 1995 have had an adverse impact on derivatives markets. The behaviour of market participants was not always consistent with their stated commitment to relationships. The surveys undertaken in both Sydney and Hong Kong provided evidence that customers have adjusted their behaviour with regard to derivatives. Customers are now less likely to choose structured derivatives products, preferring simpler transactions that can be easily understood and valued internally. Customers avoid reliance on bank marketing proposals and analysis, suggesting a lower level of trust in the industry.

Customers no longer place their trust in banks to recommend the most appropriate derivatives strategy for them. It is clear from the interviews that if the customer cannot fully understand the transaction, the transaction will not proceed. This view prevails even when the derivatives-based solution is the most efficient. According to one Sydney-based derivatives provider:

> Australian investors are now very cautious, most check pricing and when marketing, the client needs to be shown all possible downside risk, the valuation method and exit pricing.

Customers are reducing their dependence on banks by building up internal skills and spreading business between a range of different banks. Some of the end-users interviewed use up to forty banks for derivatives transactions.

The survey also provided evidence of intense competition in

the industry. As derivatives markets have matured, many financial institutions have comparable levels of technical expertise. As a large number of providers offer comparable products the balance of power in the relationship has moved in favour of the customer. In contrast to notions of reciprocity and interdependence noted in the literature earlier, the derivatives market is now 'a buyers' market'. Heavy price competition and the commoditisation of derivatives are the result.

Almost every interviewee in the survey emphasised the dominance of price in the purchase decision. Evidence for a price premium based on relationship is non-existent. These observations contrast with the relationship marketing literature which promises greater profitability and competitive advantage. The following comments are typical of those made by Australian derivatives providers:

> 'I don't see relationship marketing delivering either increased customer loyalty or decreased customer price sensitivity—customers are driven by price: they always go to the bank with the lowest price.'
>
> 'Clients are price sensitive. We rarely see cultivating a relationship resulting in higher profits.'
>
> 'We are sick of giving business for low return. It sometimes takes 3–4 months of work to put together a tender—we do not appreciate it when a customer contacts us for advice and then turns around and gives the business to someone else for one point on a very large deal.'
>
> 'We'd like to think that we'd get the first refusal in any transaction but I think in derivatives that's a fairly unrealistic ask because however strong the relationship is, price is always going to play a very important part.'

Despite this evidence, both providers and end-users said they were committed to the relationship concept. All the providers interviewed had implemented a relationship marketing program and the vast majority of end-users claimed to apply relationship principles in their buying practices. End-users saw many advantages (such as tailored proposals, high service levels and detailed knowledge of needs) in relationship banking.

The survey suggests that a relationship is a precondition to transacting. End-users prefer to buy derivatives from banks that provide other services (specifically lending) and who understand their requirements. However, since most end-users have many 'relationship' banks, the buying decision is ultimately made on price. End-users do not appear to differentiate between providers on the *quality* of the relationship, but use the *existence* of a relationship as a precondition to enter into a highly competitive tender. Relationships appear to have become a commodity in their own right.

6.3.4 *Relationships in Asia*

The study methodology allowed for some comparison between western and eastern banking cultures. To what extent do the problems experienced in western-style banking systems translate to Asian financial centres? Has Chinese business culture protected the derivatives industry from the relationship difficulties now commonplace in the west?

According to this series of interviews, relationship banking in Hong Kong is also under pressure. Traditionally, family owned businesses have tended to form business ties based on relationships. The separation of management and ownership has now created a class of professional managers who are not necessarily part of the traditional family networks. The return of many 'Asian expatriates' (ie overseas educated Chinese) has resulted in the intrusion of western business culture. Furthermore, the boom conditions of the past decade caused a very high level of staff turnover in banks detrimental to relationships.

As in Sydney, Hong Kong interviewees emphasised the importance of price in the buying decision. It is common for major corporations to maintain links with a wide circle of so-called relationship banks. While the relationship may be a prerequisite to an invitation to quote, the deal is ultimately awarded on the basis of the lowest bid.

According to one banker:

> The industry is over-banked and over-served. Competition is fierce and price sensitivity is more and more the difference between banks . . . These days, the corporates are getting interbank bids or offers . . . If there was originally a relationship oriented way of doing business before, I see that slowly eroding away . . . price means everything.

The high degree of price competition is exacerbated by keen competition from banks to enter the Hong Kong market. Hong Kong is seen as a gateway to China, and a foothold for business elsewhere in Asia. A presence in Hong Kong is often seen as vital to take advantage of the booming Asian economy. Banks have exhibited a propensity to 'buy market share' by loss-leading in derivatives transactions. While this price cutting activity aims to create relationships, it is in fact anathema to the relationship concept and encourages buyers to view derivatives as a commodity.

One end-user with a strong price orientation represented a Chinese investment company. He pointed out that their principal bank (a Chinese bank) did not provide derivatives services. Therefore derivatives services were purchased through foreign banks on a transactional basis.

Other interviewees confirmed this dichotomy between buying practices for derivatives versus lending services. One corporate interviewee was committed to relationship bankers for lending services but not for derivatives. Since relationship banking is supposed to generate cross-selling opportunities, this practice indicates a flaw in the relationship concept. He explained that he perceived little difference in the derivatives services provided by a range of large banks. Since credit lines are usually not a critical issue for derivatives, his practice was to look at the product design and then to shop around for the best price.

Most expressed the view that Asian clients prefer simpler derivatives products over complex structures. Asian investors are risk averse to new products.

There is little evidence of litigation concerning derivatives in Hong Kong compared with western financial centres. While this could be interpreted as a sign of strong relationships, one interviewee (representing a bank of European origin) disagreed:

> Certainly, there have been certain derivatives problems, particularly with Chinese corporates . . . The fact is that many disputes are not reported, because banks are in many cases dealing with companies, which according to Chinese law, are forbidden to undertake such transactions. Both the bank and customer are aware of this, which is why many such activities are secured by margin deposits. However when disputes occur, foreign banks know they will not get a sympathetic hearing from Chinese courts, so they do not publicly pursue such claims.

Bearing in mind the small sample size, the survey suggests that Hong Kong interviewees are more pessimistic than those in Sydney regarding the future of the relationship concept. Only 3 of the 11 end-users of derivatives were confident that relationships would grow in importance. The survey indicated that despite perceptions of traditional Chinese business values, Hong Kong is not an ideal place to implement relationship banking. It is thus apparent that many of the issues confronting western derivatives marketers are also of concern in Asia.

Table 6.1 Relationship banking—theory and practice

Relationship banking as foreshadowed in the marketing literature	Relationship banking as practised in the derivatives market of the mid-1990s
Trust between provider and end-user	Wariness and unwillingness to trust bankers
Mutual dependence between provider and end-user	Independence of the end-user
Superior competitive advantage and profitability	Minimal profits even for 'relationship' banks

6.3.5 *Summary of survey results*

The practice of relationship banking in the derivatives market of the mid-1990s is a far cry from that envisioned 15 years ago. Trust, mutual dependence and profitability through competitive advantage have been replaced by wariness, independence and growing commoditisation.

The marriage analogy proposed by Levitt (1983) is not descriptive of the derivatives market. The concepts of commitment and loyalty are no longer evident, even in a polygamous sense. The relationship model applied in the derivatives industry is more akin to a group of acquaintances at a party. Personal interactions help to make a more pleasant experience for everyone, but no-one is under any illusion that the friendships made are likely to develop into committed associations such as those described by McKenna (1991). Yet the relationship concept still exists and is demanded by customers.

6.4 Why have 15 years of relationship banking borne so little fruit?

The relationship concept promises a way to build trust, competitive advantage and profitability in derivatives marketing. The fact that it has failed to live up to these promises is apparent from the survey results. There would appear to be several possible reasons for the poor performance of the relationship concept. Section 6.4.1 highlights the issues which have already been discussed in the marketing literature. *Section 6.4.2* explores other areas of concern evidenced by the surveys in Hong Kong and Sydney.

6.4.1 *Relationship difficulties discussed in the marketing literature*

The marketing literature highlights the difficulty of implementing relationship marketing as follows:

a) High costs

Moriarty et al. (1983) discuss the high cost of establishing relationship banking and potential forgone profit opportunities. An investment must be made both in staff and system resources to realise the benefits of relationship marketing.

b) Account manager issues

Perrien et al. (1991) explore the impediments to relationship banking through the eyes of 57 account managers from commercial banks. Some of the specific problems which they found in implementing relationship banking are as follows:

- high turnover among account managers is prevalent and has a very negative impact on relationships;
- account managers often lack sufficient training and experience to have a deep understanding of all the products offered by a bank and of the customer's business needs;
- the workload of an account manager is often unreasonable, and too heavily weighted towards administrative tasks (rather than relationship building tasks);
- the assessment of the account manager's performance is weighted towards transactions as opposed to relationship criteria;
- the bank culture emphasises short-term profitability rather than long-term relationships; and
- account managers have inadequate authority (over product specialists) to match their responsibility.

They conclude that:

> shifting from transactional to relational marketing means more than redefining the role of contact personnel, or of account managers as in the present case. It is a major change in the seller's organisation that affects such fundamental notions as profitability, decentralisation of authority, selection of human resources, performance criteria, and corporate culture.

c) Multiple bank relationships

Eccles and Crane (1988) see multiple bank relationships as another cause of relationship breakdown. Multiple relationships cause uncertainty about the share of business that a bank will receive. Combining this fact with the 'loose linkage' problem referred to in *Section 6.2.5*, the uncertainty is even greater. A relationship bank is in danger of providing free advice and services for extended periods of time without an acceptable level of income from the relationship. This situation readily leads to more aggressive sales practices, and hence a perception that *the bank* is transaction oriented.

In a world of multiple bank relationships, maintaining many relationships can be a time consuming task. The flow of information from client to bank is often reduced, giving bankers the impression that *the client* is transaction oriented.

d) Excessive product development

Bankers need to extract profit from a relationship, but often lack sufficient information to take tailored, relevant proposals to the client. One of the easiest ways of creating an opportunity to make contact is to arrange an appointment to discuss 'an innovative new (derivatives) product'. It is hard for the treasurer to resist the opportunity to learn about a new idea which may be relevant, so the banker creates an opportunity to meet. Although it is unlikely that the current 'deal of the week' will meet the customer's need, his or her response may perhaps give some guidance regarding genuine needs. Some of the excessive product development we have seen in the derivatives industry may be seen as part of a 'trial and error' game. The objective for bankers is to try and win their fair share of client contact, to obtain crucial information and to establish personal rapport.

Since many end-users are spreading their banking relationships so thinly between multiple banks, few of the relationships can be genuinely profitable. Thus there is pressure on banks to generate revenue through higher margin products such as exotic derivatives. Bankers sometimes promote products which are more suited to the bank's own profitability than the customer's need. Some believe this was true of the Procter & Gamble transaction described in *Chapter 2*.

e) Price

Eccles and Crane (1988) also note the relationship tensions which are created by price. Relationship bankers hope that clients will take into account the value of free services and other benefits of the relationship process. Unfortunately it is difficult for the client to value the less tangible elements of the relationship in monetary terms. It is difficult for the client to resist the temptation to award the transaction solely on price. Price is more tangible than any element of a relationship.

Research undertaken by Greenwich Associates (Statius-Muller 1995) on large European corporations suggests that they are unwilling to 'pay up' for relationships. According to the Greenwich survey, these companies disagree by a ratio of 2-to-1 with the idea of accepting an offer from a relationship bank if it is more expensive (as much as $\frac{1}{16}$ per cent higher).

A major difficulty in the relationship concept is cross-subsidisation between services. This means that one service is priced at above normal profit levels to subsidise others that are priced at or below cost. This structure in fact creates an incentive for so-called 'cherry picking'. Other competitors can bid more competitively for the services which are subsidising others. The winners have been more transaction oriented banks who capture high margin business through competitive bidding.

f) Disintermediation

A further factor in the diminution of the relationship concept has been the global trend toward disintermediation. In the old days banks lent money and corporations borrowed it. Now it is common for large corporations to issue debt in their own name (as they often have a higher rating than their bankers). As more companies directly access capital markets they feel less reliant on bank services. According to the Greenwich survey of Europe's largest corporations (Statius-Muller 1995), twice as many expect to reduce their use of bank-provided short-term credit as expect to increase it. An overwhelmingly large proportion of these companies anticipate an increase in their use of commercial paper. Those expecting an increase outnumber those expecting a decline by a ratio of 6-to-1.

The problem is exacerbated in the derivatives industry where fund managers are key players. Fund managers have no need for lending services and hence less requirement for relationship banking.

g) Disparity of earnings

Adversarial elements of the client/bank interface have also hindered the relationship concept. One source of tension is the disparity of earnings between banker and client, especially taking into account age and experience. It is hardly surprising that a corporate treasurer with 20 to 40 years experience is irritated when a young banker with 2 to 5 years experience earns twice his or her salary, wears designer suits and arrives for appointments in a sportscar.

6.4.2 *Survey findings and relationship problems*

According to the survey some of the problems described above are true of the derivatives industry. However the survey points to other problems not fully explored in the literature. These are described below.

a) Corporate governance

A number of respondents to the survey referred to a new corporate governance regime affecting the marketing environment. Derivatives disasters of 1994 and 1995 caused many boards to rethink their derivatives strategy.

Today's corporate governance regime draws attention to managerial performance and accountability of the board (Pound 1995). End-users must ensure that shareholders are served by achieving the best value for money. Many companies insist that quotes are audited to ensure that the treasurer always accepts the lowest price. The following comments typify the attitude of industry participants:

> 'The industry is getting harder and harder in that price is now the market's major concern . . . Corporate governance has gone so far that very little margin can be built in. No matter if you have a good relationship or a bad relationship the best price wins . . . it makes it very hard to justify the relationships when all it is going to be is price.'
>
> 'Are relationship customers less price sensitive? No. Whilst good customer relationships will result in them nominating their side, clients are price sensitive. They have to be. They have their own performance pressures, corporate governance, and internal auditors to worry about. Transparency of customers' treasury operations means that they have to be more responsible and profitable for their shareholders.'

The survey suggests that corporate governance concerns are driving the derivatives industry to even greater price orientation.

This is having a deleterious effect on relationship banking as high-quality relationships are not adequately rewarded.

b) Erosion of trust

Corporate governance concerns combined with the events of 1994 and 1995 to cause a change in the mindset of end-user boards and managers. This issue is discussed at length in *Chapters 4* and 7. Many companies will now only enter into transactions which can be understood and managed by senior executives. The surveys in Sydney and Hong Kong strongly support the belief that a firm should not enter into a transaction which the board cannot understand. Greater accountability for decision making means that end-users are disinclined to rely on banks for advice.

The problem is exacerbated by the conflict of interest which exists for the banker. The banker advises on the transaction and is also a counterparty to it. Generally speaking, commercial bankers are not rewarded with fees associated with advice, but with transactions which result from the advice.

Many companies are now not prepared to use exotic or structured derivatives, even when they may provide an excellent solution to their needs. The financial press confirms the survey results by documenting a trend in favour of simpler transactions (Ball 1996). Those companies that do use such instruments develop internal skills to undertake internal analysis rather than relying on bank advice. Alternatively, they may seek advice from an outside consultant who is viewed as independent.

By minimising the need for bank advice, the client is also minimising the need for a relationship of trust:

> a person who believes that a partner is trustworthy and yet is unwilling to rely on that partner has only limited trust. (Moorman et al. 1993)

The events of 1994 and 1995 have reminded derivatives end-users of the old maxim—*caveat emptor*. Vulnerability to bank advice is to be avoided at all costs in a world where managers must be accountable for their actions. Moorman et al. (1992) claim that trust reflects reliance on the other partner and involves uncertainty and vulnerability on the latter's part. If there is no vulnerability and uncertainty a relationship of trust is less important.

The erosion of trust can also be explained by the growing power imbalance in the relationship. Anderson and Weitz (1990) report that an imbalance of power in relationships decreases mutual trust between parties. The survey suggests that power in derivatives markets is now very much in the hands of end-users.

c) Destroyed by its own success

Relationship banking was originally thought of as a means of creating a competitive advantage in the market. However the success of the concept has diminished its ability to achieve this. All of the derivatives providers surveyed claimed to be implementing relationship banking. Thus the relationship has actually become a commodity in the same way that derivatives themselves have.

End-users regard a relationship as a precondition to derivatives transactions. Most end-users have multiple bank relationships, dealing with up to 40 banks in some cases. Once a relationship is established, the final buying decision is based on price.

d) Evaluating performance

Earlier commentators (Perrien et al. 1991) have mentioned the need for performance measures based on relationships as opposed to transaction criteria. Performance measures will send important signals about how employees should focus their activities. Many banks interviewed have performance measures which are designed to encourage a relationship oriented approach (eg number of client visits, number of services used, share of overall business captured etc).

The problem with this approach is that marketing success must ultimately be measured by profitability. In the derivatives markets profits directly result from *transactions*. Bank shareholders do not want relationships for their own sake; if they did, they would invest in a social club. Relationships are justified as a means to achieving long-term profits. Ultimately performance measurement systems are dominated by profitability measures which are based on transactions. This encourages a transaction oriented style of business.

e) Internal bank structures

Following from the issue of performance measurement, derivatives providers highlight the need for profitability and accountability at the business unit level. Each business within a bank must pay its own way within the organisation. Business units compete not only in the external market place, but within the bank structure. This framework mitigates against the maintenance of a bank-wide client relationship approach.

Given the size of many commercial banks today and the wide range of services, the difficulty of cross-selling has skyrocketed. Even if individual staff members have an incentive to cross-sell, lack of understanding of other areas diminishes the potential opportunities.

Furthermore, individual staff members tend to have a proprietary attitude toward client relationships. Interviewees described a tendency to regard the relationship as individual territory which has been nurtured and maintained for personal use only. Many see potential risks in opening up a relationship for other areas of the bank. Cross-selling may lead to greater overall profit for the bank, but is risky at the business unit level as another area of the bank may damage the relationship through incompetent service.

The role of the account manager can also be problematic in the relationship process. Personal ties develop when transactions are discussed, structured and negotiated (File et al. 1995). Many larger customers feel that it is a waste of time to talk to 'only a salesman' as the account manager is often perceived. After an initial introduction, the customer would prefer to deal directly with the product specialists. Thus the account manager has less opportunity to develop meaningful personal links.

Bureaucracy can stifle the effective functioning of the relationship. In some cases product specialists are constrained from making client contact without the permission or presence of the account manager. The argument often made about control of the customer interface is that co-ordinating (limiting?) product specialist visits will increase client satisfaction. However it is hard to see how this state of affairs is genuinely in the interests of the bank. Surely it is in the banks' interests that client contact take place as frequently and for as long as possible. The more transactions that are discussed, the greater the possibility that some will be completed and hence profits will be generated.

6.5 The future of the relationship concept—lessons

The survey of derivatives end-users and providers suggests that many of the benefits traditionally attributed to relationship marketing have not been realised. The industry appears to be characterised by low levels of trust, interdependence and profitability. This has occurred despite the fact that industry participants are generally committed to a relationship approach, and have been so committed for up to 15 years. The derivatives example shows that there are significant challenges to the relationship concept even in an industrial/services marketing context.

As *Section 6.4* indicated, the disappointing performance of relationship banking as a framework for derivatives marketing can be explained by a range of factors. Although some of the factors are discussed in the marketing literature, the survey brings to light other problems. Some of these factors may be specific to the derivatives industry in the context of the events of 1994 and 1995. However similar issues may arise in other segments of the finance industry and other industries.

Does this mean that relationship banking should be abandoned? The answer to this question is 'no'. End-users surveyed overwhelmingly support the relationship concept because it creates potential for a detailed knowledge of their needs and hence more tailored proposals. Since customers demand relationship orientation, providers will inevitably offer it. Providers also need relationships so that they can monitor credit risk and gather the market information they require to manufacture financial services.

Nevertheless, two questions remain. Firstly, can the performance of relationship banking be improved by superior implementation? Secondly, can the relationship concept be adapted to work effectively in the derivatives industry and other similar situations? In addressing these questions there are a number of issues to be researched:

- stringent corporate governance environment. Corporate governance concerns encourage end-users to reduce their reliance on banks. How can relationships be adapted to function effectively in this environment?
- advice from banks is seen as biased since banks are rewarded through transactions. One possibility would be to separate the advice element from the transaction to avoid potential conflicts of interest. Advice could be offered on a consulting basis rather than as part of the transaction package. This is already happening to some extent, with accountancy firms and banks competing for consulting business (Ball 1996)
- product maturity and intense price competition result in decreasing margins. To what extent can relationships provide an effective means of differentiation to arrest this trend?
- relationship banking has become a near-commodity offered by almost all commercial banks. Can banks provide different types of relationship that allow for genuine differentiation? If so, can these differences be perceived by customers?

- profitability pressures within banks and competition between business units add to the difficulty of relationship banking. How can banks more effectively manage the tension between accountability and relationship management? and
- performance measures by providers now generally include relationship criteria. However these measures tend to be dominated by transactional criteria since transactions are more directly correlated with profits. What improvements can be made to performance measures?

It is hard not to conclude that the overall optimism of the marketing literature on relationship marketing is misplaced. Since the so-called derivatives crisis, factors have combined to create an environment quite hostile to a relationship approach. Further research is needed on the implementation of relationship marketing in such adverse circumstances.

References

Anderson, E. and Weitz, B. 1990, 'Determinants of continuity in conventional industrial channel dyads', *Marketing Science*, vol. 8, Fall, pp. 310–23

Ball, M. 1996, 'Waters look inviting but are they safe?', Guide to Australian Corporate Finance 1996, Supplement to *Corporate Finance*, September, pp. 27–8

Bank for International Settlements, Monetary and Economic Department 1996, *Central Bank Survey of Foreign Exchange and Derivatives Market Activity, 1995*, Basle

Board of Banking Supervision 1995, *Report of the Board of Banking Supervision Inquiry into the Circumstances of the Collapse of Barings*, HMSO, London

Braas, A. and Bralver, C. 1990, 'An analysis of trading profits: How most trading rooms really make money', *Journal of Applied Corporate Finance*, vol. 2, no. 4, Winter, pp. 85–90

Brady, S. 1994, 'Procter & Gamble vs Bankers Trust', *Corporate Finance*, December, pp. 21–5

Business Week 1995, 'The Bankers Trust Tapes', 16 October, pp. 48–53

Carroll, P. 1991, 'The fallacy of customer retention', *Journal of Retail Banking*, vol. XIII, no. 4, Winter 1991–92, pp. 15–20

Christopher, M., Payne, A., Ballantyne, D. 1991, *Relationship Marketing—Bringing quality, customer service and marketing together*, Butterworth Heinemann, Oxford

Eccles, R. and Crane, D. 1988, *Investment Banks at Work*, Harvard Business School Press, Boston

The Economist 1995, 'Bankers Trust: Shamed again', 7 October

Edwards, F. and Canter, M. 1995, 'The collapse of Metallgesellschaft: Unhedgeable risks, poor hedging strategy, or just bad luck?', *Journal of Futures Markets*, vol. 15, no. 3, May, pp. 211–64

Ennew, C., Watkins, T. and Wright, M. 1995, *Marketing Financial Services*, Butterworth Heinemann, Oxford

Fay, S. 1996, *The Collapse of Barings*, Richard Cohen, London

File, K.M., Mack, J.L. and Prince, R.A. 1995, 'The effect of interactive marketing on commercial customer satisfaction in international financial markets', *Journal of Business and Industrial Marketing*, vol. 10, no. 2, pp. 69–75

Gronroos, C. 1994, 'From marketing mix to relationship marketing: Toward a paradigm shift in marketing', *Management Decision*, vol. 32, no. 2, pp. 4–32

Gummesson, E. 1987, 'The new marketing—Developing long-term interactive relationships', *Long Range Planning* vol. 20, no. 4, pp. 10–20

Hakansson, H. 1982, *International marketing and purchasing of industrial goods*, Wiley, New York

Haubrich, J. 1989, 'Financial intermediation: Delegated monitoring and long-term relationships', *Journal of Banking and Finance*, vol. 13, pp. 9–20

Holland, J. 1992, 'Relationship banking: choice and control by the multinational firm', *International Journal of Bank Marketing*, vol. 10, no. 2, pp. 20–40

Jorion, P. 1995, *Big bets gone bad: Derivatives and bankruptcy in Orange County*, Academic Press, San Diego

Juttner, U. and Hans, P. 1994, 'Relationship marketing from a value system perspective', *International Journal of Service Industry Management*, vol. 5, no. 5, pp. 54–73

Kuprianov, A. 1995, 'Derivatives debacles', *Economic Quarterly (Federal Reserve Bank of Richmond)*, vol. 81, no. 4, Fall, pp. 1–39

Levitt, T. 1981, 'Marketing intangible products and product intangibles', *Harvard Business Review*, May–June

—— 1983, 'After the sale is over . . .', *Harvard Business Review*, September–October, pp. 87–93

Loomis, C. 1995, 'Untangling the derivatives mess', *Fortune*, vol. 131, no. 5, 20 March, pp. 50–68

Maister, D. 1991, 'How clients choose', *The American Lawyer*, October

McKenna, R. 1991, 'Marketing is everything', *Harvard Business Review*, January–February

Moorman, C., Deshpande, R. and Zaltman, G. 1992, 'Relationships between providers and users of market research: The dynamics of trust within and between organisations', *Journal of Marketing Research*, vol. 29, August, pp. 314–29

—— 1993, 'Factors affecting trust in market research relationships', *Journal of Marketing*, vol. 57, no. 1, pp. 81–101

Moriarty, R., Kimball, R. and Gay, J. 1983, 'The management of corporate banking relationships', *Sloan Management Review*, Spring, pp. 3–15

Perrien, J., Filiatrault, P. and Ricard, L. 1991, 'The implementation of relationship marketing in commercial banks', *International Journal of Bank Marketing*, vol. 10, no. 7

Pound, J. 1995, 'The promise of the governed corporation', *Harvard Business Review*, March–April, pp. 89–98

Reichheld, F. and Sasser, E. 1990, 'Zero defections: Quality comes to services', *Harvard Business Review*, vol. 68, no. 5, September/October, pp. 105–11

Shirreff, D. 1995, 'Can anybody fix Bankers Trust?', *Euromoney*, April, pp. 34–40

Statius-Muller, R. 1995, 'Here today, gone tomorrow', *The Treasurer*, March, pp. 42–5

Storbacka, K., Strandvik, T. and Gronroos, C. 1994, 'Managing customer relationships for profit: The dynamics of relationship quality', *International Journal of Service Industry Management*, vol. 5, no. 5, pp. 21–38

Turnbull, P. and Gibbs, M. 1987, 'Marketing bank services to corporate customers: The importance of relationships', *International Journal of Bank Marketing*, vol. 5, no. 1

Watson, I. 1986, 'Managing the relationships with corporate customers', *International Journal of Bank Marketing*, vol. 4, no. 1

Zineldin, M. 1995, 'Bank-company interactions and relationships: Some empirical evidence', *International Journal of Bank Marketing*, vol. 13, no. 2, pp. 30–40

Notes

1. In their 1983 article Moriarty et al. (1983) describe a relationship banking process as applied by commercial banks.
2. Problems in the derivatives industry in 1994 and 1995 are described in *Section 6.2*.
3. According to the Bank for International Settlements (1996), Hong Kong rates 5th and Australia rates 10th in a world-wide survey of daily volumes traded in the derivatives markets.
4. Research was undertaken by Financial Products Research Group on derivatives use by banks and large corporations.

7

Confronting the legal dimension

SHEELAGH McCRACKEN

Editors' Note

In the past the legal risk involved in structuring derivatives has often been ignored by industry practitioners, despite the fact that it can result in the collapse of an otherwise sound commercial relationship between provider and end-user. The process of re-examination and control of risk described in previous chapters extends also to the legal arena.

This chapter explores how the contractual nature of the various products makes them vulnerable to claims that they are unenforceable, either because they infringe general statutory insolvency or gaming legislation or because a counterparty may lack the requisite capacity or authority to enter into a proposed transaction. It also examines the circumstances in which the courts may impose on the provider a duty to exercise care towards the user and, on the latter, a duty to act in the best interests of its stakeholders as a whole.

The author contends that legal risks are still not as widely understood as they might be. In some areas legal reforms are needed to reduce these risks.

> . . . derivatives by their nature do not introduce risks of a fundamentally different kind or of a greater scale than those already present in the financial markets. Hence, systemic risks are not appreciably aggravated, and supervisory concerns can

> be addressed within regulatory structures and approaches. Where the official priority should be placed, in the view of [this Study by the Group of Thirty], is in clarifying legal uncertainties, and resolving legal inconsistencies between countries, that may impede risk-reduction procedures . . .
>
> Paul Volcker, Chairman, Group of Thirty
> (*Derivatives: Practices and Principles*, 1993)

7.1 Introduction

A good commercial relationship between provider and end-user, the importance of which was emphasised in the previous chapter, requires a sound legal foundation. Without it, commercial expectations may founder, and costly and time-consuming disputes may ensue. There are two key questions which, in an ideal world, should be asked by potential participants to any derivatives transaction: What legal risk does this transaction entail? How does the law determine who may be responsible for loss suffered if the transaction subsequently breaks down?

Legal risk arises where there is uncertainty over the enforceability of a particular transaction. It is more than simply an academic matter; if a transaction is not enforceable, not only will the parties be unable to obtain performance of each other's obligations under the transaction but also there may be no remedy in damages for loss flowing from the transaction. Seventy-five or so of the world's largest banks learnt this lesson the hard way when they entered into interest rate swaps with over 130 English local councils in the 1980s.[1] An English court's decision that such councils did not, in the particular circumstances, have the requisite legal capacity to enter into swap agreements is reported to have left those banks owed some GBP500–600 millon.[2]

While legal uncertainty over the enforceability of derivatives transactions may come as a surprise to those who work on a daily basis in the industry, regulators have been acutely conscious of it for some time. As the quote from Paul Volcker at the beginning of this chapter indicates, the issue preoccupied the collective mind of the Group of Thirty in their examination in 1993 of global OTC derivatives (Group of Thirty 1993). The Group regarded it as one of the areas that required immediate resolution.[3] In the light of the growth of markets and instruments described in *Chapter 1*, the anxiety of the Group is understandable. The legal issues cut across the commercial distinctions drawn between the various types of derivatives and are relevant not only to the financial intermediaries who deal in the derivatives but also to the end-users for whom derivatives are a vital part of their treasury strategies.

The purpose of this chapter accordingly is twofold:

- to assess the degree of legal risk which arises from the use of derivatives; and
- to examine the basis on which legal rules determine the allocation of responsibility for loss.

In addressing these legal questions, reference will be made primarily to the common law rules that form the basis not only of the Australian and New Zealand legal systems but also of those jurisdictions of South East Asia which, by reason of their colonial past, share with Australia and New Zealand the legacy of the English common law, such as Singapore, Malaysia and Hong Kong. Although there are within Asia important financing centres with a significantly different legal tradition, an examination of the common law approach remains both relevant and important. Many international financing transactions are, as a matter of choice of the parties, specifically made subject to the law of a common law country. Limitations of space unfortunately preclude a comparative analysis.

Practical illustrations of the legal issues will be drawn primarily from England and Australia. Although the rules emerging in these countries are not of direct authority outside their own jurisdiction, they are nonetheless of considerable interest in indicating how courts of a common law tradition might approach the issues. As yet, there are relatively few cases which have been fully litigated. The majority of those which have come before the courts have in fact been governed by English law. Cases from American jurisdictions will not be discussed, since the legal rules are in significant respects different to those derived from an Anglo-Australian framework and, again, limitations of space prevent a comparative study.[4]

7.2 Preliminary problems of definition

In part at least, ignorance of legal risk has in the past stemmed from a failure to appreciate the legal nature of derivatives and hence to understand what legal rules will be applicable to their operation. In finance, as was shown in *Chapter 1*, two crucial distinctions are traditionally drawn: on the one hand, between forwards and options and, on the other, between instruments traded over-the-counter and those traded on an exchange. While a lawyer will certainly want to know whether a product falls within a regulatory framework and therefore whether it must comply with specific regulation, the initial question which must be asked is whether the product is in fact an enforceable contract. It is only where lawyers answer that question in the affirmative that the second question of regulatory compliance needs to be addressed.

Take by way of example this fundamental finance distinction between forwards and options. In substance, forwards and options are instruments under which the parties agree either that delivery of a product should take place or a cash adjustment should be made at some time, based on the value at that time of a commodity, financial instrument or index.[5] The difference lies in the fact that under an option the holder of the instrument is not obliged to effect the transaction. The holder simply has the right, if so desired, to buy or sell, according to the nature of the particular option.

In legal terms, both forwards and options are clearly contracts, given that they arise from an *agreement* by the parties. The fact that only a right as distinct from an obligation may be given by that agreement does not affect its contractual nature. The distinction drawn by financiers lies simply in the content of the rights passed under the particular type of contract. For the preliminary purpose of attempting to characterise the legal nature of the product, the substance of the content does not matter. The courts have in fact provided[6] examples of legal analyses of some of the more common forms of derivatives in financial markets such as swaps, reverse swaps, swap options, caps, floors and collars. In each case the courts have emphasised that at the heart of the transaction is some form of agreement.[7]

Once it is appreciated that a product is contractual in nature, general principles of contract law can be applied. The enforceability of the particular transaction will thus depend on the application of established rules, albeit within a specialised context.

The second issue of regulatory compliance can only be answered according to the specific framework of the jurisdiction under examination. In the case of Australia, for example, the relevant statutory structure is established under the Corporations Law.[8] While this will be discussed in detail in *Chapter 10*, it is worth emphasising here that the process involved in making the appropriate regulatory determination is not necessarily as straightforward as might initially appear. This point was well illustrated by the litigation between the SFE and the ASX,[9] which again is analysed in detail in *Chapter 10*.

In 1994 the SFE challenged the ASX's right to list Low Exercise Price Options (LEPOs) for trading on the Australian Options Market, arguing that LEPOs were futures contracts and therefore subject to regulation by it and not by the ASX. The Federal Court concluded, however, that LEPOs were 'securities' within the meaning of the term given by the Corporations Law and therefore properly within the jurisdiction of the ASX, since they were in substance option contracts rather than futures contracts. The intangible nature of the underlying shares on which they were based prevented them from being regarded as commodities[10] and thus took them outside the statutory definition of a futures contract.[11]

In 1995 a new legislative procedure was in fact introduced in Australia to enable particular products to be classified simply on the issue of an appropriate regulation under the Corporations Law as securities or futures contracts, irrespective of whether they actually formally fall within the existing legal definitions of those terms. The then government described this amendment as:

> particularly relevant at this time with the development of hybrid products and the responsibility of the Government to ensure adequate regulation while not retarding market innovation.[12]

It is tempting, however, to regard it rather as a telling illustration of the inadequacy of current statutory definitions.

A very recent report published by the Companies and Securities Advisory Committee (CASAC) makes two recommendations that would, if enacted, clarify the position. First, the report proposes a formal definition which, although admittedly controversial in scope and application, nonetheless has the merit of stressing that a derivatives product is a contract. Secondly, the report proposes that all derivatives should be regulated (see *Chapter 10*). It remains unclear in early 1997 as to whether these recommendations will be accepted.

7.3 Extent of legal risk

The enforceability of any financing transaction inevitably depends on the application of general legal rules governing the formation of contracts. Under these rules a party seeking to enforce a contract must prove such matters as, for example, an intention to create a legal relationship, the existence of valuable consideration, and the absence of factors which might vitiate the consent given by the other party to the contract (as where a party has procured the consent of another by misrepresentation or the exercise of undue influence). These rules will equally apply to derivatives transactions. In this sense, the legal risk pertaining to such transactions is no more, although indeed no less, than that inherent in other financing arrangements.

There are, however, two preliminary questions[13] which should be resolved prior to entering into any contractual transaction:

- does the jurisdiction permit this type of transaction to take place?
- does the counterparty have the requisite legal capacity and authority to enter into the transaction?

These apparently straightforward questions have proved surprisingly difficult to answer in relation to derivatives transactions.[14] Hence it is argued that the real legal risk lies, not at the level of the actual operation of the contract, but rather in the initial structuring of the transaction. Accordingly, it is on the two questions posed above that this chapter will focus in assessing the extent of legal risk.

7.3.1 *Importance of jurisdiction*

Assuming that there is no blanket prohibition in the particular jurisdiction on derivatives transactions, there are essentially two[15] major obstacles which currently confront parties attempting to structure a derivatives transaction in a common law jurisdiction. Firstly, the contract underlying the product may be invalidated on the basis that it is contrary to gaming legislation. Secondly, even if the contract is valid, the netting arrangements which are crucial to the practical operation of the contract may be struck down as contrary to insolvency legislation. Again, these are not simply academic questions. The strength of the threat which they pose to the enforceability of derivatives transactions can be gauged by reform proposals now actively under consideration, discussed below.

a) Gaming and wagering contracts

The question of whether a transaction is a gaming and wagering contract may strike the practitioner in the derivatives industry as strange. The relevance may not immediately be clear. Yet it is of fundamental importance. As the law stands, many derivatives contracts which are initiated over-the-counter are potentially liable to be invalidated.

Legislation concerning gaming and wagering contracts has its modern origins in the English Gaming Act 1845, from which current Australian, Hong Kong and Singaporean legislation derives.[16] Under this statute contracts of wagering were prohibited and rendered void (of no effect).

The classic definition of a wagering contract, which emanates from a nineteenth century English case,[17] is:

> A wagering contract is one by which two persons, professing to hold opposite views touching the issue of a future uncertain event, mutually agree that, dependent upon the determination of that event, one shall win from the other, and that other shall pay or hand over to him, a sum of money or other stake; neither of the contracting parties having any other interest in that contract than the sum or stake he will so win or lose, there being no other real consideration for the making of such contract by either of the parties.

While for many (although admittedly not all) the concept of wagering may initially seem far removed from the rarefied world of finance, the point was litigated very recently in England in relation to an interest rate swap agreement entered into between Morgan Grenfell & Co. Ltd and an English local council, Welwyn Hatfield District Council (Welwyn).[18] The outcome was of fundamental importance. Had the swap been regarded as a wagering contract, it could have been set aside.

The facts of the case were straightforward. As part of the overall strategy, Welwyn had entered into a further interest rate swap agreement with another local council, Islington London Borough Council (Islington). Welwyn intended to act as the intermediary and receive a profit which arose from the fact that the initial payment which Welwyn received from Morgan Grenfell was larger than that which Welwyn was obliged to pay to Islington. In previous litigation it had been held (for reasons that will be examined below) that such contracts entered into by the local authorities were void, but that payments could be recovered. In this action Islington resisted Welwyn's claim for repayment of GBP1 798 458.90 on the basis (*inter alia*) that the contract was a wagering contract and therefore Welwyn was precluded from recovering because of the gaming legislation.

The issue therefore was simply whether the swap was a wagering contract. Courts have long held that wagering contracts[19] include 'contracts for differences'; that is, contracts under which it is agreed that instead of transferring the subject matter of the contract, one party is 'to pay to the other the difference between the price on that day and the price on the contract day'. This type of contract would clearly potentially cover interest rate swap contracts. As the judge stated:

> Since [interest rate swap agreements] provide for the payment of differences they are capable of being entered into by way of gaming or wagering. They have, at least potentially, a speculative character deriving from the fact that the obligations of the floating rate payer are to be ascertained by reference to a fluctuating market rate that may be higher or lower than the fixed rate at any given time. Such a contract is capable of being entered into by two parties with the purpose of wagering upon future interest rates.[20]

The judge noted that in determining whether a contract fell within this category the English courts have traditionally looked to the interests and purposes of the parties.[21] It was thus his view that contracts which were made for a commercial purpose would not be regarded as void, even if they resulted simply in the payment of a difference.[22] In fact he went so far as to say:

> In the context of interest rate swap contracts entered into by parties or institutions involved in the capital markets and the making or receiving of loans, the normal inference will be that the contracts are not gaming or wagering but are commercial or financial transactions to which the law will, in the absence of some other consideration, give full recognition and effect.[23]

The decision thus turned on the interests and purposes of the parties. The court concluded that Islington's intent was not to speculate. Islington had budgeted to raise GBP12 million as income for the relevant year by means of a particular transaction which was not able to be effected. It thus became necessary for Islington to raise the money by some other means. Accordingly it sought to raise the finance by way of up-front payments on interest rate swap contracts. The court held that Islington's purpose was simply to:

> . . . incur a revenue liability spread over a period of ten years in exchange for an advance payment to be made at the time of entering into the contract which could be treated by Islington as a revenue receipt.[24]

The court acknowledged that there was nonetheless a speculative element to the contract because of the very nature of the contract, but held that this was a subordinate element and therefore did not affect the transaction.

As far as Welwyn's position was concerned, the court held that Welwyn was likewise not entering into a wagering contract. Welwyn had simply interposed itself in the chain, dealing on a 'back-to-back' basis with some variation which enabled it to have an assured element of profit. In this case it was the difference in the up-front payment; it might have been a 'turn' on the interest rate. The important point was that Welwyn's purpose was to realise a non-speculative profit; its profit was insulated from any type of speculative risk since it remained constant whichever way interest rates might move. Here again, interestingly, the court was prepared to indicate that *prima facie* the transactions were of a 'commercial and financial character'.[25] Hence the purpose and interest of Welwyn simply served to confirm rather than establish that the agreements were not wagering transactions.

The court expressly left open the important question of how a contrary conclusion would have affected Welwyn's ability to recover the money. A decision on that point was unnecessary for the resolution of the case. The court, however, raised briefly the competing policy issues: on the one hand, the need to prevent the misappropriation of the council's assets; on the other, the need to enforce the statutory rule that sums paid in connection with a gaming contract should be irrecoverable.

It should be appreciated that the point raised by the Welwyn litigation is far from theoretical. It is clear, from the discussion in *Chapter 1*, that financial institutions in Australia do deliberately enter into derivatives transactions on a purely speculative basis. Those contracts must be at risk. Reliance simply on the commercial context in which the transactions are effected may of itself not be sufficient to insulate the transactions from the scope of the gaming legislation.[26] Indeed, Lord Goff in a very recent case stated quite simply his view that in England interest rate swaps were clearly wagers and survived only by reason of legislative exemption.[27]

The danger of a transaction being invalidated as a wagering contract has been recognised by the regulatory authorities in Australia, Singapore and Hong Kong. In Australia,[28] for example, the Corporations Law specifically exempts certain option and futures contracts from the operation of the gaming legislation. The exemption is, however, limited in scope: essentially to those instruments which are traded on a recognised exchange or on an exempt market.[29] The restricted nature of the statutory exemption was noted by the ASC, which certainly considered that OTC derivatives could be challenged as wagering contracts.[30] CASAC recommended initially in 1995 that the Corporations Law should be amended to exclude at least those OTC derivatives which are currently regulated under the Corporations Law (CASAC 1995) and in June 1996 that all transactions which were conducted on authorised derivatives exchanges should be excluded. In November 1996 the Netting Sub-Committee of CASAC added its voice to the call for reform (CASAC 1996).

There remains a broader question which needs to be addressed: namely, whether it is still appropriate for gaming legislation generally to be applicable in the realm of financial transactions. The legislation was introduced in another era for a very different policy reason. It was not intended to deal with financial transactions. It may thus be strongly argued that consideration should be given to exempting financial transactions generally from this legislation, rather than only specified derivatives transactions. This is an approach which has now been adopted in some common law jurisdictions, such as England in 1986[31] and, more recently, Hong Kong in 1993.[32]

To argue for a general exemption for financial transactions from the gaming legislation is not to ignore any concern over the extent of speculation in the markets. Rather, the argument emphasises the need to deal with the issue of speculation directly rather than to approach it from under cover of a piece of legislation which was never designed to deal with this particular problem. What in this writer's view needs to be explored are the legal responsibilities which are currently placed on those making decisions as to the use of derivatives, such as directors and trustees. Are the current rights and obligations of themselves sufficient to prevent reckless speculation to the detriment of their institutions?

b) Netting arrangements

In its Risk Management Guidelines for Derivatives, the Basle Committee on Banking Supervision recognised that the process of netting could offer substantial advantages such as:

> a reduction in credit and liquidity risks, the potential to do more business with existing counterparties within existing credit lines and a reduced need for collateral to support counterparty obligations. (Basle Committee on Banking Supervision 1994, para 31)

Accordingly the Basle Committee urged institutions to ensure that their netting agreements were adequately documented and properly executed. It stressed, however, that credit and liquidity risks should only be monitored on a net basis 'when a netting arrangement is legally enforceable in all relevant jurisdictions' (Basle Committee on Banking Supervision 1994). In practice, this has proved to be immensely difficult to ensure.

The concept of netting is simple—as between specified parties having dealings with each other only a net balance on those dealings should be payable. Various methods are used in the markets to achieve this outcome. Reference may be made for example to *payments netting* and *credit exposure netting*. *Payments netting* is said to take place where amounts are due between the same parties in relation to the same risk management product. Under the netting arrangement, on the due date only the difference between the two amounts is considered to be payable. *Credit exposure netting* is intended to enable one party on the occurrence of a specified event, such as the other's insolvency, to terminate outstanding obligations and to set each party's loss (calculated in damages) against the other in order to ascertain what one owes the other.

Whatever their precise content, netting arrangements are clearly contractual in nature. They thus must satisfy the normal rules for enforceability of contracts within the relevant jurisdiction. The major[33] legal issue which arises in a common law jurisdiction is the extent to which netting agreements can survive the insolvency of either or both of the counterparties and dictate what is payable and when.[34] It is a fundamental rule of insolvency law that, unless creditors have taken security over the insolvent's assets, the creditors must stand in line together and prove in the liquidation for the amount owed to them. Assuming the assets of the estate are more than the liabilities, the unsecured creditors are only entitled to receive a proportionate share of the amount available for payment of the debts.

A netting arrangement has the potential to offend this policy of the insolvency legislation insofar as its effect, if implemented, is to enable the creditor who owes money to the debtor to claim that it does not have to make full payment to the liquidator. The creditor's obligation is to pay only the net balance, if any. Such a creditor is thereby enabled effectively to stand ahead of other unsecured creditors. By netting the debt it is as if the creditor had actually received payment of the debt owed. As a result, some jurisdictions preclude this type of arrangement from having any effect whatsoever. By contrast, in common law systems based on English law such as Australia, Singapore and Hong Kong, it is regarded as unjust that a creditor should not be allowed to pay simply the balance in the debtor's insolvency. Hence, since the eighteenth century, statute has recognised a limited right described as a form of 'set-off'.

Two crucial questions arise. Are netting arrangements encompassed by the notion of 'set-off'? And if so, what happens if they purport to extend the circumstances in which set-off is permitted to occur? It is clear, however, that if the netting arrangements do not amount to a 'set-off', those arrangements will be liable to be struck down as an attempt to oust the orderly administration of assets in a liquidation.[35]

It is certainly common practice to characterise netting arrangements as a form of contractual set-off. Set-off is a long established concept which allows a person to claim to be discharged from an obligation to make payment to another, to the extent to which that other owes that person a corresponding obligation (Derham 1987; McCracken 1993; Wood 1989 and 1995). In common law legal systems it may arise, however, only in specific circumstances. Where neither party is insolvent, set-off is generally permitted by statute where debts are mutual and liquidated, under general principles of equity law where it is 'just and fair', and under contract law where there is an appropriate agreement. Where one or both of the parties are in liquidation, statute sets out the circumstances in which the set-off may take place. In the absence of such authority, there is no right to 'set-off' debts.

In Australia, the statutory right available to corporations in liquidation is conferred by the Corporations Law s553C(1), which states:

> . . . where there have been mutual credits, mutual debts or other mutual dealings between an insolvent company that is being wound up and a person who wants to have a debt or claim admitted against the company:
> (a) an account is to be taken of what is due from the one party to the other in respect of those mutual dealings; and
> (b) the sum due from the one party is to be set off against any sum due from the other party; and
> (c) only the balance of the amount is admissible to proof against the company, or is payable to the company, as the case may be.

By judicial interpretation[36] this clause is regarded as mandatory and hence any contractual arrangement which purports in any way to modify the effect of this provision will be invalidated and of no effect. Although this writer has argued elsewhere (McCracken 1993; *Chapter* 9) that this is not a necessary interpretation of the legislation, nonetheless it is clear that it remains the courts' view, not only in Australia but also in England. Hence if a netting arrangement is regarded as a set-off, it must not confer a more extensive right than that available under Corporations Law s553C. If, for example, the arrangement purported to allow netting of third party obligations, eg those of a subsidiary of a counterparty, it would be avoided since the statutory right permits only 'mutual dealings' (those of the counterparties) to be the object of a set-off.

The uncertainty in this area has caused considerable concern amongst regulators globally. Some jurisdictions have in fact enacted specific legislation to allow netting to take place and hence to take it outside the insolvency regime. Wood (1995) points, for example, to netting statutes in Belgium, Canada, France and the United States, although he notes that they apply only to particular contracts specified in the particular legislation. A recent addition to this list is the Irish Netting of Financial Contracts Act 1995.

In Australia the Australian Financial Markets Association (AFMA) has approved the view that such netting arrangement as is contemplated by the ISDA agreement operative in Australia would not offend the Australian insolvency legislation (AFMA 1994). In November 1996 the Netting Sub-Committee of CASAC published a Draft Report recommending that certain financial contracts should be expressly excluded from the scope of the insolvency legislation (CASAC 1996).

One interesting argument that to date appears not to have been run in this context is that a netting arrangement set up by contract need not necessarily be structured as a set-off,[37] but rather is capable of being governed by a different legal right, namely that of combination. The recognition of a right of combination is, however, itself controversial, although it has been judicially recognised in England in relation to current accounts maintained with a bank:

> Combination of accounts is not a set-off situation, because this postulates mutual but independent obligations between the two parties. Rather, it is merely an accounting situation, in which the existence and amount of one party's liability to the other can only be ascertained by discovering the ultimate balance of their mutual dealings.[38]

This writer would argue that there is a distinction between a right of combination and a right of set-off.[39] In order for a set-off to operate, there must be two debts in existence. Hence if only one debt arises, there is nothing against which that debt can be set-off. Where transactions are conducted on the basis of a running account, the items in the account do not give rise to individual debts. To ascertain what is owed it is necessary to aggregate the credits and the debits and establish the balance. This process of aggregating the credits and debits is undertaken by an exercise of a right of combination where each credit and debit arises under accounts (or transactions) which, although initially appearing to stand alone, are in fact themselves part of a general running account.

Under netting arrangements, it is not uncommon for documentation to provide that transactions are to be established on the basis of a master agreement which is described as forming a single agreement between the parties. Depending on the precise wording used, it may be possible to argue that individual transactions do not create separate debts but rather form part of a running account under which each transaction is recorded as an item in this general account. If it could be shown that the position was governed by a right of combination, rather than that of set-off, problems flowing from the restricted application of Corporations Law s553C would no longer be relevant. This is an argument that is explored by the writer elsewhere (McCracken 1993, 2nd edn forthcoming).

7.3.2 *Importance of legal status of counterparty*

Once it is determined that the particular jurisdiction does not preclude the enforceability of the proposed transaction, the issue then becomes whether each counterparty has the ability to enter into the transaction. As a matter of practice, counterparties to derivatives transactions are likely to take the legal form of a corporation or of a trust. It is crucially important from a legal perspective to ensure both that the particular institution as counterparty has the capacity to enter into the transaction and that the person executing the agreement on behalf of that institution has the requisite authority. Lack of capacity or authority may cause the transaction to be invalidated. The problem is particularly acute where the derivatives are traded over-the-counter. As CASAC has pointed out, in the on-exchange market the *ultra vires* (lack of power) risk is assumed by the brokers who act as principals in all transactions (CASAC 1996a).

a) Capacity to enter into transactions

This was of course the issue that was raised so dramatically by the decision of the English House of Lords in *Hazell v Hammersmith and Fulham Borough Council.*[40] The respondent local authority was held not to have the capacity to enter into interest rate swap agreements. As a matter of construction of the authority's constitutional framework, swap transactions could not be construed as incidental to its borrowing function. Accordingly the swap transactions into which it had entered were held to be void. Considerable pressure was applied by the banking industry to have the decision overruled by statute, which was resisted. There are two interesting footnotes to the decision.

Firstly, English courts have over the last few years had to consider whether money which has been paid under a void contract can subsequently be recovered. The point was raised in *Westdeutsche Landesbank Girozentrale v Islington London Borough Council*.[41] Following the invalidation of yet another interest rate swap agreement entered into in excess of a local council's powers, the English Court of Appeal allowed the plaintiff German bank to recover repayment of the balance of GBP2.5 million paid by the bank to the local council at the commencement of the transaction, which amounted to some GBP1.15 million. The ground on which the bank was held entitled to recover was that if the council were allowed to retain the amount it would be unjustly enriched. The claim by the council to the contrary was given short shrift:

> Islington say that they should receive a windfall because the purpose of the doctrine of ultra vires is to protect council taxpayers whereas restitution would disrupt Islington's finances. They also contend that it would countenance 'unconsidered dealings with local authorities'. If that is the best that can be said for refusing restitution, the sooner it is enforced the better. Protection of council taxpayers from loss is to be distinguished from securing a windfall for them. The disruption of Islington's finances is the result of ill-considered financial dispositions by Islington and its officers. It is not the policy of the law to require others to deal at their peril with local authorities, nor to require others to undertake their own inquiries about whether a local authority has power to make particular contracts or types of contract. Any system of law, and indeed any system of fair dealing, must be expected to ensure that Islington do not profit by the fortuity that when it became known that the contract was ineffective the balance stood in their favour. In other words, in circumstances such as these they should not be unjustly enriched.[42]

The Court of Appeal awarded compound interest against the local authority. The local authority thereupon appealed to the House of Lords against this award, although by the date of the hearing it accepted that it was liable to pay back the principal amount. The House of Lords nonetheless discussed at length the manner in which the principal moneys could be recovered, since this affected the decision as to what type of interest was appropriate. Unfortunately their Lordships were divided as to the legal basis, leaving the law in a state of some uncertainty.[43]

Secondly, English courts have acknowledged that a recipient of money under a void transaction will not always be required to return the money. It is open for the recipient to argue that it has a defence of 'change of position'. This argument was raised in *South Tyneside Metropolitan Borough Council v Svenska International plc*.[44] In order to succeed, a defendant must show, save in exceptional circumstances (which were not identified), that a change in its position has taken place after the money has been received.

The defence is designed to protect:

> a person who receives money in good faith and who thereafter changes his position in good faith so that it would be inequitable to require him to repay part or all of the money to its rightful owner.[45]

Applying the principle to the facts the court concluded in that case:

> . . . the position is that if a net payee can show that it has altered its position in good faith after receipt of money under a swap from the net payer it might in principle be entitled to rely upon the defence of change of position. What it cannot do is to rely upon the supposed validity of the transaction because the transaction is and always has been void.[46]

Hence the bank could not rely upon the defence when the only change occurred prior to the making of the contract and related to the hedging of its position.

In Australia, it tends to be confidently assumed that the operation of the Corporations Law precludes any question being asked about the capacity of a company. The statute states that a company incorporated under that law has the legal capacity of a natural person.[47] It should, however, be noted that it remains open to a company in its constitution to place a restriction or prohibition on the company's power.[48] While such a restriction cannot invalidate the ability of the company to enter into a transaction in contravention of that restriction, there are two points that need to be borne in mind:

- the authority of the directors to approve the transaction may be challenged by the shareholders acting as the company in general meeting (see below); and

- the fact of the breach can lay the ground for certain subsequent actions, the most important of which from a counterparty's point of view is that an injunction may be sought to restrain the company from entering into the agreement. Those entitled to bring an injunction are stated to be not simply the Australian Securities Commission but also 'a person whose interests have been, are, or would be affected by the conduct'.[49] The Court has a discretion as to whether it will grant the injunction and may do so 'on such terms as the Court thinks appropriate'.

The statutory protection against claims of *ultra vires* in Australia differs in nature from that available in other jurisdictions such as Singapore. Following the English approach, Singaporean legislation does not confer full capacity on the company itself, but rather seeks to protect a person dealing with the company from the consequences of the transaction being regarded as *ultra vires*.[50] Although in practice the same conclusion may often be reached, namely that the contract is upheld, the difference in approach can potentially nonetheless lead to differing outcomes.

It also needs to be emphasised that statutory protection, whatever its precise scope, only applies to companies incorporated under the relevant general companies legislation. The capacity of other entities depends on their constituting statute or documentation.

An ability to construe the constituting documentation of corporate entities other than those governed by companies legislation thus remains crucial. In *Hazell v Hammersmith & Fulham Local Borough Council* one of the interesting points is the limitation which the House of Lords read into the particular power to borrow. That power could only be interpreted as a power to borrow for the purpose of debt management and not speculation. The reason behind this restrictive interpretation was policy. As Clarke J pointed out in *South Tyneside Metropolitan Borough Council v Svenska International plc*[51] it was about 1987 that the Audit Commission said that swaps by local authorities were:

> within the powers of local authorities if they were part of the process of debt management but not, for example, if they were large interest rate swaps 'with front end premiums' adopted for the purpose of avoiding government controls on borrowing or if the authorities were acting as intermediaries. Thus concern was expressed about what was known as deep

discounting and about what was known as intermediating. The essence of the concern was that local authorities were thought to have no power to enter into swaps for speculative purposes.

It is far from inconceivable that an Australian court might, depending on the circumstances, read down a power to borrow in this way. Certainly the view seems to have been taken in Singapore that an express power to borrow would not be construed as authorising a governmental entity to enter into swap transactions.[52]

b) Authority to enter into transactions

The fact that a counterparty has the requisite capacity to enter into the transaction does not mean that the transaction is not vulnerable to challenge. There is a further problem that in practice appears often to be ignored and that is the question of authority: who has the authority to enter into the transaction on behalf of the counterparty?

The issue of authority is determined at two levels. In dealing with a company, the first step is to look at the objects clause in the Memorandum of Association which contains the purposes for which the company has been established (although such is no longer compulsory in Australia). If there is, for example, a restriction in the objects clause, there are, as noted above, legal consequences if that is breached. While statute may provide some protection for those dealing in good faith with the entity, that protection is only available where the conditions of the statute are met. Under, for example, a provision of the Corporations Law in Australia, people dealing with a company may assume that the memorandum and articles have been complied with. That protection is not available where the person either has actual knowledge of the matter in issue or the relationship or connection with the company is such that the person ought to know that the matter is not correct.[53] Similarly, the rule at common law, applicable equally in Singapore and Hong Kong,[54] which enables a person to assume the regularity of acts of internal management will not be available where a person is put on inquiry.

Assuming that the objects have been complied with, there is the further question of who may actually sign the contract on behalf of the company. In a company incorporated under a statutory framework such as that provided in Australia, Singapore or Hong Kong, it would be expected that the company would have a provision in its Articles of Association which would delegate the powers of management of a company to the board of directors. There would then need to be shown a specific delegation from the board to the individual who will enter into the agreement. The prudent counterparty would therefore expect evidence of that authorisation. Wallace (1994) points out that 'a particular form of authorisation or a certificate from a particular official may be required for the transaction to be binding on the counterparty', acknowledging that '[t]his of course is an unpalatable result from a swap dealer's perspective and would seem, frequently, to be ignored in practice'. In this context it is noteworthy that the Monetary Authority of Singapore requires banks to have in place policies directing staff to ensure the requisite authority of the proposed counterparty (Monetary Authority of Singapore 1995).

In the absence of express actual authority, it is possible that the signatory has either implied actual authority or indeed usual or ostensible authority (as explained below). In other words, the signatory may be regarded, by reason of the application of legal rules, as having the requisite authority in the particular circumstances. The mere fact that a person is not expressly authorised does not mean that there is no authority.

The point arose as a subsidiary issue in *AWA Ltd v Daniels*[55] (discussed in more detail below and in *Chapter 4*), where the authority of a foreign exchange dealer to raise a foreign currency loan in the course of conducting foreign exchange operations was challenged. In concluding that the dealer would have implied authority, the court looked to the practice of the foreign exchange markets[56] and accepted evidence that it was:

> the practice of the market that it was assumed that a participant ensured that its foreign exchange dealer or representative in the market was trading in accordance with any directive, policy or limitations imposed upon him by the participant.[57]

The practice developed on account of the pressure on the operators in that particular market.[58] The implied authority arose on one or other or both of two grounds: either because the borrowing of foreign currency was necessary for, or incidental to, the conduct of an FX operation or because the institution in employing a money market dealer and FX manager impliedly authorised the employee 'to do what was usual in the course of a money market manager and FX dealer's business'. In the alternative, the court was prepared to hold that the employee had in fact both usual authority and ostensible authority. Usual authority is that authority which is usual to a particular position, namely a money market manager and FX dealer. Ostensible authority arises where a person is held out as holding a particular position (even if he or she does not actually do so).

In some jurisdictions including Australia, statute provides a basis on which a person dealing with a company is protected in specified circumstances from a subsequent claim that the counterparty did not have the relevant authority. In Australia the protection is again contained in the Corporations Law and is thus restricted to transactions involving companies incorporated under the Corporations Law or its predecessors. Section 164 enables a person having dealings with a company to make assumptions about the authority of certain office holders and agents. That person may, for example, assume that a person held out to be an agent of the company has the usual authority of such an agent. This of course begs the question of what constitutes 'usual authority' for these purposes. A further problem arises insofar as a person may be precluded from relying upon s164, not simply where he or she has actual knowledge of the lack of authority but where the relationship with the company is such that the person 'ought to have known' of the lack of authority. The types of circumstances in which such a person will be precluded from relying upon s164 have yet to be conclusively defined by the Australian courts.

Even if the requisite authority is present, there is one additional issue which requires some consideration. An exercise of powers by the directors (whether directly or through their delegate) must, according to general principles of company law, be made '*bona fide* for the benefit of the company'. If it can be shown that the proposed derivatives transaction is entered into other than for the benefit of the company, the transaction may be set aside by the company (ie shareholders in general meeting). In cases of doubt the prudent counterparty would again look for evidence that the transaction would not be challenged. This would normally take the form of a shareholders' resolution approving the transaction, since the duty to act for the benefit of the company is owed to the shareholders in general meeting and therefore a breach can be cured by them. It should be noted, however, that in circumstances where the company is insolvent, or close to insolvent, the courts will not necessarily allow the ratification by the shareholders to absolve the breach if to do so would prejudice creditors of the company.[59]

The problems faced in a corporate context are echoed in those confronted in dealings with a trustee and indeed heightened by the lack of statutory protection (Adams 1994; Lanyon 1995;

McDougall 1996). It is of importance for a creditor to establish that the trustee with whom the institution dealt had the requisite authority. Generally a creditor deals with a trustee in the trustee's personal capacity and has thus no direct right to claim the assets held on trust by the trustee. However, if a trustee is entitled to be indemnified for liabilities which the trustee has incurred in the proper course of carrying out the trust activities, a creditor may in certain circumstance be entitled to stand in the shoes of the trustee (under the technical doctrine of subrogation) and claim a right to the assets on the strength of that indemnity. An indemnity will generally only arise, in the absence of express agreement, if the trustee is authorised to enter into the particular transaction.

The authority of a trustee to act in relation to trust assets stems from the trust deed under which the trust is established. In the absence of an express power to deal specifically in derivatives arising either from the deed or regulation,[60] the trustee's authority to enter into the transaction would be dependent on whether the transaction would be considered to be covered under the general investment power which one would expect to find in the trust deed. It has been pointed out that as yet there is no Australian judicial decision which confirms that derivatives can be so covered (Adams 1994). Consequently, the prudent course of action may be for the counterparty to insist that the trust deed be amended accordingly.

7.4 Legal basis for allocation of risk

The publicity surrounding recent 'disasters' in derivatives, such as the cases in *Chapter 2*, has at least had the merit of focusing end-users on the need to ensure that they have put in place adequate safeguards to enable management to control derivatives trading activities. It has also highlighted the acrimonious debates that may ensue as attempts are made to impose liability for the loss suffered. Recent newspaper reports in Singapore, for example, indicate that customers of financial institutions there have not been slow to sue institutions for loss allegedly suffering through swap transactions, although to date the cases appear to have been settled out of court.[61] There is a widely acknowledged need for the law to clarify the responsibilities of the counterparties and the basis on which liability may be allocated in the event of the transaction breaking down.

7.4.1 *Responsibilities*

The responsibilities of boards of directors under common law have traditionally been expressed in less than onerous terms. They were first formulated in the nineteenth century and reflected a then current perception of directors as gentlemen with honourable intentions. A director was bound only to take the reasonable care 'that an ordinary man might be expected to take in the circumstances on his own behalf'. He (and it was then always a 'he') did not need to exhibit 'in the performance of his duties a greater degree of skill than may reasonably be expected from a person of his knowledge and experience'. This view of a subjective standard, confirmed in *Re City Equitable Fire Insurance Co. Ltd*,[62] was generally accepted in Australia, Singapore and Hong Kong.

In Australia, however, this common law duty was subsequently supplemented by statutory duties to act honestly and to exercise due diligence. Initially, the statutory framework was interpreted as simply codification of the common law position,[63] although it did give rise to additional liability under the statute. In 1993 the companies legislation was amended to confirm that a more objective standard of care was required of a director (and indeed of senior management). The relevant provision now reads:

> In the exercise of his or her powers and the discharge of his or her duties, an officer of a corporation must exercise the degree of care and diligence that a reasonable person in a like position in a corporation would exercise in the corporation's circumstances.[64]

The amendment confirmed in Australia a clear change in attitude towards directors' responsibilities. It is interesting and, one suspects, more than coincidence that the judicial reformulation of the common law duties took place in the context of a financial transaction. The turning point was the much publicised case of AWA Ltd.

During the 1980s AWA Ltd incurred substantial losses through foreign exchange trading. Responsibility for the dealing had been left with the dealer who had caused the losses. It was clear that there had been inadequate internal supervision of his activities. AWA Ltd sued their auditors for breach of contract and negligence in not drawing to the attention of the board the weaknesses in the management system. The court at first instance held, however, not only were the auditors liable in negligence, but also that AWA Ltd itself was liable for contributory negligence and therefore liable to contribute to AWA for the damage suffered. Interestingly, the court sought to draw a distinction between the duties of executive directors and those of non-executive directors, arguing that it was:

> something of an anachronism to expect non-executive directors, meeting once a month, to contribute anything much more than decisions on questions of policy and, in the case of really large corporations, only major policy.

On appeal, the majority of the New South Wales Court of Appeal upheld the findings of negligence, but were loath to draw a distinction between executive and non-executive directors:

> A person who accepts the office of director of a particular company undertakes the responsibility of ensuring that he or she understands the nature of the duty a director is called upon to perform. That duty will vary according to the size and business of the particular company and the experience or skills that the director held himself or herself out to have in support of the appointment to the office. The duty is a common law duty to take reasonable care owed severally by persons who are fiduciary agents bound not to exercise the powers conferred upon them for private purposes or for any purpose foreign to the power and placed . . . at the apex of the structure of direction and management. The duty includes that of acting collectively to manage the company. Breach of the duty will found an action for negligence at the suit of the company.

There has been considerable discussion of what the content of this duty (and other statutory duties imposed on corporate officers) means specifically in relation to derivatives. The SFE, for example, recently published a manual entitled *Surviving with Derivatives* in which it sets out its understanding of the current position:

> The obligations placed on directors under the Corporations Law are not so onerous that Board members are required to become auditors in order to know whether the company's management is deceiving them. But they are required to exercise their obligations with care.
> ***To understand implications and risk***
> The Corporations Law requires directors to assure themselves that appropriate risk management measures are taken if their company trades in derivative markets. Directors must have at least a general understanding of the corporation's business and the effect economic change would have on it. That means that they should understand the possible effects of economic

> change on their derivative markets position, because these in turn may have a substantial effect on the company's business.
>
> Members of a corporate board do not need to understand the precise mechanics involved, and need to know what type of management information they should be receiving in order to assess whether established policies and procedures are being followed.
>
> ***Judgment, care and diligence***
> They have a duty to consider the matters brought before the board with informed and independent judgment, and they must exercise care and diligence in the performance of their roles.
>
> In practice, directors may need specialist knowledge to deal with complex situations, and may need to employ and rely on professional advice. Boards are not expected to manage the corporation's day to day business—this duty by necessity falls on the company's senior management.

The whole issue has in fact evolved into a much wider debate on corporate governance, to which reference has already been made in *Chapters 4* and 6. What is interesting to note, for the purposes of this chapter, is the courts' willingness to strengthen the duties of the board of directors at the point before the corporation enters into any transaction. The law now imposes on board members a considerable responsibility to attempt to ensure that they understand what types of transactions they are dealing in:

> The responsibilities of directors require that they take reasonable steps to place themselves in a position to guide and monitor the management of the company.[65]

The statutory duties of directors are supplemented by duties imposed by the general law under general principles of equity. The law regards the director as *a fiduciary,* that is a person in whom trust and confidence is reposed and who is required to refrain from abusing his or her position. The relevant restrictions include a duty to act honestly, to not place himself or herself in a position of conflict, and to exercise powers in good faith and for the benefit of the company.

Although there is no equivalent general statutory duty of care placed upon trustees, they are also fiduciaries and are required properly to exercise the powers given to them in the trust deed under which they are established. A trustee's fiduciary duty to the beneficiaries of the trust has, however, long been recognised as different in nature from that of a director to a company:

> . . . the duty of a trustee is to exercise a degree of restraint and conservatism in investment judgments[;] the duty of a director may be to display entrepreneurial flair and accept commercial risks to produce a sufficient return on the capital invested.[66]

Adams (1994) argues that trust funds can only be applied to derivatives transactions if:

- such application can be characterised as an investment;
- the application is permitted under the terms of the trust deed establishing the fund or under some applicable statutory regulation; and
- the use of derivatives is prudent in the circumstances.

Adams (1994) further argues, however, that it is possible to maintain that the use of derivatives as part of an investment strategy could be regarded as 'prudent', thereby satisfying the legal test of a prudent person who is required at law:

> to take such care as an ordinary prudent man would take if he were minded to make an investment for the benefit of other people for whom he felt morally bound to provide.[67]

The courts' interpretation is awaited. By way of potential analogy it is noteworthy that, in the context of superannuation funds, legislation has been introduced to codify trustee's responsibilities.[68] Under this legislation an investment strategy must be established and implemented by the trustee with regard to the fund as a whole.[69] The ISC has in fact recently issued guidelines for the use of derivatives (ISC 1996a; also see *Chapters 5* and *10*). According to the ISC (1996b), it is inappropriate for legislation to regulate the use of derivatives. Rather, it should fall to trustees to decide whether investment in derivatives is suitable for their particular funds. Where they do so decide, they will be required to issue Risk Management Statements.

7.4.2 *Liabilities*

As a matter of legal principle, it is clear that a legal risk may flow from the act of intermediation. The issue is whether the intermediary in the particular circumstances is regarded as owing a legal duty to the end-user. In general terms, that legal duty may flow from two major sources: in tort, a duty to exercise care and, in equity, a duty to act as a fiduciary. In addition, depending on the facts of the case, there may also be an action on the actual contract, such as a claim for damages for breach of a contractual duty of care or a claim for the contract to be rescinded by reason of misrepresentation or undue influence. In Australia, liability may also arise under Trade Practices Act 1974 (Cth) s52 if the intermediary has acted in a manner that is misleading or deceptive or, indeed, is likely to be misleading or deceptive.

This part focuses on the general law duty in tort. Although in theory parties may argue for recognition of a fiduciary relationship, it is considered unlikely in practice that users of derivatives will be able to establish the existence of such a relationship. The general relationship between a banker and its customer is described as that of a debtor and creditor and duties are accordingly owed on a contractual basis.[70] Traditionally, courts have been unwilling to recognise fiduciary duties on the part of banks unless there is clear evidence that the banks have specifically assumed the role of a fiduciary. As the High Court in Australia has made clear, a relationship of confidence where one person trusts another is not of itself sufficient to create a fiduciary relationship.[71] That Court has defined a fiduciary relationship as:

> . . . one which gives the fiduciary a special opportunity to exercise . . . power or discretion to the detriment of that other person who is accordingly vulnerable to abuse by the fiduciary of his position.[72]

Some members of the High Court have stressed that courts would be reluctant to find a fiduciary relationship in a commercial context where parties have entered into a transaction on an arm's-length basis.

The existence of a general duty of care in tort has been the subject of considerable debate.[73] Much of the discussion of the legal principles has taken place in the context of risk disclosure. Nonetheless, the principles are also of importance in the context of recent discussion on 'suitability'. While risk disclosure addresses the nature of the risks inherent in the particular market and its products, suitability looks to the suitability of that market and products for particular individual needs. The purpose of suitability assessments is said to be:

> [to] assist persons to determine whether contemplated transactions are appropriate for them in view of their investment objectives, financial situations and particular needs. (CASAC 1995a)

In the opinion of CASAC, such suitability assessments have the potential, if widely used and acted upon, to reduce the level of default and further promote stability in OTC markets. CASAC has called for comments on the merits of enacting a general suitability obligation, noting that where derivatives are classified as 'securities', advisers are currently required to inquire about a client's financial situation and investment objectives. Such a positive obligation would need to be imposed by statute or established under a code of practice.[74] Common law does not create such an obligation; rather, it imposes liability only if it is established that a particular duty exists and, if so, if that duty has been breached by the intermediary. Hence it is important to understand the basis on which a legal duty of care may arise.

The concept of a duty of care in the common law system has been recognised under English common law since 1932.[75] Breach of such a duty which resulted in physical injury gave rise to an action in negligence. It was some time, however, before courts were willing to recognise that a similar duty would be recognised by the law where the loss suffered was not physical damage but rather financial loss. There was concern that to allow an action for negligence in these circumstances would be to 'open the floodgates' to potential litigants, given the range of people who could be affected and the potential magnitude of the losses (Fleming 1992). In 1964 in England the House of Lords finally recognised that such a duty could exist.[76] Courts in other common law jurisdictions soon followed suit, although not without experiencing some difficulty in formulating the relevant test.[77]

The issue of a duty of care owed by financial intermediaries to their customers was raised specifically in the context of derivatives in a very recent English case: *Bankers Trust International PLC v PT Dharmala Sakti Sejahtera*. The case involved swaps entered into between Bankers Trust and the Indonesian defendant (DSS), which resulted in DSS making significant losses when US interest rates rose unexpectedly. When DSS failed to make payment under the agreements, Bankers Trust served notice of default claiming some USD64.7 million.

There were 2 features of crucial importance:

- firstly, Bankers Trust was regarded by the court as occupying a special position in the market:

> Only a few banks in the world were capable of offering [such swaps] in early 1994. The Bankers Trust group played a significant, and until 1994 apparently successful, role at the forefront of the development of such derivatives. It is a role which contrasts with the ordinary role occupied by a banker in relation to its customers, and it has inherent in it certain dangers;

- secondly, the form of derivatives which had been used, described as leveraged derivatives, were highly sophisticated and potentially capable of causing substantial financial loss.

The thrust of PT Dharmala Sakti Sejahtera's (DSS's) argument was that Bankers Trust Company (Singapore branch) (BT Co.) and Bankers Trust International plc (BTI), on whose behalf BT Co. was acting, had a duty of care to it which DSS alleged had been breached. DSS contended that the bank 'had special skill and knowledge in the operation, terms, meaning and effect of such products and as to the assessment of the risks and potential financial consequences involved for each party in accepting them', while DSS had no such relevant skill.

The judge formulated the legal position under English law:

> . . . a bank negotiating and contracting with another party owes in the first instance no duty to explain the nature or effect of the proposed arrangement to that other party. However, if the bank does give an explanation or tender advice, then it owes a duty to give that explanation or tender that advice fully, accurately and properly. How far that duty goes must once again depend on the precise nature of the circumstances and of the explanation or advice which is tendered.

On the facts, the court found that the relevant officers of DSS had 'had considerable relevant experience in the evaluation of swaps of increasing complexity, and had held itself out to BT Co. both as capable of evaluating proposals for such swaps and as concerned to do so for itself, independently of any recommendation or advice given to it by BT Co.'. The court was satisfied that the managing director of BT Co. 'did believe, as a result of [previous] contacts and what he learned and heard about the Dharmala group, that he was dealing with people who would be able and could be expected to undertake a close evaluation of the merits and risks of any proposal which he put up, and to ask questions or seek further information if they felt that they did not understand its workings or implications'.

The court concluded that DSS had failed to show that BT Co. had the relevant duty:

> The relationship was essentially commercial. DSS knew that BT Co. was soliciting DSS's custom for BT Co.'s products and for BT Co.'s and BTI's own profit. The courts should not be too ready to read duties of an advisory nature into this type of relationship. BT Co.'s conduct in proffering swap 2 as a means of avoiding loss on swap 1 and the terms in which BT Co. recommended swap 2 for consideration are factors which

> I accept tend to favour the recognition of broader advisory duties on BT Co.'s and BTI's part. But before recognising any such duty the court must consider the well-recognised, overlapping criteria of (a) forseeability (b) proximity and (c) fairness, justice and reasonableness in the context of the particular relationship and situation and in the light of the type of harm (here financial loss) against which protection is sought. The ultimate decision whether to recognise a duty of care, and if so of what scope, is pragmatic.

Accordingly, the Court concluded that BT Co. owed duties to present the terms and effects of each swap accurately and fairly. BT Co. had, however, no duty to advise about other types of transactions which might have enabled DSS to extract itself from swap 1 or have offered different protection, nor even a duty to warn DSS about the wisdom or unwisdom of this type of speculative transaction. 'It was for DSS to study and evaluate for itself the risks, always provided it was given a fair and accurate representation of the nature of the proposal.'

Australian courts have tended to formulate the duty of care in terms of assumption of responsibility for statements and reasonable reliance upon those statements.[78] As Deane pointed out in *Hawkins v Clayton*,

> . . . where the plaintiff's claim is for pure economic loss . . . the categories of case in which the requisite relationship of proximity [necessary for the establishment of a duty of care] is to be found are probably to be seen as special in that they will be characterised by some . . . element [additional to forseeability] . . . which will commonly (but not necessarily) consist of known reliance (or dependence) or the assumption of responsibility or a combination of the two . . .[79]

The question of whether or not a duty of care may be owed by a financial intermediary to its customer or client was in fact a controversial issue in Australia in the 1980s in the aftermath of the series of foreign currency loans which were made available by the banks to customers. The loans were made in Swiss francs and when the Australian dollar fell, borrowers found themselves owing more than they originally borrowed. Many thereupon made a claim on their bank alleging (*inter alia*) negligence in not having advised them to hedge.

The series of foreign currency loans was examined by the Attorney-General in giving evidence to the Martin Inquiry into banking in 1991 (Martin Report 1991). Following an examination of the cases, the Attorney-General interestingly concluded that to date no single 'universally applicable standard of conduct has been adopted'. He noted, however, that the 'standard of care to be exercised increases proportionately to the seriousness of the risk involved in any breach of duty'.

An indication of the manner of judicial approach can be found in *Mehta v Commonwealth Bank of Australia*.[80] It would appear clear that the duty arises not from the mere fact of the banker/client relationship but rather from the fact that either the parties are in an unequal bargaining position or that the bank holds itself out as providing financial advice. A number of general propositions can be drawn from this case. Firstly, if a bank does take it upon itself to advise, it must give 'a full and proper explanation of the nature and effect of the transaction'. Secondly, if the circumstances indicate that reliance would be placed on the advice and is in fact so placed, the bank may incur obligations to exercise reasonable care and skill. What constitutes reasonable care in a particular case will depend on the circumstances of the case.[81]

In March 1997 the High Court of Australia emphasised, however, that mere reliance on a statement would not in itself be sufficient to found a cause of action.[82] In the context of the provision of information or advice, reliance was said (by Toohey and Gaudron JJ) to be understood '. . . as an expectation, which is reasonable in the circumstances, that due care will be exercised in relation to that provision'.[83] Assumption of responsibility was explained as 'the assumption of responsibility for providing information or advice in circumstances where it is known, or ought reasonably to be known, that it will or may be acted upon for a serious purpose, and loss may be suffered if it proves to be inaccurate'.[84]

How this translates into practice is still unclear. As Toohey and Gauudron JJ pointed out, '[t]he decided cases do not identify precisely what it is that results in liability for economic loss suffered in consequence of the voluntary provision of information or advice'. Their Honours nonetheless gave some indication of the preconditions for the existence of a duty of care:

> . . . common sense requires the conclusion that a special responsibility of proximity marked either by reliance or by the assumption of responsibility does not arise unless the person providing the information or advice has some special expertise or knowledge, or some special means of acquiring information which is not available to the recipient. Moreover, ordinary principles require that the relationship does not arise unless it is reasonable for the recipient to act on that information or

advice without further inquiry. Similarly, ordinary principles require that it be reasonable for the recipient to act upon it for the purpose for which it is used. That is not to say that a special relationship of proximity exists if these conditions are satisfied. Rather, it is to say that the relationship does not arise unless they are.[85]

7.5 Conclusion

The above discussion would suggest that legal risk very much remains a live issue in this region. Although in principle the law provides a basis for allocating both responsibility and liability, in practice it may be difficult to predict on which side of the line parties may fall.

In part, the legal risk encountered in derivatives transactions is little different to the legal risk faced in any financial or commercial transaction. Before entering a transaction, parties should always, for example, ensure that they each have the capacity and authority to deal in the proposed manner. It is nonetheless worth noting that while many common law jurisdictions have attempted to simplify the rules relating to the capacity of corporations and the authority of their management to act on their behalf, these reforms have been effected as part of general company law reform and are not directed specifically to derivatives transactions. The question to be addressed is the extent to which further specific action may need to be taken, given the nature of derivatives trading and the potentially huge amounts of money that may be at stake. Where capacity or authority is left to be determined as a question of construction of particular constitutional documents, the process is by no means foolproof. A court's interpretation may differ significantly from that of the counterparty, or indeed from the counterparty's lawyers. A reading of the report of *AWA Ltd v Daniels*[86] leaves an impression that the court was determined to find the requisite authority. The classical law of contract does not fit easily into the practice of dealing rooms.

Derivatives transactions are particularly vulnerable to challenge as gaming and wagering contracts, although this point seems to be overlooked in practice. The line between 'debt management' and 'speculation' is fine and appears in practice to be consciously crossed not infrequently. Yet it seems inappropriate that derivatives transactions should be challenged on the basis of legislation which was intended to address a very different type of activity. There is a need for urgent re-examination of the whole issue. Piecemeal reform based on excluding particular products is, it is suggested, less than satisfactory. Re-examination of the netting rules is also clearly required to remove doubt about the practical implementation of derivatives contracts. In this respect, at least, commercial concerns have been recognised by the regulatory authorities and it is to be hoped that the draft report recently released by CASAC will be widely discussed.

As far as the responsibilities and liabilities of the parties are concerned, the courts' position is quite clear, in theory if not in practice. It is essentially for those who wish to use derivatives to ensure that they know what they are doing. On such evidence as is currently available, the courts do not appear prepared to extend the duties of intermediaries. The latter will only be regarded as having a duty of care or fiduciary duty where such obligations have been specifically assumed. In the absence of the adoption of an advisory role, the intermediaries are only required not to mislead the proposed counterparty. In reality, the crucial issue will be the drawing of the line between 'sophisticated counterparties' and others. As in other fields, the courts may be more prepared to find that a duty has been established where the status of the counterparties is markedly unequal.

It thus becomes apparent that the extent to which legal risk can be alleviated in any derivatives transaction ultimately depends at present on an identification of the legal issues, coupled with an understanding of how courts may approach those issues. Common law develops on a pragmatic basis, providing answers only to specific questions which are litigated although allowing general principles to be deduced. It remains to be seen, however, how many cases will actually come before the courts. Wallace (1994) makes the pertinent point that in fact commercial pressures may be the ultimate determinant of how legal issues may be resolved, simply because of the huge amounts involved. Analysing some of the defaults over the last decade, he concludes that considerable commercial and regulatory pressure is likely to be brought to bear on the parties concerned:

> in an attempt to ensure that those involved behave in a manner which is regarded as rational in terms of a wider market perspective rather than clinging grimly to perceived legal rights.

Yet without at least an awareness of, if not an insistence on, legal rights there can be little basis for confidence in either a proposed transaction or, indeed, the wider market itself. That confidence is, in this writer's view, a crucial prerequisite for the relationship between provider and end-user to prosper.

References

Adams, M. 1994, 'Practical Issues for Trustees in the Application of Trust Fund Moneys in the Use of Derivatives' 5 JBFLP 20

AFMA 1994, *The Australian Guide to AFMA/ISDA Standard Documentation*, Australian Financial Markets Association, vol. 1

ASC 1994, *Report on OTC Derivatives Markets,* Australian Securities Commission, May

Basle Committee on Banking Supervision 1994, *Risk Management Guidelines for Derivatives*, July

Blair and Olive 1996, 'Derivatives Sales Liability: Approach of the English and US Courts', 7 JIBL 263

Carew, E. 1995, *Derivatives Decoded*, Allen & Unwin, Sydney

CASAC 1995a, *Regulation of the OTC Derivatives Market—Discussion Paper*, Companies and Securities Advisory Committee, August

—— 1995b, *Law of Derivatives: An International Comparison*, Companies and Securities Advisory Committee, January

—— 1996a, *Regulation of On-exchange Derivatives Markets*, Companies and Securities Advisory Committee, Draft Report, June

—— 1996, *Netting in Financial Markets Transactions*, Netting Sub-Committee of the Companies and Securities Advisory Committee, Draft Report, November

Derham, R. 1987, *Set-Off*, Clarendon Press, Oxford

Everett, D. 1993, 'Multi-party Set-off Agreements', 4 JBFLP 180

Everett, D. and McCracken, S. 1997, *Banking and Financial Institutions Law*, 4th edn., LBC Information Services, Sydney

Financial Law Panel Ltd 1995, *Transactions in Derivatives, Legal Obligations of Banks to Customers, A Discussion Paper*, May

Fleming, J. 1992, *Law of Torts*, 8th edn., Law Book Co., Sydney

Group of Thirty 1993, *Derivatives: Practices and Principles*, Washington DC

Hong Kong Monetary Authority 1994, *Risk Management Guidelines for Derivatives*, December

Insurance and Superannuation Commission 1995, *Derivatives for Superannuation; Derivatives for General Insurance; Derivatives for Life Insurance*, March

—— 1996a, *Risk Management Statements for Superannuation Entities Investing in Derivatives*, April

—— 1996b, *Derivative Guidelines,* Release 1996/5

Lanyon, E. 1995, 'Derivatives and Modern Portfolio Theory: the Trustee's Duty of Investment', 6 JBFLP 58

Martin Report 1991, *A Pocket Full of Change*, House of Representatives Standing Committee on Finance and Public Administration, November

McCracken, S. 1993, *The Banker's Remedy of Set-off*, Butterworths, London
McDougall, A. 1996, 'The Prudent Trustee, Managed Funds and the Commonwealth Superannuation Industry (Superannuation) Act 1993', 7 JBFLP 93
Monetary Authority of Singapore 1995, *Guidelines on Banks' Treasury and Financial Derivatives Activities*
O'Sullivan, J. 1994, 'Derivatives—A Survey of the Law and Practice', 5 JBFLP 89
Tan, S.L. 1996, 'Swaps and Derivatives Managing Legal Risks', 11 Asia BLR 29
Wallace, I. 1994, 'Legal and Documentation Issues of Swaps and Financial Derivatives' in Das, *Swaps and Financial Derivatives*, 2nd edn., Law Book Co., Sydney
Wood, P. 1989, *English and International Set-off*, Sweet & Maxwell, London
—— 1995, *Title Finance, Derivatives, Securitisations, Set-off and Netting*, Sweet & Maxwell, London

Notes

1. See Group of Thirty 1993, Appendix 1: Working Papers, at p. 46, where it is pointed out that over 600 business relationships were involved.
2. See Carew 1995 at p. 201. Some institutions have subsequently sued in an attempt to recover payments made pursuant to the initial agreements, on the basis that the recipients have been unjustly enriched.
3. The Companies and Securities Advisory Committee in Australia also identified legal risk as a risk which has particular significance for the OTC derivatives market (CASAC 1995a, at pp. 9–10). See generally discussion of legal risk in Basle Committee on Banking Supervision 1994 and Hong Kong Monetary Authority 1994.
4. In particular, causes of action based on misrepresentation, negligence and lack of disclosure differ in scope; see for example Blair and Olive (1996).
5. This definition is based on the definition of a forward proposed by the Companies and Securities Advisory Committee (CASAC 1995a) at p. 3. It has been modified, however, to reflect within the one definition the distinction between forwards and options. Cf definition of option put forward by CASAC 1995a at p. 3.
6. See, for example, *Hazell v Hammersmith and Fulham London Borough Council* [1990] 3 All ER 33 at 63 per Woolf LJ.
7. See also the definition of derivatives in ASC 1994: 'Agreements, which establish rights and obligations relating to some underlying instrument, investment, currency, product, index, right or service.' For general discussion see O'Sullivan (1994).

8. For examples of equivalent South East Asian jurisdictions, see (Singapore) Securities Industry Act (Cap 289 Rev Ed 1985); Futures Trading Act (Cap 116 Rev Ed 1985); (Hong Kong) Securities Ordinance, Commodities Trading Ordinance.
9. *Sydney Futures Exchange Ltd v Australian Stock Exchange Ltd*, (1995) 16 ACSR 148. See generally Lawrence, 'The Regulation of Derivatives and the LEPOs Litigation', (1996) 14 C.&S.L.J. 90.
10. At law, the term commodity refers to objects which are capable of legal transfer by delivery of possession. A share cannot be transferred in this manner since it is intangible and hence incapable of possession. In fact, legal ownership of a share can only be transferred by entry on the company share register. See generally discussion in *Sydney Futures Exchange Ltd v Australian Stock Exchange Ltd*, (1995) 16 ACSR 148.
11. See *Chapter 10* for discussion of the legal definition of a futures contract.
12. Explanatory Memorandum to the Corporations Legislation Amendment Bill 1994, paras 39–40. See now Corporations Law ss72A (futures contracts), 92A (securities). See generally Donnan, 'The Share Ratio Act: Innovation or Experimentation in Securities Regulation', (1996) 14 C.&S.L.J. 101.
13. A further question could also usefully be asked: namely, does the particular industry impose restrictions on these types of transactions? The extent to which restrictions have been placed on using derivatives in particular industries will, however, be addressed in *Chapter 10*. As a matter of practice, problems are likely to arise with certain non-bank financial institutions, such as building societies and credit unions, and superannuation funds, life insurance organisations and general insurance organisations. See Insurance and Superannuation Commission (1995) and also *Chapter 5*. Under the Financial Institutions legislation in Australia, for example, building societies and credit unions can only enter into financial contracts and hedging arrangements which are approved by the Australian Financial Institutions Commission. See eg *Financial Institutions (Queensland) Act 1992* ss120, 121. Hence interest rate swap agreements will be beyond the powers of the institutions unless they are made with a bank or another approved body. In Singapore, finance companies are precluded from entering into transactions dealing in, for example, foreign currency or gold under the Finance Companies Act s23(1)(b). See generally Tan (1996).
14. It will be noted that most of the cases discussed in this context relate to swaps. This is simply an accident of litigation. There is no reason to assume that the courts' attitude would fundamentally differ at the level of general principle if they were confronted with other types of derivatives.
15. In some jurisdictions, there may additionally be requirements as to

form. In Singapore, for example, certain contracts will need to be in writing, namely, if performance is not to be made within a year: Civil Law Act s6. Such a rule used to exist in England and Australia, but has now been abolished.

16. In Australia, the legislation varies in detail from state to state. See eg *Gaming and Betting Act 1912 (NSW)*. In Singapore the equivalent prohibition is now contained in Civil Law Act s6(1). For the position in Hong Kong, see generally the Gaming Ordinance. The earlier English Gaming Act 1710 is still applicable in Hong Kong under the Application of English Law Ordinance; see generally Richardson, *Greenshields of Canada (Pacific) Limited v Keung Chak-kiu*, [1989] 1 HKLR 476.
17. *Carlill v Carbolic Smoke Ball Co* [1892] 2 QB 484 at 490, affirmed [1893] 1 QB 256.
18. *Morgan Grenfell & Co Ltd v Welwyn Hatfield District Council (Islington London Borough Council, third party)*, [1995] 1 All ER 1.
19. *Universal Stock Exchange Ltd v Strachan*, [1896] AC 166; *Re Gieve*, [1899] 1 QB 794.
20. *Morgan Grenfell & Co Ltd v Welwyn Hatfield District Council (Islington London Borough Council, third party)*, [1995] 1 All ER 1 at 7–8.
21. See eg *Earl Ellesmere v Wallace* [1929], 2 Ch 1.
22. *City Index Ltd v Leslie*, [1992] QB 98, [1991] 3 All ER 180.
23. *Morgan Grenfell & Co Ltd v Welwyn Hatfield District Council (Islington London Borough Council, third party)*, [1995] 1 All ER 1 at 10.
24. *Id.*
25. *Ibid* at 10–11.
26. Cf *Richardson Greenshields of Canada (Pacific) Ltd v Keung Chak-kiu and Hong Kong Futures Exchange Ltd*, [1989] 1 HKLR 476 where the Hong Kong High Court held that trading futures contracts on an exchange was not a game but a genuine commercial activity and therefore beyond the scope of the *Gaming Act 1710* (Eng). The fact that the investor was agreed to be a speculator was insufficient to detract from the commercial nature of the transaction. The court appears to have been persuaded by the fact that the transaction was not a 'game'. It did not consider at length the meaning of the term 'wager' which was crucial in the *Morgan Grenfell & Co Ltd v Welwyn Hatfield District Council* case. For a discussion of Australian cases, see O'Sullivan 1994.
27. *Westdeutsche Landesbank Girozentrale v Islington London Borough Council*, [1996] 2 All ER 961 at 964. No views on this point were expressed by the other members of the court.
28. For Hong Kong and Singapore equivalents, see respectively Commodities Trading Ordinance s116, Civil Law Act s6(4) and Futures Trading Act s58.

29. Corporations Law ss778, 1141.
30. ASC 1994 paras 75ff. See also CASAC 1995(a) at p. 55. Cf *Richardson Greenshields of Canada (Pacific) Limited v Keung Chak-kiu*, [1989] 1 HKLR 476.
31. Under the English Financial Services Act 1986 contracts entered into by way of business will be exempted from the gaming legislation. In *Morgan Grenfell & Co Ltd v Welwyn Hatfield District Council (Islington London Borough Council, third party)*, [1995] 1 All ER 1 Welwyn had argued that the exemption did not apply to single transactions entered into by a local authority. The argument was rejected by the court.
32. (HK) *Gambling (Amendment) Ordinance 1993* s3. Cf Irish *Netting of Financial Contracts Act 1995*. Although s4(4) states 'For the avoidance of doubt a financial contract shall not be and shall be deemed never to have been void or unenforceable by reason of the Gaming and Lotteries Acts, 1956 to 1986', it should be noted that the term 'financial contracts' is itself rather narrowly defined.
33. There is a further issue as to whether a liquidator could disclaim any particular transaction and thus make the netting obligation unworkable. In an attempt to preclude the liquidator from so acting, current practice requires the master agreement to provide that the individual transactions form part of one single contract.
34. For a discussion of some of the problems which may arise pre-insolvency, see Everett 1993.
35. See *British Eagle International Airlines Ltd v Compagnie Internationale Air France*, [1975] 1 WLR 758.
36. *National Westminster Bank Ltd v Halesowen Presswork & Assemblies Ltd*, [1972] AC 785; *Gye v McIntyre*, (1991) 65 ALJR 221.
37. In CASAC 1996 the Netting Sub-Commitee of the Companies and Securities Advisory Committee defined the process of netting in terms of a set-off. Its reasoning was stated to be set out in a Background Paper, which was not available at the time of publication.
38. *Halesowen Presswork & Assemblies Ltd v Westminster Bank Ltd*, [1971] 1 QB 1 at 46.
39. See McCracken 1993, Chapter 1. See also Derham, Chapter 10. Cf Wood 1995, Chapter 3 who characterises 'combination' rather as 'current account set-off'.
40. See discussion *supra* in text.
41. [1994] 4 All ER 890 (High Court), 957 (Court of Appeal).
42. [1994] 4 All ER 890 at 967 per Leggatt LJ.
43. The discussion focused on the nature of a claim for money had and received under an *ultra vires* contract.
44. [1995] 1 All ER 545.
45. *Ibid* at 566.
46. *Ibid* at 567.
47. Corporations Law s161.

48. Corporations Law s162.
49. Corporations Law s1324(1).
50. (Sing) Companies Act (Rev ed) s25. At the time of publication no equivalent statutory protection exists in Hong Kong, although the position is set to change with the enactment of a new statutory rule: see Deane, 1996 7JIBLN–131.
51. [1995] 1 All ER 545 at 549.
52. See Group of Thirty *supra* note 1 at p. 47.
53. Corporations Law s164(4).
54. *The Royal British Bank v Turquand*, (1856) 6 El & Bl 327; 119 ER 886.
55. (1991–1992) 7 ACSR 759; confirmed on this point on appeal in *Daniels v Anderson*, (1995) 16 ACSR 607.
56. (1991–1992) 7 ACSR 759 at 860, referring back to the discusion at 803–4.
57. *Ibid* at 804.
58. *Ibid* at 804.
59. *ANZ Executors and Trustee Company Ltd v Qintex Australia Ltd (receiver and manager appointed)*, [1991] 2 Qd R 360.
60. See eg Trustee (Unit Trust) Regulations 1986 (Vic.) under which futures contracts are regarded as authorised investments for unit trusts if they are for specified purposes, such as for protecting against movements in currency or interest rates. See Adams 1994, p. 28.
61. See cases discussed in Tan 1996.
62. [1925] Chapter 407.
63. See eg *Byrne v Baker*, [1964] VR 443.
64. Corporations Law s232(4).
65. *Daniels v Anderson*, (1995) 16 ACSR 607 at 664.
66. *Ibid* at p. 658.
67. *Re Whiteley*, (1886) 33 Ch D 347 at 355, cited in Adams 1994, p. 28.
68. *Superannuation Industry (Superannuation) Act 1993* (Cth). See generally McDougall 1996.
69. *Ibid* s52(2)(f).
70. *Foley v Hill*, (1848) 2 HLC 28. See generally Everett and McCracken 1997, *Chapter 4*.
71. *Hospital Products Ltd v United States Surgical Corporation*, (1984) 156 CLR 41.
72. *Ibid* at 97, 142.
73. For a useful discussion of potential duties of intermediaries, see Financial Law Panel Ltd 1995.
74. See eg Securities and Investments Board (UK), Statements of Principle, Principle 4.
75. It is said to date from the classic case of *Donoghue v Stevenson* [1932] AC 562.
76. *Hedley Byrne & Co Ltd v Heller and Partners Ltd*, [1964] AC 465.

77. See eg in Australia, *Mutual Life & Citizens' Assurance Co Ltd v Evatt*, (1968) 122 CLR 556 (reasoning of majority subsequently overruled); *L Shaddock & Associates Ltd v Parramatta City Council*, (1981) 150 CLR 225; *San Sebastian Pty Ltd v Minister Administering Environmental Planning and Assessment Act 1979*, (1986) 162 CLR 340; *Hawkins v Clayton*, (1988) 164 CLR 539.
78. (1986) 162 CLR 340; see also *Hawkins v Clayton*, (1988) 164 CLR 539.
79. (1988) 164 CLR 539 at 576.
80. (1991) 13 ATPR 41–103.
81. See eg *Quade & Ors v Commonwealth Bank of Australia,* (1991) 99 ALR 567, esp at 597–8 where Einfeld J set out the steps that in his view a bank would need to take to preclude a duty from being breached.
82. *Esanda Finance Corporation Ltd v Peat Marwick Hungerfords (Reg)*, (1997) 23 ACSR 71.
83. *Ibid* at 88.
84. *Id.*
85. *Ibid* at 89, cf. per Brennan at 78.
86. *Supra* n 55.

Part 3

Managing the risks

The cases described in *Part 1* raised management challenges that are still to be resolved. It is evident from *Part 2* that the process of reform in derivatives markets is far from complete. As awareness of risk grows, providers, end-users and regulators are seeking better ways to manage these risks.

Part 3 examines the path to improved risk management and analyses suggestions for reform. A range of proposals have been suggested to help avoid any repetition of the events of 1994 and 1995. The primary focus is on risk management at the microeconomic level, that is, from the perspective of an individual firm in the derivatives industry. Yet risk management is of wider significance due to the systemic risks of derivatives. Hence we also consider regulatory issues, since regulation is one manifestation of risk management at a macroeconomic level.

Management of credit and market risks has attracted enormous attention and debate in recent years. Reforms in this area have been hastened by new international regulations for banks and development of new risk measurement technologies. *Chapter 8* explains how a company can set aside appropriate capital reserves against the possibility of losses. While the details of market and credit risk assessment are technically difficult, the debate has had two welcome side effects. Firstly, risk information is much more widely available, allowing directors and senior managers to allocate resources efficiently between businesses. Secondly, the process of grappling with technical issues gives management a deeper understanding of the nature of market risk and how to manage it effectively.

Chapter 9 considers the role of the 'middle office' as a device for risk control. The middle office evolved directly from the demand from regulators and directors for independent risk assessment. Many disasters occurred because senior management lacked a detailed understanding of derivatives, and traders provided misleading or incomplete information. The middle office can be the link between the boardroom and the dealing room, with a brief to provide management information on the risks of derivatives and other instruments.

The issue of regulation is mainly dealt with in *Chapter 10*. An unrealistic approach to risk control might be to ban or restrict the use of derivatives. This would not prevent disasters and would cause loss of efficiency. Restrictions on the use of derivatives would be ineffective because any derivative instrument can, by definition, be replicated either exactly or approximately by trading in underlying instruments (see *Derivatives defined*). Moreover, risk could be increased by removing derivatives with the potential to be efficient hedging instruments. While both necessary and inevitable, regulation must be structured to encourage, not discourage, the appropriate use of derivatives.

Part 3 concludes with a discussion of management issues in new product development. The fast pace of product development in the derivatives industry is a mixed blessing. In a sense, the risks associated with, and resulting from, new product development are the same risks endemic to the industry, applying to both old and new products alike. Assiduous risk control at the stage of new product development may diminish the possibility of problems further along the product life cycle.

Part 3 gives an overview of state-of-the-art risk control, both at a technical level and at a broader managerial level. Unfortunately, state-of-the-art does not necessarily equate with a state of utopia. More remains to be done as many risks have not been adequately or uniformly addressed. Thus the process of reform must continue, as discussed in the concluding chapter.

8
Allocating capital

JOHN JARRATT

Editors' Note

Allocating capital to derivatives businesses is reliant on effective quantification of credit and market risk. Interest in quantifying credit and market risk comes from two sources, namely, regulators and senior managers. Regulators must ensure that the integrity of the global financial system is intact; that investors have confidence in the industry; and that any losses which occur are contained within a single business entity. Thus credit and market risk regulations, described in this chapter, can be viewed as risk management at a macroeconomic level.

For managers, the question of capital allocation is a broad one. It is essential that these credit and market risks are accurately measured so that appropriate capital reserves can be set aside. Quantifying risk is also essential to enable sources of risk to be identified and company resources allocated to areas which offer the most efficient risk/reward trade-off. It is self-evident that measuring risk is a necessary first step to managing it.

The quantification of credit and market risk for capital allocation can be a technical minefield. The author makes this complex area comprehensible, highlighting the most essential elements. He concludes that the debate about the use of capital, risk measurement and regulation has been extremely beneficial to the derivatives industry. Expertise in this area is now more widely spread at senior levels, reducing the chance of future disasters.

8.1 Introduction

This chapter discusses how capital can be allocated to the credit and market related risks of derivatives in a financial institution. It describes what the author sees as the most commonly used techniques in the banking industry and also incorporates, by its very nature, something of the risk management techniques used by banks for credit and market risk. It does not purport to describe all such techniques. The approach taken by regulators is also explained. Capital allocation basically has two objectives:

- to give some comfort that the institution has enough capital to withstand unexpected losses. This is of particular interest to regulators, such as central banks; and
- to allow the institution to measure the risk/reward characteristics of its various businesses and allocate a return on capital to each, if desired.

In fact, the risks of derivatives are not restricted to just credit and market risk. As described elsewhere in this book, some of the more notable derivatives disasters in financial institutions have been essentially due to a third type of risk, operational risk. It is fair to say that institutions and regulators have so far mostly (but not exclusively!) sought to control and monitor this risk by qualitative rather than quantitative means, which are not dealt with here.

8.1.1 *Credit risk*

The Basle Committee on Banking Regulations and Supervisory Practices, representing the Group of Ten Countries, published its key document entitled *International Convergence of Capital Measurement and Capital Standards* in July 1988. Since then the derivatives industry, indeed the whole banking community, has focused on the methodology to be used when measuring the appropriate amount of capital to be held against the credit and market risk associated with its business.

The Basle Committee was established by the central bank governors of the (11!) Group of Ten countries in 1975, with the Group of Ten comprising Belgium, Canada, France, Germany, Italy, Japan, The Netherlands, Sweden, Switzerland, the United Kingdom and the United States. It meets at the Bank for International Settlements (BIS) in Basle.

The output of the Basle Committee on banking supervision is a road map to the regulation of capital allocation for credit and market risk, especially for derivatives. This is because the central banks of the Group of Ten, and of other countries where major derivatives players operate, have substantially followed the methodologies of the Basle Committee for the purposes of determining capital adequacy requirements for credit and market risk. Of course, regional variations have been permitted and indeed have occurred inside the Basle guidelines.

The Basle Committee's 1988 paper did not by any means produce a methodology which was confined to derivatives. The new scheme for capital adequacy produced rules for calculating the risk adjusted value of all of a bank's assets. The intention was to relate a bank's capital adequacy to this, rather than to the gross value of assets on the balance sheet. Gross asset values were adjusted for the relative riskiness of different types of counterparty, as a first step in the process, using a weighting scheme which applied a weight of either 0 per cent, 10 per cent, 20 per cent, 50 per cent, or 100 per cent to counterparties of different perceived credit quality.

In the years prior to 1988, especially through the growth of the swaps industry in the mid-1980s, the derivatives market had increased the credit exposure of banks without adding to their balance sheets. The Basle Committee therefore also saw a need to devise a scheme which would associate an equivalent asset amount to off-balance sheet exposures. Such a scheme was incorporated in its 1988 document, with 'credit conversion' factors being assigned to different types of off-balance sheet exposure. The most difficult of these to deal with were the market related exposures created by derivatives transactions, where at one time the counterparty may owe the bank and at another time the bank may owe the counterparty, depending on the performance of market rates. This type of exposure represented a radical departure from the 'old days' of creating assets through lending money, where the borrower always owed the bank money, and led to equally radical implications for risk management and control.

Both before and after the Basle Committee's 1988 document, the derivatives industry had been working on ways to best assess the credit exposure associated with derivatives and, to a lesser extent, on ways to allocate capital against derivatives. By 1988, the larger participants in the derivatives market were already calculating the assessed exposure on market related derivatives trades for internal reasons, often in more complex ways than those proposed by Basle, and this type of development has continued. The situation remains today that there are differences between the methods used by the regulators, the smaller market participants, and the larger market participants.

8.1.2 *Market risk*

The market risk story follows that of credit risk, with the first regulatory work by the Basle Committee on capital for market risk, entitled *The Supervisory Treatment of Market Risks*, not being published until April 1993. As for credit risk, before the regulators formally introduced the idea of capital for market risk, derivatives participants had been working on this issue for some time. Indeed, the Basle scheme, which was based on 'products' rather then on 'types of risk', was rather different from many of the methods normally used in the industry for assessing market risk. It attracted a considerable amount of comment. This led to a review, with a modified version of the original Basle proposal being produced in April 1995 and finalised in January 1996. Something close to that version has been in operation since the end of 1997.

This chapter follows the story of how both the regulators and the industry's participants have dealt with the twin issues of calculating assessed exposure, and then allocating capital, to derivatives businesses. Credit risk is dealt with in *Section 8.2* and market risk in *Section 8.3*. The integration of these risks and concluding comments are discussed in *Sections 8.4* and *8.5* respectively.

8.2 Capital for credit risk

8.2.1 *The distribution of loan losses*

In the case of a loan, where the amount at risk is known, credit risk is essentially determined by two factors: the probability of counterparty default and the recovery rate upon default.

The usual approach, in a capital allocation sense, for dealing with the related uncertainty is to assume that the possible losses (or gains) from the loan exposure have a statistical probability distribution associated with them. The 'expected value' from that distribution can be factored into the pricing of the transaction. The unexpected profits or losses relating to the exposure are a function of the relevant probability distribution over time, representing the uncertainty of possible outcomes.

It is to cover these unexpected losses that a bank needs capital, as a 'buffer' against the bad times. The need to cover unexpected losses is therefore the basic premise behind capital allocation for credit risk. Analysing the probability distribution of the exposure involved is a prerequisite to calculating the capital allocation.

History provides a guide to determining the probability of default. For example, Moody's Ratings Agency publishes tables showing how many borrowers of a certain initial credit rating default over different time periods. According to figures analysed by them in 1996, covering the period 1938–95 (Moody's Investors Service 1996), a borrower who starts with an AAA rating has an average default probability of 0.13 per cent over 5 years. This compares to a probability of 0.58 per cent for a borrower who starts as an A, and one of 28.87 per cent for a borrower who starts as a B. There may be other ways of associating a probability to the default of a borrower, either subjectively or by using a model. Combining this probability of default information with information on the distribution of recovery rates in the event of a default, a statement can be made, in the case of a loan, about the expected value and the variance of the bank's possible losses from the loan.

Take a simple example, where the amount lent is \$100 with no interest payment. If the probability of default of the borrower over the period in question is 1 per cent and the recovery rate for a defaulting borrower is zero, then the loss on \$100 would be \$0 with a probability of 99 per cent and \$100 with a probability of 1 per cent. This distribution has a mean of \$1 and a variance of \$99, with a standard deviation of \$9.95. These are calculated as follows:

$$E(L) = \$0 \times 0.99 + \$100 \times 0.01 = \$1$$
$$E(L - 1)^2 = (0 - 1)^2 \times 0.99 + (100 - 1)^2 \times 0.01 = \$99$$

If the bank then factors an extra \$1 as a margin into the amount to be paid on the \$100 lent, then the expected loss is zero. However, the unexpected loss, which happens 1 per cent of the time, is \$99. Put another way, for every 100 times the bank makes this loan, on 99 of these occasions, probabilistically speaking, it makes \$1. On the 100th occasion it loses \$99, which is just covered by the 99 profits of \$1. (Incidentally, since on average this is a zero sum game, it does not represent a very good business with these numbers!)

This example illustrates the principle of how to price for expected loss. To cover the unexpected loss, the bank in this simplistic example needs to hold capital of \$99 to be certain that it could be covered.

8.2.2 *Calculating credit risk on derivatives*

The credit risk case is more complicated for derivatives, as now the amount at risk is market related and hence not definitely known. This is illustrated by the example of a bank which has a long position in US dollars (USD) against the Deutschemark (DEM) at today's exchange rate of USD/DEM 1.4800 (see *Table 8.1*). If the market moves in the bank's favour (ie USD up), but the counterparty cannot deliver on its side of the contract, then the probability of default and the recovery rate can both be measured as outlined in the loan example, but the actual size of the default amount is now also affected by how much the market has moved against the counterparty (ie the size of the asset). In this context, most stochastic market models would assume that the USD can go up or down, and that any positive exchange rate is possible with non-zero probability (see *Appendix 8.2*). The absolute 'worst case' can never be covered, and the usual approach is to work to some statistical level of confidence. In our case, if we assume a lognormal distribution for the USD/DEM rate over a 2-day period with annualised volatility of 6.00 per cent, and 260 business days in a calendar year, we get the 'one-tailed' confidence intervals for 'unexpected' loss as described in *Table 8.1*. An example of the calculations in this table, for the case of 1.96 standard deviations, is:

$$\text{Worst case exchange rate} = 1.4800 \text{ x } e^{(1.96 \times 0.06 \times \sqrt{2/260})} = 1.4953$$

The usual methodology thus chooses an appropriate (subjective) level of confidence and reduces a variable asset amount (the amount owed to us upon default) into a fixed asset amount. In this case the assessed exposure is called the 'credit equivalent' or 'loan equivalent' amount. For example, if a 99 per cent confidence interval were chosen, then the credit equivalent amount would be DEM1.83 million on a transaction amount of USD100 million, or 1.23 per cent of the principal amount.

Regulators have also addressed this problem by adopting a weighting scheme, as described later in this section, either under the 'original exposure' method or the 'current exposure' method, where interest rate and exchange rate contracts are given fixed weightings, depending on their original or remaining maturity. To better understand how this scheme relates to industry methodologies in practice, 3 'generic' examples are now considered.

Table 8.1 Assessed credit exposure for USD/DEM spot position

Confidence level	Standard deviations	Worst case exchange rate	DEM loss (mills) on USD100 million
84.0%	1.00	1.4878	0.78
95.0%	1.65	1.4929	1.29
97.5%	1.96	1.4953	1.53
97.7%	2.00	1.4957	1.57
99.0%	2.33	1.4983	1.83
99.9%	3.00	1.5036	2.36

Example 1. A forward foreign exchange contract

Take a series of forward outright contracts on USD/DEM, with the spot rate at 1.4800 and forward outright dates of one, three and five years. For a buyer of USD (seller of DEM) under these contracts, credit exposure occurs if the USD rises and the contract is 'in-the-money' at maturity. Assuming that a suitably adjusted forward rate is the mean of the distribution of spot rates at the forward date, and that the exchange rate has a lognormal distribution with a volatility of 6.00 per cent pa then, at differing levels of confidence, the assessed exposures are as shown in *Table 8.2* and *Figure 8.1 (i)*, assuming that the counterparty defaults at maturity. Credit exposures recommended by the Basle Committee are included in the table and figure for comparison, but the relativity of these to the other calculations will always be a function of volatility and one should be careful not to draw too many generic conclusions from this comparison.

The question as to what is the correct level of statistical confidence to use for the assessed exposure of the contract is crucial and lacks a definitive answer. It is clearly a subjective issue, and different institutions use different levels. Although Basle addresses this issue in the case of market risk, it sheds no real light in an analytical sense in the case of credit risk.

An institution would normally adopt a scheme which distinguishes quite finely between different time periods. Also, the volatility used for calculating assessed exposure would be updated periodically with reference to historical data.

It should also be noted that there are statistically based alternatives to the confidence interval approach. It is possible to make a case for considering the expected positive replacement cost of the contract at maturity, instead of using a confidence interval. This turns out to be closely related to the price of an option with its strike at the forward rate. Another approach is to look at the

Table 8.2 Assessed credit exposure for USD/DEM forward

Level of confidence	Number of standard deviations	Assessed exposure (% of principal) 1 year	3 years	5 years
Basle current	N/A	5.00	5.00	5.00
84.0%	1.00	6.18	10.95	14.36
Basle original	N/A	5.00	11.00	17.00
95.0%	1.65	10.41	18.71	24.78
97.5%	1.96	12.48	22.59	30.08
97.7%	2.00	12.75	23.10	30.78
99.0%	2.33	15.00	27.40	36.70
99.9%	3.00	19.72	36.58	49.55

average exposure of the contract during its life, rather than always work to the maturity date.

Example 2. Foreign exchange option

A related situation to the outright forward foreign exchange contract in *Example 1* is the case of a 1 year purchased call option on USD (put option on DEM). If the strike is at the forward rate 1.4500 then the exposure at expiry is the same as that for the forward, once the premium has been paid, since the counterparty will owe us money once the actual spot rate at maturity exceeds 1.4500. The same weightings will therefore apply. Of more interest, though, are the cases generated by different strike prices, at say 1.4000 or 1.5000. The level of confidence details are contained in *Table 8.3*.

The higher credit risk on the 1.4000 strike and the lower credit risk on the 1.5000 strike reflect the in- and out-of-the-money characteristics of these option contracts respectively.

Example 3. Interest rate swap

The first two examples have related to 'single settlement' contracts, where the final maturity date is the date on which default would most likely become apparent. An interest rate swap, however, is an example of a multi-settlement contract, where default may become apparent on any settlement date. Then the close-out value of the contract for its remaining term is the point of interest. Take a fixed-for-floating swap with quarterly reset dates over 2 years, with a fixed rate of, say, 7.07 per cent. A credit analysis of this would proceed along the lines of looking at the statistical distribution of the swap rate for the remaining term of the swap at each reset date, and then calculating the close-out value. To be

Table 8.3 Assessed credit exposure for USD/DEM one year option

Level of confidence	Number of standard deviations	Assessed exposure (%) 1.4000 strike	1.4500 strike	1.5000 strike
Basle current	N/A	9.48	7.32	6.02
84.0%	1.00	9.98	6.18	2.64
Basle original	N/A	5.00	5.00	5.00
95.0%	1.65	14.35	10.41	6.73
97.5%	1.96	16.50	12.48	8.73
97.7%	2.00	16.78	12.75	8.99
99.0%	2.33	19.11	15.00	11.17
99.9%	3.00	24.00	19.72	15.73

specific, this distribution would normally be taken to have a mean related to the forward swap rate for each reset date, with some appropriate standard deviation associated with the swap rate distribution for that date.

Such an analysis is performed in *Table 8.4* where, at inception of the swap, the quarterly forward curve is as given in Column 2, with a resulting forward swap rate for the residual term in Column 3. The 99 per cent confidence interval for the forward swap rate is based on an absolute volatility of 0.88 per cent and the close-out value assumes a constant discount rate equal to the forward swap rate implied by the 99 per cent confidence interval. A normal distribution is assumed for the swap rate.

The interesting feature of the swap exposure is that, over time, although the potential for movement in the forward swap rate increases, the number of settlement dates decreases. Hence the potential exposure peaks in the middle of the life of the swap, rather than at its end as in the case of the forward and option contracts in *Examples 1* and 2, which are single settlement contracts (see *Figure 8.1(ii)*). Because of the multiple settlement dates, the exposure is in some sense 'paid up' in part at each settlement date, and this effect counteracts the effect of the potential for greater rate movements as time passes. There is therefore a question as to the best value to take to reflect the assessed exposure of the swap. The peak value of 2.33 per cent is a candidate, as is the average value of 1.58 per cent. The number produced by the Basle Accord in this situation would be 0.50 per cent under the current exposure method and 2.00 per cent under the original exposure method.

A more complex example than the swap is generated by moving to the case of, say, a 9.00 per cent cap, assuming the same

Table 8.4 Assessed credit exposure for fixed-for-floating interest rate swap

Quarter	Forward rate for quarter	Forward swap rate for residual term	99% Confidence interval on forward swap rate	Close-out value as % of principal
1	6.85	7.07	7.07	0
2	6.65	7.10	8.13	1.71%
3	6.68	7.18	8.63	2.18%
4	6.88	7.29	9.06	2.33%
5	7.13	7.39	9.44	2.24%
6	7.34	7.48	9.78	1.94%
7	7.50	7.56	10.07	1.45%
8	7.62	7.62	10.33	0.80%

initial term structure as in the swap example. Now the residual cap at each reset date must be revalued, taking into account the potential forward rates for the residual life of the cap, since individual forwards are important for the valuation of each caplet. In fact, this situation is still more complex since, as with all options, implied volatility inputs are needed to revalue the residual cap at each reset date, and some confidence level for potential variation in these needs also to be taken into account. This is a case when two variables are involved and, to provide a theoretically sound assessment, the joint distribution of these variables should be looked at.

8.2.3 *Netting and the aggregation of exposure*

The examples of credit assessment considered above relate to individual transactions only. In fact, it is more usually the case that there is a portfolio of transactions, either with the same counterparty or a range of different counterparties, possibly across different markets.

The case for using a 'net' position applies in the credit risk case where there is an enforceable netting agreement in place with the counterparty. In this situation, adding the exposure of individual transactions would overstate the risk, since the losses from one transaction can be offset by any profits from other transactions, and it is only the net position which is a true measure of exposure.

In the case where there is no netting agreement in place, adding individual exposures is again relevant, since the liquidator of a counterparty may seek to 'cherry-pick' only those transactions

Figure 8.1 Assessed exposure for credit

(i) Assessed exposure on forwards

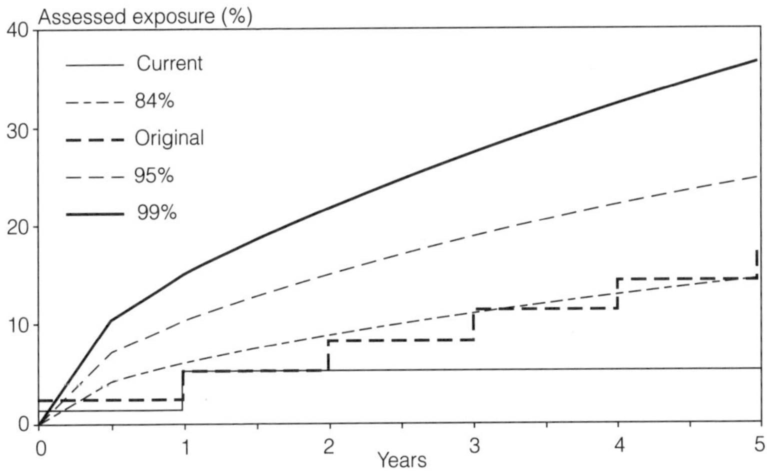

(ii) Assessed exposure on swap

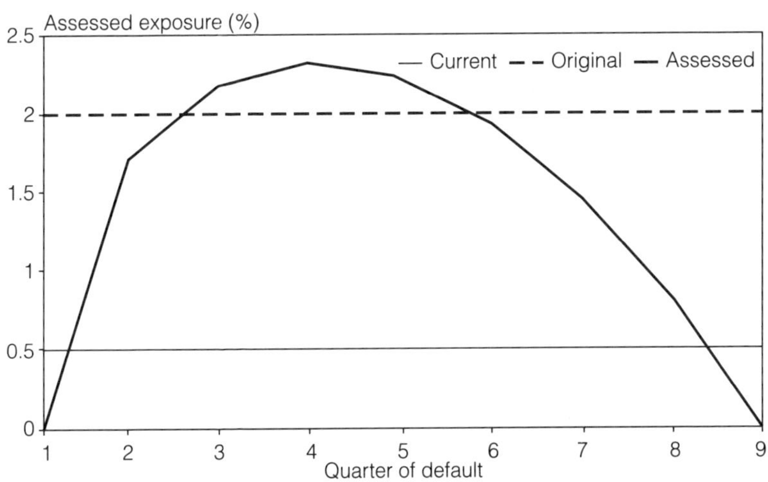

which are profitable to the counterparty and to default on all others. Some of these issues are discussed more fully in *Chapter 7*.

To illustrate these concepts by means of the USD/DEM example, suppose that a bank has a long USD position of 100 million against the DEM and a short USD position of 75 million for the same date, both with the same counterparty. From a market risk perspective, this is an effective position of only USD25 million, since any losses on the 100 million position will be offset by profits on the 75 million position. For example, if the exchange rate moves to 1.4722 by settlement date, the bank loses DEM0.78 million on one position but makes DEM0.58 million on the other.

From a credit risk perspective, if these transactions are with the same counterparty, then the offset described above will only be valid if the bank can legally net the positions upon settlement. If, instead, no netting agreement is in place and the counterparty decides to demand payment on the first contract but default on the second, then the bank is 'out of pocket' by 0.58 million. If the contracts are with different counterparties then, for credit purposes, no degree of offset could be expected, and the risk on each counterparty must be assessed separately.

The above example dealt with two contracts which matured on the same date in the same currency pair. In fact, the real world is more complex than this in general, and the 'nettable' position with a single counterparty may consist of a wide range of positions across different markets and for different dates. The statistical distribution of the net position for the purposes of calculating market risk or credit exposure to a single counterparty then becomes a complicated function of the distributions of all the market variables involved, and especially of their variances and correlations. The task of assigning an assessed exposure and thence capital allocation to the portfolio of positions necessitates either analytical or numerical techniques for studying the distribution of the aggregation of positions (see *Appendix 8.3*).

For example, if the 100 million long USD/DEM position above were combined with a short 100 million USD/JPY position, a bank's calculation may look something like that in *Table 8.5* (assuming a volatility of 6.5 per cent for USD/JPY, 6.00 per cent for USD/DEM and a correlation of 0.5 between them).

The standard deviation of the portfolio is calculated using the formula for the variance of a difference of correlated random variables, and the calculation of assessed exposure assumes normality for the distribution of the difference (see *Appendix 8.2*).

Notice that the assessed exposure of the portfolio is substan-

Table 8.5 Aggregating credit exposures

Position	Current rate	Standard deviation of position value (USD million)	Assessed exposure (99% confidence) (USD million)
Long USD vs DEM (100 million USD)	1.4800	0.53	1.23
Short USD vs JPY (100 million USD)	110.00	0.57	1.33
Both positions	N/A	0.55	1.28

tially less than the sum of the exposures of the individual transactions in it. This takes advantage of the assumed correlation between the USD/DEM and USD/JPY exchange rates and the fact that one position is long whilst the other is short USD. To put this in context, for correlations of –1, 0, 1 the assessed exposure of the portfolio would be 2.56 million, 1.81 million and 0.11 million respectively.

It is because of these advantages, both in a credit exposure and capital saving sense, that netting is such an important issue in the industry.

8.2.4 *Portfolio diversification*

As already remarked, if transactions with a single counterparty are not able to be legally netted, or if a portfolio of transactions relate to all different counterparties, then the distribution of the net position, calculated from the distributions of the individual transactions, is not relevant for credit risk exposure purposes.

There is, however, a further offset sometimes used by banks in the case of non-nettable credit exposure with different counterparties. As explained earlier for the case of a loan, the distribution of the total actual amount lost is a function of the probability of default itself. If a counterparty has a probability of default of 0.99, then the expected loan loss is 1 per cent of the principal amount and the standard deviation is 9.95 per cent of the principal. However, if the bank lends to two such counterparties, whose events of default are independent, then the situation in *Table 8.6* applies.

The expected loan loss of the portfolio is therefore 1 per cent of the \$100 lent, but the standard deviation is now only 7.04 per cent of the portfolio value. This type of portfolio diversification mitigates the risk of a portfolio where a range of counterparties is involved, especially if the default correlations of different

Table 8.6 Diversifying credit exposure

Counterparty 1 defaults	Counterparty 2 defaults	Probability	Amount of loss
Yes	Yes	0.0001	$100
Yes	No	0.0099	$50
No	Yes	0.0099	$50
No	No	0.9801	$0

counterparties are not too high. So, for example, exposure to many counterparties from a single industry grouping is more dangerous than exposure to a wide range of counterparties from different industry groupings (as many banks have found out over the years!).

8.2.5 *Capital allocation for credit risk*

The general model described here for allocating capital to credit risk first associates a weighting with each counterparty, which reflects the unexpected loss on a loan and incorporates information on the probability of default and the recovery rate. This counterparty risk weighting factor is then usually multiplied by the credit equivalent amount of a derivatives contract to produce a capital allocation, designed to cover unexpected losses. A more sophisticated model than this would look at the joint distribution of default probability with market rates, seeing some degree of possible correlation between certain rate movements and default eg a highly leveraged borrower may be more likely to default when rates rise.

In general, a financial institution will have a relatively finely tuned set of weightings representing the confidence intervals of default distributions and recovery rates for counterparties of different credit standing. To have some feeling of how these might operate, the reader is referred again to Moody's tables (Moody's Investors Service 1996), particularly Table 10 where the default tables for different credit ratings and different time periods give some idea of the complexity of the problem. A more detailed study is outside the scope of this chapter.

Also, a financial institution will normally have a probabilistic scheme for calculating the credit equivalent amount of a derivatives contract, as outlined in this section. It is now time to relate these to the Basle Scheme.

8.2.6 *The Basle 1988 Accord*

The final proposals published by the Basle Committee dealing with capital for credit risk were circulated in July 1988, after a period of industry consultation (Bank for International Settlements 1988). The basic methodology is as outlined above, involving the calculation of a risk adjusted asset value by multiplying the asset amount by a counterparty risk weighting, which could be either 0 per cent, 10 per cent, 20 per cent, 50 per cent or 100 per cent. After applying these risk weightings to the credit equivalent amount, Basle imposes a regulatory capital requirement of 8 per cent[1] of the resulting risk adjusted asset. In terms of the scheme above, this basically corresponds to a risk weighting factor of either 0 per cent, 0.80 per cent, 1.60 per cent, 4.00 per cent or 8.00 per cent, depending on the type of counterparty. These numbers can therefore be taken to represent, in some sense, the regulatory view of unexpected losses, at some level of confidence. For a loan, the credit equivalent amount is simply the face value of the loan. For off-balance sheet transactions, the credit equivalent amount is arrived at by multiplying the notional amount by a credit conversion factor.

In the counterparty risk weighting scheme, examples of exposures attracting differing weightings are:

- 0 per cent—cash, gold, claims on central governments denominated and funded in national currency;
- 20 per cent—OECD incorporated banks;
- 50 per cent—housing loans (under certain conditions); and
- 100 per cent—claims on the private sector.

These weightings are left open for final interpretation by different regulatory authorities to suit local conditions.

Credit conversion factors for off-balance sheet items deal with a range of non-market related exposures, such as financial guarantees and stand-by letters of credit by using fixed credit conversion factors.

For market related derivatives exposures, such as interest rate and foreign exchange contracts, however, the credit equivalent amount can be calculated in two ways:

- the *current exposure* method, where the current mark-to-market valuation and an estimate of potential future exposure are added together; or
- the *original exposure* method, where a single conversion factor is applied to the notional amount at inception and does not change throughout the life of the contract.

Under the current exposure method, the mark-to-market valuation would only be included if it represented a positive replacement cost, otherwise this would be taken to be zero. The potential exposure estimates, as a function of the remaining term to maturity, are defined in *Table 8.7*.

Table 8.7 Current exposure method

Remaining term	Interest rate contracts	Foreign exchange contracts
Less than 1 year	0	1.0%
1 year or longer	0.5%	5.0%

Table 8.8 Original exposure method

Original term	Interest rate contracts	Foreign exchange contracts
Less than 1 year	0.5%	2.0%
1 to 2 years	1.0%	5.0%
For each additional year	1.0%	3.0%

Under the original exposure method, credit conversion factors are defined in *Table 8.8*.

These credit conversion factors were the result of some quite detailed statistical analysis by the Basle Group, 'developed using Monte Carlo simulations of matched pairs of representative transactions and . . . intended to provide reasonable prudential coverage for a high proportion of potential exposures' (Basle Committee on Banking Supervision 1994). However, the factors were kept simple in the final proposal. Generally in the industry substantially more complex methods are used at the transactional level.

An interesting feature of the counterparty risk weighting scheme for derivatives transactions is that this weighting can never be more than 50 per cent for private sector counterparties, despite the fact that a loan to such a counterparty will attract 100 per cent. This is justified on the grounds that 'most counterparties in these markets, particularly for longer term contracts, tend to be first-class names'. Some local regulators reserve the right not to follow this particular part of the Accord and still use 100 per cent for some counterparties.

Local regulators have amended, clarified and expanded the different features of the Accord to more closely meet local requirements. The original Basle Accord has essentially had three amendments since its first introduction in 1988.

The first of these, relating to bilateral netting, was finally published in April 1995 (Basle Committee on Banking Supervision 1995b). In its final form, this amendment allows for a reduction in capital requirement for off-balance sheet items where, under certain conditions ultimately to be agreed with a bank's national supervisor, an enforceable netting agreement is in place with a counterparty. In these circumstances, under the current exposure method the mark-to-market valuation can be calculated on a net basis and the add-on for potential exposure can be calculated as a weighted sum (40% to 60%) of the gross add-ons and the gross add-ons adjusted by the ratio of current net replacement value to current gross replacement value. There was also a suitable amendment to the conversion factors to be used under the original exposure method to deal with netting.

The second amendment (Basle Committee on Banking Supervision 1995b) relates to an expanded matrix of add-on factors for use in the current exposure method. This was specifically designed to cover long dated swaps equity derivatives and commodity swaps which, it was felt, had not been adequately dealt with in the original accord.

8.3 Capital for market risk

8.3.1 *Assessing market risk*

The third amendment relates to market risk, which is the risk that money will be lost because of market movements. It is not related to credit risk in this narrow context since, in the event of a loss on a single transaction, the counterparty is owed money rather then vice versa. For example, if a bank's foreign exchange desk goes long USD and short DEM at 1.4800, then there is a risk that the bank will lose money if the USD loses value, and ends up below 1.4800 (say at 1.4600). There is also a chance, of course, that the bank will make money from this position if the USD strengthens.

It is useful to return now to *Table 8.1*, which highlights the credit risk associated with this situation. To analyse the market risk of this transaction, it is necessary to look at the confidence interval analysis of *Table 8.9*, which considers a falling rather than a rising USD.

Choice of an appropriate confidence interval will lead to an assessed exposure and a capital allocation for unexpected loss. Again, there is no choice of capital allocation which will cover the unexpected loss with absolute certainty. Included in *Table 8.9*

Table 8.9 Assessed market exposure for USD/DEM spot position over two days

Confidence level	Standard deviations	Exchange rate	DEM loss (millions) on USD100 million
84.0%	1.00	1.4722	0.78
95.0%	1.65	1.4672	1.28
97.5%	1.96	1.4648	1.52
97.7%	2.00	1.4645	1.55
99.0%	2.33	1.4620	1.80
99.9%	3.00	1.4568	2.32

are the most commonly used 'one-tailed' confidence intervals, given that it is losses, not profits, which are of interest for market exposure purposes.

8.3.2 *Calculating value-at-risk*

The discussion begun in the last section, on aggregated credit risk exposure for 'nettable' market related portfolios, is a good lead in to the question of market risk exposure. For market risk, the assessment problem is always one of measuring the assessed exposure of a portfolio of transactions over different markets with different market risk variables involved.

The context now is that of a trading portfolio, where the credit exposure to the counterparties to transactions in the portfolio is not the point of focus. The exposure to be measured is usually shorter in term than the credit case, typically about 1 day to 2 weeks, due to the assumed ability to close out mark-to-market positions in a relatively short time-frame. Again the need is to assess a 'worst case' scenario with some level of confidence. This means that, whilst recognising that any portfolio value may be possible tomorrow with non-zero probability, confidence intervals need to be determined from the probability distribution of portfolio values. Capital allocation for market risk follows from this.

In the context of market risk, the probabilistically determined amount at risk for a trading portfolio is usually called the Value-at-Risk (VAR). It is no understatement to say that an entire 'industry' has almost been built up around the VAR concept, so useful a tool is it deemed to be. This industry ranges from pure advice, to the marketing of sophisticated systems designed to handle VAR calculations for the most complex of portfolios involving the most complex of products (*Risk* 1996).

There are a range of techniques for calculating VAR which

basically divide into analytical and numerical techniques. These are discussed in *Appendix 8.3* and in summary are:

- analytical techniques
  - — monotonic function approach
  - — domain approach
  - — range approach; and
- numerical techniques
  - — simulation method
  - — historical method
  - — stress and scenario testing.

8.3.3 *How useful is VAR?—Risk measurement and management*

The VAR approach to the risk measurement of market related portfolios has wide appeal, because it produces a single number which measures the quantum of risk. This is useful for high level reporting, for measuring the relative risk between portfolios, and for comparing yesterday's risk with today's risk. It is also a useful tool for capital allocation.

However, VAR does have severe limitations. The example in *Appendix 8.4* discusses a situation where the normal VAR calculation can produce some strange results in a 'risk management' sense, even though they may be theoretically sound in a 'risk measurement' sense.

There are other more mainstream problems with the VAR approach:

- the distributional assumptions on market variables may not be valid;
- the distributional assumptions on the portfolio value may not be valid; and
- parameters estimated from historical data may not be stable over time.

It is possible to extend and modify VAR to attempt to treat some of these problems. For example, a stochastic volatility model, such as Generalised Autoregressive Conditional Heteroscedasticity (GARCH) [editors' note: see Bollerslev et al. 1992], may better model the volatility parameter and a technique such as historical simulation can avoid distributional assumptions.

Management should be careful not to rely on VAR as its only risk measure. VAR presents a useful framework for looking at risk, but it is not all encompassing as a risk measure and should not be regarded as such. It is too coarse a measure for this.

VAR is a tool which is not extensively used by risk managers in the line. They focus on structural risk measures, which might be volumes in their coarsest form but usually extend to a host of sensitivity measures (delta, gamma, vega, theta, basis point value) and 'what if' analyses and to other qualitative risk measures, relating to people and controls. A more comprehensive discussion of this is included in *Chapter 9*.

8.3.4 *Capital allocation for market risk*

The final step in the capital allocation for market risk under a VAR approach is now to determine the parameters to be used. The main quantitative parameters laid down by Basle specify a 99 per cent one-tailed confidence interval (2.33 standard deviations on a normal distribution) and a 10 day holding period. The Basle methodology would then compare this number to the average VAR of the previous 60 business days multiplied by the multiplication factor (minimum of 3) with a possible further add-on between 0 and 1. The capital charge is the higher of the two.

In their internal capital allocation systems, institutions adopt a variety of confidence levels, mostly in the 95–99 per cent region, but holding periods can be as long as one year.

By looking at examples such as those in *Table 8.9*, it is obvious that the choice of parameters makes a significant difference to the market risk exposure number and hence the capital requirement. On the one-tailed lognormal confidence interval approach in the example, the assessed exposure as a percentage of principal goes up approximately 42 per cent when moving from 95 per cent to 99 per cent confidence and the difference between a two day and a 10 day holding period amounts to a factor of approximately $\sqrt{5}$, or 2.24. It is therefore not surprising that the Basle Committee has set quantitative standards for these parameters to attempt to set a level playing field. Having said this, the capital requirement for market risk is likely to be a small proportion of that for credit risk for most institutions.

8.3.5 *Basle market risk proposal*

The amendment to the Basle Accord relating to capital allocation for market risk was first published for comment in April 1993 (Basle Committee on Banking Supervision 1993) and set out a scheme of capital allocation for market risk based on a product approach. This attracted a great deal of comment in the industry. A revised version of this proposal was put out in April 1995 (Basle

Committee on Banking Supervision 1995a) which incorporated the option for banks to use their own in-house models to calculate market risk. After a further period of consultation, the final amendment was published in January 1996 (Basle Committee on Banking Supervision 1996), to be implemented by the end of 1997.

The proposal covers market risks which pertain to interest rates and equities in the 'trading book' only, but it is intended to cover foreign exchange and commodities risk throughout the bank. There is clearly some potential for the 'trading book' classification to create a non-level playing field if it is interpreted differently by different central banks, although the Basle proposal does go to some lengths to clarify this position and provides a definition of what constitutes the trading book. Also, there is a close association made between positions in the trading book and positions which are accounted for on a mark-to-market basis, even though there is a recognition that some mark-to-market items may be outside the trading book and vice versa. The final Basle proposal for market risk allows for 2 methods of calculating capital for market risk: the 'standardised approach' and the 'model user approach'.

The standardised approach looks at the 4 markets of interest rates, equities, foreign exchange and commodities separately, and basically 'builds up' a capital requirement by looking at the different risks associated with the instruments in each market. Derivatives positions are, in general, converted into equivalent positions in the relevant underlying asset eg a fixed for floating interest rate swap is treated as 2 notional positions in securities, one (the floating side) maturing on the next reset date and the other (the fixed side) maturing on the same maturity date as the swap. Special treatment is given to options, due to the essential difficulty of incorporating them in the above framework.

The interest rate and equity sections of the standardised methodology impose 2 types of capital charge—one for 'specific risk' and the other for 'general market risk'. The specific risk charge is designed to cover the price risk relating to the individual debt or equity issuer, whereas the general market risk charge covers the risk of price movements in the market as a whole. The specific risk charge therefore allows debt and equity securities in the trading book to be excluded from the capital allocation for credit risk.

The standardised methodology for general market risk is essentially more complex for interest rates and commodities than for foreign exchange and equity products. This is because the interest rate and commodity cases incorporate charges for 'curve risk', whereas in the foreign exchange and equity case any interest rate curve risk resulting from forward positions is allocated to the interest rate section of the capital calculation.

Under the standardised methodology options always obtain special treatment, since they do not easily fit into the scheme described above, as we have mentioned. Apart from a simple approach relevant to long option positions only, there is a choice between the 'delta plus' method and the 'scenario' method. The delta plus method converts option positions into an equivalent underlying position using the delta and then slots them into the underlying position calculation as described earlier. Recognising that this approach omits gamma and vega risk, there are additional charges imposed for these. Under the 'scenario' method, a matrix analysis is performed where underlying rates and implied volatility parameters are simultaneously varied and the portfolio revalued at each point in the matrix, taking the worst case for the portfolio value. This scenario approach is the part of the standardised methodology which most closely approaches a VAR framework.

The standardised methodology, after it was first presented in April 1993, attracted considerable comment from users of the derivatives markets. Banks and financial institutions, driven by the development of derivatives technology, were already, and had for some time, been using considerably more sophisticated methods than this product based 'building block' approach. The industry thought in terms of sensitivity measures (delta, gamma, vega, basis point value) and VAR and it 'unbundled' products into their risk types, performing complex analysis on each type of risk and its correlation with other types. Option pricing theory had not only provided a means of valuing complex options, but also provided a risk measurement and risk management framework for derivatives in general. Advanced technology and systems had been developed to accommodate this approach.

The standardised methodology therefore had 2 main drawbacks. It had the potential to fail to be a sufficiently accurate measure for the risk of many institutions, resulting in a possible misallocation of capital or a mismatch between regulatory and internal capital. It also would force many institutions to develop a separate, less advanced systems environment just for regulatory reporting, at considerable cost.

Basle was asked to rethink the 1993 proposal, and the result was a revised approach (first produced in April 1995 and finalised in January 1996), which still incorporates the standardised methodology but allowed 'model users' to use their own systems, subject to certain guidelines and standards. These standards were both qualitative and quantitative. The qualitative standards relate principally to the involvement of the board and senior management in monitoring derivatives activity; the existence of an independent risk control unit to design risk management procedures and monitor positions; and the regular back testing of models to measure their effectiveness, as well as stress testing to supplement the model analysis.

The main requirements of the quantitative standards are:

- a one-tailed 99 per cent confidence interval for calculating VAR;
- a 10 day holding period; and
- historical data for calculating VAR parameters which must go back at least 1 year.

Under the model user approach, the capital requirement is the higher of the previous day's VAR number and the average VAR over the previous 60 business days, times a multiplication factor, set by the individual supervisory authority and based on 'their assessment of the quality of the bank's risk management system, subject to an absolute minimum of 3'. Moreover, this multiplication factor is subject to a 'plus' related to the performance of the bank's model. This plus can be anywhere between 0 and 1, based on the outcome of back testing, which principally involves a comparison of a bank's daily VAR measure with the actual profit and loss over historical periods. In this context, included with the January 1996 final Basle proposal on market risk is a supplement on back testing. Rather like traffic lights, back-testing results can either come up green, yellow or red indicating, on statistical grounds, whether the back-testing results are consistent with the 99 per cent confidence interval (green), could be inconsistent (yellow) or are almost certainly inconsistent (red).

Given that the model user approach is now incorporated, industry comment on the final Basle proposal of January 1996 has tended to focus on some of the quantitative standards.

A final feature of the Basle proposal for market risk is the expansion of the type of capital which may be used to cover market risk, over and above that used for credit risk. The Basle proposal allows for the use of Tier 3 capital, which is short-dated subordinated debt (at least 2 years original maturity) subject to a 'lock-in' clause preventing the payment of principal and interest in the event that the bank's overall capital would then amount to less than its minimum requirement. Some supervisory authorities (notably the Reserve Bank of Australia) have already indicated that they will not allow the use of Tier 3 capital to cover market risk.

8.3.6 *Other work by regulatory and industry groups*

As well as the Basle Accord and its amendments, there have been a number of other publications by regulators and industry bodies which have represented milestones in the development of the control environment for derivatives and the related capital adequacy issues. These are listed in the references and include, notably, the European Capital Adequacy Directive (CAD) and the Study by the Group of Thirty.

8.4 Integration of credit and market risk

The Basle capital allocation system, since the publication of the final market risk proposal in January 1996, now provides a scheme for calculating the total capital requirement of an institution relating to credit and market risk. Institutions themselves have schemes which differ in a number of key aspects. There is still much work to be done in refining these systems and making them more sophisticated, whilst retaining the essential simplicity of the output eg VAR.

One interesting question now for institutions, both in relation to the Basle methodology and in relation to their own internal capital allocation systems, is to what extent the separate capital allocations for credit and market risks are comparable ie to what extent are we comparing 'apples with apples'. For example, the credit risk and market risk numbers for a single DEM/USD 1 year forward contract calculated at 99 per cent, using a 1-year maturity for the horizon of the credit exposure but 10 days for the market risk, are quite different at 15.00 per cent and 2.78 per cent respectively. This is reasonable, since we must endure the credit risk under potential favourable market movements for 1 year, whereas the market risk under unfavourable market movements can be closed out tomorrow leaving two credit risks but no market risk.

Ultimately, the methodologies we have employed for both credit and market risk are based on the distribution of losses. They attempt to allocate capital based on the variance of this distribution, choosing a level of confidence which allows sufficient buffer for all but a small proportion of cases. The strength of the methodology as applied to each type of risk depends on the validity of the distributional assumptions and on the estimation of parameters; there are many simplifications involved in both. Although the methodologies for allocating capital to both risks have many features in common, the assumptions relating to confidence intervals and holding periods cannot always be the same or directly comparable.

8.5 Conclusion

Assessing the comparability of capital allocation to credit and market risk related businesses is critical to the task of equitably comparing the return on capital for these businesses. This is important because, whereas the regulatory approach to capital allocation may be to ensure that a financial institution has sufficient capital to cover extraordinary losses, managers should have a broader perspective. The final objective of a bank's internal capital allocation system is also to look at the returns generated by a business compared to the capital it consumes, in a full risk adjusted performance measurement (RAPM) approach. As well as credit and market risk, there is a need to look at operational and liquidity risk at least, and possibly others for this purpose, and to be able to compare the capital allocations for each type of risk.

The final questions in this chapter probably should be: Do these capital allocation systems work? Do the systems allocate enough capital for the risks encountered? In an absolute sense the questions can only be answered by experience over time. Paradoxically though, the issue of the quantum of capital provided may not be the most important. The strength of the methodology for risk measurement and risk management purposes can be an even more important feature in general. For example, the capital allocated to market risk in a particular institution may be relatively small, but the level of sophistication introduced into that institution's risk management systems to allow VAR to be calculated may carry enormous value in a risk management sense. This is not to mention the level of increased management understanding, which is hopefully induced by the whole process! This may ultimately be the best safeguard against disaster.

Appendix 8.1 The tiers of capital—The Basle definition

Tier 1

- Paid-up share capital/common stock; and
- disclosed reserves.

Tier 2

- Undisclosed reserves;
- asset revaluation reserves;
- general provisions/general loan loss reserves;
- hybrid (debt/equity) capital instruments; and
- subordinated term debt.

Tier 3 (introduced for market risk only)

Short-term subordinated debt (original maturity of at least 2 years) which satisfies certain special conditions, notably that it is subject to a lock-in clause which stipulates that neither interest nor principal may be paid if such payment means that the bank falls below or remains below its minimum capital requirement.

The sum of Tier 1 and Tier 2 capital is eligible for inclusion in the capital base, but Tier 2 must not exceed Tier 1 and subordinated debt may not exceed 50 per cent of Tier 1. Tier 3 capital is limited to 250 per cent of a bank's Tier 1 capital that is required to support market risks.

Goodwill, investments in unconsolidated banking and financial subsidiary companies and investments in the capital of other banks and financial institutions (the latter at the discretion of national authorities) are deductions from the capital base.

Appendix 8.2 Mathematical background

In general in this chapter, a stochastic process for rates is assumed as follows:

$$dS = \mu S dt + \sigma S dW$$

where W is a standard Wiener process, implying that the distribution of S_t is lognormal, given by:

$$\ln(S_t/S_0) = (\mu - \tfrac{1}{2}\sigma^2)t + \sigma\sqrt{t}Z$$

where Z is a standard normal variable.

A normality assumption is used, as opposed to lognormality, in two cases. First, in the case of the distribution of a linear combination of two exchange rates in *Section 8.2.3*. Just because the rates themselves are lognormally distributed, this does not mean that the linear combination is lognormal (or indeed normal!). However, under the range approach, the assumption of normality is frequently used in this situation for ease of calculation and we have followed this course.

The rest of the associated calculation in *Section 8.2* follows from the fact that for two variables X_1 and X_2 with standard deviations σ_1 and σ_2 and correlation ρ, then a portfolio with value $P = \alpha X_1 + \beta X_2$ has standard deviation:

$$\sigma_P = \sqrt{\alpha^2\sigma_1{}^2 + \beta^2\sigma_2{}^2 + 2\rho\alpha\beta\sigma_1\sigma_2}$$

In the example of *Section 8.2*, the assumption is that the exchange rates are lognormally distributed so the standard deviations of their distributions (in USD) over two days are:

USD/DEM: 0.003556
USD/JPY: 0.000052
The correlation is 0.5.
The portfolio standard deviation is then:

$$\sigma_P = \sqrt{0.276979 + 0.327184 - 0.301037} = 0.550569$$

Multiplying each standard deviation by the one-tailed 99 per cent standard normal value of 2.33 yields the 99 per cent confidence intervals.

The other occasion on which a normality assumption is used is in relation to the distribution of swap rates in Example 3 of *Section 8.2.3*. This is because normality, as opposed to lognormality, is a common assumption for interest rates.

Appendix 8.3 Techniques for calculating VAR

a) *Analytical approaches*

Monotonic function approach

This approach is the simplest method of calculating VAR, but it is really only usable in certain portfolios—where all contracts relate closely to a single variable, and are either increasing or decreasing functions of that variable, so that the confidence intervals of the portfolio value can be translated directly across from those of the market variable. Although the portfolio may be sensitive to other variables, the risk associated with these needs to be secondary. The examples in *Section 8.2* relating to exchange rates and swaps employ this technique. This technique can be extended to what David Rowe (1995) calls 'The Primary Risk Source Approach'.

The domain[2] approach

The domain approach is often used where other market variables clearly have a marked effect on a portfolio's value and cannot be relegated to 'secondary' status. A good example of this is a currency options portfolio. The main risk variables are spot exchange rates, interest rates and implied volatilities. Spot rates are a clear primary risk source, as are volatilities, but currency option values are less sensitive to interest rates and these can be relegated to secondary status.

An example of this approach is contained in *Table 8.10*, where a matrix of portfolio values for an options portfolio on Eurodollar futures is presented. The portfolio consists of 50 lots each of 94.00 calls and puts held short and 60 lots of 94.50 calls and 93.50 puts held long. This type of matrix is often called the 'contingent loss' matrix and corresponds to the scenario method for assessing option exposure under the Basle standardised methodology. The range of values for futures prices and implied volatilities is designed to produce a confidence region in the two dimensional joint probability space, and the worst case in the matrix (–13 000 in this case) is taken to be the VAR. Although this technique is frequently still used for options books, it has the weakness that the two dimensional 'grid' of portfolio values has the potential to miss intermediate points in the confidence region which give a worse result than those shown. To deal with this problem properly, some appropriate quantitative search technique from the field of optimisation theory needs to be adopted. Also, to ascertain the

Table 8.10 Contingent loss matrix (000s) for Eurodollar futures options portfolio (106 days to expiry)

Futures price	Implied volatility (%) 11.00	12.00	13.00	14.00	15.00	16.00	17.00
95.50	(1.5)	(1.5)	(1.5)	(1.5)	(1.5)	(1.5)	(1.4)
95.00	(13.0)	(12.6)	(12.1)	(11.6)	(11.0)	(10.3)	(9.7)
94.50	(9.0)	(8.3)	(7.6)	(7.1)	(6.8)	(6.5)	(6.2)
94.00	4.2	2.6	1.2	0.0	(1.0)	(1.9)	(2.6)
93.50	(7.7)	(7.2)	(6.7)	(6.4)	(6.2)	(6.0)	(5.8)
93.00	(10.7)	(9.8)	(8.9)	(8.0)	(7.2)	(6.5)	(5.8)
92.50	(1.3)	(1.0)	(0.7)	(0.4)	0.0	0.5	1.0

confidence interval attached to the region, assumptions need to be made about the joint probability distributions of futures prices and implied volatilities. In general, the mathematical complexity of the problems described make the domain approach difficult to apply in practice once the number of risk variables is large, although there are many cases where it clearly gives a more sensible 'risk management' perspective than the alternative range approach (discussed next).

The range approach

The range approach is the one most often used in practice when an analytical result is desired. The approach usually works by assuming that portfolio values over the time horizon in question have a known and 'tractable' distribution, usually normal. The parameters of this distribution are determined from those of the risk variables which 'drive' the portfolio's value. This technique can have the weakness that, except when the portfolio value is a linear function of the driving variables, the convenient normality assumption is suspect, especially for options.

Nonetheless, the technique is probably the most commonly used and an example of how it works for a portfolio of two exchange rate positions is included in *Section 8.2*. The mathematics of this example are included in *Appendix 8.2*.

This version of the range approach, using a normality assumption, is the one employed by J.P. Morgan in their RiskMetrics methodology. J.P. Morgan made the RiskMetrics system for measuring market risk publicly available in 1994 and it has since been widely used in the industry. The methodology in the system uses a comprehensive set of volatilities and correlations and covers a wide range of market variables to calculate VAR. The reader is referred to J.P. Morgan and Co. (1994) for a full description of the technicalities. More recently, a number of other banks have introduced products with similar characteristics (*Risk* 1996), although the methodologies are not all comparable. These include CS First Boston (PrimeRisk), Chase Manhattan (Charisma), Bankers Trust (Raroc 2000) and Deutsche Bank (db-Analyst 2.0). An example contrasting the range and domain approaches is detailed in *Appendix 8.4*.

To further illustrate some of the concepts introduced in this section, consider the Contingent Loss Matrix for the Eurodollar options portfolio in *Table 8.10*. Ignoring volatility movements for the moment, contemplation of the variation in portfolio value over a range of futures prices at the current volatility of 14.00 per cent reveals that the distribution of portfolio values is very far from normal. This is easy to see, since the portfolio value is never less than –11 600, whereas a normal distribution can take all values. The analytic range approach therefore has great difficulty dealing with such a portfolio, unless some other distribution can be easily identified. This situation is likely to occur whenever non-linear portfolio valuation functions are involved, and it is even more extreme in the case of exotic option portfolios. A numerical technique is needed for determining confidence intervals. However, even this will not avoid the problem (discussed in *Appendix 8.4*) where the range approach omits the worst case values at 95.00 (–11 600) and 93.00 (–8000), even though these are not far from the current position.

b) *Numerical approaches*

Simulation method

This technique simulates many forward paths for the market variables which determine the portfolio's value, using statistical assumptions about their distributions (again, usually normality or lognormality) and deduces confidence intervals empirically from the frequency distribution of the resulting portfolio values. A Monte Carlo simulation is the most frequently used here. The simulation technique, although computationally expensive, is clearly more comprehensive and accurate in its treatment of all the risks involved in complex portfolios than the analytical techniques above. It represents an approximate answer to the right question, whereas the other techniques, except in the case of simple portfolios, represent the right answer to an approximate question. The latter can be a dangerous approach when the portfolio is complex.

Historical method

This technique runs the current portfolio over historical data, and deduces empirical confidence intervals as for the simulation method. Since considerably less calculation is involved, it is faster than the previous method.

Stress and scenario testing

These are techniques which look at the portfolio's behaviour under certain specialised stress conditions eg major economic events. They are a supplement to the probabilistic approach implied by the techniques above. Stress testing is required under the Basle guidelines. This technique is discussed in more detail in *Chapter 9*.

Appendix 8.4 The domain versus the range approach[3]

Suppose we have a portfolio whose value P is determined by two uncorrelated market variables, X and Y, according to $P = X - Y$. Assume that X and Y are normally distributed but uncorrelated, both with a standard deviation of 1.

The range approach uses the fact that P is normally distributed with a standard deviation of $\sqrt{2}$ (see *Appendix 8.2*), and calculates a 99 per cent one-tailed confidence interval for the portfolio value as $P > -(2.33)\sqrt{2}$. This corresponds to a region in the domain of market variables given by $X - Y > -3.3$, which is the diagonally shaded region in *Figure 8.2*. In a risk management sense this region is problematic, since it omits points quite near the current position (shown as the origin) but includes points which are infinitely far away. The approach 'gathers' probability from 'distant' scenarios, without considering the situations which could produce the scenarios, at the expense of excluding much 'closer' scenarios.

The domain approach would choose a region with a more orthodox shape which has a 99 per cent probability attached to

Figure 8.2 The domain versus the range approach

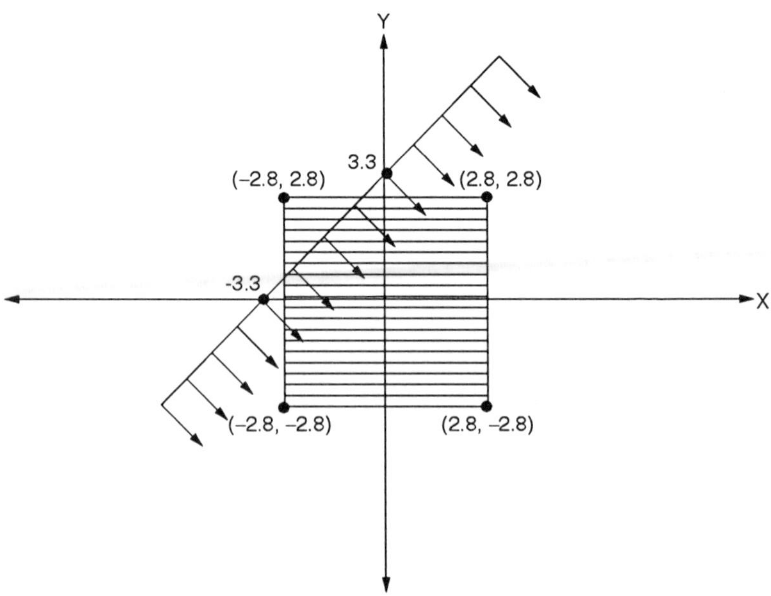

it eg the horizontally shaded square in *Figure 8.2*. Searching this region for the worst portfolio value reveals that this is at the point (–2.8, 2.8), with a value of –5.6, which is 70 per cent worse than the value –3.3 delivered by the range approach.

References

Bank for International Settlements—Committee on Banking Regulations and Supervisory Practices 1988, *International Convergence Of Capital Measurement And Capital Standards*, July

Basle Committee on Banking Supervision 1993, *The Supervisory Treatment Of Netting, Interest Rate Risk And Market Risk*, April

—— 1994, *The Capital Adequacy Treatment Of The Credit Risk Associated With Certain Off-Balance Sheet Items*, July

—— 1995a, *Proposal To Issue A Supplement To The Basle Accord To Cover Market Risks; An Internal Model-Based Approach To Market Risk Capital Requirements; Planned Supplement To The Capital Accord To Incorporate Market Risks*, April

—— 1995b, *Treatment Of Potential Exposure For Off-Balance Sheet Items*, April

—— 1996, *Amendment To The Capital Accord To Incorporate Market Risks*, January

Bollerslev, T., Chou, R.Y. and Kroner, K.F. 1992, 'ARCH Modelling in Finance: A review of the theory and empirical evidence', *Journal of Econometrics*, vol. 52, pp. 5–59

Comptroller's Handbook, October 1994, *Risk Management of Financial Derivatives*

Group of Thirty 1993, *Derivatives: Practices and Principles*, July

J.P. Morgan and Co. 1994, 'RiskMetrics', Technical Document, Global Research, New York, October

Moody's Investors Service 1996, *Corporate Bond Defaults and Default Rates, 1938–1995*, Global Credit Research, January

Official Journal of the European Communities, March 1993, *European Capital Adequacy Directive (CAD)*, Council Directive 93/6/EEC of 15 March.

Price Waterhouse 1994, *Capital Adequacy Requirements in Australia*, 2nd edn., October

Rowe, David 1995, *Derivative Credit Risk, Advances in Measurement and Management*, Risk Publications, London

Risk Special Supplement, 'Value at Risk', June 1996

Notes

1. The capital to risk weighted assets ratio required under the Basle

Accord was set at 8 per cent, with a minimum capital requirement for 4 per cent in Tier 1 capital and the rest in Tier 2, or supplementay capital. The details of the Basle definitions of Tier 1 and Tier 2 capital are included in *Appendix 1*.

2. The terms 'domain' and 'range' come from the theory of functions, but were used in this context in work done by the author and a colleague, Catriona March, at Westpac in 1994.
3. This example is adapted from one developed by the author and Catriona March.

9

Introducing the middle office

PETER HUMPHREY

Editors' Note

Regulators now insist on an independent risk management function as a vital step in the risk control process. The 'middle office' provides this function for derivatives providers, and may also have some application for end-users of derivatives. The middle office is interposed between the board room and the dealing room, giving directors and senior managers the crucial information needed to assess and control risk.

Chapter 9 *explains the functions necessary for a successful middle office. These include development of risk policies, compliance, risk measurement, verification of pricing models and profit attribution analysis. It concludes with a discussion of the challenges facing the middle office, particularly emphasising systems issues.*

In a narrow sense, the middle office may be viewed by some as a policing function. Such a view, however, both underestimates and misconstrues its potential benefits. The middle office is most effective where it educates the entire organisation concerning the sources and nature of risk, thus resulting in greater management efficiency and profitability.

9.1 Introduction

Since the latter part of the 1980s, the incidence of abnormal losses in financial institutions through misuse of derivatives[1] has grown in frequency and size.

This chapter looks at the 'middle office' function in financial institutions; the reason for its existence; its roles and responsibilities; and its role within the organisation in relation to market risk management responsibilities. It is argued that an effective middle office function is an important safeguard against abnormal losses.

9.2 Why a middle office?

Usage of the term 'middle office' varies widely between organisations and the functions discussed in this chapter may be performed within variously named departments of an organisation, including settlements, operations, financial control and internal audit. For the purposes of this discussion, 'middle office' refers to the group of functions that monitor and control market risk-taking in the trading division of a financial institution.

The need for the middle office in financial institutions arises from the maturing nature of existing financial market segments and the ongoing evolution of new segments such as derivatives.

In the developing derivatives markets, trades were often matched between end-users. Margins were fatter and banks were able to run profitable derivatives businesses without running significant market risk. To offer a more tailored and immediate product to the users, banks then began to sell derivatives to one party before matching the offsetting transaction with the second party, and to warehouse and consolidate positions using a portfolio approach, thereby introducing market risks to their books.

As markets matured, margins became thinner. The room for error in pricing and hedging became much smaller and the sophistication and exactness of portfolio valuation increased. Transaction volumes and book size tended to increase to maintain profits. This all led to an increase in the sensitivity of the value of portfolios to changes in market prices and conditions. Competitive pressure forced banks to participate in financial innovation. All banks tended to become involved in the race to develop and offer a greater variety of products to the user (often whether they were needed or not).

The traders presided over this evolution of the market. They were often the only ones within an organisation with a thorough understanding of the mechanics of the transactions that they were putting on the books, let alone their valuation and risks. Product knowledge and development, mathematical skills, pricing model development, hedging and risk management skills, market risk measurement and, sometimes, performance measurement all sat on the trading desk.

The focus and mind-set of the operations and financial control departments had been typically concentrated at the individual transaction level. Accountants and settlements staff were most often worried about an individual trade and its confirmation, settlement, valuation and accounting entries. There was often no appreciation of, or interest in, the dealers intent in entering into a transaction, nor was there often a strong concept or understanding of the behaviour of a portfolio of trades, other than possibly identifying the home of the single transaction.

This all led to the necessity of a function within the organisation which, while being independent of the trading room, had an understanding of the products and their pricing and market risks, and some knowledge of market behaviour and management of market risk for a portfolio of transactions.

9.3 The disasters

Would an effective middle office have avoided the 'derivatives' disasters in *Chapter 2*? The answer to that question is a yes, BUT. Unfortunately the case studies examined in this book—Barings, Metallgesellschaft and Procter & Gamble—must be heavily qualified in a discussion of middle office roles and effectiveness, as Metallgesellschaft and Procter & Gamble are corporations. Although these cases may in fact demonstrate a need for a middle office function in corporate financial control, it is not normally found there at present. However, for the sake of continuity in this book, we will treat them as though they were financial institutions and look at the role a middle office may have played in the disasters in that context.

The answer to the question, 'is it a middle office problem?', is yes—the author's view is that the primary role of a middle office is to actively prevent the institution suffering abnormally large market risk related losses. BUT, of course, the direct responsibility for the losses lies with the traders who put the trades on the books, the trading management who explicitly or implicitly or unknowingly approve of the trades going on the books and senior management who, in the final analysis, are responsible for everything that happens within the company.

9.3.1 *Barings*

Barings is the case that looks the least like a middle office problem. While the loss resulted from a huge market position that went wrong, the position was put on the books by fraudulent trading activity. While a functioning middle office would have been expected to catch the fact that the size of the position was beyond any measure of reasonableness, it may not necessarily have had responsibility for detecting the fraudulent act.

The Barings case appears to be an example of a missing basic control. The segregation of duties that should have been in place between the traders and trading management and operations was not in place. It seems that the trader was responsible for the trading activities as well as operations (settlements, etc) and was therefore able, through his authority in the operations area of the organisation, to hide the loss making positions as customer-based rather than proprietary.

What was lacking within Barings was the recognition, by the operations department, through confirmation and reconciliation with the futures exchange and with customers, that the organisation owned the position. Had this happened, a middle office should have valued the position and raised the alarm.

9.3.2 *Metallgesellschaft*

Had the Metallgesellschaft incident occurred in a bank, it would have been purely a case of lack of market risk measurement and control. Substantial long-dated forward oil sales were hedged with short-dated futures, hedging the oil price risk but not the 'oil interest rate' or contango risk. In a financial institution, the middle office would be expected to ensure that reasonable market risk limits were in place to measure the market risk against those limits and advise management of the breach of the limits and the extent of the risks undertaken.

This was the disaster that the value-at-risk (VAR) system (see *Chapter 8*) should have prevented. Had Metallgesellschaft identified and measured its oil 'interest rate' risk, calculated the historical variance and correlation between short dated and long dated oil 'interest rates', and fed that all into a VAR calculation, they should have seen a very large VAR number that would have raised awareness of the problem.

In this light, Metallgesellschaft was perhaps the classic middle office problem.

9.3.3 *Procter & Gamble*

Procter & Gamble bought a series of increasingly complex interest rate derivatives products from Bankers Trust. The breadth of the range of the products and the degree of their complexity was extraordinary. Procter & Gamble have said that they were not able to calculate the fair value or risk of the transaction, and that they relied on Bankers Trust to supply valuations and advise on the riskiness of the instruments. In their complaint to the United States District Court, Procter & Gamble wrote of Bankers Trust in terms of the 'trust and confidence which Procter & Gamble placed in it'.

In the banking context there would certainly never be a relationship of trust and confidence between financial institutions. In this context the trader buying an instrument would be expected to fully understand the valuation methodology and the riskiness of that instrument. It would be the trader's responsibility to ensure that he or she had the mechanism in place to be able to value and calculate the risk of that instrument.

This responsibility would, however, be shared by the middle office. Middle office's responsibilities should include the independent valuation of, or at least the verification of valuation of, all instruments on the books. Its responsibility should include the independent calculation of riskiness of the trading books.

Had Procter & Gamble been a financial institution, the middle office should have understood and replicated the pricing methodology of the instruments and noted the worsening loss position through its valuations. Middle office should have noted the abnormal riskiness of the instruments through its calculation of the risks inherent in the book.

The requirements of the VAR system would in this case be more complicated than those in the case of Metallgesellschaft. The instruments had many non-linear responses to market movements, which add significant difficulty to the calculation of VAR. Nonetheless the VAR numbers for the book should have highlighted the potential problems.

9.4 Roles in risk management and control

9.4.1 *Senior management*

The role of senior management is to set the level of risk deemed appropriate for the organisation and to provide mandates to the trading division to trade certain markets and products. Risk levels should naturally be in line with management's revenue expectations and are normally enforced by way of risk limits of various types. Senior managers then have the responsibility of being satisfied that adequate control systems are in place to ensure that the trading activities of the company operate within this level of risk.

The VAR risk measurement methodologies are a particularly useful tool at this level within the company, as in theory they provide a directly comparable view of risk across different trading operations. The VAR of the spot foreign exchange book can be compared directly to that of the government bond trading book, which can be compared to that of the interest rate option book. (Refer to the section on VAR below for further discussion of why this may not, in fact, be the case.)

In the wake of the 'derivatives' disasters there is increasing pressure on boards and chief executives from shareholders and regulators to fully understand and accept this responsibility. An example is provided by the recent moves by the Bank of England and the Reserve Bank of Australia to require a letter of assurance from chief executives stating that they are aware of the financial risks undertaken in the organisation and that they are confident of the ability of the systems and controls that are in place to measure and limit them.

9.4.2 *Trading management*

Trading management must understand the market and operational risks of the products traded. It would normally fall to them to disseminate and apportion the risk limits and trading mandates, as set by senior management, to individual desks and traders. They must be responsible for the swift implementation of disciplinary action for violation of limits and mandates. This action can range from temporarily extending a limit to the immediate discontinuance of employment.

Trading management should be aware of all significant positions in the trading room and have a very good understanding of the activities, risk profiles and profit and loss potential of individuals and desks in the room. They should ensure that middle office risk managers have sufficient understanding of the products and the trader's portfolios to effectively monitor the risks and ensure reliable valuations. It is ultimately senior management's responsibility to ensure that the company has systems and controls in place to adequately control risk. In practice, this responsibility is very much shared by both trading management and the middle office.

9.4.3 *Traders*

The trader:

- must have in depth knowledge of the market and operational risks of the portfolio and the products traded, in sufficient detail to effectively manage the portfolio;
- must stay within assigned trading limits and mandates;
- should record all trades in a timely manner for confirmation by operations and for inclusion in a trading system to measure risk and profit/loss;
- should mark positions to market at least on a daily basis;
- should have responsibility for the funding and cash liquidity of the portfolio. Even if this duty is assigned to an assistant or another department, the trader should retain the responsibility; and
- should be personally satisfied that portfolio risk under abnormal circumstances is understood by stress-testing portfolios using simulations.

9.4.4 *Operations*

The primary role of operations, in the market risk management context, is to ensure that the portfolio of trades valued for profit and loss purposes and examined for risk management purposes constitute only those trades and all of those trades that have been transacted for the portfolio. This is achieved through confirmation of each transaction with the counterparty and reconciliation of trading and risk management systems with settlement systems.

Operations of course has many other important functions, such as timely cost effective settlement of all trades, management of settlement risk and reconciliation of nostro accounts. These functions are outside the scope of this discussion.

9.5 The role of the middle office

It is now generally accepted within the industry that a middle office function is necessary to independently monitor and control market risk management. The Group of Thirty (1993) working paper recommendation 8 says:

> Dealers should have a market risk management function, with clear independence and authority, to ensure that the following responsibilities are carried out:
>
> - The development of risk limit policies and the monitoring of transactions and positions for adherence to these policies.
> - The design of stress scenarios to measure the impact of market conditions, however improbable, that might cause market gaps, volatility swings, or disruptions of major relationships, or might reduce liquidity in the face of unfavourable market linkages, concentrated market making, or credit exhaustion.
> - The design of revenue reports quantifying the contribution of various risk components, and of market risk measures such as value at risk.
> - The monitoring of variance between the actual volatility of portfolio values and that predicted by the measure of market risk.
> - The review and approval of pricing models and valuation systems used by front and back office personnel, and the development of reconciliation procedures if different systems are used.

In practice the middle office role tends to cover not only this independent measurement and monitoring of risk, but provides management information and support to trading management also.

It is the middle office view of risk across the whole dealing room which identifies concentrations and diversifications of risk. If, for instance, the forward foreign exchange desk, the interest rate swap desk and the money market desk all have the same USD interest rate position in the short dates, trading management may only be made aware of it from middle office reporting. While the individual desk positions may be well within trading limits, management may not want every desk in the room with the same position and may choose to take some action to alleviate the concentration.

The middle office will generally provide the overall view of return on risk as well. It is the middle office reporting that allows trading management to see the relative riskiness of desks' trading activities and compare the volatility of their revenues. The middle office, having the overview of the room, should be able to provide management with a comparative view of the return on risk of the various trading activities. Ideally it should be possible for trading management to optimise the use of its limited resources of capital and risk limits. If, for instance, the proprietary futures trading desk uses little capital and shows a strong, low-volatility yield on its risk limit, trading management could choose to increase this limit relative to desks with higher volatility and/or lower yielding revenues.

The sophistication of this type of measurement can be taken as far as trading management likes and is very much dependent on the style and approach of management. From the middle office view, for instance, it should be possible to apply portfolio management theory to the trading room by looking at the variance and correlation of returns across different desks and 'weighting' the 'portfolio' of desks to provide optimal overall return. The VAR methodology should be useful in such an exercise as it would, in theory, provide a consistent risk measure across all desks.

Expanding on the above Group of Thirty's recommendations and recognising the management support function of the middle office, its roles and responsibilities should then include:

- development of risk limit policies and procedures;
- calculation or at least verification of daily, independent mark-to-market profit and loss;
- calculation of provisions and deferred earnings;
- monitoring of market risks for limit breaches and abnormalities and anomalies;
- 'profit attribution'—the design and implementation of reports quantifying the contribution of all factors to changes in book value;
- design and implementation of stress test scenarios to measure the impact of different market conditions;
- monitoring and verification of the robustness of market risk measures and scenario analyses, by comparing expected, predicted profit/loss movements from price sensitivities to actual results experienced;
- establishment of controls and procedures for new products; and
- development and/or verification of valuation methodologies and models.

9.5.1 *Development of risk management policies and procedures*

In conjunction with, and on behalf of, senior and trading management, it is generally the responsibility of the middle office to develop the written policy and procedures. This requires sufficient knowledge of the products, markets, risks, strategies and of the relationship between profit/loss and risk measurements.

9.5.2 *Daily, independently verified mark-to-market profit and loss*

The foundation of risk monitoring and control of derivatives trading is the independent mark-to-market valuation of trading books.

The middle office sets out to avoid unacceptable losses from market positions. The first evidence of the presence of unacceptably risky positions is unusually large movements in profit and loss (although we could note here that there is a natural tendency to accept unusually large profits without further investigation; unusually large profits are, of course, as much a pointer to unacceptable risks as unusually large losses).

The four fundamentals of accurate, verifiable profit and loss calculation are as follows.

a) The database of deals, as confirmed with the counterparty, is available

The portfolio of deals being valued must be verified as those, and only those, that have been transacted in the name of the organisation on behalf of the portfolio concerned. It must be confirmed that there are no trades missing from the valuation that should be included, nor any extraneous trades included that should not be.

This is normally the responsibility of the operations department and is achieved by reconciling the front and middle office 'trade blotter' for the portfolio and operations records. The record of trades in operations should include only those that have been confirmed with an external counterparty or reconciled with an internal counterparty.

The systems used for settlement and valuation of the trades can often be different. If this is the case, the systems and controls implication is that the 2 systems must be reconciled on a daily basis. Depending on book size this is often effective only if done on an automated basis. To be totally sure that the book of trades being valued is equivalent to the portfolio of trades confirmed with counterparties, the author's view is that the whole portfolio must be reconciled at the individual transaction level. It is not sufficient to reconcile daily transactions. If an error does slip through (for instance, a deal cancellation in the operations system that does not make it into the trading system), it may then go undetected.

b) The appropriate market prices are used for valuation

Specific prices for individual securities may be used. Alternatively, specific prices can be implied from a set of benchmark prices such as a government bond curve or a swaps curve.

Market prices must be obtained or verified independently from the traders. Sources are competitors, brokers and exchanges, typically via the electronic information distributors such as Reuters and Telerate. The availability and reliability of prices vary widely and revaluation rate setting is often an issue much discussed between traders and middle office.

It is often particularly difficult to obtain reliable pricing for emerging markets instruments. In some cases there are no two-way quoted markets for a product at all, and it is necessary to derive a price. This may be done, for instance, by using benchmark liquid government bond issues adjusted by a historical spread to derive an interest rate swap rate.

In more extreme cases even this level of price transparency may be patchy. The decision on how to derive a price in the more extreme cases cannot be made in the middle office but must be taken by senior management, who must weigh the risks of mispriced books against the expected return of the trading activity, the assumption being that margins will be bigger in less liquid markets.

c) The correct valuation methodologies for each product are in place

The middle office must independently verify that the models in use on the trading desk produce a reasonable valuation of each type of trade, and that the system used for valuation correctly implements the model.

Valuation methodologies have typically been developed by the most innovative derivatives houses who have then brought the new products to market first. Information on the products themselves is initially disseminated in the markets. It then takes some time for the valuation methodologies to find their way into academic publications and trade journals or to be developed by other organisations.

In the recent past the quantitative practitioners have typically been found on trading desks and the middle office has struggled to keep up. Increasingly banks are placing independent quantitative skills into the middle office to verify and certify the models used. One very useful available tool is the Monte Carlo simulation, which can be used to price many financial instruments even if a specific valuation model is not available.

It should be noted that not only the model's internal arithmetic, but also differences in the inputs into black box models, can account for quite large differences in valuation. Simple issues such as the interpolation of market prices and exact treatment of all dates are very important.

d) The cash balance of the trading activity being accounted for is correct

Derivatives markets are built around the net present value (NPV) of actual and contingent cash flows. Actual cash flows are those that are certain to take place, such as the repayment of a money market loan or the payment of a fixed coupon of an interest rate swap. Contingent cash flows are those that may not take place such as the exercise of an option, or flows whose size may vary such as an interest rate swap floating coupon. The NPV of a trading book comprises the present valuation of all these actual and contingent cash flows *plus* any accumulated cash balance.

The correct accounting for, and reconciliation of, cash balances for the book is therefore vitally important in correctly calculating profit and loss. The cash balance in question must be maintained down to the portfolio level. If profit/loss is to be calculated for an entity within the organisation, the cash balance will need to be maintained to that level. Therefore if profit/loss is calculated by the dealer, cash balances at the dealer level will have to be kept. (Funding costs should also be calculated on all cash balances and attributed to the appropriate entity.)

To accurately apportion the bank's total profit or loss to the individual trading portfolios the cash balance must comprise all the cash movements related to the trading activity. This will include such things as interest rate swap settlements, foreign exchange trades and futures margins, both initial and variation.

9.5.3 *Provisions and deferred earnings*

Normal practice for mark-to-market valuation of derivatives

books is to calculate the present value of all cash flows using mid-market rates. This valuation methodology makes a number of unreasonable assumptions:

- it assumes that that the book will never suffer any losses from default by counterparties, that is, that there will never be any credit losses. Given the potential life of, for instance, an interest rate swap book, which can easily contain deals that will be on the books of the bank for 10 years, this is somewhat optimistic;
- the use of mid-market rates implicitly assumes that all positions could be closed out with a counterparty at the middle of the market bid/offer spread. In practice, if a book runner has to close a position, he or she will be forced to pay the counterparty the bid or offer spread;
- it assumes that the positions being valued can be closed out at the market rates used for valuation regardless of the size of the position. While this is a safe assumption in deep, established markets, the cost of closing a large position in a thinner, less developed market can be very high. The tendency in thinner markets is for prices to run away from the price taker as the position is unloaded;
- similarly, the NPV mark-to-market at mid-market revaluation assumes that the book runner will be able to roll forward any cash flows at the middle of the bid/offer money market cash rates. This makes no allowance for the market maker's bid/offer spread, any additional credit spread that the book runner may have to pay, or any additional costs due to the structure of the market, such as withholding taxes;
- it ignores the fact that market risks in a mismatched derivatives book will change over time, even if no new activity is introduced to the book. This will generally require adjustments to the hedges in the book, which may result in either profits or losses. In practice, these adjustments usually seem to result in a loss rather than a profit.[2] There will also be costs from bid/offer spreads, transaction fees and brokerage. The mid-market valuation assumption ignores all these costs; and
- it also assumes that the administration cost of the book will be zero over its remaining life. This is not true, as things such as option exercises and variable rate settings will have to take place, if nothing else.

These assumptions lead to initial overstatement of the portfolio's value when new trades are booked to it. This could motivate the trader to pursue deals that have an initially positive present

Table 9.1 Providing for costs

	Year 1	Year 2	Year 3
Original portfolio value	0	(100)	(150)
Provisions	(250)	100	150
Portfolio profit/loss	(250)	0	0

value but have high built-in future costs. At the very least it leads to a misrepresentation of the portfolio's performance.

The industry's answer to these problems is to include provisions for the future costs. Provisions are often made for credit losses, market illiquidity, future hedging costs, funding spreads and administrative costs.

The perfect provisioning policy would have the following effect: Imagine a 3-year derivatives instrument is purchased and hedged. The NPV of the portfolio at the end of year 1 is $0. In year 2 some hedging adjustments are made which cost $100, and in year 3 further adjustments are made at a cost of $150.

In this case the perfect provisions would total $250 at deal date, with $100 being written back in year 2 and $150 in year 3, as shown in *Table 9.1*.

It is generally the responsibility of the middle office to design the provisioning policy and either calculate, or at least verify, the provisions.

9.5.4 *Monitoring of market risks*

The most obvious role of the middle office is the monitoring of market risks in the room. There are generally two uses made of the information resulting from this activity. The first is to ensure that the level of risk in the trading room is within the limit set by senior management, and perhaps to take a qualitative view of the risks in the room to forewarn senior management of potential problems. The second is often to provide management information to trading management.

a) Types of risk

The types of market risk that should be considered are:

- Outright price risk (delta): Potential changes in NPV of the portfolio caused by changes in the price of the underlying asset. For instance, the risk of loss from a long foreign exchange, equity or futures position if prices were to fall, or the risk of loss in a position receiving fixed interest rates if the relevant yield were to increase.

- Volatility risk (vega): Changes in value of the portfolio caused by change in implied volatility of the underlying instruments. One of the inputs to the pricing model of instruments with option characteristics is volatility. If the traded implied volatility of the option changes, the instruments' value will change also.
- Convexity (gamma): The non-linear response of a portfolio to changes in price of the underlying instruments. For example, a portfolio with a net short option position will have 'negative gamma', which means it will be more likely to suffer hedging losses than a portfolio with neutral or positive gamma, especially when price movements are large (ie gapping risk).
- Basis risk: The risk of changes in the price spread between highly correlated instruments. For instance, a portfolio of short interest rate swaps may be hedged with a long government bond position. A narrowing of the spread between swaps and bonds will result in losses.
- Time decay (theta): The change in value of the portfolio over time assuming no change in market prices.

b) Types of risk measures

- Position size: A straight measure of the size of the position. Spot foreign exchange, commodity and securities positions are usefully measured in this way but it is very difficult to express other more complex risks, such as those involving term structures.
- Sensitivities: Outright price and volatility risks can be adequately measured by measuring the sensitivity of the value of the portfolio to changes in market prices and underlying volatility. This is typically done over the spectrum of the term structure, with 1 basis point (bp) shifts often used for interest rate risk and 1 percentage point for volatility risk. Using this measure a view of non parallel movements in the yield and volatility curves can also be achieved. The sensitivities are calculated by valuing the portfolio at the market yield and then shifting each point on the yield curve up a basis point and revaluing the portfolio to measure the profit/loss impact. For instance we would value a portfolio at market rates and then shift the 1 month interest rate up 1 basis point, and note the change in value. We would then reset the 1 month interest rate to market, and set the 2 month rate up one basis point. *Table 9.2* provides an example of the sensitivity of an interest rate swap portfolio to the swap par curve.

Table 9.2 Interest rate sensitivities

Par point	$
Overnight	390
1 month	(1 100)
2 months	(3 876)
3 months	(2 887)
6 months	2 504
1 year	5 600
2 years	3 400
3 years	(4 780)
4 years	(10 120)
5 years	(8 900)
Total	(19 769)

Table 9.3 Interest rate sensitivities by product

Dollar sensitivities	Futures	Cash	Government bonds	Swaps	Total
Overnight		278		112	390
1 month	–	2 499	(78)	(3 521)	(1 100)
2 months	(3 560)	3 923	–	(4 239)	(3 876)
3 months	–	(890)	(67)	(1 930)	(2 887)
6 months	2 250	670	(569)	153	2 504
1 year	2 500	250	(782)	3 632	5 600
2 years	–	–	(2 400)	5 800	3 400
3 years	(1 700)	–	(13 870)	10 790	(4 780)
4 years	–	–	(25 300)	15 180	(10 120)
5 years			(3 876)	(5 024)	(8 900)
Total	(510)	6 730	(46 942)	20 953	(19 769)

In *Table 9.2* the outright interest rate risk is ($19 769), indicating that a parallel shift of +1bp in the swap curve would result in a loss of $19 769. A shift in the 2 year swap rate of +1bp would result in a profit of $3400.

Basis risk can also be examined by constructing a matrix of sensitivities of the portfolio with term structure on one axis and each class of product on the other axis. Basis risk can be seen by looking across horizontal lines of the matrix. For example, sample interest rate sensitivities by product of an interest rate swap portfolio are shown in *Table 9.3*. In this example we can see that while the outright interest rate risk is ($19 769), we also have a bond/swap basis position and thus carry the additional risk that bond yields will move with respect to swap rates.

Table 9.4 Option portfolio sensitivities

USD/DEM spot	Currency options volatility		
	−1%	**6.70%**	**+1%**
1.5253	(22 810)	2 950	25 760
1.5203	(24 310)	(750)	23 560
1.5153	(25 780)	1 783	26 093

c) Scenario analyses

Simple scenario analyses of portfolios containing options provide a view of outright price and volatility as well as convexity risk. The risks in option portfolios are often measured by creating a matrix of scenarios with movements in price on one axis and movements in volatility on the other. The time horizon of the valuation is set one or more days in the future to catch the impact of time decay, and the portfolio is evaluated for each scenario on the matrix.

The scenario of 'decrease in volatility, decrease in price', 'decrease in volatility, no change in price' etc is thereby calculated. The middle position of the matrix, with no change in price or volatility, shows the time decay.

A limit can be set on the greatest loss in the matrix and perhaps the time decay.

Table 9.4 shows the matrix sensitivity of a portfolio of USD/DEM FX Options and FX hedging trades. In the example, the market spot rate is 1.5203 and market volatility (at some point on the volatility curve) is 6.70 per cent. If the spot rate were to move up to 1.5253 and all points on the volatility curve were to be shifted in parallel down 1 per cent, the portfolio would lose DEM22 810. Time decay is (DEM750) and the limit utilisation of the portfolio would be DEM25 780 (being the greatest loss).

d) Value-at-risk

There are a number of shortcomings with the approaches above. The 1 bp interest rate or 1 percentage point volatility sensitivity treats all currencies and commodities as though they have the same riskiness, and as though the risk is linear. A currency with very low historical interest rate volatility will be reported as having the same risk as one with a very high volatility. This may bias the traders towards higher volatility currencies, in the hope of higher returns on the same measured amount of risk. Likewise, an FX position in a highly correlated currency pair will appear as risky as one in a pair with very low correlation.

The view of curve risk obtained with the sensitivities must be interpreted intuitively. It is obvious that a 3 month versus 10 year position is riskier than 3 month versus 6 month, but there is no measure of how much riskier. Using simple risk measures, it is very difficult to get a good feel for basis risk in particular. It is virtually impossible for a middle office practitioner with responsibility for a large trading room, with many trading activities, to get a good understanding of the risks of a complex portfolio containing transactions of multiple product classes and many maturities, through the facilities described above.

VAR addresses these shortcomings by using historical volatility and correlation of the underlying instruments to calculate the statistically probable potential loss from adverse market movements. (Refer to *Chapter 8* for a more complete discussion of this methodology.)

The strength of the VAR representation of risk is that it provides a single number. This is a very powerful tool to convey riskiness of different trading activities to senior management. It is particularly useful in highlighting potential problem areas in a dealing room, and it allows the apportionment of risk limits between trading activities in a more meaningful way. This single number does very little to explain the nature and cause of the risk, however. Increasingly one of the prime roles of the middle office is to provide explanations for VAR numbers.

VAR remains a hot topic of discussion in many organisations, especially if there are discussions among traders comparing risk between desks. All VAR systems make many simplifying assumptions in order to produce a set of numbers. The period of time in which a position can be closed, for instance, is often assumed to be the same across different products. For example it may be assumed, for computational simplicity that both a USD/DEM FX position and an illiquid emerging market bond will both take one day to close.

The VAR methodology will no doubt be evolutionary in nature and we will see many refinements over time. The initial challenge facing many organisations is the effective treatment of instruments with option like payoffs. Many VAR methodologies in the market at the moment do not have an effective treatment of these types of risks.

It is important to stress that while the VAR measurement is very useful and has the advantages described above, it is not an all inclusive representation of the total risk the desk or organisation is carrying. It is only another measurement of risk. It makes many assumptions about market behaviour, the most significant being that markets will behave in the future as they have done in the past. It is not a panacea to prevent abnormal losses, only a tool.

9.5.5 *Profit attribution*

Profit attribution is the exercise of identifying the contribution of all factors to movements in a portfolio's profit and loss. The factors identified can include:

- changes in market prices, including spreads;
- time decay;
- effect of deals done today; and
- interest rate swap rate sets and similar events.

The sophistication of profit attribution varies widely. In its simplest form the various factors are analysed as follows.

a) Market price changes

The start of day sensitivities and closing market price values from yesterday are stored. At the end of day, the start of day sensitivities are simply multiplied out with the change in market price.

b) Time decay

The change in value of the book on switching the effective day of the book is noted and stored.

c) Effects of deals done today

The NPV of all deals done today is calculated at closing prices and summed.

d) Rate sets and similar events

The impact of all events that can have a profit/loss effect such as interest rate swap floating rate sets and option exercises must be calculated.

A sample simple profit attribution report is illustrated in *Table 9.5* below. The daily report shows that for the example interest rate swap book:

Line 1: time decay is ($4580). In other words, after setting today's date 1 day forward, re-setting all the market dates (6 month, 12 month date etc) and re-valuing the portfolio (without changing the market rates used for revaluation), its value falls by $4580.

Table 9.5 Daily swap book profit attribution report

Line		Sensitivity $	Previous close %	This close %	Profit/loss contribution $
1	Time decay				(4 580)
2	Swap/MM curve sensitivities				
3	O/N	112	8.4000	8.4500	560
4	1 month	(3 521)	8.4500	8.5000	(17 605)
5	2 months	(4 239)	8.4500	8.4900	(16 956)
6	3 months	(1 930)	8.5000	8.5300	(5 790)
7	6 months	153	8.5500	8.5700	306
8	1 year	3 632	8.7500	8.7600	3 632
9	2 years	5 800	9.0000	9.0300	17 400
10	3 years	10 790	9.2500	9.2900	43 160
11	4 years	15 180	9.3125	9.3625	75 900
12	5 years	(5 024)	9.5000	9.5500	(25 120)
13	Total				75 487
14	Futures profit/loss				
15	Sep96 bills				(4 500)
16	Dec96 bills				(2 507)
17	Mar97 bills				3 870
18	3yr bond				12 450
19	10yr bond				(6 350)
20	Total				2 963
21	NPV of new trades today				125 496
22	Impact of rate sets				(12 560)
23	Total forecast profit/loss				186 806
24	Actual profit/loss				186 494

Lines 3–12: sensitivities at the beginning of the day in question are as listed, based on the assumptions that:

- the market interest rates used to value the portfolio at the beginning of the day are as listed (from the previous day's close);
- the market interest rates used to value the portfolio at the end of the day are as listed;
- the estimated profit/loss resulting from shifts in market interest rates is:

  Estimated profit/loss contribution = sum of (start of day sensitivity x (closing interest rates – opening interest rates))

Line 13: the total estimated profit/loss from the impact of market rate movements is the sum of lines 3 to 12, or $75 487.

Lines 15–19: the profit and loss from positions in futures contracts are as listed.

Line 20: total profit/loss from futures positions price movements and newly opened and closed positions is $2963.

Line 21: the contribution to profit and loss of new trades is \$125 496, calculated by valuing all new trades at the closing interest rates.

Line 22: the impact of interest rate swap variable rate resets on the portfolio is (\$12 560). This is calculated by comparing the estimated value of the floating rate coupon at the previous day's closing interest rates versus the value of the coupon when set at the actual rate set rate.

Line 23: the total estimated profit/loss for the day is \$186 806; whereas

Line 24: the actual profit/loss result for the portfolio is \$186 494. This difference is not normally significant in porfolios with no option positions. It is due to the convexity of the interest rate sensitivities to changes in interest rates. A book with option-like instruments presents a greater computational challenge and the greater convexity of the portfolio has to be taken into account in estimating profit/loss also.

The value of the above report is twofold. One is that if such reports are not available, the middle office staff can spend a good deal of time answering trader's profit/loss queries (for example 'you have reported my profit/loss as down \$50 000 whereas I believe I made \$50 000').

Secondly, and more importantly, it provides the link between the risk estimates calculated in the middle office and the profit/loss numbers that are ultimately the primary concern. In this way the profit attribution can be extremely valuable. Without trading the book and knowing the positions and being very aware of the movements in market prices, as the traders are, the risk numbers can very easily be bland and uninformative.

The profit attribution exercise serves to educate the middle office about the trading books and the reasons for profit/loss movements which, after all, are the product of the risks in question and the reason for all the attention given.

The sophistication of the profit attribution process tends to be evolutionary. The illustration above would serve as a starting point. It is descriptive only of the mechanical valuation process. It basically proves the profit/loss number, but makes no attempt at tying profit/loss to trading strategies or specific positions. It may be useful, for instance, to look at the futures and swaps as a spread position, and attribute profit/loss to the shift in the spread instead of measuring the profit/loss from the individual components.

9.5.6 *Stress testing*

The risk measures described above are necessary and useful, but they are all reasonably static measures of risk. VAR goes furthest in quantifying total market risk born by the organisation but even it is an incomplete solution to risk measurement. Statistically we may have (say) 97 per cent confidence that our losses tomorrow will not exceed a certain level, but we are left with 3 days in a hundred where our losses can be *expected* to exceed this level. In addition, estimates of variances and correlations may prove inaccurate.

Markets can and do make substantial moves in very short periods of time. The Group of Thirty recommended that stress tests be applied to analyse the impact of abnormal market movements that could, for instance, fall outside the confidence interval of the VAR measure. The function of the stress test is to give trading management and the middle office a feel for the behaviour of portfolios under unusual market conditions, and the extent of the profit/loss swings that could be seen if such conditions were to occur. This can be particularly useful for books with option instruments, as their response to market changes is not linear and can be severe in extreme market conditions.

Performing stress tests simply entails performing book revaluations using a range of market scenarios and looking at the results. There is nothing particularly scientific about it and, as with most of the described measures of risk, its usefulness depends on how the risk manager interprets the results.

The author has always had trouble designing appropriate scenarios. How far should one shift markets? Should the USD yield curve be shifted a percentage point? Fifty basis points? Where should we shift the FX rates to? Having invented some scenarios of significant shifts and observing large swings in profit or loss, how should we interpret the results? Is a USD10 000 000 swing unacceptable in this scenario? If so, what is the likelihood of this scenario taking place?

For this reason, the idea of capturing market conditions around the time of financially significant historical events and using these as scenarios is attractive. This would entail capturing all the relevant market rates and prices just prior to and just after the event. The book of trades is valued at the 'prior' set of rates and prices, and then at the 'post' set. The difference in valuation (or profit or loss) is the scenario result. With such a system it would be possible to evaluate a book of trades against the 1987 Crash or the Gulf War scenario. We would then have an answer to the question 'with this book of trades, what would happen if we had another Gulf War tomorrow'. It at least provides a mental tag on which to hang the results of the evaluation.

9.5.7 *Comparing risk measurement forecasts to actual profit/loss*

The exercise of comparing profit/loss movements forecast in the various risk measures to actual results serves the dual purpose of testing and tuning the validity and robustness of the risk measurements and improving the middle office's intuitive understanding of the measures themselves.

The first purpose is obvious: if a risk measurement predicts a result for a certain market circumstance and, having occurred, that circumstance produces a different result, there is something wrong with the measurement that needs adjustment.

The ultimate purpose of the risk measurement and monitoring activity is to improve the profitability of the trading activity. It can be effective in helping to avoid unknown or misunderstood risk, as this may lead to unfavourable surprises in profit/loss results.

It follows therefore that the job of the middle office is to understand and synthesise the risks of the traders. As previously mentioned, it is very difficult to get a good intuitive grasp of the many books without actually trading them and all the risk reports in the world will not add any value to the organisation if they are not understood.

The comparison exercise serves very well to educate the middle office practitioner's understanding of the risks and, most importantly, the size of the risks that he or she is looking at in the measurements that they produce.

9.5.8 *Controls and procedures for new products*

There should be a process of analysis and sign off by the middle office for any new products to be introduced into the trading room. Traders and trading management should share the responsibility to make sure that the middle office has a good understanding of the risks involved in any new product. This issue is discussed in detail in *Chapter 11*.

9.5.9 *Verification of valuation methodologies and models*

The middle office should initially satisfy itself that valuation methodologies and models are appropriate for the instruments to which they are applied. This implies that the middle office must either have appropriate quantitative skills or have access to those skills independently of the traders.

Having satisfied itself as to the veracity of the models and methods, it should then be the responsibility of the middle office to ensure that the models and methods as signed off by them are used for the actual valuation of the books. This necessitates that either the models within the system used for valuations are not accessible to the traders or that they are verified from time to time by middle office.

9.6 Systems

The middle office problem is basically a systems problem. While risk management theories may be relatively easily developed, effective implementation of these theories is much more problematic.

It would probably be fair to say that in all professional trading organisations the dealing room uses a wide variety of systems, with different systems in different desks and often multiple systems supporting a single trading activity. This difficulty is magnified and exacerbated in the middle office because it must draw and consolidate data from all the systems in use. At best, this means building interfaces from these to a purpose built or bought middle office system. At worst, it means trying to get all the systems in use to produce the desired reports and consolidating information manually.

Organisations invariably have a nicely bound information technology strategy describing the utopian situation of integrated, normalised, interfaced front, middle and back office systems. They are invariably somewhere along the path of implementing it, but typically nearer the start than the end. The resulting mix of systems tends to have 2 implications for the middle office. The first is a lack of process efficiency. There tends to be a lot of manual calculation of, or at least manual consolidation of, risk numbers across many product oriented systems. The second is related to the first, in that while energy is expended on producing the numbers, middle office practitioners are not able to spend time analysing, understanding and using them.

9.6.1 *Evolution of derivatives systems*

The derivatives markets would not exist as we know them if not for the IBM personal computer and Lotus 123. Prior to the introduction of the personal computer and the spread sheet, mainframe computers and information technology departments ruled the technology and dictated what could and could not be developed. There were big backlogs of development requests and they were ever increasing.

The personal computer empowered traders and quantative experts with the ability to develop software. They were able to develop their own pricing and hedging models and portfolio management support. Trading operations were often started with little more systems support than spread sheets. It would not surprise the author to find spread sheet systems performing significant roles still in many organisations.

The development of the derivatives industry has gone hand in hand with the increasing availability and price performance of computing power and increasing sophistication of software tools. From the early stages of stand alone personal computers running Lotus 123 it is now quite routine for the traders' spread sheet to extract data in real time from both organisation-wide databases and market price information systems.

In-house software development groups and software houses are now beginning to catch up with the traders and there are now some very sophisticated systems on the market. This is true at least for the more generic products. The challenges in designing systems to support the rapid product development, complexity and variety of more exotic products remain significant.

9.6.2 *Desirable features of middle office derivatives systems*

Some aspects of a systems utopia from a middle office perspective are as follows.

a) Commonality of front and middle systems

Ideally the system used in the front office and middle office for a trading activity should be one and the same. If this is not the case, any discussion about risk positions between front and middle offices is much more difficult and time consuming. With different systems it is always necessary to first translate the middle office view of risk into something that the dealer is familiar with and aware of before discussions can commence.

If the same system is in use it is simply a matter of calling up the position information on the system in front of the trader and getting straight down to meaningful dialogue.

b) Product coverage

All products used by a trading activity should be covered by the system used by that trading activity. It is difficult, expensive, time-consuming and error-prone to manually consolidate profit and loss and risk numbers for a portfolio from a number of different, product centred systems.

This often tends to be the case as systems typically betray their origin. A swaps system will offer great utility for swaps but will struggle to book the bond hedges. It may capture futures trades but they will also have to be entered into a futures specific system to calculate brokerage and margins. To produce profit/loss and risk numbers in this scenario would require consolidation across the 3 systems.

c) Single source of valuations

Ideally the trade valuation in the system used to display the profit and loss to the trader should be used by both middle office for management reporting and financial accounts for financial reporting. In other words, there should be only one system used to value outstanding trades. If this is achievable the often difficult and time-consuming task of front and back office profit and loss reconciliation becomes infinitely easier and many tasks become redundant.

Capture and entry of revaluation prices and rates, for instance, need only be done once. The settlement system, which is often the source of profit and loss for financial accounting purposes, can concentrate on settlement issues rather than revaluation rates and methodologies. It should therefore be cheaper to maintain and easier to enhance.

A single source of profit and loss is an important concept because of the importance of the profit and loss number itself. Quality earnings over the long-term is the goal of most organisations. If the trader and trading management knows that the profit and loss displayed to them is the real trading revenue of the bank, with no additional funding costs or brokerage or other add ons, they will be better able to maximise that profit because they will be more aware of all the ways that it can be affected. As a side benefit, the organisation will also be more efficient.

d) Data model

The data model is the description of the world contained in the systems' databases. The model includes descriptions of the instruments and markets that the system is concerned with. It often brings short-term gain in the system design process to make simplifying assumptions about products and markets and market practices. These invariably lead to difficulties later in the design process or, worst still, when the system is in production.

An example may be a simple assumption that futures are only traded with expiry in March, June, September and December. This may be true for the markets that the designers had in mind, but inevitably the first trade a dealer will want to book will be a USD one month London inter-bank offered rate (LIBOR) contract—expiring in July.

It is very important in any system development to get the data model correct. The resulting system will tend to be more useful and flexible over a longer period of time.

9.6.3 *The holy grail*

Most of the issues above point towards the holy grail of trading systems support units: the integrated, all products, all markets single system for all trading activities. Until we all achieve this system we will continue to compromise requirements and put 'interim solutions' in place.

9.7 Conclusion

The middle office provides independent monitoring and control of market risk. When effectively implemented with clear authority and effective 'teeth', the author believes that the middle office is an important safeguard against unforeseen losses. As well as avoiding unforeseen losses, one of the primary goals of the middle office should be the optimisation of normal trading profits. Most derivatives market participants now accept the value of a middle office function, although in many organisations its effectiveness and authority are still evolving.

In the author's opinion, the major challenge facing the middle office is the need to better understand dynamics and sources of day-to-day profit and loss in the dealing room. The biggest impediment to the pursuit of that challenge remains the difficulty of achieving effective computer systems to make the risk and return information available in an accessible way across product and business lines.

Acknowledgments

Many thanks to Richard Williams of Wolseley Treasury Pty Ltd for his input and assistance.

References

Group of Thirty 1993, *Derivatives: Practices and Principles (including Working Papers)*, Global Derivatives Study Group, July

Notes

1. The blame for any disaster in financial institutions involving financial market instruments has come to be attributed to 'derivatives', even though the cause has often been related to the use of straight forward 'primary' instruments or controls around trading practices that could have as easily caused problems in primary instrument trading.
2. Editors' note: These consistent losses may be attributed to the fact that many financial institutions are net sellers of options and therefore portfolios have negative gamma.

10

Focusing on regulation

NUNCIO D'ANGELO AND SARAH DOW*

Editors' Note

This chapter examines from a legal perspective the regulatory framework within which derivatives transactions are conducted. It takes a critical view of the extent to which the risks commonly identified by the various regulatory bodies in Australia represent an appropriate subject for legislation, arguing that risks other than that arising from legal uncertainty are more properly a matter for self-regulation.

There is, however, a clear need for existing legal uncertainty to be resolved. The uncertainty arises, in the authors' view, largely from the fact that existing legislation has not kept pace with the development of the derivatives market. In particular, the attempt by the Corporations Law *to regulate derivatives according to the time-honoured distinction between a futures contract and a security has proved inadequate to encompass current market products. There are very many derivatives now unregulated because they do not fall within the legal definitions. Recent proposals for reform are accordingly examined. The chapter concludes with a consideration of 2 further areas currently of concern to both international and national regulators: namely, the lack of available information about the industry and the need to protect unsophisticated investors.*

---

* The authors thank Megan O'Rourke for her assistance.

Throughout their discussion, the authors point to the competing interests between, on the one hand, the protection of markets and investors and, on the other, freedom for the industry to continue to develop and innovate. It is the balancing of these interests which, they argue, will provide the challenge for regulators in the future.

10.1 Introduction

The spate of highly publicised financial scandals involving derivatives, discussed in *Chapter 2*, has highlighted the issue of the regulation of the derivatives industry.

In recent years, discussions, enquiries and proposals concerning the operation of derivatives have been initiated by a range of national and international bodies including, in Australia, the Reserve Bank of Australia (RBA), the Australian Securities Commission (ASC), the Australian Financial Markets Association (AFMA), the Insurance and Superannuation Commission (ISC), and the Companies and Securities Advisory Committee (CASAC); in the US, the Securities and Exchange Commission (SEC); and, internationally, the Basle Committee on Banking Supervision and the International Organisation of Securities Commissions (IOSC).

The tax and accounting treatment of derivatives has also been under review. In the 1992–93 Budget, the Government announced that it would issue a consultative document outlining a comprehensive new legislative regime for taxing financial arrangements, which would include derivatives.[1] Following its release on 22 December 1993 (Dawkins 1993), the Australian Taxation Office and the Australian Commonwealth Treasury have been involved in protracted consultation with industry and professional groups. A further issues paper is due to be released shortly with legislation to be introduced into Parliament subsequently.[2] From an accounting perspective, the Australian Accounting Standards Board has been drafting a new standard to cover derivatives and their disclosure for accounting purposes.[3]

This chapter focuses on the concerns of regulators currently influencing both national and international proposals for changes to existing regulatory structures. Although the chapter deals mainly with the Australian market (with references to Singapore and Hong Kong), many of the Australian regulators' concerns and proposed solutions reflect those of overseas and international regulators. The chapter initially examines the current regulatory framework, outlining the principal regulators which have the potential to impact the derivatives markets and discussing the concerns of these regulators in the context of a review of the risks allegedly inherent in derivatives activities. Thereafter attention is drawn to, and an analysis made of, the legal uncertainty in Australia, which it is argued has been created by the fact that the Corporations Law has not kept up with the development of the market itself. Legal problems have been compounded by the lack of information available to the market and to regulators. Accordingly the chapter also examines proposals made to address this deficiency. Finally, the chapter examines the additional concerns of regulators arising from the perception that unsophisticated investors require protection.

The conclusion (and, indeed, the theme of this chapter) is that derivatives regulation is not simply inevitable but, in the case of legislative reform, also in fact quite necessary. Nevertheless, it is important to emphasise that this conclusion does not seek to undermine the clear move in the market towards a certain degree of self-regulation. This self-regulation has, however, tended to be focused on issues of internal risk management and control, in particular through the development of industry guidelines and codes of conduct. Yet it is a positive development which should be encouraged, given that measures which affect the internal operation and structure of an organisation will only be effective if they are enthusiastically adopted by the relevant organisations. The best way to encourage adoption would seem to be to allow the relevant organisations to have some say in the development of the policies. At the same time, it is acknowledged within the industry that there should be some level of supervision of these self-regulatory measures, because of the wider implications of the risk of systemic failure.

In the writers' view, there are some issues and objectives within the sphere of derivatives regulation that are more appropriately dealt with by public intervention. Obviously, rectification of the deficiencies in the Corporations Law falls within this category as do, perhaps more controversially, measures aimed at ensuring investor protection and public disclosure of information. There is a risk that the market would not have the incentive to provide what may be viewed as the correct or appropriate levels of protection and disclosure, simply because it is not in its direct interests to do so. Against these valid objectives, however, lies the public interest in financial markets that develop and grow without unnecessary impediments through public intervention. It is the balancing of these conflicting public interests that represents the challenge faced by derivatives regulators.

10.2 The regulatory framework

10.2.1 *Who are the regulators?*

In Australia, there is a surprisingly large number of bodies with regulatory powers which can affect the derivatives markets. In other common law jurisdictions in the region, the number is much lower. In Singapore and Hong Kong, for example, the main regulatory bodies are the central banks of those countries being, respectively, the Monetary Authority of Singapore and the Hong Kong Monetary Authority, although stock exchanges and futures exchanges also play an important role. The principal Australian regulators are as follows.

- Australian Securities Commission
  The ASC is an independent governing body accountable to the Commonwealth Parliament through the Attorney-General. One of the ASC's main objectives is to administer and enforce the Corporations Law throughout Australia. There is an overriding philosophy that the interests of companies and investors are protected by providing information about companies and taking action against offenders. Major functions of the ASC include the regulation of securities markets, licensing of securities dealers and advisers, registration of auditors and liquidators, and investigation and enforcing of the corporate and securities laws (ASC 1991; ASC 1992).
- Reserve Bank of Australia
  The RBA is Australia's central bank. It is responsible for the maintenance and integrity of the financial system and the protection of depositors. It exercises a supervisory role over the banking system and Australian banks and sets prudential requirements (including capital adequacy standards) which must be observed by Australian banks.
- Sydney Futures Exchange
  The SFE is approved as a futures exchange under section 1126 of the Corporations Law. It has its own rules of conduct and oversees the conduct and licensing of traders and enforces compliance with its rules by traders and participants.
- Australian Stock Exchange
  The ASX is presently a non-profit organisation. Its members are corporations that have been licensed as stockbrokers, and organisations and individuals who have been admitted as stockbrokers. The role of the ASX includes surveillance of market trading to monitor compliance by its members with ASX listing and trading rules. The ASX reports breaches of

the Corporations Law to the ASC. In conjunction with the ASC, it regulates the entrance requirements for its members (Australian Stock Exchange 1993; Australian Stock Exchange 1994).

- Australian Financial Institutions Commission
  AFIC supervises building societies and credit unions throughout Australia. AFIC has two main objectives: firstly, the support of the state-based financial institutions whose efficiency and integrity it promotes; secondly, the protection of the interests of depositors (Australian Financial Institutions Commission 1992).
- Insurance and Superannuation Commission
  The ISC now encompasses the former offices of the Insurance Commissioner, the Life Insurance Commissioner, the Australian Government Actuary, the Occupational Superannuation Interim Group, and a branch of Treasury which advised the government on insurance and superannuation matters. The functions of the organisation include the supervision of insurance companies, insurance brokers and superannuation funds, and the provision of general and actuarial advice to commonwealth departments (particularly the Treasury), statutory authorities, and other agencies (Insurance and Superannuation Commission 1992; Insurance and Superannuation Commission 1991).
- Council of Financial Supervisors
  The Council of Financial Supervisors was created in 1992 for the sole purpose of promoting discussions and the exchange of information among Australian supervisors and regulators. The Council consists of representatives from the RBA, ISC, ASC and AFIC. This body provides a forum in which unintended overlaps, inconsistencies and gaps in the supervision of the financial system can be identified and eliminated, and the regulatory regime improved upon. The Council is not, however, a regulatory establishment in its own right, and does not assume the responsibilities of each of the members in the Council (Reserve Bank of Australia 1994).
- Companies and Securities Advisory Committee
  CASAC was established under Part 9 of the Australian Securities Commission Act 1989 to advise the federal Government and to make recommendations in relation not only to companies but also to the securities and futures industries, and to initiate proposals for improving the efficiency of the securities and futures markets.[4] Following the release of the ASC *Report on Over-the-Counter Derivatives Markets*, CASAC com-

menced a review of derivatives in mid-1994 with a view to recommending appropriate regulation of the Australian derivatives market. To this end, it published a discussion paper in August 1995 entitled *Regulation of the OTC Derivatives Market* and a draft report entitled *Regulation of On-Exchange Derivatives Markets* in June 1996. A further report on the regulation of the OTC derivatives market is due to be published in 1997.

10.2.2 *Areas of concern to regulators*

Many reports, studies, discussion papers, surveys and articles have been written about the derivatives industry and regulatory issues in recent years. This volume of literature can be explained, at least in part, by the rapid growth of the industry worldwide[5] and the regulators' lack of knowledge and information about both the market and the extent of its participants' activities. The large and unexpected losses incurred in recent times by companies such as Metallgesellschaft, Procter & Gamble and Barings have also focused the attention of many groups and writers on derivatives in general and their regulation in particular.

The concerns of regulators can be classified into 4 groups:

- those arising from the nature of the risks associated with derivatives products;
- those arising from the legal uncertainty created by existing legislation which has not kept up with market developments. Reforms to the legal regulatory scheme have been proposed by various bodies in answer to these concerns;
- those arising from the lack of information available to market participants and to regulators about the derivatives activity of counterparties or institutions. This has led to calls for the imposition of disclosure guidelines; and
- those relating to the need to protect retail end-users.

Each of these concerns will be discussed in turn and the proposals for dealing with them will be outlined and assessed.

10.2.3 *Nature of the risks associated with derivatives*

A major focus of regulators' concern is the nature of the risks associated with derivatives activity and the ability of participants to manage those risks. It is acknowledged that the risks associated with derivatives are essentially the same as those inherent in any other financial product. Derivatives regulators have, however, tended to emphasise risk management because the consequences of failing to manage those risks are, in the case of derivatives, profound given the concentration of interests and the perceived possibility of a domino effect.

Intermediaries often act as dealers in a transaction by taking on positions themselves and seeking to manage the risks incurred. Hence, the risks associated with derivatives activity can be concentrated in a relatively small group of intermediaries (ASC Report 1994). Regulators are concerned that due to a concentration of these risks or to the consequential failure of a major intermediary a domino effect could be triggered. That impact could be felt by other intermediaries in a related futures or physical market or within the national or international financial community. This is often referred to as 'systemic risk'. Therefore, despite the apparent 'familiarity' of the risks, regulators generally feel that the systems used to regulate and monitor the inherent risks associated with derivatives need to be more comprehensive than in the case of more traditional financial products.

The risks described below are those commonly identified by regulators[6] as being of particular concern in the OTC derivatives market (and of lesser concern in on-exchange markets[7]):

- Market risk—the risk that movements in the price of an underlying asset such as interest rates will adversely affect the value of the derivatives contract (see *Chapter 8*).
- Counterparty credit risk—the risk that a counterparty will default on its financial obligations. Unlike on-exchange markets, OTC markets do not have clearing house facilities or defalcation compensation funds to provide protection from this risk.
- Liquidity risk—the risk that a counterparty will be unable to fund its current obligations (this is the converse of counterparty credit risk). For instance this may occur through market liquidity risk, which arises where a party cannot promptly complete or close out its position at, or close to, its true market value due to a lack of available counterparties or off-setting positions. Liquidity risk may also arise through funding risk, which arises where a participant's derivatives positions impose undue adverse funding or cash flow pressures.
- Legal risk—the risk that a counterparty's performance obligations will be legally unenforceable, for example, as a result of its legal inability to enter the contract in the first place, a breach of regulatory requirements, inadequacy of legal docu-

mentation (particularly in cross-border transactions), or ineffectiveness of the netting provisions under insolvency laws.

- Managerial risk (also described as Management and Control risk)—the risk that an internal risk management system (such as the setting of credit limits) is inadequate or will otherwise fail through human error, fraud or technological breakdown resulting in poor financial decisions.
- Market liquidity risk—the risk that a derivatives transaction cannot be sold or replaced quickly at or close to its true value (ASC Report 1994). This is not such an issue in relation to on-exchange traded products which usually have greater 'depth' than OTC markets. The ASC Report notes that market liquidity risk is more important in the less liquid markets such as those based on mineral commodities or energy.
- Settlement risk—the risk that a counterparty to whom delivery of assets or money has been made will default before meeting its own obligations, or that technical difficulties interrupt delivery or settlement even if the counterparties are able to perform (ASC Report 1994). Settlement risk exposes a party to counterparty credit, market and liquidity risk. At an international level, concern has been expressed that a major default could result in settlement 'gridlock' because of the interdependencies of the transactions involved (*Institutional Investor* 1992).

The primary response of overseas and national regulators in the face of these risks has been to impose new capital adequacy standards which have regard to market risk and credit risk. These standards flow from the recommendations by the Basle Committee, described more fully in *Chapter 8*. In some cases large exposure or concentration limits for derivatives transactions have been established. The American and European authorities have, for example, established such limits and the RBA has implemented similar restrictions in Australia (Reserve Bank of Australia 1989).

In January 1996, the Basle Committee released its Amendment to the Capital Accord to Incorporate Market Risk. The amendment was summarised by the Committee as follows:

> The objective in introducing this significant amendment to the Capital Accord is to provide an explicit capital cushion for the price risks to which banks are exposed, particularly those arising from their trading activities. Introducing the discipline that capital requirements impose is seen as an important further step in strengthening the soundness and stability of the international banking system and of financial markets gener-

ally. Also part of the Amendment and underpinning this is a set of strict qualitative standards for the risk management process which apply to banks basing their capital requirements on the results of internal models. The Committee sees these qualitative standards as reinforcing the continued efforts within the supervisory community to achieve improvements in risk management techniques across the full range of financial market participants'. (Basle Committee on Banking Supervision 1996, para 2)

This Amendment, and the Accord itself, are not without their critics. In July 1996 Viki Fitt, the Deputy Director of the US Securities and Futures Authority, described directives such as the Accord as essentially political documents that represent arbitrary and irrational compromises. She further questioned the basis for the motivation behind the Accord, arguing that it was based on:

> . . . regulators' desire to set capital requirements. But in so doing, they dangerously confuse risk management and regulatory capital, as though they were interchangeable. The discipline of having capital to back risk is clearly necessary. Risk management is, however, entirely different and indeed more valuable. At the end of the day it is risk management, not capital, that protects a firm.

Other responses to risk include encouragement by regulators of the adoption of best internal risk management systems to minimise the possibility of managerial risk, or market risk resulting from lack of segregation of duties, unreliable pricing models, or from deliberate mispricing by traders (ASC Report 1994, p. 17, para 36).

In December 1994, the Hong Kong Monetary Authority wholly adopted the Basle Committee's recommendations on sound risk management as guidelines for institutions that fell within its jurisdiction. In May 1996 the Authority issued further guidelines that focus more on the operational aspects of risk management. The Monetary Authority of Singapore has also issued Guidelines on Banks' Treasury and Financial Derivatives Activities. These guidelines largely implement the recommendations of the Basle Committee in terms of risk management.

In Australia, the RBA initially took some steps to reduce the operational risks associated with derivatives. In 1994, for example, the RBA commenced a program of on-site visits to banks to ensure that banks have in place systems and controls to address market related risks, and to seek corrective action where these are not considered adequate. The RBA's supervision of the operational and management of risk control is assisted by the fact that external auditors of banks are required to give the RBA an opinion on the adequacy of internal management systems and controls. Auditors advise on whether the banks' management systems to control and limit credit, liquidity and foreign exchange risk are effective and are being observed. In December 1996 the RBA issued its guidelines on prudential standards for Australian banks. As anticipated, these are consistent with the approach recommended by the Basle Committee (RBA 1996).

In summary, regulators are concerned that the types of risk that affect all markets are particularly prevalent in the derivatives market, and fear that if those risks are realised the consequences may be felt in the national and international economy. From this, a justification for regulatory intervention is provided, namely, to avoid the collapse of the wider financial community as a result of an aggregation of risks.

10.2.4 *Assessment of regulators' concerns*

The avoidance of systemic risk is clearly a worthy objective of regulatory intervention. Yet there are 2 key questions to be asked. Are these risks suitable regulatory targets? Will regulation aimed at these risks actually operate to reduce or eliminate potential systems failure?

In the Australian context, CASAC has stated that it is not aware of any evidence that a systemic risk problem exists in this country, or that such a problem is even likely to arise. Despite this acknowledgment, CASAC considers that regulation directed at minimising these risks is justified in order to maintain confidence in the OTC market (CASAC 1995a, p. 11, para 0.25).

As was stressed in the previous section, the first point to reiterate is that the risks discussed above are not confined to derivatives transactions. Virtually all of these risks are an incident of commercial arrangements in a market-based environment. As the RBA has stated:

> A fundamental point and one most overlooked is that the nature of risk associated with derivatives is identical to that faced by banks in their traditional areas of activity. (Reserve Bank of Australia 1993)

These risks are of a type which banks and other participants are used to dealing with as part of their everyday business. For that reason, such risks are likely to have been built into the participants' preliminary consideration of the transaction. Therefore, regulation directed at those risks may not actually operate to reduce the likelihood of failure of a participant because, from commercial experience and necessity, participants have already built safeguards into the transaction. In this sense, regulation aimed at risk management may be viewed as merely regulating ordinary commercial good management, and therefore represents unnecessary public intervention into the market.

Further, most of the above risks are of concern in OTC transactions, rather than in exchange traded transactions. The OTC market is substantially a wholesale market (at present, the retail market is largely non-existent). Therefore, the participants in OTC transactions are likely to be sophisticated and experienced and the transactions based on arm's length relationships.

In such circumstances, regulation aimed at 'investor protection' by a reduction in inherent risks is inappropriate. Each party can and should take responsibility for their commercial activities and ensure that they understand the risks associated with them. It may be argued that market forces effectively limit excessive risk-taking and encourage disclosure of pertinent information and the implementation of sound risk management practices. If this is accepted, there is little justification for regulation and the consequent imposition of artificial barriers on market activities. In these circumstances, it is not the role of regulators to overcome the consequences of poor investment decisions, a point that is acknowledged by CASAC (CASAC 1995a, p. 9, para 0.23).

An analysis of the 5 risks which the regulators identify as warranting further regulatory intervention shows that all except legal risk may be argued to fall within the category of risks for which participants should take individual responsibility. On this view, the reduction of the inherent risks associated with derivatives is more properly a matter for self-regulation. The arguments are as follows:

- Market risk: The sole responsibility for monitoring and protecting against market risk should fall to the party exposed to it. It should not be the responsibility of the counterparty to keep the other party apprised of market movements. Additionally, reports of both national and international regulators indicate that market participants do not themselves consider market risk to be sufficiently problematic to warrant regulation (Bank for International Settlements 1992, p. 16; ASC Report 1994, p. 17). The ability of the OTC market to absorb the extreme market movements in October 1987 is presented as evidence of the fact that market risk is not an issue which should provoke regulators' concern. This ability has been further enhanced by the new Basle Committee Guidelines on capital adequacy.

- Counterparty credit risk: This must be assessed by the individual participant which is responsible for establishing appropriate limits on trading activities with any particular counterparty. For instance, in relation to counterparty credit risk, the ASC recognises (ASC Report 1994, p. 16) that the major intermediaries in the OTC derivatives market place particular emphasis on credit assessment of counterparties, and have stringent procedures in this area. Such intermediaries argue that both the cost of this process and the emphasis on credit quality restricts the involvement of non-professional participants in the market. If this is the case, regulation (beyond that already introduced) designed to counter this risk is unwarranted and may in fact impose additional unnecessary barriers to the activities of participants and the market.
- Liquidity risk: This is something entirely within the control of a particular participant which must take responsibility to ensure that it has sufficient funds on hand to meet obligations.
- Managerial risk: Managerial risk is clearly an issue to be dealt with by participants themselves. Boards of directors already have clearly defined legal obligations to manage their companies' affairs prudently and establish risk management systems. Those that fail to do so will be weeded out of the system. As the regulators appear to acknowledge, it is not the regulator's role to seek to protect participants against bad management practices (CASAC 1995a, p. 9, para 0.23; ASC Report 1994, p. 18). This issue again appears to be more appropriately dealt with by self-regulatory organisations rather than by the imposition of inevitably blanket regulations on a wide range of different intermediaries.
- Legal risk: Unlike the other forms of risk, this is an area where further regulation appears appropriate. Particularly in the well-established markets, matters of legal uncertainty (some of which are discussed in *Chapter* 7) are well documented.

10.2.5 *Role of self-regulation*

A vocal advocate of self-regulation is the Australian Financial Markets Association (AFMA), as is evident in its Financial Markets Self Disciplinary Program Discussion Papers (AFMA 1995). Phil Gray, AFMA's Chairman in 1994–95, has defined the Association's task as promoting:

> . . . a marketplace based on proper and sound standards—a marketplace which is responsive to customers' needs in a responsible self-disciplined way. The Association believes that

> this is superior to legislatively-based regulation which, typically, fails to adjust over time to either market innovations or the opportunities to 'do things better and cheaper'. The preservation of an efficient, innovative and competitive market place, meeting customers' needs, is paramount.

Among other things, AFMA has considered and produced discussion papers on:

- a code of conduct which incorporates the issue of segregation of duties, which was identified in the studies that followed the Barings collapse as a major requirement for internal risk management;
- market risk, which endorses and prioritises the recommendations of the Group of Thirty in a prescriptive manner; and
- disclosure, which provides 8 recommendations for the public disclosure of information.

AFMA's intention is that the essential features and recommendations of the Self-Disciplinary Program will be published in a Financial Markets Handbook.

There does appear to be merit in the development and institution of measures for the industry by the industry. It is to be expected that such measures would be 'internalised' to a greater extent by participants, since those very participants would actually formulate policies. The attractive consequence is that the measures should therefore be more effective. This would seem to hold most true in terms of internal management/risk control type measures, where a detailed practical knowledge of the industry and its inherent limitations must be a necessary starting point for regulation of any kind.

The RBA has itself publicly stated that fundamental to its supervisory philosophy is the belief that:

> . . . The prime responsibility for effective management of banks, and for the introduction of systems which effectively control or limit risk, rests with the bank itself, its management and its board. (Reserve Bank of Australia 1995a)

Despite this philosophy, the RBA has taken some steps to monitor the operational risks associated with derivatives, through its on-site visits to banks and review of external auditor's assessments (discussed above).

The ISC has introduced guidelines for superannuation funds and life insurers who invest in derivatives, which are aimed at reducing the risks associated with such activity (see *Chapter 5*).

These guidelines require fund managers and life insurers to prepare formal Risk Management Statements. Arguably, however, the introduction of these regulations may be explained on the basis of the constituency of the ISC, rather than on the universal need to introduce such regulations. At least in the case of superannuation funds, the guidelines are aimed at encouraging funds to review their policies so that they satisfy the covenants in section 52 of the Superannuation Investment (Supervision) Act (1993) (which requires the trustee to formulate and effect an investment strategy that is in the best interests of beneficiaries). Accordingly, the regulations may be viewed as unique, given that the subject of their operation is already under special fiduciary and legislative duties.

It is also important to note that regulators such as the ASC and the Bank of England (ASC Report 1994, p. 15) acknowledge that most of the potential problems discussed above arise because the derivatives industry is relatively new and has experienced rates of growth far beyond the regulators' development of supervisory frameworks. The ASC quotes a report of the Bank of England on derivatives (ASC Report 1994, p. 15):

> several of the problems exhibited by the markets are common to new activities: data on many areas are lacking (with opacity reinforced by the off-balance sheet nature of the derivatives); market practices, including documentation, are often not standardised; some areas of the law are untested; the markets can be shallow and volatile; management of risk may lag behind product innovation; and the requisite skills are not widely spread. (Bank of England 1993)

In this context, a more appropriate focus for regulators may be the issue of disclosure of adequate information to the market (see *Section 10.4*), solving the legal uncertainty resulting from out-of-date legislation (see *Section 10.3*), and providing investor protection (see *Section 10.4*). Adequate levels of information combined with adequate internal management systems should largely alleviate many of the regulators' concerns.

10.3 Legal uncertainty

The legal uncertainty created by existing legislation which has not kept up with development of the markets has raised the regulators' concern in Australia. Quite clearly, the correction of legal uncertainty is an area that is quite properly a matter for public regulation and intervention, albeit in consultation with industry.

10.3.1 *Legislation affecting the derivatives market in Australia*

A number of different laws currently affect the derivatives industry in Australia. They include:

- Corporations Law: Derivatives (and derivatives markets and the conduct of market participants) are regulated by the Corporations Law only if the derivative in question falls within the definition of a 'futures contract' in s72 of the Corporations Law or of 'securities' in s92 of the Corporations Law. A derivative which fits neither definition remains outside this regulatory framework.
- Insurance and Superannuation legislation: The Life Insurance Act 1995 (Cth) governs the activities of life insurance organisations.[8] The Superannuation (Supervision) Act 1993 (Cth) imposes an obligation on trustees to formulate and give effect to an investment strategy in the best interests of beneficiaries.
- Australian Financial Institutions legislation: This legislation restricts the use of derivatives by building societies and credit unions and links capital adequacy requirements to a building society's or credit union's exposure.
- Banking legislation: Under the Banking Act 1959 (Cth), the RBA imposes capital adequacy requirements and limitations on credit exposure of Australian banks.
- Common law and the Trade Practices Act 1974: The conduct of end-users and participants may be affected by the common law and the Trade Practices Act 1974 (Cth) (see *Chapter 7*).

The main legal issues arising in the Australian regulatory system stem, however, from the Corporations Law. This section discusses some of the principal issues which Australian regulators are currently attempting to address.

10.3.2 *Current regulation of derivatives under the Corporations Law*

In order to understand the starting point for reform, it is important to look at how the Corporations Law currently copes (or, to state it with greater precision, fails to cope) with the regulation of derivatives and the industry. This requires a review of several technical definitions in the law. Currently (as pointed out in *Section 10.3.1*), derivatives are regulated in Australia if (and only if) they fall within either the definition of a 'futures contract' in s72 of the Corporations Law or, alternatively, within the definition of 'securities' in s92 of the Corporations Law.[9]

If a derivative is a 'futures contract', it will be regulated according to the regulatory regime applying to futures contracts generally. This means (among other things) that the derivative must be traded on a futures exchange; futures advisers and futures brokers who deal in the derivatives must be licensed; and futures advisers and futures brokers must comply with the rules and by-laws of the futures exchange of which they are a member.

If the derivative falls within the definition of 'securities' in s92 of the Corporations Law, similarly the regulatory regime applying to securities will affect the activities of brokers and advisers who deal in such derivatives and the derivatives will be required to be traded on a securities exchange.

a) What is a 'futures contract'?

Under s72 of the Corporations Law, a 'futures contract' is defined as:

- an eligible commodity agreement. This is a standardised agreement under which a person has an obligation to make or accept delivery at a future time, of a particular quantity of a commodity at a particular price where it appears likely (having regard to matters such as common commercial or market practice) that the contract will be settled otherwise than by physical delivery;[10] or
- an adjustment agreement. This is a standardised agreement under which a person has an obligation to pay, or to receive, an amount of money where the amount of money payable will depend on a state of affairs that relates to fluctuations in the value or price of a commodity or other property, or in an index or other factor;[11] or
- a futures option. This is an option over an eligible commodity agreement or an adjustment agreement; or
- an eligible exchange traded option. This is a contract entered into on a futures exchange where one party purchases an option or right to purchase or sell a specified quantity of a commodity at a specified price. Alternatively, it is an option or right to be paid or to pay an amount of money to be determined by reference to the ASX All Ordinaries Index or a prescribed index.[12]

However, s72(1)(d) specifically excludes certain derivatives from the definition of a 'futures contract'. They are consequently not regulated under the regime applying to 'futures contracts'. The following are not 'futures contracts' so long as an Australian bank or a merchant bank is a party:

- currency swaps;
- interest rate swaps;
- forward exchange rate contracts; or
- forward interest rate contracts.

b) What are 'securities'?

Under s92, 'securities' include 'an option contract within the meaning of Chapter 7 but not a futures contract or an excluded security.'

In summary, an 'option contract within the meaning of Chapter 7' is defined in section 9 as:

- a contract where one party acquires an option or a right to buy from, or to sell to, another party a number of specified securities at a price which is determined under the contract; or
- a contract entered into on a stock market (or an exempt stock market), where one party to the contract acquires an option or right:
    - (i) to buy or sell an amount of a specified foreign currency, or a quantity of specified commodity, at a price determined under the contract; or
    - (ii) to be paid an amount of money which is determined by reference to the amount by which the level of an index (such as the All Ordinaries Index) at the exercise date is greater than or less than the level of the same index at the time the option was purchased.[13]

10.3.3 *Problems arising from the Corporations Law*

The regulation of derivatives based on a definitional distinction between 'futures contracts' and 'securities' has given rise to several problems, the more troublesome of which are outlined below.

a) Regulatory gaps

A fundamental problem widely identified by commentators and industry participants is that the present regulatory regime leaves 'grey' areas. In other words, simply because some derivatives fall outside the definition of a 'futures contract' or 'securities', they are not caught under either of the regulatory systems.

An example, commonly discussed, is that of off-exchange compulsorily cash settled options. They fall outside the regime because they are not a 'futures contract' and they are not a security.

These products are not 'futures contracts' within the definition in s72 for the following reasons:

- They are not eligible commodity agreements because one of the essential elements of a 'commodity agreement' (being an obligation to make or accept delivery) is not satisfied. As the product is compulsory cash settled, there is no *obligation* on a party to make or accept delivery and the product therefore does not fall within the definition of an eligible commodity agreement;[14]
- They are not adjustment agreements because the courts have held that to satisfy the definition of an adjustment agreement, each party must be obliged either to pay an amount of money or to receive it, based on a future event. The buyer of an option has an obligation only to pay the premium when the contract is entered, but has no obligation to pay money based on a future event. The buyer only has a *potential* right to receive money based on that future event. If the option is 'out-of-the-money' and therefore lapses, neither the buyer or seller will have an obligation to pay an amount of money nor any right to receive it. The product therefore falls outside the definition of 'adjustment agreement';
- They are not futures options as they are not options over either an adjustment agreement or an eligible commodity agreement; and
- They are not eligible exchange traded options as they are not traded on an exchange.

They are not 'securities' because they do not fall within the definition of a Chapter 7 option contract, since:

- they do not give a person a right to buy or sell securities at a specified price since the buyer of the option has no right to buy the securities themselves;[15]
- they are not traded on a securities exchange (or an exempt stock market) and also do not give a person a right to buy a specified currency itself;[16] and
- they are not traded on a securities exchange.[17]

The off-exchange compulsory cash settled option may simply

be one product that falls between the gaps in the Corporations Law. It is conceivable that other products currently traded, and others yet to be created, are not and would not be regulated by the existing framework.

What is the significance of these regulatory gaps? On a micro level, the obligations and safeguards provided under the Corporations Law may not regulate the parties to some derivatives agreements. In a more macro sense, horizontal inequities in the financial market are created. Products that perform very similar functions and are aimed at achieving the same economic ends are not treated similarly at law. While regulation inevitably leads to expense for those regulated, horizontal inequity may lead to the development of economic inefficiencies in the market. Funds will be directed *not* to the product that provides the best return (and is therefore the most efficient use of scarce financial resources) but to the product that is not governed by the Corporations Law. Clearly, these inequities and inefficiencies must be remedied for the sake of an optimally functioning economy.

b) Problems connected with the section 72(1)(d) exclusions

As noted in *Section 10.3.3a*, s72(1)(d) of the Corporations Law exempts certain derivatives from the definition of 'futures contract', removing them from the scope of Chapter 8 of the Corporations Law. The original purpose of this exemption was to ensure that ordinary banking and commercial transactions were not regulated where these transactions were not ordinarily considered to be futures contracts. It was argued that such transactions were usually conducted between sophisticated participants and that regulation was unnecessary as concerns relating to the protection of retail investors did not arise. The exemption has, however, given rise to some problems in practice.

Firstly, the exclusion does not exempt other types of derivatives (for instance, commodity swaps and equity swaps) which are commonly traded only between sophisticated participants. Nor does it allow for the exclusion of other products that may be developed in the future, even where those products would satisfy the original rationale of s72(1)(d) by being traded only between sophisticated parties in the ordinary course of banking and commercial business. This different treatment of similar instruments leads (and will continue to lead) to similar inequities and inefficiencies as discussed above.

Secondly, those products listed in s72(1)(d) are not exempted under the Corporations Law from the effects of the gaming and wagering legislation in each of the Australian States and Territories and may thus run the risk of being held to be unenforceable (see *Chapter 7*).

Thirdly, the exemption requires only *one* of the parties to be a sophisticated participant. The exemption applies even if the other party is a retail investor, a result which is at odds with the concerns of the regulators relating to the protection of retail and unsophisticated investors, discussed below.

c) Whether particular types of transactions are 'futures contracts' and, if so, whether persons arranging the transaction are conducting a 'futures market'

A further uncertainty stemming from the difficulties over the categorisation of derivatives as futures contracts or securities lies in the fact that participants cannot be sure whether they are conducting a 'futures market' for the purposes of the Corporations Law. If they are, and the market is not authorised by the ASC, the participant risks liability to criminal penalties and the contract will be tainted with illegality and potentially invalidated.

Under the Corporations Law, it is an offence to establish or conduct or assist in establishing or conducting an unauthorised futures market.[18] The term 'futures market' is defined widely as 'a market, exchange or other place at which, or a facility by means of which, futures contracts are regularly acquired or disposed of'. It need not be a physical place such as an exchange or other place. It could exist simply as a facility by means of which futures contracts are regularly made.

No matter how the market is conducted, whether contracts are traded on an exchange or, for example, by interlinked computer systems, it is illegal under Australian law to establish or conduct the futures market without authorisation. Therefore, if an institution provides a facility by means of which futures contracts are regularly acquired or disposed of, there is a risk that it may be held to be carrying on an unauthorised futures market in contravention of the Corporations Law. The possible risks of a contravention of the unauthorised futures market provisions include:

- prosecution by the ASC; and
- an action by a counterparty to avoid its obligations under a contract on the basis that the contract was entered into in circumstances tainted by illegality, being the fact that it was entered into on an unauthorised futures market. There may

be significant incentives for a counterparty in a loss position or for a liquidator to raise such an argument.

A related problem is that, as a result of a technical reading of the definition of 'futures market', internal corporate treasuries may be operating a 'facility by which futures contracts are regularly acquired or disposed of' and, consequently, conducting an unauthorised futures market.

d) Different regulatory treatment of products with similar functional characteristics

The Corporations Law is, by reason of the definitions of a 'futures contract' and 'securities', 'product focused' rather than 'functionally focused'. Hence it is possible that a product that behaves or *functions* the same way as a 'futures contract' will nonetheless not be a 'futures contract' because it is structured in the same way as an options contract and will thus rather fall within the definition of 'securities' in the Corporations Law. As a result, products with similar functional characteristics will be regulated in 2 different ways under two different regulatory regimes.

This problem arose in *Sydney Futures Exchange Limited v Australian Stock Exchange Limited.*[19] The Full Federal Court held that LEPOs, which function in the same way as futures contracts and which have the same characteristics as futures contracts, are nevertheless not futures contracts and are therefore not regulated under the regulatory regime applying to futures contracts.

The facts of the case were undisputed. In May 1994, the ASX announced that it intended to list a new product, LEPOs, for trading on the Australian Options Market. LEPOs are legally structured as options. However, in contrast to other equity options which typically have nominal premiums and substantial exercise prices, a LEPO has a substantial premium and only a nominal exercise price. Accordingly, a LEPO is closer to a 'futures contract' in its function, as the taker of the option holds a position similar to buying the underlying shares at a future time.

The SFE claimed that the product fell within the definition of an 'eligible commodity agreement' in paragraph (a) of the definition of 'futures contract' in s72 of the Corporations Law. It was submitted that, since the product was a 'futures contract', a market by which LEPOs were regularly acquired and disposed of constituted a 'futures market' within the meaning of s9 of the Corporations Law. Accordingly, the ASX would be conducting an unauthorised futures market by allowing these products to be traded there. However, for various technical legal reasons, the court held that a share is not capable of delivery and is not a commodity and therefore falls outside the definition of an 'eligible commodity agreement'. By extension, it falls outside the definition of a 'futures contract'.

The result of this case is that it is possible for 2 products that function in the same way to be regulated under two different regulatory regimes. As George Harris and Lynne Saunder have commented, the case also 'highlights the difficulty of interpreting statutory provisions to accommodate a product which was not in existence at the time the relevant definitions were drafted and passed by Parliament'.[20]

This different treatment of functionally similar products has the potential to distort the allocation of resources in the financial sector, because of the inequalities and inefficiencies that flow from the different legal treatment.

e) Standardisation—does use of ISDA mean a derivative contract cannot be traded OTC?

A key element of the definition of 'futures contract' in s72 is the *standardisation* of the product. A number of market participants have been concerned that their use of ISDA documentation will mean that their transactions fall within the definition of futures contract and therefore attract the regulatory regime imposed by the Corporations Law.

ISDA terms and documentation are in fact very widely used in the industry, as to a lesser extent are AIRS and ABAFRA terms. This increases the chance that OTC derivatives transactions incorporating such terms will be regarded as standardised and that the use of this kind of documentation may result in OTC derivatives falling within the regulatory structure imposed on exchange-traded derivatives.[21]

Several submissions to the ASC and to CASAC have suggested that the requirement for contracts to be standardised should be amended to require 'fungibility' instead of 'standardisation'. A contract is fungible if it can be replaced by, or is a substitute for, another contract, whereas standardisation focuses on the conformity to other contracts of key elements of the specific contract. It is possible for a contract to be standardised but not fungible if, for instance, it contains a provision preventing the assignment of the contract.

f) Which regulator has responsibility?

Some derivatives participants are regulated by different bodies in relation to the same transaction. An example which is often used is the provision by a bank of a loan with an embedded option (CASAC 1995a, p. 15). In this case, at present, both the RBA and the ASC would have jurisdiction.

CASAC has proposed that the existing 'lead regulator' arrangement should continue so that a regulator can exempt an entity over which it has regulatory jurisdiction from certain matters where derivatives are involved, if another regulator is more appropriate.

10.3.4 *Proposed changes to the regulatory regime imposed by the Corporations Law*

CASAC has proposed a number of changes to the regulation of on-exchange derivatives which also affect OTC derivatives, in particular:

- that a new definition of 'derivative' be inserted in the Corporations Law. It will include all derivatives transactions, regardless of whether they are traded on or off exchange and will specifically exempt particular classes of derivatives transactions that are not to be regarded as derivatives, in accordance with commonly accepted market practice and understanding;
- that all derivatives other than those which are fully negotiable be transacted on an approved exchange;
- that derivatives should be dealt with in a separate section of the Corporations Law, thus removing the current distinction between 'futures contracts' and 'securities' with their corresponding regulatory regimes. It is proposed that the new section should be divided into 2 parts, one dealing with on-exchange transactions and the other with OTC transactions;
- that the current division between the licensing of securities dealers and that of futures brokers be merged, resulting in a single financial markets licensing system for all on-exchange derivatives and securities broking and advising activities (CASAC 1996, p. 55, para 9.3);
- that all derivatives brokers be required to give risk disclosure statements to all end-users with an exception made for sophisticated end-users who have waived their risk disclosure rights (CASAC 1996, Draft Recommendation 13, p. 70); and
- that derivatives brokers be subject to an obligation to consider the suitability of the particular transactions for retail clients in on-exchange derivatives transactions (CASAC 1996, Draft Recommendation 14, p. 76). This suitability obligation will

be based on ss 851 and 852 of the Corporations Law which currently apply only to securities advisers.

Several of these proposals require further consideration because they give rise to potential problems. Of particular concern is the new definition of 'derivative'.

a) Definition of 'derivative'

CASAC has recommended that a derivative should be defined as follows:

> any agreement:
> - the value of which is derived from, or varied according to, the value of another asset or the level of a rate or index (*derived value element*), and
> - where at least one party could (but not necessarily would) be required to provide cash or other consideration (including entry into some other obligation), but excluding an initial or fixed periodic consideration, during and/or at the termination of the contract (*liability element*),
>
> unless the agreement would not be regarded as a financial agreement by the commercial community. Any statement by the ASC that an agreement is not so regarded should be taken as *prima facie* evidence of that fact. (CASAC 1996, p. 20) [emphasis added]

The derived value element and the liability element of the definition reflect the essential characteristics of a derivative. The definition is, however, very wide and potentially catches transactions which would not commonly be regarded as derivatives in commercial practice.

The first problem with the proposed definition is that it is difficult to determine (much less to prove) what type of agreement 'would not be regarded as a financial agreement by the commercial community'. Who comprises the 'commercial community'? Which members, or which representatives, of the commercial community will be regarded as being most persuasive or knowledgeable in stating what is, and what is not, regarded as a derivative?

These questions have the potential to create grave difficulties for legal advisers. While the concept of the 'reasonable person' and the 'reasonable business person' are not unknown to the law, it is sometimes argued that these ostensibly objective touchstones are somewhat illusory and are used by the courts in any particular case to substantiate a decision reached on the merits. It would be inordinately difficult for a legal adviser to be able to advise with any certainty what view the commercial community would hold in relation to a particular type of agreement.

Another problem with this definition has to do with the fact that any statement by the ASC that an agreement is not regarded as a financial agreement by the commercial community 'should be taken as prima facie evidence of that fact' (CASAC 1996, Draft Recommendation 1, p. 20). This implies that such a statement by the ASC may be rebutted if sufficient evidence to the contrary is adduced. However, for the reasons discussed in the paragraphs immediately above, it could be very difficult (or at least expensive) for any party to adduce sufficient evidence to rebut the ASC's assertion.

Thirdly, the new definition of 'derivative' seeks to cover OTC derivatives as well as exchange-traded derivatives. This means that a distinction must be made between the two markets. In distinguishing between OTC derivatives and exchange-traded derivatives, CASAC recommends that the OTC market should be limited to those derivatives which are 'fully negotiable' (CASAC 1996, p. 26, para 5.6). 'Fully negotiable derivatives' will be 'those derivatives all of whose material economic terms (that define the parties' rights and obligations), not just price and volume, are negotiable (whether or not negotiated in fact)' (CASAC 1996, p. 28, para 5.10). This definition gives rise to a potential problem where standardised ISDA terms and documentation (or other similar documentation) is used in OTC transactions. The use of such documentation may mean that, technically, the terms are not actually 'fully negotiated'. This technical problem is hopefully one which should be capable of clarification before adoption of the new definition.

In summary, the proposed definition could become a recipe for litigation. By casting the prescriptive net initially too widely, while simultaneously allowing the ASC the jurisdiction to narrow it by administrative action, the definition could inadvertently pave a pathway to the courts, to be travelled by regulators and participants (and their legal counsel) accompanied by phalanxes of market and financial experts determined to prove to the satisfaction of the courts that some product or other is or is not 'regarded as a financial agreement by the commercial community'.

10.4 Lack of information

Many of the concerns of the regulators arise because of the lack of information available in relation to the derivatives industry.

Information is required by market participants on a range of issues in order to make reasonable judgments about potential counterparties and to assess the financial consequences of a derivatives transaction both to themselves and others. It also is required by regulators to carry out their supervisory activities by, for instance, monitoring the adequacy of prudential guidelines such as capital adequacy standards. At present, the level of available information is generally thought to be inadequate for both these purposes.

10.4.1 *Public disclosure of information*

As observed by the Bank for International Settlements:

> Financial markets function most efficiently when market participants have sufficient information about risks and returns to make informed investment and trading decisions. However, the evolution of financial trading and risk management practices has moved ahead of the public disclosures that most firms make of information that is relevant for such decisions. As a result, a gap exists between the precision with which a firm's management can assess its financial risks and the information available to outsiders. This asymmetry of information can cause a mis-allocation of capital among firms and can also amplify market disturbances. During episodes of market stress, this lack of transparency can contribute to an environment in which rumours alone can cause a firm's market access and funding to be impaired. (Bank for International Settlements 1994)

At present, an entity's financial statements do not have to disclose the following in any detail: the level of activity in derivatives; the current or future potential exposure to derivatives and risks relating to derivatives; risk management techniques relating to derivatives; the volatility of derivatives-based revenue; purposes for which derivatives are used (for instance, hedging, trading or investment); or financial risks which are *not* hedged by the use of derivatives.

It must be noted that the RBA does have access to some information about derivatives in respect of the institutions that fall within its jurisdiction. External auditors of banks must provide the RBA with an opinion on the adequacy of internal management systems and controls. The auditors advise the RBA as to whether the banks' management systems to control and limit credit, liquidity and foreign exchange risk are effective and are being observed. Nonetheless, the provision of information to the RBA is not in itself sufficient. Many entities other than those that are under the RBA's jurisdiction engage in substantial derivatives activities. Further, the information provided to the RBA is not freely available to members of the public who have an interest in derivatives.

A number of solutions have been proposed by various Australian and overseas bodies, including the Group of Thirty, the Institute of International Finance, the Bank for International Settlements, Australian Society of Corporate Treasurers and Australian Society of Chartered Practising Accountants. Many of the proposals recommend disclosure of the following information in financial statements and annual reports:

- the specific purposes for which derivatives are used and the extent of these transactions;
- the entity's current exposure to derivatives; and
- the degree of risk involved in the transactions and the entity's risk management policies and controls.

In addition, the Bank for International Settlements proposed that financial institutions should publish information relating to:

- the potential for further exposure to risk should market prices fluctuate significantly;
- the extent to which revenues of an institution have been derived from market activities; and
- the volatility of derivatives-based revenues (Bank for International Settlements 1994).

In Australia in June 1995 the Australian Accounting Standards Board released the Exposure Draft of an accounting standard dealing with the disclosure of information relating to derivatives (ED65). Under that accounting standard, reporting entities would have to disclose information in their financial reports relating to:

- the nature, terms and conditions of the derivatives;
- the purpose for which the derivatives are held (for instance, as part of a risk management strategy);
- details of hedges;
- the aggregate net market value at balance sheet date including disclosure of the valuation methods used; and
- maximum counterparty credit exposure as at the balance date.

CASAC generally agreed with the requirements of ED65 and appeared to be prepared to rely on the accounting standard, as far as public disclosure is concerned. CASAC also suggested that *all* sophisticated participants (intermediaries, financial institutions, government bodies, institutional investors, investor groups and large corporations) should be required to comply with the disclosure requirements of ED65.

CASAC also agreed with the view of the Australian Society of Chartered Practising Accountants that financial risks *not* hedged against by the use of derivatives should also be disclosed. Although this idea certainly makes sense, in that an entity may be taking large risks by not covering its position by using appropriate derivatives products, it would be impracticable if entities were statutorily obliged to report such risks (CASAC 1995, p. 42).

10.4.2 *Supervisory disclosure requirements*

As discussed above, regulators require access to information in addition to that required by the market and participants.

In May 1995, the Basle Committee and IOSC proposed that national derivatives regulators introduce standard disclosure frameworks and capital standards requiring financial institutions to disclose:

- their total activity in the derivatives market;
- credit risk which is comprised of:
  - current credit exposure (the replacement cost of the cash flow if the counterparty fails) and potential credit exposure (exposure which may be realised over the remaining term of the contract due to movements in the value of the underlying asset);
  - credit enhancement (security sought to reduce current and potential credit exposure);
  - concentration of credit risk (based, for instance, on a counterparty's credit rating or currency risk);
  - counterparty credit quality; and
- liquidity risk comprised of market liquidity risk and funding risk.

In Australia, CASAC supported these proposals and considered that intermediaries should be required to comply with them (CASAC 1995a, p. 42). It appears to be CASAC's view that such supervisory disclosure obligations should also be imposed on other sophisticated participants, which would permit a nationally consistent regulatory framework to be developed.

A further issue relating to the disclosure of information relevant to supervisory activities is the trend towards the sharing of information between the regulators of different countries. Regulators recognise the cross-border nature of derivatives transactions and the fact that often entities (or parent entities) which are involved in transactions in one country are based in another country. They are realising that, by sharing information among themselves, systemic risk on an international scale may be avoided.

On 14 March 1996, the ASC and the SFE announced the signing of two international arrangements for the bilateral sharing of information about the trading of multinational futures trading firms on futures exchanges. The ASC signed the Declaration on Co-operation and Supervision of International Futures Markets and Clearing Organisations. The SFE became a signatory to the International Information Sharing Memorandum of Understanding and Agreement. These agreements are the first multilateral international agreements for information sharing signed by Australian capital market regulators. They provide for the more timely and complete sharing of information amongst futures regulatory authorities and self-regulatory organisations. For example, information may relate to large futures exposures on exchanges that might put a trading firm, a related firm or a whole market at risk. The agreements were drafted as a result of the issues that were raised at the Windsor Conference in May 1995. At that conference, representatives of regulatory bodies from 16 countries responsible for supervising the activities of the world's major futures and options markets met to discuss the wider implications highlighted by the Barings collapse.

A further example of this trend is the co-operation between the US SEC, the US Commodity Futures Trading Commission (CFTC) and the UK Securities and Investments Board (SIB). In a Joint Statement published by the 3 bodies, the authorities agreed to 'work actively with other national and sectoral regulators'. In relation to the exchange of information, they agreed to:

> . . . exchange financial and operational information regarding major securities and futures firms with regard to whom SIB and either the SEC or the CFTC . . . have regulatory responsibilities and who conduct securities or futures business within their jurisdictions upon:
>
> (i) the triggering of a specifically defined early warning event that indicates . . . that [such a] firm . . . may be experiencing significant financial or operational difficulties; or
>
> (ii) a request of one of the Authorities based upon reasonable grounds for concern that the financial or operational condition of [such a] firm may be materially affected by a related entity.[22]

10.5 Protection of unsophisticated or retail investors

One of the main concerns of regulators, both in Australia and overseas, is the protection of unsophisticated or retail investors in derivatives products. This is consistent with the development of the law in many other areas of the commercial and financial markets. For instance, in Australia in the 1980s the courts began to impose a duty of care on lenders in contracts made with unsophisticated clients, independently of the actual terms of the particular contracts.[23]

In relation to the derivatives industry, regulators are becoming more concerned about the need to protect unsophisticated investors in derivatives markets because studies conducted by various overseas and Australian bodies indicate that the demand for access to the derivatives market by retail or unsophisticated investors is likely to increase (CASAC 1995a, p. 21; ASC Report 1994, p. 29).

Investor protection is a sound motivation for public intervention into the derivatives market. Without such regulation, investors would not be protected to the same level as is generally considered appropriate for the public good. It is not necessarily in the interests (at least in the short term) of the sophisticated participants to provide protection to unsophisticated investors as this is costly.

However, it is interesting to note that the Hong Kong Monetary Authority, in its regulations issued in May 1996, sought to make investor protection a private concern. The Authority asserted that financial institutions face a 'reputation risk' that clients who lose money on a derivatives agreement will complain publicly or even take legal action. While the fear of a loss of reputation may inspire some interest in investor protection without regulation, it is submitted that this is questionable, as indeed is the further issue of whether the appropriate level of protection would in fact be provided.

In a Discussion Paper on the Regulation of the OTC Derivatives Market published in August 1995, it was CASAC's view that the increasing presence of unsophisticated investors in derivatives markets necessitated greater intervention by regulators because unsophisticated investors differ from sophisticated investors in having:

- less expertise in OTC products;
- less capacity to assess counterparty credit risk;
- fewer funds to satisfy their OTC commitments; and

- fewer resources to enforce legal remedies in the event of default (CASAC 1995a, p. 21).

10.5.1 *CASAC proposals*

A number of possible regulatory responses were considered by CASAC in its Discussion Paper (CASAC 1995a, pp. 22–3):

- restricting access of retail end-users to less exotic or complex derivatives products. This raised a number of regulatory concerns including the following:
  - — there is no clear division between 'plain' and 'exotic' products;
  - — retail end-users may be unduly disadvantaged by being denied particular derivatives products;
  - — exotic derivatives could be replicated by using combinations of other, permitted, derivatives;
  - — retail end-users can sustain substantial losses even on 'plain' derivatives;
  - — the contractual rights of retail end-users and counterparties who enter into prohibited exotic products would be uncertain; and
  - — to impose a prohibition would require a continuing regulatory role to classify new products and enforce the prohibition;
- requiring that retail end-users have a good credit rating, at least for contingent liability OTC derivatives, which may require the unsophisticated investor to meet further financial obligations. This was directed at a possible lack of financial resources to meet potential costs, although it was recognised that any legislative prescription of this nature might eliminate many retail end-users from the OTC market;
- limiting retail end-users to 'non-contingent liability' obligations (where the retail end-user is only required to make a single complete payment at the commencement of the transaction) except under OTC contracts entered into with a sophisticated counterparty. This was directed at the possible lack of financial resources of retail end-users to meet their potential liabilities. The sophisticated counterparty could assess the creditworthiness of the retail end-user. It was recognised, however, that this option might restrict the opportunity of retail end-users to deal in certain products. Uncertainties would also arise as to the legal consequences of entering into prohibited contingent liability transactions;
- limiting retail end-users to hedging rather than speculative

transactions. For instance, AFIC restricts the use of derivatives by building societies and credit unions to the reduction of market risk. Difficulty lies in clearly distinguishing between hedging and speculation and attempting to enforce such a restriction in the OTC market;

- limiting transactions to parties who have specifically opted out of the protections otherwise afforded to retail parties. This may put pressure on parties to forgo appropriate protections;
- banning transactions between retail end-users. In consequence, retail end-users could transact only with sophisticated counterparties. This would enhance market stability by protecting retail end-users from the increased possibility of loss as a result of transacting with other retail end-users. It might also reduce the possible level of failure in the OTC market and any adverse contagion effects. CASAC recognised, however, that banning could be difficult to enforce and would leave unresolved the legal status of prohibited transactions; and
- imposing a particular risk disclosure requirement for contingent liability transactions between retail end-users. Any involved intermediary would have to disclose to the retail end-user the specific counterparty credit risk of dealing in contingent liability transactions with a retail counterparty. This would be in addition to any other disclosure obligations.

10.5.2 *Risk disclosure obligation*

CASAC concluded that the last option was sufficient to provide a necessary warning to retail end-users at the least regulatory cost. It continued to support this proposal in its Draft Report published in June 1996, suggesting that *all* participants, not just unsophisticated investors, should be entitled to receive risk disclosure statements, either generally or for particular classes of derivatives products. CASAC also proposed that sophisticated participants would be entitled to waive their right to receive such statements (CASAC 1996, p. 68, para 11 onwards), but that those who did not and, in any case, retail end-users should receive 2 forms of risk disclosure:

- a general standardised statement of the risks inherent in transacting on a derivatives exchange, the contents of which could be prescribed by regulation; and
- specific standardised statements of risk inherent in each class of derivatives, the content of which and the accompanying client agreement forms could be prescribed by the business

rules of the appropriate exchange (CASAC 1996, p. 68, para 11.7).

It further proposed that the risk disclosure statement should be given to the client at the commencement of the broker-client relationship and that the legislation should require clients to provide written acknowledgment that they have read and understood the risk disclosure statements. CASAC did not propose that brokers should be required to enquire further into whether or not their clients actually understood the disclosure. It also did not support the imposition of a mandatory delay period after receiving the disclosure before trading could commence.

Whether risk disclosure statements actually achieve anything is a topic of some debate in legal and commercial circles. This issue is particularly pertinent in relation to this proposal as there is no requirement on brokers actually to ensure that their clients have understood the risk disclosure statement. In this situation, the imposition of a risk disclosure obligation on brokers may be an artificial barrier which will serve no useful purpose. In addition, in practice it may be found that it is not the failure to provide a risk disclosure statement that is the cause of a client's loss. Rather, it is inappropriate, inadequate or negligent advice which is more likely to be the cause of loss to that client.

CASAC also proposed that a criminal penalty will be imposed on brokers who breach their risk disclosure obligations. They will be subject to liability for damages where the clients have incurred losses through the broker's failure to provide a risk disclosure statement. If a risk disclosure statement is not a particularly effective method of protecting investors, the question should be asked as to whether a criminal penalty is warranted in this situation.

As superannuation funds and life insurers are now required to provide risk disclosure statements, the effectiveness of such statements may be ascertained in this section of the market before (and indeed if) such obligations are uniformly imposed.

The Monetary Authority of Singapore's Guidelines on Banks Treasury and Financial Derivatives Activities provides for risk disclosure as a major tenet of sound business practices. The Authority suggests that banks should provide customers with a risk disclosure statement which explains the transaction and the risks.

The Hong Kong Monetary Authority's Guidelines on Risk Management of Derivatives and other Traded Instruments do not specifically require the preparation of a risk disclosure statement.

Nonetheless, they do provide that as part of the normal credit analysis that is undertaken it is expected that an institution will:

- analyse the expected impact of the proposed transaction on the counterparty;
- identify whether the proposed transaction is consistent with the counterparty's policies and procedures with respect to derivatives transactions, as they are known to the institution; and
- ensure that the terms of the contract are clear and assess whether the counterparty is capable of understanding the terms of the contract and fulfilling its obligations under the contract.

The Authority suggests that financial institutions should be conscious of the fact that their role (and other consequent duties) will differ depending on the nature of the counterparty and the complexity of the transaction. It suggests that an institution owes a wide duty of care to tender its advice fully, accurately and properly, particularly when a relatively unsophisticated counterparty is involved.

10.5.3 *Suitability obligations*

In its draft report published in June 1996, CASAC also proposed that derivatives brokers and advisers should be subject to a suitability obligation similar to that currently imposed upon securities advisers under the Corporations Law.[24] Securities advisers who breach the statutory suitability obligation may be liable to compensate a client who suffers loss or damage as a result of reliance on a recommendation of that adviser. The consequence of a breach of the suitability obligation is possible revocation of the adviser's licence.

The suitability obligation is thought to be appropriate for derivatives transactions as it imposes obligations which are more far reaching than current common law or Trade Practices Act obligations. The suitability obligations impose a 'know your client' obligation on the derivatives provider to give advice which is adequate and appropriate for a particular client's investment objectives, financial situation and particular needs.

CASAC concluded, however, that a suitability obligation should be imposed upon derivatives brokers:

> only where there is a compelling consumer protection justification. This does not apply to sophisticated end-users. Those participants can, or reasonably should, be able to protect their

> own interests by implementing procedures to appropriately manage the risks involved in on-exchange derivatives transactions. Also they would be more likely to have access to information to assist in this suitability assessment. Furthermore, they may be better placed than retail participants to negotiate the standard of advice to be provided to them and any remedies for default.' (CASAC 1996, p. 74, para 12.7)

By way of contrast, the Monetary Authority of Singapore requires that banks ensure that they have a reasonable basis for recommending a transaction and have disclosed the basis and the assumptions on which a recommendation is based. The Authority recognises that the customer has the ultimate responsibility for entering into a transaction. It suggests, however, that if the bank does not believe that a transaction is appropriate for a particular customer, but that customer still wants to enter into it, then the bank should carefully document its analysis and the information that is provided to the client. Similarly, the Hong Kong Monetary Authority suggests that when a financial institution believes that a transaction is inappropriate for a client, the client should be informed of this opinion. If the client still proceeds, the institution should fully document its discussions and advice.

10.6 Conclusion

The regulation of the derivatives industry in Australia and overseas is in a state of flux. The existing regulatory structures have not kept pace with the rapid growth and development of the domestic and global financial and derivatives markets. There is international support for global reform of the regulatory regimes applying to derivatives and rapid and dramatic changes can be expected over the next decade.

In Australia, this process is still in its comparatively early stages. Yet, the pace of the push towards reform is quickening as evidenced in May 1994 by the issue of a major report on the OTC derivatives markets by the ASC and, in August 1995 and June 1996, by the publication by CASAC of the results of extensive consultations with industry representatives, regulators, representatives of professional associations, lawyers, accountants and academics. The RBA has also been conducting studies and surveys of the derivatives industry and of the practices of the financial institutions for which it has supervisory responsibility.

Regulation of the derivatives industry is seen by most as inevitable. Nonetheless, regulators do recognise that a sensible balance must be found between the competing interests of, on the one hand, the protection of investors and the maintenance of the stability and integrity of domestic and global financial markets and, on the other hand, the industry's need for sufficient freedom in order to continue to develop and innovate.

Aside from legislative reforms necessitated by the legal uncertainty created by outdated legislation, the main changes in the regulatory environment will arise from a recognition by regulators, both domestically and internationally, that more information is required by markets and regulators, and that the use of derivatives by unsophisticated investors will necessitate the imposition of suitable protections. These changes will not occur without regulatory intervention into the market, because it is not in the interests of the institutions involved to adopt internally such 'public interest' reforms. The challenge for regulators in coming years will be to find appropriate solutions to these problems, a task that is made even more difficult because of the international or cross-border nature of the derivatives markets.

Authors' Note

In June 1997, after this chapter was submitted for publication, the Companies and Securities Advisory Committee (CASAC) issued a final report titled *Regulation of On-Exchange and OTC Derivatives Markets*. This report expands upon the issues raised in the Draft Report (1996) and the Discussion Paper (1995a), both of which are referred to in this chapter. In particular, the reader should note the following:

- The discussion of risks associated with the OTC derivatives market in 10.2.3 of this chapter should include an additional reference to 'large exposure' risk. This is discussed in paragraphs 2.37 and 2.38 of the Final Report.
- The Final Report has addressed concerns expressed in this chapter about the definition of 'derivative'. The reader is referred to paragraphs 3.27 to 3.36, 3.55 to 3.65, and Recommendation 4 of the Final Report.
- Exposure Draft 65 is now finalised as accounting standard AASB1033/AAS33 Presentation and Disclosure of Financial Instruments.
- The CASAC Proposals discussed in 10.5.1 of this chapter are substantially incorporated in the Final Report, with the excep-

tion of the final point concerning contingent liability transactions between retail end-users. The reader is referred to paragraph 2.67 of the Final Report.

References

Asia Money 1994, 'Derivatives Guide', *Asia Money Hong Kong*, May

Australian Financial Institutions Commission 1992, *Annual Report 1992*

Australian Financial Markets Association 1995, *Financial Markets, Self Disciplinary Program—Discussion Papers*, Discussion Papers for presentation at the AFA National Convention and Annual General Meeting, Sydney, 14–15 September

Australian Securities Commission 1991, *Annual Report 1990–91*

—— 1992, *Annual Report 1991–92*

—— 1994, *Report on Over-The-Counter Derivatives Markets*, May

Australian Stock Exchange 1993, *Annual Report 1993*

Australian Stock Exchange 1994, *Annual Report 1994*

Bank of England 1993, *Derivatives: Report of an Internal Working Group*, April

Bank for International Settlements 1992, *Recent Developments in International Interbank Relations*, Basle, October

—— 1994, *Public Disclosure of Market and Credit Risk by Financial Intermediaries*, September

Basle Committee on Banking Supervision 1996, Overview of the Amendment to the Capital Accord to Incorporate Market Risks, January

Board of Banking Supervision 1995, Report of the Board of Banking Supervision Inquiry Into the Circumstances of the Collapse of Barings, Return to an Order of the Honourable The House of Commons, 18 July

Companies and Securities Advisory Committee 1995a, *Regulation of the OTC Derivatives Market—Discussion Paper*, August

—— 1995b, *Law of Derivatives: Australian and International Comparisons*, January

—— 1996, *Regulation of On-Exchange Derivatives Markets Draft Report*, June

Cookson, R. 1992, 'The Great Escape', *Risk*, vol. 5, no. 5, May, pp. 32–7

Dawkins, J. 1993, *Taxation of Financial Arrangements—A Consultative Document*, December

Hong Kong Monetary Authority 1996, 'Guideline on Risk Management of Derivatives and other Traded Instruments', *Hong Kong Monetary Authority Quarterly Bulletin*, May

Institutional Investor 1992, 'Why Derivatives Rattle the Regulators', September, p. 59

Insurance and Superannuation Commission 1991, *Annual Report 1990/91*

—— 1992, *Annual Report 1991/92*

International Securities Institute 1994, *Handbook on Financial Futures and Traded Options in Asia*, Hong Kong

Martin Report 1991, *A Pocket full of Change,* House of Representatives Standing Committee on Finance and Public Administration, November

—— 1994, 'Risk Management Guidelines for Derivatives', December

Monetary Authority of Singapore 1995, *Guideline on Banks' Treasury and Financial Derivatives Activities*

Reserve Bank of Australia 1989, *Supervision of Bank's Large Credit Exposures*, Prudential Statement No. E1, August

—— 1993, *Bulletin*, August

—— 1994, *Payments Systems*, July, pp. 7–8

—— 1995(a), *Bulletin*, May

—— 1995(b), *Bulletin*, October

—— 1996, *Capital Adequacy of Banks; Market Risk Prudential Statement No C3*, December

Satyajit, D. 1994, *Swaps and Financial Derivatives*, 2nd edn., Law Book Company, Sydney

Notes

1. The original consultative document only dealt with some derivatives. However, discussions with the Treasury indicate that as a result of industry consultation legislation to be introduced will cover all derivatives.
2. The rationale for the introduction of special legislation for the treatment of financial arrangements is that the existing tax law is viewed as inadequate in that it is too reliant on legal form rather than economic substance, and it is thought that this results in tax driven decisions. Further, like the Corporations Law (which is discussed in detail in the text of this chapter) it is generally felt that the rapid development of sophisticated financial instruments has led to uncertainty as to the application of the tax law to these instruments. It is interesting to note that the consultative document is based on the assumption that the correct response to this uncertainty is a new legislative regime, and other remedies are not canvassed at all.
3. Discussed in more detail in *Section 10.4.1* below.
4. Australian Securities Commission Act 1989 section 148.
5. The ASC report notes (at page 10) that the world-wide volume of exchange traded products increased six-fold in the period from 31 December 1986 to 31 December 1991 and the volume of OTC products increased eight-fold during the same period.
6. For instance, see CASAC Discussion Paper pp. 9–11 and ASC Report pp. 14–20. The meaning of each of the risks listed is taken from the CASAC draft paper and the ASC report.
7. For instance, counterparty credit risk is not a major concern in

on-exchange markets because of the existence of clearing house facilities.

8. Although the Act does not expressly restrict the use of derivatives by life insurance companies, the Act imposes a requirement to report potential exposures to the Insurance and Superannuation Commission.
9. Since 1995 it has also been possible by regulation for particular products to be deemed to fall within one of these categories, even if they do not satisfy the definition (see Corporations Law ss72A and 92A).
10. See Corporations Law section 9, definition of 'commodity agreement' and 'eligible commodity agreement'.
11. See *ibid* section 9, definition of 'adjustment agreement'.
12. See *ibid* section 9, definition of 'eligible exchange traded option'.
13. See *ibid* section 9, definition of 'option contract'.
14. See *Carragreen Currency Corporation Pty Limited v CAC (NSW)*, (1986) 11 ACLR 298; (1987) ACLC 148.
15. See Corporations Law section 9, definition of 'option contract', paragraph (a).
16. See *ibid* section 9, definition of 'option contract', paragraph(b)(i).
17. See *ibid* section 9, definition of 'option contract', paragraph (b)(ii).
18. *Ibid*, section 1123.
19. (1995) 128 ALR 417.
20. *George Harris and Lynne Saunder, Sydney Futures Exchange Limited v Australian Stock Exchange Limited*, (1994) 126 ALR 209, (1995) 6 JBFLP 61 at 63. See now Corporations Law s72A and s92A which attempt to deal with the problem by enabling particular products to be classified by a new regulatory procedure as either a futures contract or a security.
21. The ASC has highlighted the problem being increasingly experienced in the industry:

    > The increasing use of the ISDA documentation, the trend towards greater homogeneity in basic products, and the wide interpretation given to the concept of standardisation by the courts, mean that uncertainty about whether or not a transaction is a futures contract will remain a major market issue.

    See ASC report para 65.
22. See Joint Statement of the Securities and Exchange Commission, the Commodity Futures Trading Commission and the Securities and Investments Board.
23. See, for instance, the foreign currency loan cases in Australia in the late 1980s (collated and discussed in 'A Pocket Full of Change', the so-called Martin Report, published by the House of Representatives Standing Committee on Finance and Public Administration in November 1991) and discussion in *Chapter 8*.
24. See Corporations Law section 851.

11

Developing derivatives products

KEVIN JAMESON

Editors' Note

This chapter focuses on how new products are developed. Understanding the development process is of importance for both providers and users, creating a more informed relationship. The key steps in the process are examined in detail, with the author contending that omission of any one of the steps in a transaction is likely to provoke problems in the future. These steps are equally appropriate for the creation of single or multiple products although in the latter case additional considerations come into play, which are briefly outlined.

In guiding the reader through the process, 2 examples are used to illustrate some of the issues commonly arising: the Procter & Gamble/Bankers Trust 5/30 year swap (discussed in Chapter 2*) and an Inverse Floating Rate Note. The author's interest relates not just to the technical peculiarities of these transactions, but rather to broader lessons for management. It is only by learning these broader lessons that future disasters can be avoided.*

The author emphasises that while product development can clearly perform a valuable role in, for example, promoting and expediting the transfer of risk between parties in accordance with their wants, the justification for its use in any particular transaction should always be clarified. The financial community is unlikely in the long term to benefit from products which have been created merely to circumvent regulations or shore up dealers' bonuses.

11.1 Introduction

'Those who cannot remember the past are condemned to repeat it.'

George Santayana

The above quote relates as much to financial markets as any other field of human fallibility. It is only partly true that it is the 'newness' of financial products that led to such disasters as Procter & Gamble, described in *Chapter 2*. If the only lesson we learn is to understand the details of derivatives products (and derivatives disasters) better, we will avoid some future problems but by no means all.

In particular, it is as much the process of the development and adoption of new products as the products themselves that has caused the disasters. For example, many problems in foreign exchange markets in the 1980s have similar features to derivatives problems in the 1990s. A list of the causes of the difficulties of AWA in Australia in 1987 (see *Chapter 4*) and Procter & Gamble in the US in 1994 would have many items in common: products outside the experience of the organisation, a lack of informed management, oversight, ill-defined objectives, reliance on key individuals, lack of a risk reporting framework, lack of a proper mark-to-market accounting environment, and so on. The paradox is that at the start of the 1990s many users had well-controlled foreign exchange operations but poorly controlled derivatives units; in other words, they had learned the narrow lessons from problems in the foreign exchange markets, but not the broad lessons of how to introduce new financial products into organisations.

The risk therefore is that markets will now learn the narrow lessons from the derivatives disasters, but not those broad lessons. We will see fewer problems in the area of interest rate management using complex products by borrowers, or structured notes for investors, yet problems of the same fundamental nature may erupt in new areas, such as credit derivatives perhaps. Different people and departments within an organisation may be responsible for such new products. They may have to re-learn the lessons of history unless their organisations find ways of codifying the risks that arise out of new products generally, rather than any specific single product.

Consequently, an understanding of the product development process is important at 2 levels. Firstly, at a technical level, what steps are required successfully to introduce a new financial product? Secondly, at a management level, what broader issues need to be considered by organisations entering into new financial products, either on a one-off or on an ongoing basis?

This chapter will deal with the design and development of new products at both of these levels, discussing not only the technical issues but also the practical issues that arise, in the hope that George Bernard Shaw's comment that 'we learn from history that we learn nothing from history' isn't really a more appropriate opening quotation for later editions of this chapter.

11.1.1 *The nature and role of product development*

It is helpful to start by considering the question: Why do new products need to be developed at all?

To highlight the issue, consider the benefits of 'old fashioned' products, such as vanilla swaps, for example. They tend to have liquid markets (at least relatively speaking), allowing easy entry and exit; to have low associated dealing costs (particularly bid-offer spreads); and to be transparent in the sense that the effect of the product is reasonably clear to a financially literate observer. In addition, there exist pools of people who can settle, account for, audit etc the products and the accounting and regulatory treatment of the products tends to be reasonably clear cut. On the other hand, new products tend to offer none of these characteristics. In fact, on each count the reverse usually applies.

Why therefore would anyone want to use a new, complex product? It is tempting to suggest that the reason must be to invent new, customised payoffs that are not available using standard products, yet in general this is not the case. It is possible in many, if not most, cases for the user to replicate the financial behaviour of the new, complex product with a portfolio of standard products. The user thus achieves the payoff being sought while only holding simple, liquid, transparent instruments.[1] If so, why would anyone want to enter into a new product when they can usually replicate (at least the essential terms of) its behaviour synthetically?

The answer to this question rarely lies in the payoff (in other words the financial behaviour) of the new product. This payoff can almost always be replicated dynamically, if not on a fully locked-in basis. This must be the case, because in the absence of back-to-back trades this is precisely how the providers hedge their transactions with users. The answer will rather tend to arise out of the following list:

- a payoff genuinely unavailable by other means (for example, an exposure to a commodity not usually traded, and only available in embedded form in a structured product);
- high costs of replication (as a simple example, a borrower may be able to replicate a swaption synthetically, but in practice will deal in the swaption market because the costs of replication exceed any benefits);
- pricing advantages available by using the structured product. For example, a copper producer may find that the cheapest way to short copper is to embed a call in a structured bond sold to retail investors, or indeed to issue such a bond and buy back the call in the OTC market to generate (risk-free) funds at a rate lower than otherwise available (see *Sections 11.2.3* and *11.2.6* of this chapter);
- access to markets or counterparties. For example, a lowly rated counterparty may be able to gain access to a ten year swap market by being prepared to accept regular settlement of mark-to-market losses, or an early termination in the event of rating downgrade;
- regulatory or legal 'arbitrage'. For example, an investor prohibited from dealing in options may obtain an option-like payoff by dealing in structured bonds where the 'option' is embedded in the cash flows of the bond; and
- taxation or accounting 'arbitrage'. For example, in an environment where there is asymmetry between the taxation (or for that matter financial or management accounting) treatment of capital gains and income, income can be converted to capital gains (or vice versa) by lowering the coupon of a structured bond and increasing the redemption amount by a corresponding amount (either outright, or in an option-like manner).[2]

The construction of this list starts to bring out the problems that new product development generates. A slightly harsh re-statement of this list is that many new products are entered into by users because they do not wish to go to the expense of setting up an infrastructure to handle the risks of the new product in synthetic form, or else they want to circumvent a regulatory, legal, taxation or accounting treatment of standard products that the user finds 'unsatisfactory'—hardly an encouraging starting point. This issue will be the subject of further discussion in *Section 11.2.9*.

As well as considering the user's viewpoint in addressing the question of why anyone would enter into a new financial product, it is necessary to consider the viewpoint of the provider. It is not only users who will have their motivations for entering into new transactions, but also providers. Clearly the latter want to meet the needs of their customers, so the preceding list may also motivate those providers. Providers, however, face an additional temptation. As a general rule, the spread (and therefore profit) they can obtain from a transaction is least when the product is highly standardised and liquid, and most when it is highly structured and illiquid. The point should not be pushed to unnecessary extremes, as the unit costs associated with structured products are much higher and volumes much lower, so that it may make perfect business sense for providers to encourage customers to use standardised products (as is clearly observable on a day-to-day basis). However, this issue of relative margins must be addressed, as in a narrower 'marginal' context providers will generally be much happier if a borrower transacts a highly structured swap than a vanilla swap, because of the much larger spreads that can be charged by the provider in the structured market than in the liquid, public vanilla swap market (see *Section 11.2.9*).

To conclude these opening remarks, bear in mind (before becoming too pessimistic or cynical about the process) that many products regarded as standard and certainly useful, such as swaps and interest rate futures, were new only a little more than 20 years ago. Clearly the process can have benefits. The key is to identify appropriate development and then to find ways of maximising the benefits while minimising the costs.

11.1.2 *Scope of the chapter*

In attempting to deal with these issues, this chapter will take a sequential approach, and attempt to track the process of developing a new derivatives product from concept to launch (and beyond).

Some difficulty arises in establishing the scope of this chapter, as the very words 'new', 'derivatives' and 'product' are subject to their own ambiguities. 'New' might, for example, mean a brand new underlying risk but it might equally mean an old risk packaged in derivatives form. 'Derivatives', as defined earlier, refers to instruments like swaps and forwards, whose value is derived from underlying assets. The term also includes packaged solutions combining underlying assets and derivatives, such as a swap/option embedded in a Medium Term Note (MTN).[3] Finally, 'product' has an obvious meaning, but we should define the concept broadly enough to include the synthetic version of a product: a portfolio of simple products that behave in an analogous fashion to a single product.

All of these observations lead to a key conclusion: in derivatives markets generally, but particularly in the development of new products, it is vital to maintain a clear distinction between form and substance. The substance is the economic payoff of the product, and the form is the documentation within which the payoff is embedded. Part of the reason that derivatives can cause such problems within organisations is the ease with which virtually any payoff can be documented as a derivative within the normal range of activities and approvals of the organisation. (The Procter & Gamble/Bankers Trust swap was a classic case of a transaction recorded and documented as a 'swap', but with wildly different behaviour to that which we would expect from the name alone.)

Unfortunately, these ambiguities also mean that 'new product development' in derivatives markets covers a vast range of possibilities. To give the chapter some focus we will need to restrict these possibilities. In particular, in an effort to achieve depth rather than breadth, this chapter will narrow its attention to derivatives providers developing debt instruments and debt-related derivatives for issuers and investors. While the detail will tend to reflect this approach, it should be noted that the principles hold for any other form of product development.

Again for purposes of focus, much of the discussion in this chapter will relate to the development of a single transaction, usually within a bank or other derivatives provider. This by no means lessens the usefulness of the remarks in this chapter for users, for two reasons. Firstly, new product development can be carried out within the user's organisation rather than that of the provider. In this case, apart from some institutional detail, this chapter applies quite straightforwardly. Secondly, even if users are not carrying out product development themselves, it is a major contention of this chapter that they should understand in detail the process from the point of view of the provider. Such an understanding leads, for example, to a proper recognition of what constitutes good or bad pricing but, more broadly, it leads to a recognition of the forces that drive providers and the sorts of products that such forces tend to encourage. This allows for a more informed dialogue between user and provider relating not just to the pricing of products, but also to the kinds of appropriate products.

Despite this focus on the development of a single product, it is frequently the case in practice that a product developed for a specific client and purpose is readily applicable to other situations or groups of clients. This gives rise to the concept of new product development as a business process, rather than as an isolated exercise. Yet there is an important difference between, on the one hand, creating single transactions and perhaps marketing them in a low-key way to a few prospective clients and, on the other, developing a new product with the intention of marketing it widely, through a number of channels, over an extended period of time. For that reason the implications for banks carrying out product development as a major line of business is also considered.

A number of issues that could have been discussed here have been omitted, partly for reasons of length and partly because they have been dealt with elsewhere in this book. The marketing of new products is an example (see *Chapter* 6).

In keeping with this narrow focus, two archetypal examples are used throughout this chapter:

- the Procter & Gamble/Bankers Trust 5/30 year swap, described in *Chapter* 2.[4] Note that on occasions statements may be made about possible motivations for each of the parties to the transaction. No claim is made that such possible motivations were the actual motivations—the intention is rather to use the transaction as a case study, and to bring out the issues in a generic rather than specific sense; and
- an Inverse Floating Rate Note (FRN).[5] This is a security with a coupon determined by a formula in the form of K–LIBOR, usually with a minimum coupon of 0 per cent. K is a fixed interest rate (for example 15 per cent), determined by the yield curve at the time the deal is struck. If rates rise the coupon falls, and conversely if rates fall the coupon rises. While this product is no longer really new,[6] it was implicated in the problems of Orange County in 1994 and has some characteristics which bring out dramatically some of the problems associated with the use of new financial products. It is assumed that the reader is familiar with the idea of decomposition of financial instruments, and that an Inverse FRN can be decomposed as a normal FRN, 2 swaps for the face value of the Inverse FRN where the fixed rate is received, and a bought interest rate cap.[7]

11.2 The product development process

The key steps in the process can be summarised as follows:

- understand the objectives of the user;
- understand the objectives of the provider;
- understand the objectives of the transaction, and set up the payoffs;
- analyse the market risks of the product;
- embed the payoff in a vehicle;
- consider the hedging or distribution of the transaction and its pricing;
- fine tune the product;
- reflect on where the value is coming from;
- assess the alternatives;
- consider the operational implications;
- determine whether approvals, limits and appropriate controls are in place;
- consider the suitability of the transaction;
- execute the transaction; and
- put in place on-going monitoring and review of the transaction.

It is not claimed that all product development goes through these steps sequentially. However, it is claimed that each of these steps is important, and should be dealt with at some point in the process. The order may well change, or even take place in a parallel manner, but omission of any step is a likely source of problems. With that caveat, each step is now considered in turn.

11.2.1 *Understand the objectives of the user*

This topic might seem to border on the self-evident on first inspection. A provider can only advise a user about new products, and a user can only make its choice about new products based on an understanding of the user's objectives.

This is to a large extent true, and the topic is not dealt with in this chapter. The reader is referred to *Chapters 4* and *5*, written from the viewpoint of borrowers and fund managers respectively, for more discussion on this point. However, there are 4 (related) points worth considering.

Firstly, it would be a bold user who assumes that the provider understands their objectives fully. At worst, a 'bucket shop' mentality may exist; the provider seeks to sell, irrespective of need. Even if the provider does genuinely care about the position of the user, the provider will never possess full information, either because the user does not (or cannot) disclose all relevant information or because the provider is not expert in the user's industry, for example. Moral: both the user and the provider must take responsibility for ensuring that products match objectives.

Secondly, as 'good practice' has evolved, and continues to evolve, it might be argued that providers have an incentive to not understand the objectives of the user. As is described later in this chapter (and within its proper legal framework in *Chapter 7*), there is arguably a greater duty of care in an advisory relationship than in a transactional relationship, where a new product is offered on a transactional or 'take it or leave it' basis. This leaves a choice for providers: avoid giving advice, but no doubt have a poorer relationship with the user, or work with the user in developing the product but have a greater on-going liability if problems arise in the future.

Thirdly, a bland statement along the lines of 'make sure that transactions entered into match the objectives of the user' are clearly true, but mask a multitude of real-life complexities. For example, exactly whose objectives? Boards set objectives, but usually not at a level of detail that would distinguish between different types of products or transactions. As described above, there may be a perfectly acceptable synthetic alternative to a new product, so what 'objectives' are being used to adjudicate between them? Clearly, rational tests can be established to help in this process (see *Section 11.2.9*). Equally clearly though, human nature will be in operation. Highly educated dealers in the user's treasury will often have a natural (and understandable) tendency to want to try out new products and techniques, both for the good of the organisation, their own job satisfaction and their own careers. Making sure that the objectives of dealers are aligned to the objectives of the firm is not trivial, notwithstanding a system of fully risk adjusted performance measures such as that described in *Chapter 8*.

Finally, the issue of the role of the provider in alerting the user to potentially flawed objectives needs consideration. For example, to what extent should Bankers Trust have alerted Procter & Gamble to the consequences of their view on interest rate movements being incorrect, or the lack of any 'risk adjusted' benefit to the transaction? The question is potentially enormous, and is unresolved; further consideration is deferred until *Section 11.2.12*, where the concept of 'suitability' is discussed.

11.2.2 *Understand the objectives of the provider*

Clearly, any provider needs to understand the objectives of a potential user. It is less obvious but equally true that users need to understand the objectives of providers. The reasons are quite commercial.

At a superficial level, any user must address the issue of the extent to which its interests are aligned with the provider due to the possibility of encountering a 'bucket shop' mentioned previously. Furthermore, the user will want to reflect upon past transactions, the broader relationship with the provider and so on to determine an appropriate level of trust (see *Chapter* 6).

Equally importantly, understanding how the provider manages its business will allow the user to make better judgments about the product being offered. This is in fact of benefit to both parties. An understanding of such matters as the costs of running a business, the hedging process, credit assessment and capital treatment will help a user understand that 'mid-market' is not an appropriate benchmark for the pricing of financially engineered transactions.

11.2.3 *Understand the objectives of the transaction, and set up the payoffs*

In *Section 11.1.1*, the possible motivations for new product development were briefly considered. This section extends that discussion, and attempts to understand the specific objective a user may have when looking for a new product. The possible objectives may be categorised as follows:

a) Customised cash flows

Timing of cash flow rather than market risk is the issue. An example is an amortising swap.

b) Exotic or specific payoff (including speculation)

The transaction is driven by a desire to take on a new risk because of a view that money will be made as a result. It may relate to a single market price, rate or index, the relationship or spread between 2 (or more) such prices, or the impact of a change in the underlying price on the value of the transaction (including gearing). The Procter & Gamble/Bankers Trust 5/30 year swap is an example.

c) Risk management related

The transaction is driven by a desire to take on a new risk to offset an existing risk. An example is provided by Magma Copper issuing bonds where the coupon is linked to the price of copper in such a way that the issuer benefits if the price of copper falls, offsetting its natural exposure to falls in the price of copper (Smithson et al. 1995, Chapter 16).

d) Cost of funds/return on investment applications

The transaction is not driven by a desire to take on a new risk, but rather by a desire to 'strip out' the complex features of the product and leave a simple product which generates an advantageous transaction (for example, cheap funds for a borrower, or an excess return on funds for an investor). For example, a typical AAA borrower issuing an Inverse FRN is usually entering into a set of hedging transactions with a derivatives provider to strip out the unwanted, complex payoff and leaving what amounts to an FRN at a rate lower than could be obtained directly from the floating rate market.[8]

Note that we need to distinguish carefully between such transactions which genuinely belong in this category and transactions which merely claim to be for risk management. For example, the Procter & Gamble/Bankers Trust transaction, which claimed to generate funds (say) at the Commercial Paper rate less 0.75 per cent, only did so because Procter & Gamble had taken on a geared exposure to rises in rates beyond a breakeven level.

e) Tax, accounting and benchmark 'arbitrage'

The transaction is driven by a particular tax, accounting or performance measurement treatment, rather than a genuine mark-to-market benefit. A simple example would be a borrower entering into a zero coupon swap (ie pay fixed in a single amount at the end of the swap, and receive floating each 6 months during the life of the swap). In a mark-to-market environment, such a swap will behave roughly the same as a standard swap. However, if the tax, financial or management accounts are prepared on a cash basis, this transaction will 'look' advantageous as income will be received each 6 months, but the corresponding payment (as a future value) will not be paid until the end of the life of the swap.

Other examples include transactions designed to convert income into capital gains (or vice versa) because of some asymmetry in the treatment of income and capital gains, or transactions designed to obtain a particular accounting or disclosure treatment (for example, because they were structured as a swap).[9]

f) Legal and regulatory 'arbitrage'

Similarly, a transaction may be driven by a particular legal or regulatory treatment, rather than a genuine mark-to-market benefit. For example, a money market fund prohibited from buying bonds but allowed to purchase FRNs could take on a bond-like exposure by purchasing an Inverse FRN, which in fact behaves like a *geared* exposure to the bond market![10]

As can be seen from this brief review, new derivative products tend in practice to fall into one of the following 3 categories:

- genuinely complex payoffs in derivative form, where the primary objective of the transaction is related to the payoff (for example, the Procter & Gamble/Bankers Trust 5/30 year swap);
- fairly simple payoffs packaged in derivative form, which superficially look complex but in fact are equivalent to a portfolio of simple products (for example, Inverse FRNs); or
- fairly simple payoffs packaged in derivative form, where the primary objective is the legal, regulatory, taxation or accounting treatment of the derivatives documentation (for example, swaps where the fixed cash flows are uneven, being loaded to either the beginning or end of the transaction for tax acceleration or deferral purposes).

Note that these categories are not mutually exclusive; an Inverse FRN may be purchased to achieve a certain regulatory outcome (bond exposure packaged as a money market instrument) as well as for the payoff.

The above discussion is meant to try to apply some structure to the sorts of 'ideas' which may drive a new product. Transactions in the third category are driven primarily by the form of the product rather than the manipulation of the payoff, and are therefore fairly simple to set up. However, the payoff is central to products in the first 2 categories, and the process by which they are developed is worth some consideration.

All design must commence with a central idea: the purpose that the proposed product is intended to achieve, and some conception of the potential users of the 'idea'. Frequently the original idea will come from an end-user. Typically, the end-user will have a problem to be solved or outcome to be achieved, and is prepared to disclose enough information to an intermediary to allow it to work on the problem. It should be noted that banks take endless pains to develop relationships with clients of sufficient depth to allow this sort of dialogue to take place. Sometimes an existing product will be sufficient to solve the problem, but at other times financial engineering will be required to tailor an existing product or develop a new product.

The successful development of new products leads to a second source of ideas: mimicry (otherwise known as 'reverse engineering'). In practice, it is difficult to keep any structure 'secret' for very long (it is in fact surprising how soon many products become public, presumably at least in part for reasons of advertising or profile building, both corporate and individual). Exposure of a structure to the market leads very quickly to reverse engineering of that product. By seeing enough of the structure it is usually not difficult to re-invent the structure, along with its pricing and hedging. The task then is to market this structure to end-users, hoping that the initial developers have not had too long a lead time or else that your pricing or relationships are better than theirs.

A third source of ideas is 'pure research', which may discover pricing anomalies, relationships that appear out of line, or mathematical techniques that allow exotic options (for example) to be priced and hedged. Similarly, research into legislative, taxation or accounting standard changes may allow a financial engineer to spot an opportunity which can be presented to a potential user. Unfortunately, while this tends to be the 'pure' approach, many organisations find this approach ultimately less profitable than reverse engineering on an organised basis. On the cost side academic researchers are sought after and tend to know their worth, and the support costs are not trivial. On the revenue side new products are only infrequently developed this way and, unlike other markets where research and development are commonplace, there is little or no practical protection via patent or copyright laws for new financial products (further encouraging the reverse engineering route).

Whatever the source of the idea, the heart of the development of many new derivatives products is the modification of the cash flows of the instrument to create the desired payoff. This will in turn lead to the fulfilment of objectives.

11.2.4 *Analyse the market risks of the product*

In many cases (such as the Procter & Gamble/Bankers Trust swap), unusual market risk is a key feature of the new product. In such cases, it is vital that both the user and the provider understand the market risk characteristics of the product.

As the product is new it may not have 'simple' market risk, which we might define as an outright (or option related) exposure to a single rate, price or index. Rather, it may incorporate an exposure to a second factor (quite unrelated to the primary factor), or be based on a spread or other relationship between two such factors, or perhaps incorporate indirect risk factors such as volatility or even correlation. Although the Procter & Gamble/Bankers Trust 5/30 year swap was stuctured and documented as a 5 year swap, its risk factors included exposure to not only 5 but 30 year Treasury Bond rates, 5 and 30 year Treasury Bond volatility, and in addition the correlation between 5 and 30 year Treasury Bond rates.

Although a detailed consideration is well beyond the scope of this chapter, some comments are appropriate.

- once the risks have been analysed and understood, they must be quantified for limit and management review purposes. This leads to 'value-at-risk' techniques;
- it should be carefully noted and understood that when analysing new products, the name of the product provides virtually no guidance. For example, the Procter & Gamble/Bankers Trust transaction was called a 'swap' but had quite different characteristics. Amongst other issues, the gearing and 'linearity' of a new product might be quite radically different to anything previously seen by the organisation in question;
- for complex products, the risk and price behaviour of the product may be determined by modelling, but with no useful history to which to refer. If the model is incorrect, either conceptually or in its implementation, then the risk and price of the products being used may be seriously flawed;
- any measurement of market risk carries with it an assumption about liquidity: how long will it take to exit the product? For complex new products, this is unknown but likely to be quite lengthy. Indirect liquidity is available by hedging rather than selling the product, but that brings with it additional basis risk. This practical issue needs to be considered; and
- in practice, there is an important linkage between market risk and other risks usually regarded as 'non market', such as personnel and systems risk. The management of the risk of a new complex product is often in the care of a handful of key personnel, and heavily reliant on a specially created system (for example, a spreadsheet written by those key individuals).

Bear in mind that as described previously, market risk may not be a key feature of a new product; it may be driven by a tax or regulatory requirement. Nevertheless, the product should still be reviewed as described in this section to ensure that no unexpected risks have appeared as a result of any structuring that has taken place.

11.2.5 *Embed the payoff in a vehicle*

If not already done, the transaction should be embedded in an appropriate vehicle. In some cases, the choice of vehicle will be a central part of the engineering and will drive the transaction (for example, to achieve a certain regulatory treatment). In other cases the vehicle may be a secondary issue, allowing the transaction to be packaged in different ways.

For example, the payoff of the Procter & Gamble/Bankers Trust 'swap' was embedded in standard swap documentation even though it didn't behave like the 5 year swap it purported to be. This choice of swap documentation was arbitrary as the payoff could just as easily have been embedded in bond documentation. In fact, in the initial stages, this is how it was presented to Procter & Gamble.[11]

Note that unless there is a very specific requirement, it is usual to embed the transaction as far as possible in an existing product form, rather than developing new documentation. For example, Bankers Trust documented their very non standard swap in a standard ISDA master agreement). There are a number of reasons for this.

Firstly, there is the issue of cost. It is cheaper to take a vehicle 'off the shelf' than to incur legal and other fees in developing a new vehicle. Secondly, a standard vehicle introduces no new risks associated with the documentation, which presumably is familiar and tested. Thirdly, the use of a standard form will assist liquidity in the future, should the product need to be unwound. Liquidity is always an issue when dealing in new, complex products because there may be a need to exit the product at some future date. Embedding a complex payoff in a proprietary document can only exacerbate this problem.

Off-balance sheet structures are commonly embedded in an ISDA swap-like agreement. The form of the agreement is identical to that for a vanilla swap (and in fact can be within the same master agreement, with all the potential benefits of netting), but the nature, frequency and amount of the cash flows are dealt with by way of an explicit schedule. Note that the payments need not be interest rate related: they can be driven by any underlying index or price. This technique will also work for any other form of swap or derivatives documentation with which the counterparties are comfortable.

Structured products which involve funding can be embedded in virtually any debt instrument. Public issues are less common, because of costs and the difficulties of attracting a significant pool of investors at a time, but any instrument which can be issued on tap is a suitable contender. In recent years, many issuers have set up flexible MTN programs which can be tapped to provide structured notes tailored to the demands of investors (a process commonly referred to as 'reverse inquiry'). The investor will normally keep the Note in its issued form, while the issuer will probably unwind the Note to generate standard floating or fixed funding in the required currency.

It should be borne in mind that a synthetic alternative to a new product usually exists. Accordingly, accepting the documentation of each of the underlying standard products is also a viable alternative, provided that the objective of the transaction is related to payoff rather than the form of the transaction.

11.2.6 *Consider the hedging or distribution of the transaction and its pricing*

The moment of truth arrives when the bank checks how the proposed product will be sold or hedged and then priced. It is only if the pricing is appropriate, and the product can be distributed by way of a matched transaction, or unbundled and hedged, do the glimmerings of a viable product exist.

Bear in mind that every financial transaction must have 2 sides. A borrower can only raise funds if it can issue debt or securities, and an investor can only acquire assets if it can find an issuer who will issue, or has issued, a suitable instrument. A similar analysis prevails for off-balance sheet instruments, although an intermediary will probably transact with the parties as principal. (It is worth noting, in passing, that this ability to stand as a principal does not remove the need for distribution. The appetite of even the biggest derivatives houses for being an end-taker of outright risk is surprisingly modest. While their ability to warehouse secondary risks such as basis risk is greater, it is not limitless and in any event needs to be turned over to allow for future transactions.)

Consequently, for a transaction to work we need to decide:

- Will the transaction be kept in its original form by both parties?
- Will it be unbundled by one or both parties and sold or hedged in pieces? and
- In either event, is the price demanded by the originating side commensurate with the price that will be demanded when the transaction is distributed or hedged?

For example, in a straight bond raising, the issue will only work at a level where the investors are happy with their yield and the borrower is happy with the cost of funds, and these rates (neglecting fees and costs of the issue) are identical. This motivation may apply equally to a structured bond product.

If the instrument is issued in its original form, the exercise is one of simple distribution. Inquiries can be made of potential investors (if the transaction is being driven by a borrower), and a rate at which the issue would be purchased can be clearly ascertained. If this is acceptable to the party driving the transaction, the deal can proceed. This is a common scenario for transactions engineered for tax, accounting or regulatory consequences. An instrument is developed in a form which meets the needs of one party, and is subsequently offered to potential counterparties (who are indifferent to tax and other consequences, presumably operating under a different regime) who will effectively price the issue. If the pricing is acceptable, it proceeds; if not, it either stalls until new investors or a fresh twist can be found, or else it fails.

It is more common for one (less commonly both) side of the transaction to be unbundled. This happens most frequently when the transaction is driven by a borrower looking for 'below market' funds or, sometimes, by an investor looking for 'above market' yields. A transaction is created which meets the needs of the other party, but is then unbundled to create a traditional borrowing or investment. The rate of that borrowing or investment takes into account the costs incurred in hedging the unwanted components.

For example, as described in *Section 11.2.3*, a borrower may be prepared to issue an Inverse FRN, not because of a rate view, but because it can be unbundled into its component parts: one of which may be equivalent to a sub-LIBOR borrowing, and the rest of which can be hedged in the market.

The first issue is therefore 'Can the relevant parts be hedged?' Issues that need to be considered include:

- is the structure hedgable in theory? For example, the investor may want to be granted an exotic option, but if this cannot be unbundled and hedged (assuming for the time being the borrower does not want to accept that risk), the transaction will not work; and

- is the structure hedgable in practice? For example, we may be able to devise a method of unbundling the transaction but face practical hurdles such as:

  — are credit lines available?
  — is there a market at the maturity required?
  — is there sufficient liquidity in the market?
  — is it too expensive to hedge effectively (eg bid/offer spreads)?

Assuming there is a practical hedging strategy, the issue is priced to see if it works. In practice this is attempted by deriving all the cash flows and calculating the effective cost of the residual 'traditional' instrument. This is often a key step in the process, particularly where hedging is possible over time, but in the short term the bid/offer spread is wide, or liquidity means that the position will need to be warehoused. Frequently, pricing on a worst-case basis may mean the business is missed or accusations of price gouging are levelled. On the other hand, these costs can be real and significant, particularly if warehousing or dynamic hedging are required for a protracted period.

Bear in mind that factors other than pricing can determine whether a product can be distributed. For example, the rating of the issuer or counterparty and the form of documentation required by each of the counterparties can become fatal impediments.

Finally, it is important to understand that all products do not 'work' all the time. It is typical for a new product to be developed to exploit some opportunity and for it to enjoy huge popularity for (say) a matter of months, only to disappear from sight completely. Such windows of opportunity may (rarely) include genuine arbitrage situations, or more commonly a perceived anomaly or imbalance in a price or relationship between 2 prices. Tax, accounting and regulatory windows may open from time to time (and will usually close if the product becomes too popular). Increased retail demand for a particular company, sector, country, commodity and so on can be catered for (and thus exploited) by professional participants.

11.2.7 *Fine tune the product*

It is highly unusual to arrive at the final form of the product after only one iteration. A number of iterations are invariably required, for a number of reasons.

Firstly, most products are developed from the point of view of only one (or perhaps even none) of the parties to the final transaction. Once both sides have been spoken to, there is invariably some tailoring required to meet the needs of the other party.

Secondly, as suggested above, there may be a theoretical or practical impediment to unbundling the product. Consequently, the transaction may need to be modified from to its original concept to make it more amenable to unbundling (or straight distribution).

Thirdly, engineering may throw up unintended consequences which need to be dealt with. For example, the first iteration of an Inverse FRN may have been an FRN with a coupon of 15 per cent-LIBOR, say. The unintended consequence is that if LIBOR exceeds 15 per cent, the investor will pay the borrower a coupon, which is not only 'emotionally' unsatisfactory for the investor, but also leads to the borrower having credit risk on the investor! The second iteration is therefore to put in place a minimum coupon of 0 per cent.

Fourthly, the pricing of the transaction may not be acceptable to one (or even both) parties. This can be for a number of reasons: firstly, the idea simply may not work (the market may not bear the pricing being demanded, in which case the transaction cannot proceed); or it may be that the transaction has been over-engineered and can be restructured. One possibility is that the issuer may have placed constraints on the transaction which are not central to his or her requirements, but which make it unviable. For example, an investor may demand that the asset he or she acquires is a public Eurobond issue, but for reasons of cost and profile the borrower is only prepared to issue as a Euro-MTN. If the requirement for a Eurobond is not central (because of some internal limitation, for example) tailoring the transaction by substituting a Euro-MTN may make the transaction viable. (Note, by the way, that tailoring a transaction to make the pricing acceptable is not the same as taking on additional risk to achieve a target rate.)

Finally, the product may be workable in principle (to an investor, for example), but there may be difficulty in finding an appropriate borrower to issue securities, or in finding a form of documentation acceptable to both parties.

11.2.8 *Reflect on where the value is coming from*

Once a transaction has been developed and tailored, it is worth all parties reflecting upon why the deal works from the point of view of both sides. Understanding this will ensure that they have properly understood the deal, as well as giving assistance in dealing with 'marginal' transactions.

Firstly, we can rule out certain extreme cases. Any deal which looks too good to be true probably is. Warning signs can be the presence of physical cash or bearer instruments, rates which are well outside of market, unfamiliar intermediaries, counterparties or jurisdictions, unwillingness to commit terms to writing and so on. In such situations, reflect and take careful advice on whether the transaction is 'state of the art' financial engineering, or old fashioned money laundering or fraud.

If the terms seem too good to be true and there are no warning signs, it is likely that the transaction may not have been understood correctly. Most commonly, a risk exists that has not been correctly analysed. Bear in mind that new product development is largely a zero sum game. Value cannot be created out of thin air; it must come from (or go to) one of the parties to the transaction, an intermediary, or third parties such as taxpayers etc.

Traditionally, product development (including very early examples such as the swap market) were driven by comparative advantage, that is, fixed and floating borrowers of different credit ratings effectively arbitraged differences in risk premia at different parts of the curve to each generate a lower cost of funds than otherwise possible. In this case, the investors are supplying the value. They have given up the difference in risk premia back to the borrowers (and a bank which may also stand in the swap transaction).

However, there are other sources apart from comparative advantage which frequently drive transactions. We also need to look to these to see where value in a transaction is coming from:

- there is a tax angle, and the taxpayers in some jurisdiction are subsidising the transaction;
- one of the parties suffers from constraints or a lack of alternatives, and needs to give up value in order to achieve his or her objectives, reflecting the cost of alternatives;
- one of the parties has insufficient information and is subsidising the other party inadvertently;
- the advantageous cost of funds is illusory and in fact represents fair pricing for the risks being taken; and

- what one party regards as a 'significant' spread the other party regards as insignificant or a normal transaction cost.

Any of these can be acceptable reasons in the right circumstances. However, if either party does not understand where the value is coming from, that party runs a serious risk of entering into a mispriced or unsuitable transaction.

Finally, do not assume that it is only end-users who should be looking for the source of value in a transaction. When reverse engineering a product, banks also need to ensure that they have fully understood the dynamics of the pricing and hedging of the product. Missing a subtlety of this nature can be very expensive if discovered after one or more trades have been completed.

11.2.9 *Assess the alternatives*

The need to assess alternatives has already been mentioned. This is worth careful consideration, as there is an ever-present danger in new product development of becoming involved in development for its own sake. In product development increased flexibility invariably brings with it additional costs.

In certain situations there may well be no alternative. This is common where there are tax or regulatory implications, for example, or where the aim is to shift cash flows.

However, where the structure is a means of expressing a market view, more care is required, particularly where this is combined with a desire to create 'cheap' funds. In such situations, there is almost certainly an 'unbundled' alternative which should be considered. (This flows from the presumed ability of the arranger to hedge the transaction, demonstrating the need for end-users of these instruments to be able to understand transactions down to the level of pricing and hedging.)

For example, while an investor may purchase a reverse floater for its payoff, it is likely that the issuer is unbundling it to create cheap funding that derives solely from the spread that the investor gives up in the transaction. Why would an investor do this, when it could purchase the unbundled alternative of an FRN, 2 received swaps, and a bought cap? An even simpler alternative, with similar (but ungeared) interest rate exposure, would be to purchase a traditional bond.

Unacceptable reasons would include ignorance and an inability to understand or price the alternative. Nevertheless, there may be reasons which justify this implicit cost:

- a retail investor, while not ignorant in the above sense, has no alternative, and invariably faces a retail mark-up;
- the investor may not be of sufficient credit quality to obtain a swap credit line, making the first alternative impossible. Investment restrictions may eliminate the second alternative;
- the investor may want the gearing in the instrument, making the second alternative unappealing; and
- the investor may not be able to book the alternatives because of internal systems constraints, or because unbundled they may have an unacceptable accounting treatment.

In such cases, the investor (or borrower in the analogous situation) can measure the costs against the benefits on an informed basis. However, in all cases it should be recalled from *Section 11.1.1* that unbundled products do have certain advantages, such as:

- liquidity;
- lower transaction costs, including bid/offer spread;
- transparency of pricing;
- transparency of accounting, tax, regulatory etc treatment; and
- ease of booking and control within a more traditional environment.

Similarly, always remember that apart from unbundling, there is the alternative of simpler financially engineered structures. As a rule of thumb, each level of complexity adds to the sunk cost of the transaction, both on entry and on any future unwinding. This is partly because of real costs involved in hedging and risk management, but also because of the decreased transparency of the structure which tends to lead to reduced price competition. There may be features which are nice rather than central. Apart from their own cost, what cost do they add to the overall transaction?

As a stark demonstration of this point, consider the Procter & Gamble/Bankers Trust transaction. Given that Procter & Gamble were keen to exploit what they felt was the unlikelihood of a significant rise in rates, why did they embed their view in such a complex transaction? Why not simply buy an equivalent amount of futures contracts or sell put options on futures prices, or perhaps enter into a receiver's swap or sold payer's swaption for equivalent terms and amounts?[12] All of these are standard products, and had they been used the issues which caused so many problems for Procter & Gamble, such as mark-to-market accounting, transparency for management, liquidity and so on would simply not have existed!

An implication of this discussion is that an end-user should manage relationships with arrangers of financial engineering structures with great care. There may be a preference for one house because of a lending relationship or historical associations. However, it is difficult to get a balanced view of alternatives when talking to one house only and, as suggested above, pricing may tend to suffer. There is a fine line here; there is value to be had in a close relationship with a good investment bank, which may result in a range of quality transactions being offered. It is not suggested that all end-users will want to have an adversarial relationship, or that they should obtain alternative quotes on proprietary structures offered from the market. However, non-proprietary structures should be priced competitively and, at the very least, end-users should be able to replicate structures so that they can price independently from observable market parameters such as zero coupon and volatility curves. If for some reason it seems necessary to carry out a transaction whose pricing cannot be tested, great care should be exercised, as the only source of mark-to-market data will be the provider of the structure. At the very least, great attention should be paid to the terms upon which the transaction can be closed in the future, as this will convey information about both market risk and the spread to the dealer.

11.2.10 *Consider the operational implications*

There will need to be agreement from those responsible for running specific areas such as the back office, accounting, and computer systems that they can support the proposed product. It needs to be understood that these areas in general cannot vary their level of support as quickly as a front office can build volumes, so that there needs to be agreement as to business plans for some time into the future.

The agreement of such support areas needs to be informed, and not driven by undue pressure from business areas. A clear strategy needs to be in place to provide both current support and future support if volumes grow in accordance with the business plan. Particular care needs to be taken if the product area is very new or complex, rather than a natural evolution from existing products.

There are a number of issues that should be given careful consideration in the context of product development, such as:

- excessive reliance on particular individuals or resources. Are there single or small groups of individuals whose departure would threaten not only new transactions (unfortunate but acceptable), but the management of the portfolio of existing transactions?

- contingency arrangements. Given that many new products are very heavily reliant on systems, for example, what arrangements are in place to support the business if there is a short-term or long-term disruption to those systems? and
- the audit program and the overall control environment, taking into account the complexity of the product, and the possibility that traditional audit and control personnel may lack the market and quantitative skills, for example, to monitor the businesses fully.

11.2.11 *Determine whether approvals, limits and appropriate controls are in place*

It needs to be established that all appropriate approval, limit and control issues have been identified and dealt with before launch. Again bear in mind that the risk associated with missing a tax implication (say) for a large portfolio is much greater than for a single product, so that a level of control needs to offset the entrepreneurial instincts of the business area.

In practice, it is virtually impossible for senior management to be involved in every transaction, so that responsibility must be delegated to front line management. However, there should be a mechanism for senior management to clear products which have the potential to have a significant impact on the operations of the bank in some way.

To fulfil this function, senior management needs to be supported and advised by independent specialists who can analyse the product and the way it has been developed, but who are separate from the business area. With such support, senior management will be looking for confirmation that the business plan is satisfactory, that all appropriate steps have been taken in setting up the product, and that the product is one that the bank should be involved in (particularly given the interests of broader stakeholders and interested parties such as shareholders, the customer base of the bank and regulators), and that it is correctly balanced with the other businesses and risks of the bank.

The apppropriate level of clearance should be in proportion to the significance of the product. All products should be cleared by management not involved in the dealing or selling process, but the level of clearance may range from a divisional head to a full board depending on the issues.

11.2.12 *Consider the suitability of the transaction*

Historically, this has been regarded as the responsibility of the (end-user) parties to the transaction, with the provider making the assumption (at least in the case of large professional counterparties) that it is for the end-users to assess risks and suitability. It is not easy to predict whether courts will find that an intermediary in a particular transaction does in fact owe an additional legal duty towards the user—namely, a duty to exercise care in its dealings with the user. Hence it is not just the user but also the arranger who need to reflect on the issue of risk and suitability. This is particularly so in situations where the financial engineer has a broader relationship with the end-user and so, for example, where it plays a role which could be construed as that of an advisor.

There can be no definitive checklist to confirm whether a transaction is suitable and appropriate, but as a minimum it is suggested that the issues noted below need to be considered. They should be examined not only by management of a party about to enter into a financially engineered deal, but also, albeit to a more limited extent, by management of the intermediary not involved in dealing and selling.

- Does the transaction fit with the party's objectives? For example, if a corporate treasury has a board mandate to be an active, risk-taking profit centre, a sub-LIBOR funding driven by an option granted on a commodity may be suitable, whereas it would seem more dubious for a small, match-funding Treasury. Similarly, a geared structured note may be suitable for a hedge fund, but not for the management of surplus cash.
- Has the transaction been approved at an appropriate level, involving management, board and perhaps regulators?
- Are the market risks understood, have they been tested under a range of scenarios, and does the party have the ability to absorb losses which may arise?
- Are the secondary risks such as liquidity, credit and settlement risk understood, and have appropriate measures to deal with them been put in place?
- If the transaction relies on interpretation of tax, accounting or regulatory rulings, have independent opinions been sought, and is the aggression of interpretation suitable for the party?

- Does the party have the management, and operational and control structure to support the proposed transaction?
- Does the transaction add shareholder value, or are management's interests being served ahead of those of the shareholders?
- Does the transaction give rise to potential reputational risk, in excess of the benefit of the transaction or the appetite of the party?
- Do the parties come to the table as equals, or does one party have such superior information that would cause discomfort should the transaction be scrutinised independently at a later date? This can apply to banks dealing with less sophisticated corporations, but will equally apply to borrowers raising funds from a retail market.
- Has the pricing of the transaction been independently tested, either internally or in the market?
- Have alternatives been examined? For example, is there a simpler way of achieving the objectives of the transaction? What value does the engineered structure add, to whom, and at what cost?

It is unlikely, unless in an extreme situation, that such an analysis will definitively allow a transaction to proceed or be stopped. Nevertheless, such analysis (at an appropriate level of management) will at least identify potential issues and enable them to be tackled directly.

11.2.13 *Execute the transaction*

If the end of this process is successfully reached, the transaction is ready to be launched. This will involve final pricing, confirmations and the exchange of formal documentation.

Once the transaction has been closed, the organisation should review regularly the performance of the transaction in the context of the organisation's objectives. In addition, the organisation will need to deal with such matters as booking the transaction, making on-going accounting entries, providing appropriate management accounting information to senior management and establishing the control environment. All of these requirements need to be considered explicitly by management, as they can all give rise to losses at a future date if not correctly handled.

11.2.14 *Ongoing monitoring and review of the transaction*

Users and providers will need to put in place a process to ensure the transaction is appropriately monitored during its life.

Users will want to ensure that the transaction meets the objectives originally set. For example, if a transaction is entered into for hedging purposes, the efficiency with which the underlying risk is hedged in practice should be regularly monitored. Any residual risk needs to be understood, and any failure in the hedge needs to be dealt with.

Providers also need to monitor transactions and their associated risks during their lives. Compliance with the approvals, limits and controls that have been established (see *Section 11.2.11*) must also clearly be monitored. An appropriate performance measurement environment should be established. Clearly, basic profit and loss will be a useful measure. However, account should be taken of:

- return on capital;
- return on market risks;
- return on credit utilised;
- volume growth, both in absolute terms and compared with the business plan and the market generally; and
- analysis of the raw profit and loss, to ascertain whether the profits are driven by client spread, hedging, outright speculation, and whether there are parts of the business subsidising other parts.

11.3 New product development as a business process

This chapter has concentrated on the process of developing a single product or transaction. The issues discussed remain valid whether one or 100 products are developed. However, if the provider is developing many products on an ongoing basis, product development becomes a business in its own right, and issues arise above and beyond those relevant to a single transaction. In particular, repeating a transaction implies concentrations of risk, and often an inability to change direction quickly because of size and commitment to customers. A full discussion is beyond the scope of this chapter, but examples of such concentrations of risk include:

- major market risks: which may be quantified by scenario analysis at varying levels of probability (from expected, to 'normal' worst case, and disaster scenarios). An analysis of the correlation of these risks with other risks the bank runs would be helpful. An analysis of the experience and abilities of the individuals managing risk and marketing the product would also be appropriate here;

- basis, correlation and residual risks: where the product is hedged on a portfolio basis, and there are gaps or imperfections in the hedging. These risks appear minor but have the potential to develop into significant pockets of risk;
- pricing risk: where the pricing of a product is determined by competitive pressures. The issue becomes whether the product can be managed (incurring hedging costs) within this pricing;
- model risk: the risk that the mathematical underpinning for pricing or hedging may be either flawed in theory, or incorrectly implemented. While serious for a particular transaction this can be disastrous for a product portfolio;
- credit risks: which may be quantified, for example, by counterparty, term, industry or country to ensure that there is sufficient appetite for such risks. Ideally, if there is a lack of appetite because of existing exposures, there should be an analysis of the marginal revenue being derived by all internal users of credit lines to ascertain whether there should be a reallocation;
- operational risks: arising from the impact of the product on such matters as back office, systems and control structures if the product is complex, or will generate high volumes;
- reputational risk: which may result from adverse publicity or comment associated with actively promoting a product which relies on aggressive interpretations of tax law; and
- other risks: such as those which may arise if an unsuitable product is sold to a client.

Risk analysis is a two-stage process. The actual identification of risk is not the issue, as all institutions accept risk as part of their normal business activities. Of more concern is the measurement and management of that risk.

Before becoming too involved, the provider should conduct a fairly careful analysis of the costs and benefits of the proposed product. These can be more than the simple direct revenues and direct costs of the product.

A full analysis of revenues would need to include:

- direct revenues or margins from the product;
- indirect but measurable revenues, for example, those derived

from book management or the favourable impact on other products; and
- unmeasurable benefits, such as bank-wide benefits which derive from having the bank seen as a provider of solutions.

Similarly, a full list of costs would include:

- direct and indirect costs of individuals and resources involved in the development;
- direct and indirect costs of supporting the product when developed;
- an allocation reflecting the credit and capital usage of the product;
- an analysis of the resources required to support the product, including the number and type of personnel, premises requirements, computer hardware and software, information services, support services and so on; and
- a fuller study of the cost of the product, if the resources required to support it increase non-linearly. For example, support staff can be hired one by one, but if volumes push a computer system past its capacity, the marginal cost may be impossibly high in the short term.

This financial analysis must be in the context of a comparison between the product under consideration and the alternatives, that is, other uses of resources that are available at that time. It must also be in the context of competing institutions, both at present and in the future.

11.4 Conclusion

In conclusion, some final thoughts on the potential pitfalls of product design and development follow.

It is the process of developing individual transactions and then products that has led to the current proliferation of financial instruments. Products that were once innovative (for example swaptions) are now standard and even liquid. There is no reason to believe that this process will stop now. This process performs certain valuable roles, for example, it promotes and expedites the transfer of risk away from those who don't want it towards those who do. Adding value through new products requires, however, all users and potential users of these instruments to be focused on their needs and to avoid excessive or inappropriate use. Just because a product can be used doesn't mean that it should be used.

There are other consequences of product development that tend to be harder to justify. The use of product development to circumvent local regulations and tax codes may have a role in developing more free and efficient markets, but it involves placing the users and promoters of such products above local authorities. This is clearly a cause for valid debate.

There should be no misunderstanding as to the historical and potential profitability of new product development. The hand of the banking community is not strengthened by excessive profitability, just as arguments as to suitability of products or regulatory arbitrage, for example, are diminished by their self-serving character. This is particularly so in the 'bonus culture' that has developed in many if not most providers, where there is a very direct link between individual transactions and (frequently sizeable) bonuses on the dealing desk of the provider. Such a linkage may be commercially sensible for the provider, but can only lead to a climate of distrust between user and provider.

It is not being suggested that new products will always cause problems for the user. It is, however, being suggested that there are usually many more bad uses than good uses of new products. It is therefore incumbent on both users and providers, at the levels of both senior and dealing room management, to ensure that the considerable potential benefits of new products are not lost within a general attitude of mistrust between providers and users, perhaps exacerbated by informed or uninformed intervention by regulators or legislators.

This chapter concludes with a third alternative quotation, alongside those appearing in the first section of this chapter. Perhaps it is the closest to the truth of all three:

> History teaches us that men and nations behave wisely when they have exhausted all other alternatives.
>
> Abba Eban

Appendix 11.1 Product decomposition

A key technique in product development is decomposition. Many new products can be broken down into their component parts. In other words, it is possible to produce a (static) portfolio which replicates the cash flows of that product.

In other words, if we call our new product X, we can find standard products A, B, C . . . such that X = A + B + C + . . ., where we interpret '=' to mean identical in cash flow terms and '+' to mean 'add to the portfolio'.

The importance of decomposition cannot be overstated. If a structured bond X can be decomposed as Bond + A + B (in other words, X as a portfolio made up of a straight bond, as well as products A and B), then:

- X is simply the sum of its parts, leading to a better *understanding of X*.
- X–Bond–A–B = 0; in other words, X can be *hedged*.
- Bond = X–A–B; in other words, the structured bond can be turned into a straight bond.
- It would be nice to be able to say that the *price* of X is equal to the sum of the prices of the bond, and A and B. Unfortunately, this may not be true as there may be tax, regulatory and other considerations which in some circumstances give the structured bond a greater value than the sum of its parts. However, the main factors contributing to the price of X may be understood, and the mark-to-market value of its cash flows may be calculated as the sum of the mark-to-market values of X, A and B.
- Following on from this last point, the exposure of X to movements in an underlying price, rate or other factor will be equal to the sum of the exposures of the Bond, A and B to that factor.

In other words, decomposing a product tells virtually all there is to know about the way that product behaves in a financial sense (as opposed to tax, legal, regulatory etc sense), and simplifies dealing with that product. Any new product which can be decomposed in this way (so long as this is understood) is unlikely to cause problems.

As an example, it can be shown that the Inverse FRN referred to in *Section 1.3* can be decomposed as 2 straight bonds, a short FRN, and a bought cap with a strike rate of K per cent, where K is the fixed amount used to determine the coupon.[13] This starkly demonstrates the power of the technique. We can now see that an Inverse FRN is actually equivalent to a geared bond exposure (along with a short term exposure and an out-of-the-money cap, which do not contribute greatly to the market risk, at least at the outset). This understanding was not obvious from the product description, yet dealing with an Inverse FRN is now easy. We can hedge it, turn it back into a straight bond, carry out a mark-to-market valuation etc easily.

Contrast this with the Procter & Gamble/Bankers Trust swap. This cannot be decomposed (as the exposure to 5 year and 30 year rates cannot be separated in an additive sense), so that problems easily arise. For example, to hedge the transaction, Procter & Gamble were forced to revert to Bankers Trust. It is impossible to value the transaction easily, meaning that daily movements in profit and loss could not be monitored.

References

Finnerty, J.D. 1988, 'Financial Engineering in Corporate Finance: An Overview', *Financial Management*, Winter

Peng, S.Y. and Dattatreya, R.E. 1995 *The Structured Note Market—The Definitive Guide for Investors, Traders and Issuers*, Probus Publishing, Chicago

Smithson, C.W., Smith, C.W. and Wilford, D.S. 1995, *Managing Financial Risk—A Guide to Derivative Products, Financial Engineering, and Value Maximization*, Irwin

Notes

1. Contrast this with Procter & Gamble who, as described in *Chapter 2*, entered into a remarkably complex transaction to express a quite simple view of rates (see *Section 11.2.9* of this chapter for further discussion).
2. See Finnerty (1988) for a detailed discussion of the motivations behind a range of financial innovations.
3. See *Section 11.2.5* for an example taken from the Procter & Gamble/Bankers Trust transaction.
4. Information on this case comes from court papers from the US District Court, Southern District of Ohio, Western Division, Case C–1–94–735.
5. See, for example, Peng and Dattatreya (1995), Chapter 5, for a more detailed description of inverse FRNs, and a range of other variants of basic FRNs.
6. The first issue was by SallieMae in 1986.
7. See *Appendix 11.1* at the end of this chapter for some further discussion of these issues.
8. In other words, using the decomposition of an inverse FRN as a normal FRN, 2 swaps for the face value of the inverse FRN where the fixed rate is received, and a bought interest rate cap described in *Appendix 11.1*, the borrower would issue the inverse FRN but then receive the fixed rate on 2 interest rate swaps (or one swap for twice the face value) and buy an interest rate cap to synthetically return the structured note to 'normal' form. The issue price and/or coupon would be chosen to ensure that the yield on this synthetic 'normal' FRN is advantageous to the borrower.
9. Transactions like the Procter & Gamble/Bankers Trust transaction could be aggregated with all other swaps to prevent their explicit disclosure, as well as potentially qualifying for hedge accounting treatment rather than mark-to-market treatment, which would be the case if the payoff was achieved using futures contracts, for example.

10. Geared by a factor of 2, because the key components of the decomposition are 2 straight bonds.
11. For example, a bond issued by a borrower with coupons given by CP – 0.75% + margin, where the margin is the same as defined in expression (1) in the Procter & Gamble case study in *Chapter 2* would have given the borrower the same exposure as Procter & Gamble, but in bond form.
12. While the transaction cannot be fully decomposed, it is assumed for the moment that 5 and 30 year rates are perfectly correlated (certainly in practice the correlation is high, and was particularly so during the period in early 1994 when Procter & Gamble sustained their losses), then the transaction can be decomposed as a geared bundle of sold call options on 5 year rates and 30 year rates (or sold put options on 5 year and 30 year treasury bond prices).
13. This is equivalent to the decomposition as a normal FRN, 2 swaps for the face value of the inverse FRN where the fixed rate is received, and a bought interest rate cap mentioned in *Section 11.1.3*, but makes the point more starkly.

Conclusion
The risks that remain

ELIZABETH SHEEDY

Two friends enjoyed a successful week of big-game hunting in a remote area. Their pilot for the return journey told them the plane could not carry all the game they had bagged. The hunters protested that the plane that had carried them out the previous year had carried a similar load, so the pilot reluctantly agreed to try. After loading the plane and taking off it transpired that the plane was indeed too heavily loaded and the plane crashed. As they stumbled from the wreckage, one hunter asked the other if he knew where they were. 'Well, I'm not sure,' replied the second, 'but I think we are about two miles from where we crashed last year.'

Anonymous

The fundamental question underlying this book is plain: can the derivatives industry learn the harsh lessons of experience, or is it condemned to repeat past mistakes like the hunters in the above anecdote? Our conclusion is that the derivatives industry is in a state of transition. While many lessons have been learned, the process of change is far from complete.

In this chapter we summarise:

- the major risks remaining;
- the reforms highlighted throughout the book; and
- issues for further study.

Growth in Asia-Pacific derivatives markets

Our examination of the current state of the industry commenced with a study of the Asia-Pacific region, arguably the home of the most rapidly developing derivatives markets in the world. Australia, Japan, Hong Kong and Singapore are sophisticated financial centres, providing home or regional bases for the world's financial institutions. While these 4 financial centres offer the most mature infrastructure for derivatives markets in Asia, other centres are growing even faster than the established markets.

The main drivers of growth in newer derivatives markets are deregulation, increasing volatility in financial prices, rapidly growing economies and the transfer of technology from established centres. These trends are evident in countries such as the Peoples' Republic of China, Malaysia, Thailand, South Korea, Indonesia and Taiwan.

Chapter 1 concluded that these rapidly developing derivatives markets offer exciting prospects for all participants, but also large risks. Legal, operational and market risks apply in these markets, resulting mainly from lack of infrastructure. Some events (such as the suspension of bond futures trading on the Shanghai Stock Exchange in March 1995) show that growth can outpace infrastructure, to the detriment of all concerned.

Catalysts of change

Chapter 2 discussed 3 case studies which we believe should be, and to an extent already are, catalysts of change for the industry world-wide. Barings, Metallgesellschaft and Procter & Gamble were widely publicised due to the size of the losses. We believe these cases deserve to be re-examined now that more information is available regarding their underlying causes. They illustrate the dangers of management complacency, inappropriate use of exotic instruments, inadequate controls, lack of risk assessment/understanding and the erosion of trust between providers and users of derivatives. Participants need to examine their use of derivatives in the light of these events. Derivatives providers were the starting point for this examination in *Chapter 3*.

Professional dealing desks

Derivatives dealers in earlier times were often noted for their 'cowboy' mentality. A range of factors necessitated an evolution in this approach, including greater complexity of derivatives products and increased competition. The latter led to a reduction in profit margins, requiring greater volumes to maintain revenues and hence more sophisticated risk control.

This 'professionalisation' of the derivatives dealer has been accompanied by the disappearance of 'the black box'. Specialist knowledge of derivatives products has disseminated from the dealing desk throughout the industry: to lawyers, accountants, tax advisers, credit assessors, regulators, risk managers, senior managers, corporate treasurers and fund managers. *Chapter 3* argued that this dissemination of knowledge has further strengthened the capacity of the industry to avoid and withstand losses.

Despite these encouraging developments, there are a number of outstanding issues. One is the establishment of effective performance measures and incentives. Also, senior managers struggle to promote co-operation between business units, especially when each is separately accountable for its own profitability. These and other issues provide ongoing challenges for derivatives providers.

The long term success of derivatives use, however, requires reforms by end-users as well as providers of derivatives, as discussed in *Chapters 4* and *5*.

Corporate treasuries

According to *Chapter 4*, corporate treasuries have fundamentally changed their approach to derivatives. The losses of 1994 and 1995, not to mention other earlier disasters, led to a questioning of the use of derivatives, and even the role of hedging. While most (if not all) participants now accept the importance of hedging, various conditions must exist for the successful use of derivatives.

One precondition is a detailed assessment of risk and exposure. In the past, derivatives were often employed without such an assessment, resulting in unforeseen adverse consequences in some cases. Informed managerial oversight is a second precondition for the use of derivatives. In today's stringent corporate governance environment, shareholders and regulators will not accept ignorance by directors as an excuse for losses.

There is also a need for review of performance objectives for corporate treasuries. Many high profile losses (eg Procter & Gamble) were arguably caused by aggressive benchmarks that inadvertently encouraged risky behaviour. As a result, the number of profit-centre treasuries diminished greatly, and debate continues on selection of appropriate benchmarks.

A further area for reform is that of management reporting. Requirements of derivatives providers drive many of the developments in risk quantification (discussed in later sections). Unlike banks, corporations have natural exposures to financial prices. Corporations require reporting of cashflow-at-risk, not just mark-to-market valuations of derivatives. In other words, the net effect of derivatives and underlying exposures must be reported, preferably on a portfolio basis.

Fund managers

Applications for derivatives are growing rapidly in funds management, as discussed in *Chapter 5*. Derivatives offer the potential to improve the efficiency of unit trusts, superannuation funds, hedge funds and life companies if used appropriately. If anything, derivatives are still under used in this industry, especially in the Asian region.

Fund managers have been forced to grapple with many of the same issues as corporate treasurers. The requirement to protect unsophisticated investors has, however, heightened the need for such a re-evaluation. In Australia, for example, all workers are reliant to some extent on the funds management industry for their retirement savings. Not surprisingly, regulation has been used (or considered) in some cases to protect these investors.

Consistent with earlier chapters, *Chapter 5* argued that fund managers have increased their capacity and skills to manage derivatives strategies. The industry is still, however, grappling with issues such as:

- the need to ensure that the use of strategies is suitable for a given situation;
- informed management oversight and risk controls;
- dissemination of intelligible information to investors to aid investment choices;
- realism by investors in terms of the risk implications of high return investments; and
- performance measures that encourage suitable risk-taking behaviour by fund managers.

Relationships between users and providers of derivatives

Marketing relationships between providers and users of derivatives have also evolved. Both parties agree that derivatives ought to be transacted in the context of a relationship, and many have implemented relationship strategies for 20 years or more. Despite these efforts, recent evidence from the derivatives industry in both Sydney and Hong Kong suggests that the benefits of relationships are not as great as many had hoped.

Impediments to more productive relationships include:

- the stringent corporate governance environment which discourages end-users from relying on providers for advice and encourages price sensitivity;
- intense competition and commoditisation in derivatives markets which further encourages an undue focus on price, and diminishes banks' chances of recovering the costs of providing relationship services;
- perceived conflicts of interest for derivatives providers who seek to provide advice regarding risk management, yet are rewarded for this advice by transactions; and
- performance measurement systems and other structural issues that mitigate against a relationship.

All of these factors, along with others discussed in *Chapter 6*, erode trust in the relationships between providers and end-users. While this trend has not prevented growth in the volume of derivatives traded, it has resulted in narrower margins and therefore a business environment more conducive to disasters. The main challenge for derivatives marketers is to find ways to improve the relationship concept.

Legal risks

Legal risks always exist for participants in the derivatives industry, but there is now an increasing awareness of these risks. Along with this awareness is a growing desire for reform to reduce these risks.

Chapter 7 highlighted legal risk and the need for reform in several areas. Derivatives contracts may be unenforceable if they infringe general statutory insolvency or gaming legislation, or if a counterparty lacks the necessary capacity or authority to enter into a transaction. Already there are detailed proposals on netting rules, considered critical from a commercial standpoint. *Chapter 7* also argued for reform of gaming legislation. Such legislation was introduced to address a different type of activity, but now may have unintended adverse consequences for derivatives participants.

The events of 1994 and 1995 emphasised the possibility that

courts may impose on the provider a duty of care for the end-user. On current evidence, it appears that such an imposition is, however, unlikely when both parties are 'sophisticated' unless an advisory role is specifically assumed. Providers may nonetheless find that a significant inequality in the status of a counterparty could form a basis on which courts might find a duty of care. In common law jurisdictions, the legal environment will continue to evolve as (or if) cases come before the courts.

Allocating capital—quantifying credit and market risks

Quantifying credit and market risks has developed remarkably in the last decade. Credit risk was addressed in the late 1980s after some major defaults highlighted the significance of counterparty risks for derivative markets. Efforts to quantify market risk are a later development. Regulators now seek to ensure that banks set aside sufficient capital reserves to prevent insolvency from market and credit related losses.

Quantification of risk is a prerequisite for effective risk management, yet measuring risk is in itself a difficult task. Debate on the technical aspects of risk measurement has raged in the industry, along with debate concerning new regulations. This debate has benefited the industry, educating participants regarding the nature of risk and providing management with better information for efficient allocation of company resources.

Chapter 8 explored the problems of quantifying credit and market risks in relation to derivatives. While the debate on some issues has largely run its course, further change is likely at the implementation level. Sophisticated industry participants have excellent procedures to quantify risk, but these skills have yet to be disseminated to all participants, especially in less developed markets. Further progress is also likely in applying this new information, with senior managers using it to manage their organisations more efficiently.

Middle office

A major change in the industry in recent times has been the birth of a new risk management profession—the 'middle office'. The middle office is another initiative, supported by regulators, to control the risks for derivatives providers. It may be viewed as the link between the dealing room and the board room, informing senior management about the nature of risk. Such a link has been deemed necessary given the lack of knowledge of senior managers as a contributing factor in a number of derivatives disasters.

Chapter 9 explained how the middle office can help prevent unforeseen losses such as those discussed earlier. The role of the middle office includes:

- developing risk policies;
- ensuring compliance with risk policies;
- measuring market risk;
- running stress scenarios to identify the implications of major adverse market movements;
- analysing variance between predicted risk and actual experience;
- reviewing pricing models;
- attributing (risk adjusted) profits between business units; and
- controlling the new product process.

For most providers, the middle office is an evolving element of the risk control process, but lack of integrated systems inhibits its effectiveness. *Chapter 9* argued for improved systems and an increased role for the middle office to support management decisions as better information becomes available.

Regulatory issues

One far-reaching reaction to the events of 1994 and 1995 is the trend towards greater regulation of derivatives. While investor protection is often the rationale, some forms of supervision may reduce investor welfare or limit investor choice. Limits on the use of derivatives may be ineffective since, by definition, a portfolio comprised of physical assets can replicate any derivatives strategy. Further, regulation can create a moral hazard by giving participants a false sense of security that risks are adequately controlled. To the extent that further regulation is introduced, it should encourage rather than restrict the appropriate use and management of derivatives.

Chapter 10 acknowledged the role of self-regulation. Self-regulation promotes development and innovation in derivatives markets. Imposition of new regulations is, however, inevitable. Some derivatives are currently completely unregulated because they do not fall within legal definitions made obsolete by rapid market developments. Reform in regulatory regimes for derivatives is expected to be rapid and dramatic over the next decade. Some reforms will target the protection of unsophisticated investors and the need for more information required by markets and regulators.

New product development

The disasters of 1994 and 1995 called into question the development and use of exotic derivatives instruments. While innovation has often been a positive feature of derivatives markets, proliferation of exotic derivatives with no genuine justification has been criticised. Not only are exotic derivatives more difficult for managers to monitor, they are often regarded as self-serving attempts by dealers to enhance their bonuses, or as a means to circumvent regulations.

Chapter 11 argued that development of new derivatives products can enhance market efficiency and satisfy genuine needs. What must change, however, is the nature of the new product development process to avoid the problems referred to above. These steps were examined in turn, including the need to question the use of complex products. Both the user and the provider should consider what exactly is the justification for using complex derivatives (as opposed to simpler versions) and should identify where the value is being added.

Users, as well as providers, must understand the new product development process. If each party understands the motivations and needs of the other, more informed and productive relationships are possible. Diligent risk control at the stage of new product development may diminish the possibility of problems further along the product life-cycle.

Managing agency risk

In this book a wide range of issues have been identified for further managerial, legislative or regulatory reform. We have discussed likely and desirable directions for the derivatives industry, with reference to each specific field of endeavour. One issue, however, that arises in almost every chapter of the book is that of agency risk, often in the guise of performance measurement problems. It is arguably the most pressing issue still facing the industry. Yet it remains poorly understood, especially compared with, say, market and credit risks.

An agency relationship arises when one party, the principal, engages another party, the agent, to perform some service on its behalf. Examples of such relationships abound in the derivatives industry. Derivatives dealers, for example, are agents for senior managers and directors of banks, who are in turn agents for bank shareholders. In a similar way, corporate treasurers are agents acting for directors and shareholders of corporations. When a provider of derivatives advises an end-user on a derivatives strategy, the provider in a sense becomes the agent of the end-user. Fund managers are agents acting on behalf of investors.

Agency problems often occur because each individual acts in such a way as to promote his or her own interests. Not surprisingly, agents often do not act in the best interests of the principal. For example, *Chapter 4* showed how hedging with derivatives may be in the interests of the corporate treasurer (acting as the agent) but not in the interests of the shareholders. Many of the derivatives disasters (especially Barings and Procter & Gamble) can be regarded as agency problems where agents (employees) failed to act in the best interests of their principals (shareholders).

Appropriate organisational structure can address agency problems (Brickley, Smith and Zimmerman 1997). Three important aspects of organisational structure are:

- assignment of decision rights;
- evaluation and control systems; and
- remuneration and reward systems.

For example, position limits are used in banks as a device to assign decision-making responsibility appropriate to the expertise of the individual. Responsibility for trading and settlement are normally separated in order to provide appropriate checks and balances. The use of effective position limits and the separation of trading and settlement responsibilities would have helped to avoid losses in the case of Barings.

Remuneration systems can provide the agent with incentives that help align the interests of the agent and principal. The derivatives industry frequently uses performance bonuses; for example, payment of bonuses related to profits encourages dealers to write more profitable business.

A performance bonus based on transactions can, however, create its own adverse consequences. *Chapter 6* showed that transaction-based bonuses can encourage behaviour by providers which is damaging to long term business relationships with customers. Similarly, *Chapter 4* discussed how aggressive performance benchmarks in corporate treasuries can encourage excessive risk-taking and thus lead to disasters such as Procter & Gamble. The same thing happens in the funds management industry (described in *Chapter 5*) when managers take excessive risks to earn incentive payments. Linking incentives to long-term performance (which is generally more closely aligned to the interests of the principal) can reduce this problem.

A further problem in designing performance incentives is the issue of whether to pay incentives based on individual or group performance. The former method encourages non co-operative behaviour within the firm. Individuals may compete aggressively, sometimes to the extent that the customer suffers. Payment of incentives based on group (or firm) performance can cause free-rider effects. That is, since lazy and hard-working individuals all earn the same bonus, there is little incentive to work hard. Clearly, structuring effective incentive contracts to reduce agency risk is a complex issue.

Final comments

The process of reform we have described is encouraging to all those concerned with the integrity of individual firms and markets (be they managers, boards, individual investors or supervisors). Yet the transition of the industry towards secure, well-managed ground requires further change in many areas. It is essential that the lessons learned are not narrowly based around the technical aspects of past disasters. Lessons must be learned at a broader, managerial level so that they are applied to new products and situations that arise as the industry matures.

Above all, a transformation is required in the mindset of all participants regarding the nature and management of risk. The best regulatory regime can never rule out the possibility of loss. Risks of derivatives should not be isolated, but integrated into an overall risk management policy taken seriously at all levels and in all organisations. While this transformation has already occurred within some institutions, there is in our view need for further change throughout the industry.

References

Brickley, J., Smith, C., Zimmerman, J. 1997, *Managerial Economics and Organizational Architecture*, chs. 7–10, 12, Irwin, Chacago

Index

Note: numbers in bold type refer to a major discussion of the topic.